Bestellgrüße

Inclusion and Exclusion in the Liberal Competition State

This book examines the increasingly international division of labour that promotes transnational integration. It analyses the change in worker solidarity as it moves from collective national welfare to a transnational inclusion of workers from various links in the production chain.

Examining three types of welfare regimes within the USA, Germany, Denmark and Sweden, the author addresses how and why globalization is furthering the change from the welfare state to the competition state. The book considers in particular the change to solidarity taking place because of the internationalization of labour division; a change away from the segmented and differentiated system of nation states with strong internal national solidarity to broader, more inclusive and cross-border labour identity and inclusion. Analysing the deeper moral consequences of a globalized labour society, such as the paradigms of inclusion and justice, this book considers the implications of transnational labour on national welfare politics, and looks at the increasing significance of the transnational and national politics of inclusion in social policy, education, minority rights, immigration and gender equality.

Inclusion and Exclusion in the Liberal Competition State will be of interest to scholars and students of political science, sociology and social policy studying welfare state change.

Richard Münch is Professor of Sociology at the University of Bamberg, Germany.

Routledge research in comparative politics

1 **Democracy and Post-communism**
Political change in the post-communist world
Graeme Gill

2 **Sub-state Nationalism**
A comparative analysis of institutional design
Edited by Helena Catt and Michael Murphy

3 **Reward for High Public Office**
Asian and Pacific Rim States
Edited by Christopher Hood and B. Guy Peters

4 **Social Democracy and Labour Market Policy**
Developments in Britain and Germany
Knut Roder

5 **Democratic Revolutions**
Asia and Eastern Europe
Mark R. Thompson

6 **Democratization**
A comparative analysis of 170 countries
Tatu Vanhanen

7 **Determinants of the Death Penalty**
A comparative study of the world
Carsten Anckar

8 **How Political Parties Respond to Voters**
Interest aggregation revisited
Edited by Kay Lawson and Thomas Poguntke

9 **Women, Quotas and Politics**
Edited by Drude Dahlerup

10 **Citizenship and Ethnic Conflict**
Challenging the nation-state
Haldun Gülalp

11 **The Politics of Women's Interests**
New comparative and international perspectives
Edited by Louise Chappell and Lisa Hill

12 **Political Disaffection in Contemporary Democracies**
Social capital, institutions and politics
Edited by Mariano Torcal and José Ramón Montero

13 **Representing Women in Parliament**
A comparative study
Edited by Marian Sawer, Manon Tremblay and Linda Trimble

14 **Democracy and Political Culture in Eastern Europe**
Edited by Hans-Dieter Klingemann, Dieter Fuchs and Jan Zielonka

15 **Social Capital and Associations in European Democracies**
A comparative analysis
Edited by William A. Maloney and Sigrid Roßteutscher

16 **Citizenship and Involvement in European Democracies**
A comparative analysis
Edited by Jan van Deth, José Ramón Montero and Anders Westholm

17 **The Politics of Foundations**
A comparative analysis
Edited by Helmut K. Anheier and Siobhan Daly

18 **Party Policy in Modern Democracies**
Kenneth Benoit and Michael Laver

19 **Semi-Presidentialism Outside Europe**
A comparative study
Edited by Robert Elgie and Sophia Moestrup

20 **Comparative Politics**
The principal-agent perspective
Jan-Erik Lane

21 **The Political Power of Business**
Structure and information in public policymaking
Patrick Bernhagen

22 **Women's Movements**
Flourishing or in abeyance?
Edited by Marian Sawer and Sandra Grey

23 **Consociational Theory**
McGarry and O'Leary and the Northern Ireland conflict
Edited by Rupert Taylor

24 **The International Politics of Democratization**
Comparative perspectives
Edited by Nuno Severiano Teixeira

25 **Post-communist Regime Change**
A comparative study
Jørgen Møller

26 **Social Democracy in Power**
The capacity to reform
Wolfgang Merkel, Alexander Petring, Christian Henkes and Christoph Egle

27 **The Rise of Regionalism**
Causes of regional mobilization in Western Europe
Rune Dahl Fitjar

28 **Party Politics in the Western Balkans**
Edited by Věra Stojarová and Peter Emerson

29 **Democratization and Market Reform in Developing and Transitional Countries**
Think tanks as catalysts
James G. McGann

30 **Political Leadership, Parties and Citizens**
The personalisation of leadership
Edited by Jean Blondel and Jean-Louis Thiebault

31 **Civil Society and Activism in Europe**
Contextualizing engagement and political orientation
Edited by William A. Maloney and Jan W. van Deth

32 **Gender Equality, Citizenship and Human Rights**
Controversies and challenges in China and the Nordic countries
Edited by Pauline Stoltz, Marina Svensson, Zhongxin Sun and Qi Wang

33 **Democratization and the European Union**
Comparing Central and Eastern European post-Communist countries
Edited by Leonardo Morlino and Wojciech Sadurski

34 **The Origin of Electoral Systems in the Postwar Era**
A worldwide approach
Krister Lundell

35 **The Globalization of Motherhood**
Deconstruction and reconstructions of biology and care
Edited by Wendy Chavkin and JaneMaree Maher

36 **Parties, Elections, and Policy Reforms in Western Europe**
Voting for social pacts
Kerstin Hamann and John Kelly

37 **Democracy and Famine**
Olivier Rubin

38 **Women in Executive Power**
A global overview
Edited by Gretchen Bauer and Manon Tremblay

39 **Women and Representation in Local Government**
International case studies
Edited by Barbara Pini and Paula McDonald

40 **The Politics of Charity**
Kerry O'Halloran

41 **Climate Policy Changes in Germany and Japan**
A path to paradigmatic policy change
Rie Watanabe

42 **African Parliamentary Reform**
Edited by Rick Stapenhurst, Rasheed Draman and Andrew Imlach with Alexander Hamilton and Cindy Kroon

43 **The Politics of International Law and Compliance**
Serbia, Croatia and The Hague tribunal
Edited by Nikolas Rajkovic

44 **The Funding of Political Parties**
Where now?
Edited by Keith Ewing, Joo-Cheong Tham and Jacob Rowbottow

45 **Parliamentary Oversight Tools**
A comparative analysis
Riccardo Pelizzo and Frederick Stapenhurst

46 **Inclusion and Exclusion in the Liberal Competition State**
The cult of the individual
Richard Münch

Inclusion and Exclusion in the Liberal Competition State
The cult of the individual

Richard Münch

LONDON AND NEW YORK

First published 2012
by Routledge
2 Park Square, Milton Park, Abingdon, Oxon OX14 4RN

Simultaneously published in the USA and Canada
by Routledge
711 Third Avenue, New York, NY 10017

Routledge is an imprint of the Taylor & Francis Group, an informa business

© 2012 Richard Münch

The right of Richard Münch to be identified as author of this work has been asserted by him in accordance with sections 77 and 78 of the Copyright, Designs and Patents Act 1988.

All rights reserved. No part of this book may be reprinted or reproduced or utilized in any form or by any electronic, mechanical, or other means, now known or hereafter invented, including photocopying and recording, or in any information storage or retrieval system, without permission in writing from the publishers.

Trademark notice: Product or corporate names may be trademarks or registered trademarks, and are used only for identification and explanation without intent to infringe.

British Library Cataloguing in Publication Data
A catalogue record for this book is available from the British Library

Library of Congress Cataloging-in-Publication Data
Münch, Richard, 1945–
Inclusion and exclusion in the liberal competition state: the cult of the individual/Richard Münch.
  p. cm. – (Routledge research in comparative politics; v. 46)
  Includes bibliographical references and index.
  1. Division of labor. 2. International economic integration. 3. Labor movement. 4. Liberalism. I. Title.
  HD51.M86 2012
  338.6–dc23
                                                                    2011026127

ISBN: 978-0-415-67153-8 (hbk)
ISBN: 978-0-203-14484-8 (ebk)

Typeset in Times New Roman
by Wearset Ltd, Boldon, Tyne and Wear

Printed and bound in Great Britain by
TJI Digital, Padstow, Cornwall

Contents

List of figures	viii
List of tables	x
Acknowledgements	xi

	Introduction: inclusion and exclusion in the emerging world society	1
1	Economic change: from incremental to radical innovation	11
2	The change of solidarity: the causes and consequences of international labour division	37
3	Symbolic change: the new cult of the individual	90
4	Institutional change: liberal, conservative and egalitarian adjustment to international labour division	140
5	Relative exclusion and disintegration: convergence in the liberal competition state?	213
	Conclusion: the interdependent change of economy, solidarity, politics and justice	246
	References	264
	Index	297

Figures

I.1	Interdependent fields of social change	6
1.1	Patent specialization, Germany and USA 2006–2008	13
1.2	A comparison of innovation regimes in social and liberal market economies	16–18
1.3	Medium high technology 1988–2008 and employment rate 1988–2008	31
1.4	Employment in services 1988–2008 and employment rate 1988–2008	34
2.1	Public expenditure and economic openness OECD	44
2.2	Population, transport, communication, world trade, INGOs, ratification of ILO Conventions, GATT and WTO accession 1960–2010	51
2.3	Gini ratio, USA	61
2.4	*Question 1: V153 Status differences are acceptable, by education over time*	69
2.5	*Question 2: V152 Income differences raise motivation, by education over time*	70
2.6	*Question 3: V169 State is to supply provision in case of illness, hardship, unemployment and old age*	77
2.7	*Question 4: V197 Should social benefits be cut in the future or should they be extended*	78
3.1	The double structure of authority in the national and transnational fields of politics	96
3.2	State and civil society I	124
3.3	State and civil society II	124
4.1	Unemployment rates 1980–2008 Germany, Denmark, Sweden, United States	146
4.2	Employment protection and employment rate	151
4.3	Employment protection and women employment rate	152
4.4	Share of aggregate income 1967–2009	153
4.5	Net migration rate – employment ISIC 6	155
4.6	Net migration rate – earnings dispersion	156
4.7	Union density and earnings dispersion P90/P10	157

4.8	P50/P10 percentile ratio of gross earnings and annual job growth	158
4.9	Crime rate in the USA	159
4.10	Incarceration rate in the USA	159
4.11	Earnings dispersion and property crime	160
4.12	Crime and incarceration	161
4.13	Household and family is women's job	180
4.14	Costs of childcare and fertility rate	181
4.15	Children (0–3 years old) in day care and fertility rate	182
5.1	Total robberies (1975–2008) in selected OECD countries	219
5.2	Incarceration rate and crime rate in the USA	220
5.3	Unemployment rate and qualification, West Germany/West Berlin	223
5.4	Unemployment rate and qualification, East Germany/East Berlin	224
5.5	Educational attainment and unemployment	224
5.6	Trade union density	226
5.7	The rise of service sector employment	227
5.8	Gross foreign direct investment (% of GDP)	229
5.9	Hourly labour costs in manufacturing (US$) 1980–1995	230
5.10	The decline of industrial sector employment	231
5.11	De-industrialization, globalization, relative exclusion and deviance	235
C.1	Class structure and results of the Hessian state elections of 25 September 1983	253
C.2	Class structure and results of the Hessian state elections of 18 January 2009	254
C.3	Education and voting behaviour at the Hessian state elections on 18 January 2009	255
C.4	Causal factors, pathways and stations of societal change	260
C.5	Interdependent processes of societal change	263

Tables

1.1	Indicators of education and research, government action, economic achievement and inclusion in the labour society	25
1.2	Share of the technology industry in manufacturing exports 2008/2009	26
1.3	Germany's industrial R&D sectors in an international comparison from 1991 to 2005	29
1.4	Growth of OECD trade in production depending on industry and technology intensity 1996–2005	30
1.5	Correlation matrix	32–33
1.6	Employment rate 1988–2008	35
2.1	Basic features of three welfare states	46
2.2	Poverty rates in OECD countries	62
2.3	To be national/European in the future (% by demographics)	67
2.4	Activities of the state in selected fields of social and economic policy	76
3.1	Volunteering in the USA (I)	125
3.2	Volunteering in the USA (II)	126
3.3	Volunteering in OECD countries	128
4.1	GDP growth, public social expenditure and labour market performance of different countries	144–145
4.2	Attitudes towards equality of opportunity and equality of outcome	148
4.3	Attitudes towards activities of the state	149
4.4	Inequality of income within different groups of education in the USA 1973–2001	154
4.5	Relative volume of strikes (cross-national)	163
5.1	Robberies: detailed results for measuring inequality according to OECD	242–243
5.2	Robberies: detailed results of WIDER measurements of inequality	244

Acknowledgements

This book has emerged from a myriad of discussions in the interdisciplinary setting of the graduate programme "Markets and Social Systems in Europe" at the University of Bamberg, which was funded by the German Research Foundation from 2002 to 2011. I am grateful to both colleagues and students for providing a stimulating atmosphere for writing this book. In some parts, it draws on my German study *Das Regime des liberalen Kapitalismus* (Frankfurt/New York: Campus, 2009). André Ortiz and Len Ole Schäfer assisted in gathering, updating and analysing data from various sources, Christian Baier did so in Chapter 1. Many thanks to all of them! I am especially grateful to Brigitte Münzel for translating various chapters and for her assistance in editing the book.

Introduction
Inclusion and exclusion in the emerging world society

The crash of the financial market in Autumn 2008 has called for enormous coordinated state activities in order to restabilize the world economy. This historical moment has brought back to our minds that no stable economy can exist without rules established and controlled by coordinated state power. Some commentators have used this crisis to argue for re-establishing coordinated state control of the economy on a broader scale including the state's responsibility for people's welfare. To meet such claims would, however, draw back the deep-going processes of liberalization that have taken place everywhere over the past two decades. Such a return to the status quo ante is very unlikely to occur. It is the goal of this study to find out whether and why this is the case.

We aim at understanding and explaining the change of the old welfare state towards the new liberal competition state, which is taking place in the context of the globalized "knowledge-based" economy (Cerny 1990: 204–232; 1997, 2000, 2005, 2010). The competition state is an "enabling state" (Gilbert and Gilbert 1989) and a "social investment state" (Giddens 1998). This change of the state's role is part of the rise of neo-liberal governmentality (Lemke 1997; Dean 1999; Rose 1999; Jessop 2006; Foucault 2008; Miller and Rose 2008) in the framework of the global knowledge society (Stehr 1994; Jakobi 2007). The special focus of this study is on the moral consequences of international labour division, which can be summarized as a change from collective national welfare to individualized transnational and national inclusion. The study addresses particularly the change of solidarity taking place on the tracks of the internationalization of labour division. It is a change away from the segmentally differentiated system of nation states with strong internal national solidarity and weak transnational solidarity, complemented by the strict differentiation between the in-group morality of widely shared equality of results within nations and the out-group morality of inequality of opportunity and results between nations. The change goes in the direction of a new network solidarity both across and within nations, which is accompanied by the increasing significance of justice as fairness in the sense of rewarding achievement under the condition of equal opportunity within and between nations as well. This change of justice by way of transnationalization implies a turn away from the prominence of the national politics of welfare and towards greater significance of the transnational and national politics of inclusion in the broader sense of not addressing exclusively problems of social policy, but also – and with increasing significance – education, minority rights, immigration and gender equality.

Because the change is rather deep-going we can speak of a change of the paradigm of inclusion and the paradigm of justice. In a nutshell: the modern "cult of the individual" (Durkheim 1964: 172) is being transnationalized to reach beyond the solidarity of the citizens of nation states. The cult of the individual makes the dignity of the human individual a sacred and untouchable thing. The human individual is conceived as a moral person capable of leading an autonomous and responsible life respecting the dignity of any other person. For a long time, this cult was institutionalized exclusively in the constitution of the modern nation state and was shared exclusively by national citizens. In the meantime, however, it has been transnationalized by processes such as the increasing inclusion of non-national residents in the sharing of basic rights on the territory of the nation state (Soysal 1994), particularly promoted by jurisdiction (Joppke 1999); the active promotion of human rights by the United Nations' Declaration of Human Rights and the European Convention on Human Rights as well as the extension of individual rights beyond national borders within the European Union's single market by the jurisdiction of the European Court of Justice and the World Trade Organization's turning down of trade barriers.

In the emerging societal order beyond the nation state, moral universalism joins the ethics of individualism in a novel way. This development goes beyond economic liberalism and includes the global realization of human and civil rights which, however, do not possess the substantiation they had in the nation state, and even more so, the national welfare state. The formal rights to freedom and equality are given priority over political and social rights. Transnational economic integration and the rise of a global society under the auspices of human rights are two sides of one and the same coin and cannot be separated from each other. Hence, both sides affect each other.

We observe a new development boost towards moral universalism and ethical individualism, which pushes the moral particularism based on preferring one's own fellows, and the ethics of obedience to authorities to the background. Moral universalism relies on the principle of justifying fundamental norms for interpersonal relationships through general agreement in an open and egalitarian discourse; the ethics of individualism designates the appraisal of a lifestyle marked by self-responsibility and mutual respect. The human and civil rights form the concrete legal frame for the entanglement of moral universalism and the ethics of individualism; ever since the United Nations' human rights declaration of 1948, these rights have witnessed increasingly wider acceptance worldwide (Habermas 1992: 15–60; Dunne and Wheeler 1999; Risse *et al.* 1999; O'Brien *et al.* 2000). An elite of moral pioneers creates the new yardsticks, which are spread beyond the existing national borders across national societies by transnational actors. This includes transnational social movements committed to the worldwide acknowledgement of human rights, but also scholars advancing the global scientific discourse; experts cooperating in the development of international standards for the global trade and the protection of health and environment; and, not least of all, the managers of multinational businesses creating a worldwide network of trade and labour division. These are the "cultural others" representing the principles of the "world polity" and advising national governments in an apparently "disinterested" way (Meyer 1997; Meyer et al. 1997). The moral pioneers become carriers of moral universalism, because they meet the necessary requirements of socialization in an exemplary way: the broadest reach and the highest number of social groups to participate in (Simmel 1908/1992: 456–511, 791–863). In that way, they acquire the highest possible level of individuality while, at the same time, getting acquainted more than others with justifying their decisions in the light of their consequences on the most distant and highest possible number of affected parties. The scope of the – at least imaginary – discourse on justifying their own decisions tends towards universality. This means that they will approach most closely the situation in which they can choose only such principles as a guideline of their actions, which would meet with the agreement of any potential participant in a discourse that would be open basically to everybody and to any argument (Habermas 1981). Under these terms it is not possible to grant an advantage to one party that would be denied to another party without any restriction to particular groups. Each and everyone is entitled worldwide to acquire a share of the globally produced wealth in the same way (cf. Münch 2001b; Brunkhorst 2002; Koenig 2005).

It is getting increasingly difficult to justify the collective allocation of wealth, because it does not take the individual contribution to the whole as a criterion of assessment, but the mere membership in a group blessed by affluence. Under these conditions, all that can be justified is, first of all, the distribution of the share of wealth in proportion to the individual achievement contributed to the global whole – no matter how this proportionality is measured. This idea is inseparably linked with the principle of keeping the door to the allocation of wealth open to each individual. It would be a contradiction in itself if the shares in wealth were distributed according to achievements, but if access to the provision of achievements were not offered to each and every one at equal terms. It is also necessary to support those people who are impeded in contributing through no fault of their own, because it would be another contradiction in itself if remuneration was made according to achievement while those who are less capable through no fault of their own were treated just like those who are more capable right from the start. In this case, it would not actually be their individual achievement that is being assessed, but instead a result of their efforts that has been determined by disadvantaging outside factors.

But what about the differences in achievement that remain despite all measures of support? What should be the extent of income or wage differentials in order to trace the differences in achievements adequately? What share should be given to the least capable people? It will hardly be possible to find generally valid answers to these questions. The solution will depend on how weak performance is being interpreted; what consequences are expected to result from more or less wage or income differentials and from a higher or lower baseline for the whole society; furthermore, it is important to see what idea of the human individual is being envisioned. If everyone is considered equally capable, if equal opportunity is offered to him/her as to all others, then a distribution depending on capability alone is justified. The baseline need not guarantee more than the subsistence level and what is required to keep society from drifting towards rebellion or crime. If people are considered ready to achieve only if they are given a sufficient amount of incentives, a higher wage or income differential will be opted for. All those, however, who assume basically existing inequality, will concede a higher level of collectively shared wealth to less capable people. This will be the case even more, the more it is coupled with the assumption that people can achieve more, if they are supported by recognition through society that is largely independent of achievements. It is easy to note that the first argumentation involves a preference for a "liberal" model of society as it has been realized most strikingly in the United States. The second argumentation, instead, leads us to a preference for the Continental European "social" model of society. The principle of the liberal model is the *individual* participation in wealth under the terms of achievement, equal opportunity and fairness on the basis of a minimum level of commonly shared wealth. The principle of the social model is the *collective* participation in a large base of shared wealth beyond which only a smaller part of wealth is distributed individually under the terms of achievement, equal opportunity and fairness (Lessenich and Ostner 1998; Zukunftskommission der Friedrich Ebert Stiftung 1998; Goodin *et al.* 1999; Alesina and Angeletos 2005).

The central question arising in this context regards the impact of the increasing international labour division on the structure of solidarity and the viability of the liberal or social model of society. Does international labour division undermine national and promote transnational solidarity? Does it favour the liberal model of society instead of the social one? Or will different cultural traditions and institutional settings maintain different models of society? Will the United States continue with the liberal model, while Europe will go on with the social model (cf. Scharpf and Schmidt 2000; Alber 2006)?

Without any doubt, the institutional order of the transnational economic space will not be stabilized without introducing widely acknowledged legitimatory principles. As long as the Europeans believe in the legitimacy of the social model, they will continue to support its establishment in the legal regulation of economic transactions. The question arises, however, as to whether this can be done successfully in the long run, when the cultural superstructure loses the necessary structural foundations of the segmentary differentiation into national economies and nation states. In that case, a tension will arise between the collectivistic ideas of the superstructure on the one hand, and the individualization of the social structure and the actual living conditions on the other hand. In this context, the transnationally acting moral pioneers play a crucial part. They ensure an opening to the outside, which makes competition for scarce goods fiercer on the inside. Human rights, civil rights and wealth must be shared with more people now than in the past. Hence, the problem of "moral hazard" becomes more heated. Since everybody is exposed to fiercer competition, and since the moral pioneers put the alien on an equal basis with the familiar, fears are growing that support independent of achievements will be exploited frequently. The necessary collective solidarity, which would be in a position to carry a large base of commonly shared wealth, is lacking. The emergence of a transnational economic space levels the difference between in-group and out-group morality and calls for the same ethical standards both inside and outside, which necessarily create a wider scope for individual inclusion according to achievement, equal opportunity and fairness as opposed to the ethic of the welfare state thus pushing back to the same extent collective inclusion in the sense of equal participation in the collectively produced wealth (cf. Mackert and Müller 2007).

The balance between collective and individual inclusion shifts toward the individual one. The modern "cult of the individual" as specified by Emile Durkheim (1964: 172; 1973a, 1973b), or in the words of Talcott Parsons and Winston White (1964): "institutionalized individualism", actually reach their global dimension (Meyer and Jepperson 2000; Münch 2001a). This need not necessarily mean, however, that American conditions will prevail in Europe all of a sudden. Yet it does mean that the tension between the segmentary welfare ethic and the opening to the outside generates legitimation conflicts and nationalistic countermovements, which accompany the structurally enforced path towards the liberal model. After all, the European welfare states are in a position to interpret the liberal model in such a way that they add new bonds from their own tradition to the new reality, which do not exist in the United States, but which are nevertheless adequate in structural terms. As this development is driven by moral pioneers, it appears unavoidable that a lot of time will pass until practicable new symbioses will be found between structural conditions, legal regulations and cultural traditions in the wake of the new legitimation conflicts. It will take some time until the global economic space will be characterized less by anomie and will attain a new, structurally adequate institutional order.

The study carried out in this book tries to understand and explain the paradigmatic change of inclusion and justice and the transnationalization of the cult of the individual in five major steps. The first four steps are focused on one basic field out of four interdependent fields of change, which together make up the whole process of change: economic change, change of solidarity, symbolic change and institutional change (Figure I.1). Each of these four basic fields of change will be investigated in the book's first four chapters. The fifth chapter will focus on the disintegrative consequences coming about with the outlined transformation of solidarity. We will especially look at relative exclusion within national societies emerging from the turn away from collectivistic forms of social inclusion (family, class, trade unions) and towards individualized forms (educational and occupational achievement) in the global and post-industrial economy. Relative exclusion implies increasing rates of delinquency. Because collectivistic forms of social inclusion have lost legitimacy and effectiveness in the global and post-industrial economy, liberal strategies of activation and deterrence (e.g. policies of zero tolerance) gain in significance, legitimacy and effectiveness.

6 Introduction

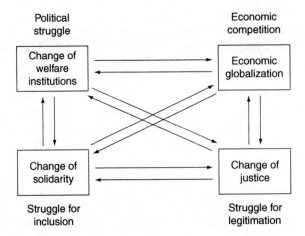

Figure I.1 Interdependent fields of social change.

The change addressed in this study is a change of welfare regimes in the context of the globalized knowledge-based economy with expanding international division of labour. A welfare regime consists of institutions designed to fulfil the task of social integration by way of the social inclusion of individuals and groups in the shaping of rights, especially social rights along with civil rights and political rights. A welfare regime is a special case of a more comprehensive inclusion regime. It specializes in inclusion through social policy. Beyond social policy there are policies of education, immigration, gender equality or minority rights, which are all devoted to solving special problems of social inclusion. In the process of change under scrutiny we observe an increasing coordination of social policy with these other policies of inclusion. That means social policy is losing some of its long-lasting dominance to give way to a broader concept of inclusion policy within which social policy is but one of several areas. We may also say that social policy is losing prominence in as much as other inclusion policies such as gender equality, minority rights and education policy gain in significance.

Institutions representing inclusion regimes or welfare regimes consist of a set of rules established to solve problems of inclusion. The rules making up institutions are linked together by common basic ideas, guidelines and principles, which confer a common meaning and coherence to the set of rules. We can speak of a *paradigm* making up the deep structure of an institution (Hall 1993). The core of that paradigm consists of basic principles. This core is surrounded by special *programmes* that carry out the basic principles in practical action. An institutional paradigm is embedded in a vocabulary of ideas, concepts and remedies used in addressing problems to be solved by institutions. This is the *rhetoric* guiding discourse on institutional performance. The more such rhetoric forms a coherent and closed language that determines the way in which problems are perceived and tackled, the more we can speak of a *semantic* dominating the discourse on institutions.

What shall be demonstrated is the emergence of a New World of Welfare Capitalism, in which the conservative as well as the social democratic regimes approach the liberal regime in the extent to which social inclusion becomes a matter of equal opportunity and individual achievement. There are as many ways of exploring the change of inclusion or welfare regimes as there are theoretical approaches in social science. To focus the analysis, the study in this book will address the four interdependent fields of social change mentioned above: (1) economic change; (2) change of solidarity; (3) symbolic change and (4) institutional change. These are four battlefields that interact in the production of social change.

Economic change results from the global expansion of markets and the concomitant intensification of competition for market shares. Innovation is central for maintaining market shares. In the past, the innovation regime of the social market economy supported a special type of innovation, namely *incremental* innovation as the refinement of established technologies. Moreover, it was coupled with a high level of structural persistence. The fiercer international competition in the global economy enforces a transfer of production jobs in the branches of industry following the pattern of incremental innovation to more cost-effective locations. Hence, the highly developed economic venues can only take the bull by the horns by investing in top technologies and replacing a lack of production jobs with service jobs. Nevertheless, this involves a paradigmatic change of the economic order, an approach to the innovation regime of the liberal market economies, which is geared towards radical innovations producing a fast, thorough social change. The disintegration trends of the no longer adjusted old regime, namely the separation of the national and transnational societies into insiders and outsiders, and the disintegration trends of the new regime, namely the marginalization of the little skilled workforce, require specific reintegration measures: the conversion from a deactivating to a new, activating social policy. In this way, the discrepancy between far-reaching national equality and extreme international inequality is being removed, and a step is made towards a convergence of the internal and external social orders according to the ideas of justice of achievement, equal opportunity and fairness.

The *change of solidarity* starts from the condition that inclusion or welfare regimes represent the solidarity structure of society in fulfilling the function of social integration. This solidarity structure of classes, strata, gender, religious, ethnic or regional groups forms the material basis of a welfare regime that itself works back on reproducing/transforming the solidarity structure. In as much as this structure of solidarity is changing, established welfare regimes come into conflict with the solidarity structure so that there is pressure of change. The emerging structure of solidarity determines what kind of regime change will be adapted to the new structure of solidarity and what kind will not be adapted, and thus will have more limited chances of selection and stabilization in the long run. We have to take into account, however, that welfare regimes and solidarity structures shape each other so that welfare regimes are not simply adapted to changing solidarity structures, but at the same time exert a formative influence on their production, reproduction and change. National welfare regimes produce national solidarity and contribute to maintaining national solidarity in a globalized economy. Nevertheless, in the context of globalization national solidarity is undermined by cross-border division of labour so that national welfare regimes are losing some of their control of the structuration of solidarity. The material dimension of change is, however, incomplete. Factual change does not necessarily result from maladjustment. It rather needs further complementing factors to produce factual change.

Symbolic change starts from the misfit between solidarity structure and welfare regime as a rule. In such a situation the legitimacy of established regimes is being questioned. The struggle for defining the situation and legitimating continuity or change of regimes is being opened. The preservation or change of a regime depends on who succeeds in the "symbolic" struggle on the definition of the situation. Change can be more or less deep and pervasive. It can remain on the level of *rhetorical change*, which means the introduction of a new vocabulary of ideas, concepts and remedies for coping with problems of welfare and inclusion. *Semantic change* occurs when a new coherent language is established determining the way in which problems of welfare and inclusion are perceived and tackled. *Programmatic change* takes place as far as new programmes of providing for welfare and inclusion are introduced in legislation, administration and practical action. Eventually, we speak of *paradigmatic change* when the change of some programmes spills over to changing other programmes broadly. This means that the core of basic principles of welfare or inclusion can no longer provide for coherence and a common meaning of welfare or inclusion programmes and, as a result, basic principles are changed to regain coherence and a common meaning of welfare or inclusion programmes.

Such symbolic change from rhetoric up to paradigms results from symbolic struggles on the definition of the situation. Success in these struggles depends on three basic conditions: (1) Rhetoric, semantics, programmes and paradigms have to adjust to a situation that is primarily determined by the structure of solidarity in the context of this study, which addresses the change of welfare and inclusion regimes. (2) They have to attain legitimacy within a cultural horizon of basic world views and values in a discourse stretching increasingly beyond the national on to the global level. (3) They need powerful carrier groups. Established rhetoric, semantics, programmes and paradigms are maintained by the incumbents of power positions in a field of discourse. In the context of this study these include social policy experts of parties, specialists in labour and social law and national welfare organizations. New challengers must replace the incumbents in power positions in order to enact symbolic change (cf. Fligstein 2001). In our context, such challengers include economists, consultants and international NGOs. Like material change, symbolic change is but one part of four basic dimensions of change and does not produce factual change without complementation by structural and institutional change. It is itself largely shaped by material struggles of inclusion and processes of institutional change.

In the perspective of sociological institutionalism (Meyer 1997; Meyer *et al.* 1997; Drori *et al.* 2003; Beckert 2010b), the nation state has been constructed as a legitimate actor by complying with the basic principles of good modern responsible statehood. For about fifty years the welfare state has become the model of good statehood. This model is changing with the growing understanding of solidarity and justice as accommodating international and national solidarity and justice. In this perspective, collectivistic national solidarity and its institutionalization in social security systems do not only lose in effectiveness, but also in legitimacy. With the establishment of a world polity and regular international benchmarking and assessment of institutions by international experts legitimacy may even overrule functional effectiveness and define how it is conceived of. Because the latter is difficult to assess anyway, conforming to legitimate principles of good responsible statehood has become even more important. This means that with the establishment of international benchmarking a world polity made up by international experts (scientists, consultants, managers) is being established exerting increasing pressure on national governments to conform to the globally established models of good governance. In this respect, material change enhances the dynamics of the process while symbolic change determines its direction.

What comes to the fore when we focus on *institutional change* is path dependency and inertia of established institutions because of the traditional legitimacy of what is given, the transaction costs of change and vested interests, which are served by established institutions (Pierson 2004; Beyer 2006). What has to be addressed above all is the fact that global functional pressure of adjusting welfare institutions to changing solidarity structures and transnational symbolic change are always transformed into institutional change within national societies in the context of an existing paradigm and institutional programmes, which determine largely the outcome of social change (Berger and Dore 1996; Goff 2006). Functional pressure and symbolic change can be resisted within national borders, they can be absorbed to be framed by the existing paradigm and institutional programmes, and they can be layered around the historically established paradigm and programmes to build hybrid forms (Thelen 2002; Streeck and Thelen 2005b). Institutional path dependency is, however, only one force out of the four basic fields of change focused in this study. Material and symbolic change might become powerful enough to break through institutional inertia and vested interests in a radical revolutionary overturn or incrementally with every new programme layered around the given institutions to affect eventually even the core of basic principles and to produce deep and far-reaching institutional change.

The driving force of change in this nexus of interdependent fields is economic globalization. Nevertheless, each of the other fields makes its own contribution to institutional change and filters the influence of the other fields on itself (cf. Beckert 2010a). Economic globalization undermines national solidarity, which is in itself being reconstructed in the context of the emerging world society. It also calls into question the differentiation between in-group morality and out-group morality in the field of legitimation struggles, which is itself the battleground for changing the notion of justice. Economic globalization also puts national welfare regimes under financial pressures, which are being turned into reform programmes in political struggles. Furthermore, these struggles are influenced by the change of solidarity and changes in the notion of justice.

The sociological approach to studying the change of the welfare state towards the liberal competition state in the context of the emerging world society differs from the political science approaches ruling this field in that there is a special interest in a long-term and more comprehensive structural change. This is considered part of a more comprehensive change of state, economy, social structure and culture on the path from the system of nation states towards a world society. It is not simply a matter of reducing welfare state-related security nor of simply spreading liberalization, privatization and marketization programmes. It is, instead, a material change of the economy, a structural change of solidarity, a paradigmatic change of justice as well as an institutional change of social policy and, also, their interrelation. A fundamental change of society as a whole should be made understood in its meaning, its forms of presentation and its consequences. Doing so makes it necessary to introduce social theory into the investigation of welfare state change (cf. Dörre *et al.* 2009; Vobruba 2009). This is precisely what this study tries to undertake.

In this frame of reference, questions of political constellations are also relevant. For instance, historically cooperative relations between capital and labour produced proportional representation which, in its turn, favoured centre-left governments and their preference for comprehensive welfare state security. In contrast, antagonistic relations between capital and labour ensured that the middle class tended to opt for a majority vote which, in its turn, supported centre-right governments and their trend towards restricting welfare state arrangements (Iversen and Soskice 2006; Cusack *et al.* 2007; Iversen and Stephens 2008). According to the party difference hypothesis, the different length in the participation of conservative or social democratic parties in government is to be held responsible for the more or less comprehensive extension, but also the dismantling of the welfare state (Huber and Stephens 2001; Swank 2002). Many veto players in the political system (Tsebelis 2002) make an extension of the welfare state difficult, but also its dismantling, if it has been institutionalized. These explanatory approaches offer the advantage of direct access to political events, but also the disadvantage of being short-sighted. No structures are discernible, no comprehensive relationships and no long-term processes. Though they may be justified in themselves in their approach, they nevertheless require complementation by a sociological perspective as to the width, depth and length of the ongoing societal change (cf. Mahoney and Rueschemeyer 2003; Streeck and Thelen 2005a, 2005b). In this interest in broader social change, political economy and economic sociology should join forces (Swedberg 1998, 2003; Beckert 2009a, 2009b; Berger 2009).

1 Economic change

From incremental to radical innovation

According to an analysis by Hall and Soskice (2001), "liberal" market economies differ from "coordinated" and/or "social" ones not by their generally better capacity for innovation, but merely by a different type of innovation (cf. also Albert 1992; O'Sullivan 2000: 11–40). While liberal market economies tend to support more radical innovations involving profound change, the special quality of coordinated market economies rests in incremental innovations of the permanent refinement of products and processes without any profound change. This contrast can be assessed when taking into account that the quota of openings and closures of companies in the research-intensive industry in coordinated market economies like Germany, Japan, Switzerland, Sweden and Finland is clearly lower than in liberal market economies such as the UK and the USA. A similar trend can be discerned for knowledge-intensive services, where coordinated market economies like Denmark, the Netherlands and France display nevertheless high levels of openings and closure (EFI 2008: 58). Each of these two types of market economy possesses its very special qualities with regard to its capacity for innovation. Hence, according to Hall and Soskice, both types can assert themselves only with their own specific policies strengthening their own qualities against competition, which has been aggravated by globalization. From this point of view, the type of coordinated market economy has good opportunities to cope with the challenges of globalization. We are going to discuss this thesis in this chapter.

First of all, the two contrasting innovation models differ due to their *technological specialization*. Germany is specialized in incremental innovation, which originates from the perfection of high-quality, established technology in automotive construction, machinery construction, electrical engineering and chemistry and is based on knowledge gained by experience. It is geared towards patenting inventions designed to secure the technological lead for existing products. The USA, in contrast, is specialized in radical innovation resulting from the production of top technology in micro-electronics and biotechnology, which originates from scientific knowledge and concerns the patenting of inventions designed to create new markets.

In Germany, the *organization of innovations* includes the tight entanglement of innovations and production inside established enterprises. Innovations are controlled by production. Applied research dominates, which is not linked with basic research. Stable, long-term production and innovation networks, which are regionally concentrated and closely entwined, and which are frequently organized by associations, dominate the field. Innovations are a matter of traditional small, medium-sized and large enterprises with a vast potential of accumulated technical knowledge. In the top technologies developed by the USA, innovations occur outside production through independent fields of research and development and newly established businesses. They trigger new products and innovation-controlled production. Applied research is closely linked with basic research at university research centres. The innovation networks are free, short-term cooperations that are not organized by associations; they are targeted towards marketable inventions and may also include international alliances. Newly established start-up businesses act as pioneers being taken over by the large enterprises if they are successful.

The contrasting innovation patterns of coordinated and liberal market economies

Summarizing, we can say that the German model of coordinated market economy and the American model of liberal market economy differ through contrasting innovation patterns: incremental versus radical innovations. One side is strong exactly where the other side is weak. This is underlined by an assessment of patents for 1983/1984 and 1993/1994 in a detailed comparison of Germany and the United States. Both sides behave inversely with a clear increase in differences recognizable during the period of ten years under scrutiny. The same result is achieved by an examination of the patent specialization in Germany and the USA from 1986 to 2000 (Legler 2004: 80). Up until the present time, no fundamental changes have been made in Germany's patent specialization (EFI 2008: 54) (Figure 1.1).

Germany has increased in strength in all established technologies of the old industries such as structural and civil engineering; consumer goods; arms; nuclear energy; transport; agricultural machinery; mechanical parts; machinery; machine tools; environmental technology; thermal engineering; material processes; coatings; production engineering; chemical elements; and electrical energy. In contrast, weaknesses can be discerned in agriculture and foodstuff; new materials; biotechnology; polymers; organic chemistry; medical technology; optics; semiconductors; information technology; telecommunication; and audio-visual technologies. Pharmaceutical products have remained unvaried on a medium level. A slight improvement can be discerned for control systems. In the United States, the picture is mirror-inverted (Hall and Soskice 2001: 42–43, figures 1.5 and 1.6; cf. also O'Sullivan 2000: 135–144). The prevailing strategies for defying competition on the market correspond to these different innovation patterns. In Germany, the strategy of diversified quality production prevails (Streeck 1991), while in the United States innovations dominate the growth markets and price struggles the stagnating markets. In Germany, the established industry attempts to assert its world market position in automotive construction, machine tool construction and in chemistry through the diversification and perfecting of established products. In the United States, a new industry in microelectronics, biotechnology, medical technology and information technology has developed within a very short time, while the old-established industry has chosen the path of price competition, above all facing goods from Japan (Casper 2001).

A comparison between Germany and the UK supplies similar differences in the relationship of the share of exports of certain product groups in all exports of the country in question and the share of all exports of these product groups in all

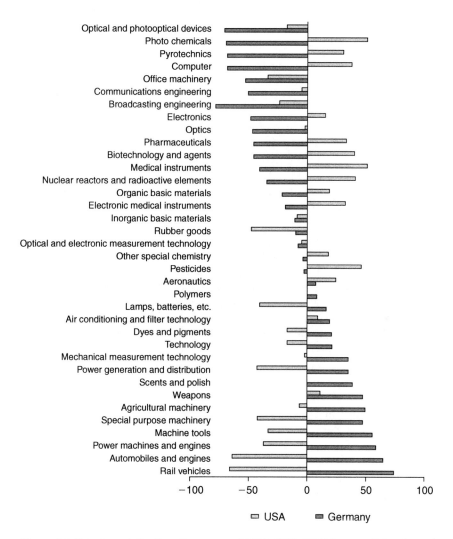

Figure 1.1 Patent specialization, Germany and USA 2006–2008 (source: Frietsch *et al.* 2011: 13, table 2).

industrialized countries among the OECD nations. In Germany, exports in chemistry, automotive construction and mechanical engineering rank clearly ahead of resource-intensive, labour-intensive and knowledge-based exports. In contrast, in the UK, resource- and labour-intensive exports – and even more so knowledge-based exports – attain higher shares than in Germany. The scale-intensive fields of chemistry and automotive construction along with the field of specialized mechanical engineering are ranked at an approximately equal level as resource- and labour-intensive products in the UK. Moreover, they are clearly behind the volume achieved in Germany. This pattern remained relatively stable between 1970 and 1990. The most obvious change occurred in the field of knowledge-based products whose export share in the UK continued to grow from an already higher level, while it dropped slightly in Germany. It is also striking to note that resource-intensive exports have increased but slightly in the UK, but substantially in Germany. Also, in the UK, labour-intensive products dropped from a higher level to the level of Germany, where they grew marginally. Exports of machine tools fell notably in both countries (Fiöretos 2001: 222, figure 6.1).

Differences in the weighting of general and vocational education, the protection of the workforce against dismissals and the protection of the unemployed against income cuts are correlated with the different innovation and export patterns of coordinated and liberal market economies. In the coordinated market economies, vocational education, the protection of the workforce against dismissals and the protection of the unemployed against income cuts are more important than in liberal market economies. Blatant contrast can be established between Germany, Austria, Belgium and Sweden on the side of the coordinated market economies and in the United States, the UK, Australia, New Zealand, Canada and Ireland on the side of the liberal market economies. Special cases with regard to coordinated market economies can be found in Denmark, the Netherlands and Switzerland, which offer a medium protection of employment, but a high income guarantee for the unemployed; the situation is exactly the other way round in Italy and Japan. Between these poles, we find the coordinated market economies of Norway, France and Finland offering a slightly more than average protection of employment and unemployment (Estevez-Abe *et al.* 2001: 173, figure 4.2).

Another obvious relationship can be established between the significance of vocational training in a country and its income differentiation, measured by the distance between the top and the bottom 10 per cent. In Germany, Finland, Denmark, Italy, Norway, Sweden, the Netherlands and Belgium, greater significance of vocational training is accompanied by lower income differences, while in the United States, Canada and Ireland – and slightly less in the UK – a reduced significance of vocational training is linked with higher income differences (Estevez-Abe *et al.* 2001: 173, figure 4.3). It is shown that vocational education guarantees higher incomes to the lower and medium qualification levels. An international comparison gives evidence of the fact that early school leavers achieve better results in an international test in educational systems emphasizing vocational training than early school leavers in systems attaching less importance to vocational training (Estevez-Abe *et al.* 2001: 173, figure 4.5).

Without any doubt, the manufacture of high-quality products in chemistry, automotive construction and mechanical engineering by a great number of highly skilled workers is a production regime making the growth in wealth a collectively supported matter. Even workforce from the medium and lower levels contribute their expertise so that they achieve a higher share in wealth than the workforce in regimes of simple mass production, where we find a wider gap between the knowledge of production managers and the knowledge of production workers. Nevertheless, these are educational and production regimes focused on male jobs in production work. Compared to the United States, in particular, it is therefore striking to see that there are fewer women in production work and in higher management, administration, technical jobs and the professions. A comparison of data from the second half of the 1980s reveals, for instance, that women account for a 22 per cent share in professions and technical jobs in the United States, but only for 15 per cent in Germany. As far as administration and management jobs are concerned, these figures are at 26 and 11 per cent respectively; for office management, they are at 70 and 59 per cent; and for production jobs at 30 and 21 per cent. In contrast, they are at 33 and 52 per cent respectively for sales activities, and at 30 and 67 per cent for simple service jobs (Estevez-Abe *et al.* 2001: 173, figure 4.6).

Research along the Varieties of Capitalism approach has confirmed the established connections between specific educational regimes, welfare systems and income inequality (Iversen 2005). A typological sharpening of the argument along the lines of Esping-Andersen's (1990) three types of welfare regimes helps us to differentiate between three types of human capital formation (Iversen and Stephens 2008). The liberal regime, which supports the market, prefers high private investments in general competences, average public spending on education and little redistribution. The family-centred conservative regime is focused on moderate redistribution, a high level of social insurance, strong company- and job-specific competences and medium public spending on education. The social democratic regime, which relies on the state, represents comprehensive redistribution, high social security and high public spending on general, company-specific and job-specific education.

As we can see so far, liberal and coordinated (or social) market economies differ with regard to technological specialization, the organization of innovation, company management, education and job structure and work relationships. Figure 1.2 summarizes the essential differences in a systematic manner:

Adjustment to open markets in liberal and coordinated market economies

Let us now turn to the question as to whether the specific institutions and their typical innovation, export and inequality patterns are subject to a pressure of transformation by processes of market opening and the fiercer competition

		Social market economy	Liberal market economy
Technological specialization	Innovation pattern	Incremental innovation by perfecting high-quality established technology. Automotive, machinery construction, chemistry	Radical innovation by producing top technology. Micro-electronics, biotechnology
	Knowledge basis	Experimental knowledge	Scientific knowledge
	Patenting strategy	Patenting to secure technological advance for certain given products	Patenting to secure market lead for new products

		Social market economy	Liberal market economy
Organization of innovations	Relationship between innovation and production	Innovation closely linked with production and within established businesses product-driven innovation	Innovation outside production through independent R&D departments and newly-established companies as a stimulus for new innovation-driven production
	Appl. and bas. res.	Applied research without a connection to basic research	Applied research linked with basic research
	Type of innovation network	Stable Longer-lasting Regionally-focused Production and innovation networks	Free Short-term Not association-organized Result-oriented cooperations right through to international alliances
	Type of business	Traditional small, medium and large enterprises with a vast potential of accumulated technical knowledge	Newly-established smaller enterprises

Figure 1.2 A comparison of innovation regimes in social and liberal market economies.

		Social market economy	Liberal market economy
Company management	Corporate control	Through supervision and co-determination	Through the market
	Relation between banks and ind. comp.	Interdependency of banks and enterprises (Germany inc.)	Low interdependency of banks and enterprises
	Management philosophy	Rule of expert knowledge Long-term stability of the enterprise	Rule of financial economy Short-term return of the enterprise
	Opportunity for hostile takeover	Strict controls against hostile takeovers	Few opportunities of defence against hostile takeovers
	Stock market capitalization	Low stock market capitalization	High stock market capitalization
	Financing by banks	Comprehensive, long-term financing by banks (patient capital)	Low financing by banks, only at short and medium term
	Venture capital	Little available venture capital Company financing depending on entanglement with banks Patient capital	Company financing depending on market achievement Transparency of yields for investors (information) Shareholder value
	Shift of funds	Slow shift from low-profit to high-profit companies	Radical shift from low-profit to high-profit companies
	Birth and death rates of companies	Low birth and death rates of companies	High birth and death rates of companies

		Social market economy	Liberal market economy
Educational system and vocational structure	Education	Specialized vocational training Dual, school and in-firm training	General education
	Vocational organization	Engineers, technicians and skilled workers with a common specialist understanding	Natural scientists and engineers as competing specialists Production workers without any specialized expert knowledge
	Carrier of innovation and production	Integration of levelled specialist qualifications into an organic entity	Gap between top-level education and routine qualification
	Change of company and job	Few changes of company and job	Frequent changes of company and job
	Acquired knowledge	Long-accumulated expert knowledge of engineers, technicians and skilled workers as a source of continued innovation	Theoretical basic knowledge of natural scientists as a source of radical innovations

Figure 1.2 continued

		Social market economy	Liberal market economy
Company management	Association structure	Uniform trade unions and uniform industry associations	Pluralism of trade unions and entrepreneurial associations
	Level of organization of association	Medium to high level of organization	Low level of organization of associations
	Legalization	Legal structuring of labour relationships	Voluntarism
	Workers representation	Corporatism as part of bargaining autonomy institutionalized in-plant workers representation	Dualism of decreasing interest representation by trade unions and human resource management
	Level of wage agreements	Sectoral wage agreements	Decentralized, on company level
	Job security	High job security for insiders Marginalization of outsiders	Low job security
	Commitment of staff to company	Long-term commitment of staff to company Low inter-company mobility	Short-term commitment of staff to company High inter-company mobility
	Recruiting and dismissal	Slow recruiting and slow dismissal depending on profits	Fast recruiting and fast dismissal depending on profits
	Payment regulations	Collective, status-related payment	Individual, achievement-related payment
	Wage differences between companies	Little wage differences between companies depending on profits	Greater wage differences between companies depending on profits
	Recruiting of top executives	Slow guidance of top executives to new growth markets in top technology	Fast guidance of top executives to new growth markets in top technology
	Staff participation in innovation	Participation in technical perfection based on status security and long-term accumulated knowledge	Innovation as a result of high orientation to achievement of top executives

Figure 1.2 continued

arising in their wake (Münch and Guenther 2005; Guenther 2007). A much discussed question is, above all, as to whether the regime of the liberal market economy possesses competitive advantages over the regime of the coordinated market economy in the open world market, and whether the latter regime is thus constrained to adjust to the liberal regime by adopting deregulatory measures. A frequently raised argument refers to the higher social costs that may turn out a locational disadvantage for enterprises in coordinated market economies. It is argued that to cut these costs, enterprises shift their production venues to locations with lower social costs so that the coordinated market economies are forced to lower social costs by deregulatory measures in order to keep production venues in their own country. Hall and Soskice (2001: 54–62) object to this argument claiming that international labour division offers an opportunity to coordinated market economies to specialize on diversified quality production, e.g. in the classic fields of chemistry, automotive construction and mechanical engineering, which depends on a different institutional setting than the development and production of knowledge-based top technologies and standardized mass products. Diversified quality production requires a kind of vocational training that guarantees a great share of knowledge – and, hence, a stronger position of power – to skilled workers, too, so that they are in a position to attain higher wages, secure jobs and higher unemployment benefits. Their position of power, which is anchored in qualified vocational training, and their higher share in the number of employed people in an international comparison forms the basis for the greater stability of the trade unions. While in the liberal market economies the level of unionization has dropped along with the greater shift of employment from production to service jobs, it has remained on a higher level in the coordinated market economies, and in Germany, in particular, due to the less marked shift of employment. Hence, the position of power of qualified production workers is supported by relatively strong trade unions, which participate still very actively in forming the production regime in cooperation with the employers and the state.

In contrast, the level of unionization of the workforce in liberal market economies has dropped substantially as has their influence on the formation of the production regime. Both in the United States and in the UK, the company-specific agreement on wage levels has gained the upper hand on sector-wide wage agreements. In the United States, an increasing number of businesses negotiate their wage levels with their staff directly without a trade union being involved at all. In the UK, agreements are meanwhile being concluded mostly with a single trade union instead of several trade unions, on the company level instead of the sector level, in part even without the participation of any trade union. The closed shop – forced membership of employee groups in a trade union – has ceased to exist. Frequently, the shop steward is no longer the unionized representative of the staff, but the link between the management and the workforce. Hence, the liberal regimes have advanced even further towards the market-type determination of the employment relationship. With these changes, they responded to the increased competitive pressure on the global market. The liberalization and deregulation policies have supported the strengths of the liberal market economies: faster shift of investments to knowledge-based top technologies; lower wage and labour costs for standardized mass production; and employment growth due to the easier transfer of capital and staff from the production sector to qualified and simple service jobs (Swank 2002: 218–242). The way of a diversified quality production with a lower dispersion of qualifications and wages – which existed in the coordinated market economies – would not have been available for them, since they would have lacked the necessary stability of company financing (patient capital) and the commitment and qualification of the skilled workforce.

20 Economic change

Hall and Soskice argue, however, that it is the availability of this structural arrangement that opens up a different path to the coordinated market economies for meeting the challenges of globalization. Above all, they would need to focus on their own strengths: solid financial markets with patient capital; cooperation between workforce, trade unions and the state; great significance of vocational training with highly qualified skilled workers; and a close cooperation of research institutes and enterprises in the development, transfer and standardization of technologies. The diversified quality production and the incremental innovations in the key sectors of chemistry, automotive construction and mechanical engineering provide them with a policy to maintain their position in international competition without having to put their emphasis on comprehensive liberalization and deregulation. On the contrary: the more they accept these, the more they destroy – according to Hall and Soskice – precisely those institutions that guarantee their specific capability for incremental innovation.

To corroborate their claim, Hall and Soskice refer to the fact that the structural arrangements, innovation and export patterns in the liberal and coordinated market economies have not converged up until today. While the liberal market economies have become even more liberal, the coordinated market economies did not experience a significant change of the institutions which characterized them. An international comparison proves that the growth they attained between 1985 and 1998 went from 2.3 to 3.2 per cent on average. This increase is 0.9 per cent below that of the liberal market economies. In the decade from 2000 to 2009, the average growth rate was 3.7 in Ireland, 2.9 in Australia, 1.8 in the USA, 1.7 in the UK, 1.7 in Austria, 1.6 in the Netherlands, 1.4 in France and 0.8 in Germany (OECD 2011e). The growth rates for previous periods had been at 2.4 and 2.5 per cent from 1974 to 1984 respectively, and at 5.1 and 4.3 per cent between 1961 and 1973 respectively. After all, the unemployment rates for the earlier periods are lower on average for coordinated market economies than for liberal market economies: 1.3 and 3.2 per cent from 1960 to 1973 respectively; 3.6 and 6.7 per cent between 1974 and 1984 respectively; and 6.1 and 8.9 per cent from 1985 to 1998 respectively (Hall and Soskice 2001: 20, table 1). These average values are meaningful to a certain extent only, since Ireland, for instance, represents a strong outlier among the liberal market economies featuring an unemployment level of 14.1 per cent between 1985 and 1998; the same goes for Japan in the field of coordinated market economies showing a level of 2.8 per cent. Moreover, at the end of the 1990s, the situation in the coordinated market economies of Sweden and Germany deteriorated once again. They were positioned at around 10 per cent for a shorter (Sweden) or longer (Germany) period of time, although they are listed at 4.8 and 8.5 per cent in the table. If we compare the United States and Germany, the ratio is at around 5.6 to 10 per cent for 2002. Moreover, the unemployment rate is not meaningful as the sole indicator of social integration. We have to take into account, above all, the average time of unemployment. In Germany, the quota of people being unemployed for one year and more among all unemployed people amounted to 51.5 per cent in 2001, in Sweden to 22.3 per cent and in the USA to 6.1 per cent (OECD 2003a). The percentages in 2009 were at 45.5 in Germany, 12.8 in Sweden and 16.3 in the USA

(OECD 2010c). The overall employment volume is just as important, which was clearly higher in the United States (73.1 per cent) than in Germany (65.2 per cent) in 2001 (OECD 2003a). However, Germany outranks the USA and comes close to Sweden in the meantime. In 2009, the employment rate amounted to 70.4 per cent in Germany, 72.2 per cent in Sweden and 67.6 per cent in the USA (OECD 2010c). The same kind of difference can be established for most other coordinated or liberal market economies, too. This claim holds less true, however, for the Scandinavian countries as is underlined by Sweden's employment rate of 75.3 per cent (OECD 2003a). If we relate the employment volume to income inequality according to the Gini index, we discover that in the liberal market economies of the United States, Australia, Canada and the UK higher employment levels go hand in hand with higher inequality – with Japan being the only outlier. In contrast, we establish the inversed relationship for the coordinated market economies of Germany, Norway, Sweden and Finland (Hall and Soskice 2001: 22, figure 1.2).

In view of the now obvious liberalization trends of coordinated market economies, advocates of the Varieties of Capitalism approach identify, above all, the declining capability for coping jointly with the fiercer global competition as the main reason of change (Hall and Thelen 2009). In line with their theory, a lack of coordination has involved a dualism between the still protected industrial core and the evolved unprotected periphery outside the regular wage agreements (Thelen and Kume 2006). Objecting to Hall and Soskice's claim of specific competitive advantages of the liberal and coordinated market economies, we might say that several changes have undermined the institutions of coordinated market economies: the growing market capitalization of enterprises in the coordinated market economies; the loan policy, which is getting more restrictive in the wake of the international banking agreement Basel II, since it requires more capital stock depending on risk assessment; the disentanglement of banks and companies; and further reforms of the financial market that exert an opening effect. These changes have made the financing and control of companies in coordinated market economies more dependent on the market (O'Sullivan 2000: 278–288). Hence, they are required to pursue a stronger orientation to the shareholder value, which, in its turn, opens the doors wide to a faster up and down of investments. The growing number of hostile takeovers in the German economy is considered proof of this development. The most spectacular case in this context was the takeover of Mannesmann by Vodafone in 2001 (Höpner and Jackson 2003). Indeed, reforms of the financial market loosened the close entanglement of staff and assets among German enterprises during the 1990s. The number of asset holdings dropped from 186 to 152 between 1996 and 1998 alone among the 100 biggest German enterprises (Heinze 2001: 663–664). At the same time, emission of shares in an enterprise's financing has increased, as has the share of investment funds and insurances in shareholding while, on the other hand, the share of enterprises in other firms has declined (Heinze 2001: 661–662). The number of takeover bids rose from thirteen to fifty per year between 1996 and 2000 alone. Qualifying these statements we have to say, however, that these figures concern mainly the complementation of shares that have already existed for some time (Heinze 2001: 665–666).

22 Economic change

A look into the Mannesmann case proves that this is somewhat an exception than the start of a complete conversion of entrepreneurial control from the model of entanglement to the market model. This is because Mannesmann was a strongly internationalized and market-capitalized company of the New Economy (telecommunications), which was listed on eleven foreign stock markets with 99 per cent of shares owned by various stockholders (Heinze 2001: 655). Within a relatively short period of time, the company had been transformed from a classic industrial company into a telecommunications provider. Only around 10 per cent of the 100 biggest German companies meet similar requirements. The same findings emerge when assessing the 558 biggest German companies (Heinze 2001: 667). We can, therefore, say that the system of company funding and company control has moved towards the market model to a limited extent only, but nevertheless visibly – also in view of the reforms of the financial market – and that the model of entanglement has persisted to some extent (cf. Bornschier 2005; Beyer 2006). In the short and medium term, we can expect a co-existence of the market model for the field of the New Economy and of the liberalized model of entanglement for the classic industrial enterprises. Accordingly, the pressure of the market hits the classic industrial enterprises from the field of diversified quality production in an alleviated form only. We can assume that the institutions supporting this production regime are subjected to a – limited – pressure to change. This assumption is confirmed, after all, by the only small institutional changes that have taken place. Despite this persistence, the changes are obvious: The "Germany AG" as an internally entangled and externally shielded stronghold has undergone a process of dissolution to some extent (Höpner 2003; Höpner and Jackson 2003; Höpner and Krempel 2003; Streeck and Höpner 2003; Streeck 2009).

It is above all the unemployment rate of around 10 per cent, which was given for about twenty years, that has damaged the model's legitimatory bonus. For Hall and Soskice (2001: 64), the major cause of this crisis is the fact that the grown internationalization of the production chains working according to the just-in-time principle, implies that production downtimes result in high losses so that the large internationalized companies can no longer afford to accept longer strikes or lock-outs as countermeasures. Moreover, the internationalization of production offers them the opportunity of transferring too expensive jobs to cheaper countries. Hall and Soskice suppose that the big companies did not display the necessary steadfastness during the 1980s and 1990s to avoid high wage agreements. As a result, medium and smaller companies felt obliged to leave the wage agreements which, in turn, restricted the effectiveness of sector-wide wage agreements. To counteract this trend, opening clauses have been added to wage agreements. Moreover, legal stipulations and agreements are concluded between the collective bargaining partners that introduce a higher level of flexibility into the employment situation (part-time, marginal employment, working hours).

Doubts have cropped up increasingly as to whether the innovation regime of the social market economy will remain competitive without any major changes under the terms of a large-scale market opening. In an international comparison, Germany still holds an outstanding second place in the export of R&E-intensive goods, accounting for a share of 14.9 per cent. The country is behind the USA, which leads the ranking holding a 19.4 per cent share of exports in global trade, but is placed ahead of Japan, which reaches 12.4 per cent, the UK with 7.5 per cent and France with 7.2 per cent (Legler et al. 2005: 15).

The greatest part of German R&E exports covers the classic high-quality products from the fields of automotive construction, mechanical engineering and chemistry; only a minor part is allotted to products from top technology, i.e. electronics, IT and biotechnology. Knowledge-based services are also represented but weakly. Nevertheless, top technologies and knowledge-based services are the specific sources of a greater growth dynamism. They are also those fields where the highly developed economic locations can create new jobs, while they cede jobs to venues in developing, newly industrialized and transformation countries in areas of long-established technologies, as these countries feature wage costs of 1–20 per cent of the German level. If opportunities for catch-up development are to be granted to developing, newly industrialized and transformation countries, this involves an increasing significance of investments in radical innovations in the field of top technologies in Germany (Legler et al. 2005: 22).

As we learn from a comparison between the two innovation regimes of the social and liberal market economies, this does not only imply the financial support of specific investments, but also a further-reaching institutional change, which ensures that elements from the liberal innovation regime are incorporated into the regime of the social market economy. Increasing market capitalization, hostile takeovers and the disentanglement of banks and industrial enterprises suggest an approach to the liberal regime of corporate control (Streeck and Höpner 2003). The exit of companies from the collective wage agreement, falling membership levels for the trade unions and employers' associations, the expansion of general education and the increased investment in linking basic research and applied research – also carried out by shifting research and development to the best locations in the USA – show that essential pillars of the regime of the social market economy are losing in vitality. The continuing high unemployment level has undermined the legitimacy of the regime, especially in view of the achievements of other comparable countries on the job market. Accordingly, two thirds of the citizens anticipated fundamental reforms in 2004. Nevertheless, with each reform that has been implemented, they have withdrawn their support, as nobody is prepared to forego established privileges (Süddeutsche Zeitung 2004). The old regime has lost much of its legitimacy, and no legitimately recognized new regime has emerged so far, although its outlines are recognizable already. They show that the concomitance of innovation and structural persistence is losing significance. Instead, the concomitance of innovation and structural change has become more important (cf. Armingeon 2005; Dörre and Brinkmann 2005; Manow 2005; Traxler 2005).

Despite these changes, the crisis has not yet been overcome. It is obvious that the historically grown institutional arrangement is geared towards a certain segment of the economy, namely to the segment of production work in the classic German showcase industries such as chemistry, automotive construction and electrical engineering, but that it is less suited for other branches of the economy. The same institutional arrangement is, however, less viable in labour-intensive production sectors and in the fields of qualified and simple services or top technologies (Streeck 1999). Its inherent stability has ensured that capital had been tied up in heavy industry too long, which is no longer competitive in the open global economy in the long run. Hence, it was not available for investments in growth markets, which hampered the inevitable structural change for a long time. Serving as a generally binding model, this structural arrangement has also seen to it that a lot of financial resources were invested in the support of unproductive instead of productive life in a very wide sense of the term.

Since a further transfer of labour-intensive production to the developing countries can be expected in the context of the global economy, and since the highly productive German showcase industries of chemistry, automotive construction and electrical engineering will do with less workforce instead of hiring more, a wider inclusion of working people in gainful employment can only be reached in the long run, when new fields of knowledge-based top technologies and qualified or simple services are tapped alongside the continued advancement of diversified quality production (Legler et al. 2005: 61). To this end, reforms are indispensable aiming at a shift of investments from unproductive to productive life. They do not have to remove the basic structures of diversified quality production. It is important, instead, to rob them of some of their rigidity and enrich them with new elements (Scharpf 2000). Martin Heidenreich (2004a) has shown that a "third path" has been developed in the Scandinavian countries, which includes both high investments in research, development and general education, and the promotion of vocational training and high social security. We can observe in this context that social policy is increasingly geared to activating instead of deactivating the working population, which results in clearly falling unemployment rates (Schmid 2002). Obviously, a way is open to the European societies that links innovation dynamics with structural change and social security. Social security will, however, be led more than before by activation, empowerment and employability instead of the deactivation of the individual (Table 1.1).

The ideal types of a liberal market economy targeted at radical innovations and of a coordinated market economy geared towards incremental innovations, as they have been sketched by Hall and Soskice (2001), comply with the actual situation only in a single comparison between Germany and the USA or the UK, but not in a group comparison between liberal and more conservative or more social democratic market economies. Table 1.2 shows the percentage of top technologies, medium high, medium low and low technologies in the industrial exports of the OECD countries for 2008/2009. We can see that among the nine countries situated above the OECD average there are four nations – the USA, the UK, Ireland and Hungary after its post-socialist radical change – that can be categorized as liberal market economies, on the one hand. On the other hand, there are also four countries – Switzerland, Korea, the Netherlands and Japan – that can be assessed more as conservative, or as conservative/social democratic in the case of the Netherlands. Finland, Sweden and Denmark as social democratic coordinated market economies, and France and Belgium as conservative coordinated market economies are close to the

Table 1.1 Indicators of education and research, government action, economic achievement and inclusion in the labour society

	Germany	Sweden	USA
Education and research			
Percentage of population between 25 and 64 years, 2008			
with university education[1]	25	32	41
with secondary education II[1]	52	48	48
with secondary education I[1]	9	11	8
Expenditure on educational institutions as a percentage of GDP (2007)[2]	4.7	6.3	7.6
School achievements of 15 year old students according to PISA 2009, score from 300 to 600			
Competence in reading (2009)[3]	497	497	500
Mathematics (2009)[4]	513	494	487
Sciences (2009)[4]	520	495	502
Government action			
Total expenditure of general government, percentage of GDP (2008)[5]	43.7	53.1	38.8
Economic achievement			
Annual rise of the real GDP in per cent, 2000–2007[6]	1.7	3.6	3.0
Inclusion in the labour society			
Employment rate 2009 in per cent of the population 15–64 years[7]	70.4	72.2	67.6
Employment rate 2009 in per cent of the population 55–64 years[7]	56.1	70.1	60.6
Unemployment rate 2009 in per cent of the population 15–64 years[7]	7.8	8.5	9.4
Long-term unemployment rate 2009 (longer than one year) in per cent of all unemployed people[8]	45.5	12.8	16.3

Sources:
1 OECD (2010): Education at a Glance, Indicator A1: To what level have adults studied?, retrieved 27 March 2011, from http://dx.doi.org/10.1787/888932310092.
2 OECD (2010): Education at a Glance, Indicator B2: What proportion of national wealth is spent on education?, retrieved 27 March 2011, from http://dx.doi.org/10.1787/888932310301.
3 OECD Statistics, retrieved 27 March 2011, from http://dx.doi.org/10.1787/888932343133.
4 OECD Statistics, retrieved 27 March 2011, from http://dx.doi.org/10.1787/888932343152.
5 OECD StatExtracts, retrieved 27 March 2011, from http://stats.oecd.org/Index.aspx? – National Accounts – National Accounts at a Glance - 2009 edition : 5. General government.
6 OECD StatExtracts, retrieved 27 March 2011, from http://stats.oecd.org/Index.aspx? – National Accounts – GDP, volume – annual growth rates in percentage.
7 OECD StatExtracts, retrieved 27 March 2011, from http://stats.oecd.org/Index.aspx? – Labour – LFS by sex and age – indicators
8 OECD StatExtracts, retrieved 27 March 2011, from http://stats.oecd.org/Index.aspx? – Labour – Incidence of unemployment by duration.

OECD average and are slightly ahead of Germany and Austria. Nevertheless, market economies that have been characterized as liberal for quite a while or more recently such as the Czech Republic, Canada, Australia, Poland, Slovakia, New Zealand and Iceland, are ranked clearly below the OECD average. This is proof of the fact that the relationship constructed by Hall and Soskice between radical innovation and liberal market economies or between incremental innovation and coordinated market economies does not exist in reality in such a generalized form.

Table 1.2 Share of the technology industry in manufacturing exports, 2008/2009

	High technology	Medium high technology	Medium low technology	Low technology
Ireland	49.01	34.46	3.63	12.89
Switzerland	44.04	31.65	10.93	13.38
Hungary	30.96	45.88	12.98	11.08
United States	30.75	43.41	16.16	13.32
Mexico	30.17	44.43	14.01	11.38
Korea	29.14	34.32	31.44	5.10
United Kingdom	26.37	46.87	19.84	14.76
Netherlands	25.76	29.84	24.21	20.19
France	22.87	45.21	18.78	18.91
OECD average	**21.71**	**43.48**	**21.15**	**15.77**
Japan	21.29	55.75	19.50	3.45
Finland	19.77	32.80	25.80	21.63
Slovak Republic	19.57	42.65	24.75	13.36
Czech Republic	19.40	44.94	20.94	14.72
Sweden	19.02	37.38	23.57	20.03
Germany	18.40	51.10	17.67	13.38
Belgium	18.22	52.33	23.27	18.35
Denmark	17.48	31.84	17.87	32.82
Canada	13.61	38.19	28.17	20.02
Austria	12.55	46.00	23.56	21.76
Greece	11.95	18.34	39.60	30.11
Australia	11.52	20.81	46.61	25.34
Norway	11.00	24.82	49.98	14.20
Iceland	10.54	5.33	46.72	37.42
Portugal	10.35	30.92	23.60	34.58
Spain	10.19	43.34	24.86	21.61
Poland	9.99	39.78	26.26	23.96
Italy	9.34	41.64	24.53	24.97
Luxembourg	6.83	23.18	51.72	17.95
New Zealand	5.50	11.28	11.73	71.49
Turkey	3.16	30.60	38.10	28.14

Source: OECD (2011e).
Share of the technology industry in manufacturing exports 2008 retrieved 18 September 2011, from http://stats.oecd.org/Index.aspx? – Industry and Services – Structural Analysis (STAN) Databases – STAN Archives – STAN Indicators 2009.

Notes
High technology, medium high, medium low and low technology 2008 is calculated as share of technology industries in manufacturing exports of goods.

Obviously, there are both liberal and coordinated market economies where top technologies account for a high share of the exports of industrial products, just as the opposite is true as well. Likewise, more or less high shares of medium high technologies in the export of industrial products can be found among both types of the market economy without any fixed pattern. Only two conservative coordinated market economies stand out from this field, namely Japan at 55.75 per cent and Germany at 51.1 per cent. After all, the scores achieved by the liberal market economies of Canada, the USA and the UK, which are between 38.19 and 46.87 per cent, are close to the OECD average of 41.8 per cent. Moreover, some strongly or largely (in the case of the Netherlands) social democratic coordinated market economies are represented in this category with far below-average values between 24.5 and 29.5 per cent, namely the Netherlands, Finland, Denmark and Norway. This means that radical innovations can flourish in a coordinated environment, too, as can incremental innovations in liberal surroundings. The thesis launched by Hall and Soskice saying that both innovation types require an individual institutional environment cannot be maintained in a strict sense. Nor can the thesis be maintained claiming that coordinated market economies have to cling to their institutional arrangement to be able to play their trumps in international competition. This eliminates an argument against the global pressure of liberalization.

With all these ideas in mind we have to take into account, however, that industrial production geared towards medium low to medium high technology has formed the core of corporatist capitalism. The secured normal work contract in the private economy has its roots here. If this branch of business shrinks and is not compensated for by the extension of likewise secured civil service contracts, but is replaced with highly paid but less secure jobs in top technologies and with very poorly paid insecure jobs in the private service sector, the regime of the coordinated market economy will crumble. The related liberalization of the employment order might then also spill over to the old core of industry jobs in medium technologies, especially as these are very much prone to competition with less regulated newly industrialized and transformation countries. Korea and Mexico, Hungary, the Czech Republic, Poland and Slovakia are on equal terms with Germany in the field of medium low to medium high technologies. In part, they attain even higher scores altogether. Korea, Mexico and Hungary are ranked even further ahead of Germany in top technologies. This situation mirrors Germany's special position within the OECD's realm of marked concentration on medium high technologies. The latter is shown by Germany's 51.1 per cent share in exports of industrial products of medium high technology, which is exceeded by Japan only. After all, top technologies at 18.4 per cent, medium low technologies at 17.7 per cent and low technologies at 13.4 per cent are represented rather weakly when compared with other countries (cf. EFI 2008).

Table 1.3 provides a survey of the period from 1991 to 2005. We can see that Germany is between 7.2 and 10.7 below the OECD average in R&D expenditure on top technology over the entire period under review, while it is between 22.6 and 27.3 above that average in the field of higher applied technology. In both technology fields, the distance has even grown in the period under scrutiny. Accordingly, German industrial production has specialized even more on higher applied technology. In the same vein is the great distance from the OECD average in the service sector, which has grown from 11.8 to 15.6 per cent. The precariousness of this special position of Germany in the OECD realm can be assessed when taking into account that the maintenance of the leading position in the field of medium high technologies is due exclusively to the unusual growth of R&D expenditure in automotive construction, while the latter has dropped slightly in mechanical engineering and industrial chemicals and strongly in electrical engineering.

It should be noted in this context that the OECD trade (imports and exports) in the field of top technologies has grown far more strongly than in the field of medium high, medium low and low technologies, as is underlined by Table 1.4 for the period from 1996 to 2005. Accordingly, we can show for a group of twelve leading OECD countries that their economic growth recorded between 1994 and 2004 was higher in those fields where R&D investments were made (Legler and Krawczyk 2007: 11). The strong benchmarking by the OECD statistics exerts additional normative pressure on Germany to come closer to the OECD average model. This model features a shrunken centre in medium low to medium high technologies, a growing top in top technologies and knowledge-based services, and a likewise growing bottom in simple, mainly privatized services such as postal delivery or the telephone services provided by call centres. However, several of the knowledge-based services have meanwhile become hazardous financial products, which have been identified as some of the culprits of the global financial crisis. Higher growth rates always involve higher risks.

In this OECD model, the normal working condition as represented by the centre is reduced in volume both from the top and from the bottom and is delegitimated with regard to its exemplary function. With this, the coordinated market economy loses one of its essential pillars. This applies irrespective of whether or not radical innovations will unfold better in a liberal market economy. The decline of the centre robs the regularities of the coordinated market economy of some of its fertile ground anyway. The fact that we have discovered four coordinated market economies among those boasting an above-OECD-average share of top technologies in exported industrial goods does not mean automatically that they were as coordinated in 2003 as they had been ten or twenty years before. The global wave of deregulation, liberalization and privatization hit the coordinated market economies, too. Hence, we cannot deduct from the related finding that the old type of coordination can easily go hand in hand with the cut of medium technology and the extension of top technology.

The normal working condition of medium technologies and public services as the core of the coordinated market economy loses significance, since its basis shrinks along with the extension of top technologies and knowledge-based services on the one hand, and the extension and privatization of simple services on the other hand. In line with this development, society's class structure is changing in that a global elite withdraws from national bindings at the top and a new

Table 1.3 Germany's industrial R&D sectors in an international comparison from 1991 to 2005

Sector	OECD[1]							Germany						
	Vertical structure[2] (in %)							Horizontal structure[3] (in %)						
	1991	1995	1997	1999	2001	2003	2005	1991	1995	1997	1999	2002	2003	2005
Top technology	**42.1**	**42.6**	**44.5**	**40.0**	**39.1**	**39.1**	**41.3**	**8.8**	**7.0**	**6.5**	**6.8**	**6.9**	**6.8**	**6.3**
Pharmaceuticals	6.8	8.1	8.1	7.9	7.4	9.0	12.3	8.8	5.2	6.9	7.0	6.8	7.9	6.0
Office machinery/EDP	7.9	5.8	8.1	5.3	5.2	4.7	3.9	6.6	6.1	2.4	3.2	2.7	2.5	3.0
Communications engineering	11.5	13.6	14.5	13.2	15.8	12.8	13.7	13.4	6.7	6.7	7.3	6.2	6.0	5.3
MSR technology	5.6	6.5	6.4	7.3	6.8	6.9	6.2	3.2	8.3	6.9	6.0	8.7	8.9	9.2
Aerospace engineering	10.2	8.6	7.4	6.3	4.0	5.6	5.1	8.5	8.5	9.8	9.3	11.0	7.9	8.5
Higher commodity technology	**30.4**	**30.9**	**29.1**	**27.8**	**26.5**	**26.3**	**26.0**	**18.6**	**15.9**	**15.2**	**16.9**	**18.6**	**18.1**	**16.9**
Industrial chemicals	8.3	7.4	6.5	6.0	5.4	5.1	5.0	18.2	16.5	16.2	16.0	16.4	15.1	13.1
Mechanical engineering	5.5	6.0	5.9	5.5	5.5	5.4	5.8	20.6	17.1	16.0	16.3	16.8	16.3	15.6
Electrical engineering	5.5	4.8	4.4	3.8	3.8	3.0	3.1	19.9	13.5	5.9	7.2	8.9	8.3	8.2
Automotive construction	10.7	12.2	11.9	11.9	11.2	12.2	11.6	17.4	15.7	17.4	20.9	23.1	23.2	21.8
Other vehicles	0.3	0.4	0.5	0.6	0.7	0.5	0.6	12.4	20.7	25.8	12.3	15.5	6.9	7.7
Other branches of industry	**11.1**	**10.4**	**10.0**	**8.8**	**8.8**	**8.7**	**9.1**	**8.0**	**7.0**	**6.6**	**7.7**	**7.5**	**7.3**	**6.7**
Services	**14.2**	**13.9**	**14.1**	**20.8**	**24.0**	**24.1**	**21.8**	**1.8**	**2.3**	**3.3**	**3.5**	**3.1**	**3.1**	**3.9**
Rest of the economy	**2.0**	**2.2**	**2.3**	**2.6**	**1.8**	**1.8**	**1.9**	**9.1**	**4.8**	**4.3**	**3.4**	**3.0**	**2.7**	**2.7**
Total	**100**	**100**	**100**	**100**	**100**	**100**	**100**	**10.7**	**9.0**	**8.6**	**8.9**	**8.9**	**8.9**	**8.5**

Source: Legler and Krawczyk (2009: 76, Tab. 2.4.1). Based on: OECD, ANBERD Database (DSTI/EAS Division) – STI Database – Calculations and estimates by Niedersächsisches Institut für Wirtschaftsforschung.

Notes
1 1991: seventeen big countries, since 1995: twenty-four big countries.
2 Share of sector-related internal expenditure in R&D in the total expenditure of the economy (in %).
3 Share of Germany in the seventeen and/or twenty-four big OECD countries in (%).

lower class is outdistanced at the bottom, while the middle class is compressed to a smaller volume and more modest living conditions that are less geared to upgrading both from above and from below. Hence, society lacks a wide centre forming the basis of a comprehensive welfare state that is in a position to absorb risks and compensate for failures. The foundation of the coordinated market economy thus loses some of its customary capacity. Accordingly, the paradigmatic change of the economic order is accompanied by a paradigmatic change of the social order, which we will discuss in the following chapter.

We can summarize the results obtained in this chapter by saying that the OECD countries are constrained to compensate for job losses in industrial production in the field of simple to medium high technologies by building jobs in the field of top technologies and, even more so, in services in order to face the global competition with each other and with the developing, newly industrialized and transformation countries. This implies a partial abandoning of the old unity of innovation and structural persistence in the coordinated market economy and a turn towards the unity of innovation and structural change in the liberal market economy. Scatter diagrams show that the employment quota in services is related

Table 1.4 Growth of OECD trade[1] in production[2] depending on industry and technology intensity 1996–2005

Industry	Average annual growth rate (in %)	Technology intensity
Pharmaceuticals	13.8	High technology
Petrol refining	12.2	Medium low technology
Scientific instruments	7.9	High technology
Railroad and transport equipment	7.4	Medium high technology
Radio, TV, communication	7.2	High technology
Shipbuilding	7.0	Medium low technology
Motor vehicles	7.0	Medium high technology
Rubber and plastics	6.8	Medium low technology
Chemicals	6.5	Medium high technology
Basic metals and metal products	6.5	Medium low technology
Other manufacturing	6.3	Low technology
Electrical machinery	6.2	Medium high technology
Aircraft and spacecraft	6.0	High technology
Machinery and equipment	5.2	Medium high technology
Non-metallic minerals	4.7	Medium low technology
Office machinery and computers	4.4	High technology
Wood	4.3	Low technology
Food, drink and tobacco	4.2	Low technology
Paper and printing	3.5	Low technology
Textiles and clothing	3.5	Low technology

Source: OECD (2007: 213); OECD, STAN Indicators database | OECD, International Trade by Commodity Statistics, May 2007, retrieved 5 April 2011, from http://dx.doi.org/10.1787/120423112608.

Notes
1 Excluding Luxembourg and Slovak Republic.
2 Average values of OECD exports and imports of goods.

far more with the overall employment quota than the export share of medium high technologies. Apart from a few outliers such as Switzerland, Greece, Turkey and Poland, we can recognize a negative correlation for the export share of medium high technologies (Figure 1.3). As far as the employment quota in services is concerned, the correlation is positive (Figure 1.4).

Bivariate correlation analyses and multiple regression analyses covering the relationship between the employment rate in the service sector; the share of different technology levels in exports; the rate of tertiary education; and public social expenditure on the one hand, and the employment rate on the other hand confirm the above thesis for thirty OECD member states. Looking at the following correlation table (Pearson's r), we establish a strong relationship between the employment rate in services and the overall employment rate alongside a still recognizable positive relationship between the overall employment quota and the export share of top technologies, and a likewise recognizable negative relationship with the export share of medium high technologies (Table 1.5).

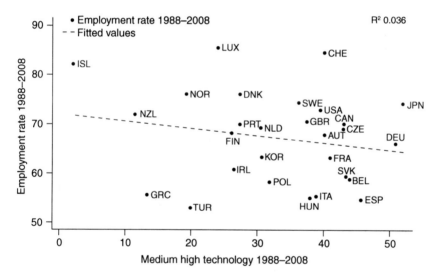

Figure 1.3 Medium high technology 1988–2008 and employment rate 1988–2008 (source: DSI 2010; OECD 2010c, 2011e).

Notes
Employment rate 1988–2008 rate retrieved 14 June 2011, from http://stats.oecd.org/Index.aspx – Labour – Labour force Statistics – Annual Labour Force Statistics – ALFS Summary tables.

Medium high technology 1988–2008 retrieved 23 June 2011, from http://emedia.ub.uni-bamberg.de/NetManBin/nmwebclt.asp?CONFIGID=OECDSTATWIN&DT=2&LANGUAGE=German – Industry, Science and Technology – STAN Indicators Database.

Employment rate is defined as Total employment/population at age 15–64. Medium high technology is calculated as share of medium high technology industries in manufacturing exports of goods. Indicators are calculated as averages at related periods of time per country.

Correlation and R2 is not significant in the related regression model with $p > 0.1$.
No control variables added. Own calculations.

Table 1.5 Correlation matrix

	Employment rate 1988–2008	High technology 1988–2008	Medium high technology 1988–2008	Medium low technology 1988–2008	Low technology 1988–2008	Employment in services 1988–2008	Tertiary education 1998–2008	Public social expenditure 1988–2007
Employment rate 1988–2008	1							
High technology 1988–2008	0.1577 0.4229	1						
Medium high technology 1988–2008	−0.1902 0.3323	0.3495 0.0631	1					
Medium low technology 1988–2008	0.0958 0.6276	−0.5351 0.0028	−0.3513 0.0617	1				
Low technology 1988–2008	0.0229 0.9061	−0.6056 0.0005	−0.7861 0	0.0131 0.9461	1			
Employment in services 1988–2008	0.6936 0.0001	0.2834 0.152	−0.1768 0.3777	0.0975 0.6286	−0.1112 0.581	1		
Tertiary education 1998–2008	−0.0123 0.9495	0.1209 0.5323	−0.2803 0.1408	−0.1533 0.4273	0.2919 0.1175	0.0674 0.7383	1	
Public social expenditure 1988–2007	0.2487 0.1934	−0.0992 0.6087	0.1695 0.3794	−0.007 0.9712	0.0711 0.7087	0.4187 0.0297	0.0041 0.9827	1

Source: DSI (2010); OECD (2010c, 2011e).

Notes

Employment rate 1988–2008 rate retrieved 1 June 2011, from http://stats.oecd.org/Index.aspx – Labour – Labour Force Statistics – Annual Labour Force Statistics – ALFS Summary tables.

High, medium high, medium low and low technology 1988–2008 retrieved 23 June 2011, from http://emedia.ub.uni-bamberg.de/NetManBin/nmwebclt.asp?CONFIGID=OECDSTATWIN&DT=2&LANGUAGE=German – Industry, Science and Technology – STAN Indicators Database.

Employment in services 1988–2008 retrieved 14 June 2011, from http://stats.oecd.org/Index.aspx?DataSetCode=MEILABOUR – Labour Force Statistics (MEI).

Tertiary Education 1998–2008 retrieved 24 June 2011, from http://stats.oecd.org/Index.aspx?DataSetCode=RGRADSTY – Education and Training – Education and Skills – Graduates by field of education and http://stats.oecd.org/Index.aspx – Labour – Labour force Statistics – Annual Labour Force Statistics – ALFS Summary tables.

Public Social Expenditure 1988–2007 retrieved 19 May 2011, from www.oecd.org/document/24/0,3343,en_2649_34637_2671576_1_1_1_1,00.html#data and http://dx.doi.org/10.1787/550420773523.

Employment rate 1988–2008 is defined as Total employment/population at age 15–64.

High technology, medium high, medium low and low technology 1988–2008 is calculated as share of technology industries in manufacturing exports of goods. Employment in services calculated as the division of total employment in services by total employment. The data is level, rate or quantity series over all persons. Tertiary education 1998–2008 is calculated as tertiary education divided by total population. Tertiary education is defined as Tertiary-type A and advanced research, over total programme destination, over all educational programmes of programme duration, total over all fields of programme orientation, total over all fields of study of field of education, total over all males and females. Public social expenditure 1988–2007 is defined as government social spending and is calculated as total public social expenditure as a percentage of GDP. Indicators are calculated as averages at related periods of time per country. The underlined values are significant with $p < 0.05$. Own calculations.

34 Economic change

A multiple regression using the employment rate in services, high technology, medium high technology, tertiary education and public social expenditure from 1988 to 2008 or 2007 as independent variables explains 48 per cent of variance in the employment rate from 1988 to 2008 according to R^2, and 46 per cent of this variance according to the adjusted R^2 (Table 1.6).

Nevertheless, we are on a high level of aggregation here. Other relevant factors interact with the factors under scrutiny so that we cannot be really sure. We can learn from such analyses that there is some pressure of coordinated market economies to replace jobs that have been lost in the industry of medium high technology by jobs in high technology and in the service sector. Nevertheless, such a policy meets its limits where it would undermine the social conditions for high quality production in medium high technology. This is where we still find truth in the varieties of capitalism approach. And we also see that there are indeed a variety of ways to cope with intensified economic competition and that there is still leeway for coordinated economies not to turn completely to the liberal model. However, there are other forces exerting pressure of change which

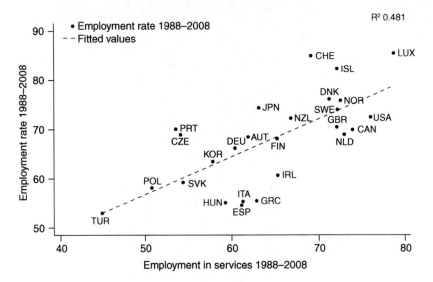

Figure 1.4 Employment in services 1988–2008 and employment rate 1988–2008 (source: OECD 2011e).

Notes
Employment rate 1988–2008 rate retrieved 1 June 2011, from http://stats.oecd.org/Index.aspx – Labour – Labour force Statistics – Annual Labour Force Statistics – ALFS Summary tables.

Employment in services 1988–2008 retrieved 14 June 2011, from http://stats.oecd.org/Index.aspx?DataSetCode=MEILABOUR – Labour Force Statistics (MEI).

Employment rate is defined as Total employment/population at age 15–64. Employment in services is calculated as the division of total employment in services by total employment. The data is level, rate or quantity series over all persons. Indicators are calculated as averages at related periods of time per country. Correlation and R2 is significant in the related regression model with $p < 0.001$.

No control variables added. Own calculations.

Table 1.6 Employment rate 1988–2008

Employment rate 1988–2008	I	II	III	IV	V
Employment in services 1988–2008	0.75***	0.77***	0.76***	0.75***	0.75**
High technology 1988–2008		−0.06	−0.04	−0.02	−0.03
Medium high technology 1988–2008			−0.03	−0.05	−0.04
Tertiary education 1988–2008				−304.75	−302.67
Public social expenditure 1988–2007					−0.01
Constant	19.62+	19.13+	20.45	23.17	23.06
Observations	26	26	26	26	26
R^2	0.481	0.485	0.486	0.491	0.491
Adjusted R^2	0.459	0.441	0.416	0.394	0.364

Notes
+ $p<0.10$, * $p<0.05$, ** $p<0.01$, *** $p<0.001$

we will deal with in the following two chapters. These are the forces of changing solidarity and the forces of changing ideas about justice and the position of the individual in society.

Concluding remarks

We clearly see that the way towards higher employment rates beyond traditional industrial labour proceeds across top technology to a very limited extent only, but includes overwhelmingly an expansion of the service sector. Since traditional industrial work has been the heart of the regime of incremental innovation with a simultaneously reigning structural persistence, this regime loses its support. The extension of top technology and services comes strongly along the path of the regime of the radical innovation of the liberal market economy. The Scandinavian countries prove, however, that there is a way towards higher employment rates even within coordinated market economies that uses top technologies and, to an even higher extent, the service sector. They have proceeded along this way with a substantial flexibilization of their employment by attaching less importance to employment guarantees and more to the workforce's employability. This policy has, above all, been adopted by Denmark. Accordingly, productive investments in lifelong learning have increased the employability of the wide mass of working people in Denmark. In Germany, in contrast, a consumptive social policy focused on the shrinking part of insiders has protected normal employment, while a growing part of outsiders was thus relegated into precarious employment. One crucial explanation of this development results from the fact that the Scandinavian trade unions feature an up to 90 per cent level of organization thus representing almost the entire workforce. In contrast, the German trade unions, which feature a level of organization of less than 30 per cent, represent the insiders at the expense of the outsiders. Tobias Schulze-Cleven (2009) has demonstrated this in a comparative study of Germany and Denmark.

In spite of the great effectiveness of the model of diversified quality production in the past, this model has failed to solve the new social problems of the present time, presumably just because of its great success. It solved the problem of social integration in a way that cannot be transferred smoothly to the solution of the new social problems. We are going to tackle these questions in the following chapter. In doing so, we must also bear in mind the integration of developing countries into the global economy and the effect of the competition between industrialized and developing countries on the industrialized nations.

2 The change of solidarity
The causes and consequences of international labour division

The European welfare states owe a substantial part of their welfare to their external economic links and their international political cooperation. What is presently being discussed as globalization is, in fact, a persistent process, an integral part of the modern world's development. The present crisis of the European welfare state, which is ascribed to globalization, underlines that the process has now reached a stage that calls collectively shared welfare based on national solidarity into question. The cross-border division of labour involves a differentiation of solidarity into global, supranational, national, regional and local solidarity relationships. These further-reaching and more differentiated relationships can no longer be integrated by means of an in-depth policy of approaching equal living standards within the national collective only, but rather by formal and abstract principles of justice reaching beyond national borders. To the same extent as solidarity becomes more differentiated, the value system is changing away from the principle of a far-reaching equality of results as well as away from the principle of remunerating status groups according to their attributed functional importance within an organic whole and towards an emphasis on the principles of achievement, equal opportunity, fairness and minimum help in need. Both the collectivistic and the organic models of the European welfare states are forcibly being pushed some way towards the individualistic model of an open and liberal society. The driving force behind this development is the growing global division of labour. The driving force behind the advancing global division of labour is not the resulting quantitative growth in the supply of disposable goods and services, especially as this also includes social, cultural and ecological losses, but the increasing competition for scarce and non-renewable resources which goes hand in hand with the diminishing distance between people due to the extension of ways and means of transport and communication. Competition necessitates specialization. The global division of labour transforms the lethal struggle for survival into a peaceful competition for consumers. Therefore, established life-worlds have to be converted out of necessity into excessive commodity worlds geared towards an ever more short-lived enjoyment by means of permanent "creative destruction" (Schumpeter 1983, 2004).

As a result of globalization, the nation state loses some of its capacity to regulate and redistribute, which cannot be restored to the same extent on either a European or a global level. The state's withdrawal requires compensation by the mobilization of civic associations and activities in order to retain a minimum level of social integration. The active society of empowered citizens is emerging as a guiding idea of global modernity in public discourse across nations with different cultural traditions. In this sense we observe convergence along different cultural tracks of development.

This chapter will address the change of the welfare state in the globalized economy as an effect of increasing international labour division based on Emile Durkheim's (1964) classical study. The main argument will develop as follows: with worldwide population growth and shrinking distances between people in the wake of improving means of transportation and communication, pressure on specialization and division of labour within and across nations rises. Therefore, the national welfare state is losing internal integrative power and is increasingly an obstacle to accommodating transnational and national integration. Accordingly the welfare state is an increasingly deficient institution when it comes to fulfilling exclusively the function of social integration in the global multilevel society emerging on the tracks of international labour division. On these tracks a change of solidarity takes place away from the segmentally differentiated system of nation states, which are internally integrated by mechanical solidarity. This change goes towards organic – or, rather, network – solidarity both across and within national borders. It is accompanied by a change of justice away from strong internal national justice of sharing post-market equality of results in the sense of national social citizenship or sharing status security within a meritocratic organic whole. Instead, there is a turn towards fairness in terms of sharing pre-market equal opportunity across and within national borders and remuneration according to individual achievement.

We will develop the outlined argument in five steps. In the first step, we will start with an analysis of the historical establishment and the change in the structural conditions that made the nation state the centre of social integration. The second step points out the effects of the global division of labour on the restructuring of market access, poverty and inequality between industrial and developing countries in the broad sense. Step three addresses the consequences of global labour division for the welfare state, namely disintegration and increasing pressure of structural change. The fourth step deals with the change of the notion of solidarity and justice in the process of increasing global labour division. Finally, the fifth step brings together the main theoretical argument, which explains the change described in the previous steps.

International trade and strong sovereign nation states: a model for the future?

The removal of trade barriers that accompanies both European integration and globalization is changing the foundations of social integration. According to Emile Durkheim (1964), we can basically differentiate between two dimensions of social integration: negative solidarity and positive solidarity, which correspond with negative and positive freedom from the viewpoint of legal philosophy (Kant 1956; Höffe 1999: 40–57).

Negative solidarity means harmonizing people's rights to act in such a way so that conflicts are avoided. The unambiguous establishment of property rights avoids quarrels about access to property. Each determination of rights to act, which are free from conflicts, represents negative solidarity. People can follow their tracks like celestial bodies without hindering each other, according to Durkheim (1964: 117). This negative solidarity, however, is but one side of a coin whose other side is positive solidarity. Without this counterpart, no negative solidarity would be possible at all. Positive solidarity, which corresponds to the establishment of rights to act, includes the mutual recognition of such rights in particular, and of the common maintenance of legal authorities supervising the mutual respecting of these rights.

In the discussion about European integration and the opening of the world market, the term "negative integration" is being used to characterize that form of integration that results from the removal of trade barriers. The flow of goods, services and capital, which is made easier in this way, leads towards cross-border relationships that are guided by interests. The state-controlled intervention into market relationships aiming at controlling the undesired side effects such as, for instance, too much inequality, social, ecological and technical risks, is interpreted as positive integration. There is some parallelism with Durkheim's term in as far as both negative integration and negative solidarity are based on the granting of private rights of freedom, above all property rights, whereas positive integration and positive solidarity are founded on cooperation aiming at collective decision on the latitude of individual action (Tinbergen 1965; Scharpf 1996, 1997a; Jachtenfuchs 1998).

Positive solidarity always includes a form of cooperation. It means that people (1) acknowledge their mutual rights to act and correspondingly grant each other a greater range of opportunity for the free pursuing of interests, namely civil, political, social and cultural rights; (2) settle conflicts peacefully according to legally stipulated procedures; and (3) maintain commonly supported legal authorities, which are able to sanction deviations from the rules effectively. The integration medium of positive solidarity, which corresponds with negative solidarity, is the law. Both the volume and recognition of civil law and the volume and power of civil jurisdiction can be regarded as indicators of this form of positive solidarity. Hence, we may speak of *legal* solidarity.

A form of positive solidarity that must be distinguished from legal solidarity is shown in the following: (4) collective bonds, which above all include a dense division of labour, a commonly shared civic spirit, close social cooperation and a common cultural life-world; (5) comprehensive readiness to share the welfare gained with all members of society; (6) priority of the collective over the individual; and (7) priority of one's own collective over other collectives. The integrative force of this form of positive solidarity is the feeling of belonging together. We may describe this as *emotional* solidarity. Indicators of an emotional positive solidarity are, for instance, the density of the division of labour, political consensus, amount of welfare budgets and cultural homogeneity.

The more the items (1) to (7) are met and the more completely they are accomplished, the stronger will be the integration of a society. The more social integration represented in items (4) to (7) is realized, the narrower will be the latitude for the individual pursuing of interests, and the more limited will be the personal freedom of choice. The greater the range of opportunities that are left to the individual's freedom of choice, the larger will be the number of negative external effects that cannot be corrected. The more latitude is given to the individual pursuing of interests, the more opportunities to act will be distributed in an unequal way according to the individual's capabilities; this, in turn, involves an ongoing accumulation of inequalities to the effect that past achievements or failures are producing future achievements or failures. Too great an extent of social integration cuts a society from the outside, narrows down the individual's latitude of action and hinders innovations. Too small an amount of social integration prevents cooperation where it is necessary, involves a lack of infrastructures, leaves people who are less capable unprotected and produces trouble spots of alienation, hopelessness and anomie (lack of rules), which are reflected by refusal to cooperate, cynicism, refusal to achieve and crime.

In modern times, the nation state has become the central unit of strong social integration with the corresponding embedding of negative solidarity into a comprehensive positive solidarity (Marshall 1964). The nation is a historically evolved and/or politically constructed community with a spirit of solidarity, which overcomes internal differences between groups (regions, ethnic groups, religious communities, classes, strata, etc.), and which demarcates on the outside towards other nations. The state is a unit of rulership (*Herrschaftsverband*), which successfully claims the monopoly of power for a delimited territory. The nation state unites national solidarity and territorial rule. The right to citizenship forms the point of intersection of state and nation (Meinecke 1907/1962; Deutsch 1953/1966; Weber 1976; Smith 1986; Anderson 1988; Gellner 1991; Hobsbawm 1991; Brubaker 1992).

The integrative power of the nation state has emerged in the following processes in a historic-genetic way:

- Formation of a wider-ranging territorial rule through incorporation and/or submission of smaller territorial powers in the course of military conflicts (Elias 1976).
- Successful maintenance of the established territorial rule against competitors.
- Inclusion of the masses into warfare and, consequently, the exercising of power: the struggle against external and internal enemies brings the nation to the awareness of the masses as a unit of solidarity. The granting of liberty, equality and fraternity creates a link between nation, legality, democracy and welfare. The united nation is the collective resource from which the nation states take their ability to act and their power of forming and integrating society by way of legislation, tax levying and redistribution.

- Internal homogenization through political-administrative penetration of all regions and legal unification.
- Cultural homogenization through uniform official language, school education and mass communication.
- Restructuring of regions existing side by side to form a relationship of centre and periphery, sometimes also referred to as internal colonization (Münch 1993a: 15–33).

The nation state, which is obliged to legality, democracy and welfare, breaks all particular group bonds and converts social integration into the mutual respect of individual civil, political and social rights and their coordination by the law. Particular feelings of solidarity are replaced with contractually formed, legally coordinated and administratively regulated relationships. Law ousts the particularistic feeling of belonging together as a factor of integration (Parsons 1971).

Nevertheless, the nation state not only replaces the particularistic solidarity of regions, ethnic groups, religious communities and classes with law, but also creates a new unit of solidarity, without which it could not interfere in society through law in the far-reaching and redistributing way it does. National solidarity is the non-legal basis of a society, which is otherwise integrated by law, just as the law is the non-contractual basis of the contract – as Durkheim (1964: 206–219) stated – and as the contract is the binding element of the labour dividing society with its order of market economy. In Durkheim's terms, organic solidarity, which is based on the growing division of labour, has been embedded into a marked mechanical solidarity in the welfare state. Its mechanical solidarity is represented by the level of independence from the market (decommodification) of the individual's standard of living in the case of unemployment, sickness or old age (Esping-Andersen 1990). It is most marked in the social democratically formed Scandinavian welfare states; it is weaker in the conservative welfare states on the European continent, and is weakest in the liberal welfare states, above all in the United States (Schmid 1996; Schmidt 1998).

The construction of the social democratic welfare state in Sweden has been the work of a united labour movement of the Social Democratic Party (SAP) in close relationship with the trade unions assembled in the Swedish Trade Union Confederation (LO). The labour movement forged a coalition with the farmers in the early twentieth century and subsequently also with the middle class. Thus the SAP was able to construct national solidarity across the working class, the farmers and the middle class. The Swedish "Volksheim" became the basic idea legitimating the egalitarian welfare state across classes. The conservative welfare state in Germany was primarily being shaped by Bismarck's model of social insurance as means of stabilizing a society having been mobilized and having become prosperous and more risky at the same time on its way to rapid industrialization in the late nineteenth century. This conservative basis was being extended by Christian centre parties and the Christian idea of subsidiarity of family and state in maintaining social security, particularly after the Second

World War. It has been additionally extended along its track by Social Democratic coalition governments since 1966. What has emerged in this context is national solidarity across status groups forming an organic whole, which means organic solidarity within the confines of mechanical national solidarity in Durkheim's (1964) terms. In the United States neither conservative nor socialist political forces were able to gain a majority over the liberal forces prevailing in the Republican and Democratic parties. Only the deep economic crisis of the 1930s enabled President Roosevelt to create a residual welfare state in Richard Titmuss's (1958) terms with his politics of the New Deal (Esping-Andersen 1990: 16–34). Immigration has created a far more pluralistic solidarity structure than in European countries with ties of solidarity fragmented according to class, ethnicity, national origin and religion (Gordon 1964). The middle class has been conceived as stretching across a wide variety of groups and does not leave space for successful working class politics. Solidarity has therefore emerged as a complex structure composed of a multiplicity of personal ties of the single individual.

Thus different solidarity structures and their transformation into political and ideological forces have produced different types of welfare states. In Sweden national solidarity across classes and its construction and representation by the Social Democratic Party and the idea of the "people's home" have created the comprehensive "institutional" welfare state in Richard Titmuss's (1958) terms. In Germany the solidarity of classes and status groups has been transformed into an organic whole by conservative leaders and Christian parties and their idea of subsidiarity to form a status reproducing and securing welfare state. In the United States the predominance of the middle class, continuous immigration and the multiplicity of differentiation into class, religion and ethnic as well as national origin have produced a kind of market solidarity. This type of solidarity is focused on enabling the single individual to achieve on the market. Social benefits are limited in amount and duration. In this sense the welfare state is residual, only designed for the limited and temporal support of the very needy. The major pillars of this type of welfare state were being constructed by F.D. Roosevelt's New Deal in the 1930s and by the Democratic Party. The underlying ideology is liberalism, which aims at enabling the single individual and also at enabling society through the productivity and creativity of the individual.

The question arises as to how far the different types of welfare states will be able to continue along their paths of providing collectively shared welfare under the condition of external globalization and internal pluralization and individualization. Globalization, pluralization and individualization are the major forces of change. They are closely linked with each other. Globalization implies pluralization and individualization of nation states, because it imports a greater plurality of values, ideas and interests in the nation states, and because it extends the latitude of action for the active individual. Pluralization makes nation states similar to each other in one global world. Individualization is internally being promoted by broad educational upgrading in particular. It produces empowered individuals, who are ready for global entanglement. The more we assume that external globalization and internal pluralization and individualization set closer limits to the nation state's provision of collectively shared welfare, the more the question arises as to how far the nation state's shrinking capacity in this respect can be compensated for by a corresponding growth of this capacity on the levels of the European Union and the emerging world society. In public discourse on the social and cultural effects of globalization, the "good old world" of the nation states is frequently being invoked. On the one hand, they are considered a stronghold of national, inter-group and inter-class solidarity, and, on the other, a guarantee of equality. The European welfare state has become a symbol of social integration which seems to dissolve everywhere in the global economy. Hopes are now being pinned on the legal, democratic and social extension of the European Union and on global cooperation as a substitute for the nation state's dwindling capacity for social integration.

Yet, the welfare state did not create its abilities for social integration by shutting itself off from the outside, but above all by the process of a growing economic linkage with the outside, of bilateral and multilateral cooperation with other states right through to the formation of supranational units. The European Union is the most advanced example of this type of supranational integration. The success of the European welfare states is closely related to European integration and the securing of peace in the framework of the Western alliance. Economic links with the outside and international cooperation have become quality seals of nation state policy since the end of the Second World War. There is, however, only a weak correlation between general government total outlays in per cent of nominal GDP in 2007 and economic openness in terms of import and export quota of GDP in 2008 (Figure 2.1).

The correlation between the openness of economies and state expenditure as well as welfare expenditure has been understood as proving the linkage between external economic integration and internal social integration. The prevailing interpretation says that a high level of collectively shared social security is being demanded from national governments as compensation for increased employment risks in the wake of international trade (Rodrik 1996). What is more directly implied is the increasing ability for collective investments the more the per capita income rises beyond the level of a decent private income and living standard in an open economy. With rising per capita income there is greater latitude for redistribution and collective infrastructure.

Agell (1999: F 155) shows that the openness of economies in terms of "the logarithm of the sum of exports and imports divided by GDP in 1980–4" is positively correlated with union density, centralization of wage bargaining, higher minimum wages, generosity of social benefits, strictness of job protection, lower wage inequality and lower income inequality (Agell 1999: F 156–F 159). Such data underlines that a high level of collectively shared welfare was linked with cross-border economic entanglement in the past. However, it does not prove at all that this will be the same in the future with continuously growing international trade and labour division, as we will argue

44 The change of solidarity

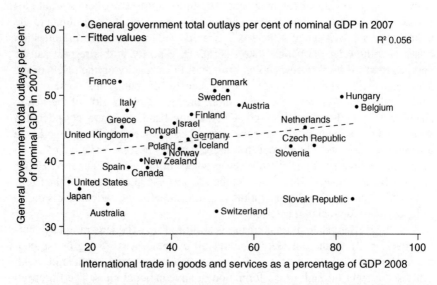

Figure 2.1 Public expenditure and economic openness OECD (source: OECD 2010d, 2011e. General government total outlays retrieved 14 March 2011, from www.oecd.org/dataoecd/5/51/2483816.xls. International trade in goods and services retrieved 14 March 2011, from www.oecd-ilibrary.org/sites/factbook-2010-en/03/01/01/index.html?contentType=/ns/StatisticalPublication,/ns/Chapter&itemId=/content/chapter/factbook-2010-24-en&containerItemId=/content/serial/18147364&accessItemIds=&mimeType=text/html).

Note
Ireland, Korea and Luxembourg excluded as extreme values. Own calculations.

in the following sections. The positive correlation between a high level of collectively shared welfare and economic openness does not confirm the interpretation that social protection is all the more politically demanded and provided by itself, the more open the economy is. Such a functional interpretation disregards the fact that institutions are neither created by function itself, nor simply by demand of voters from governments, if there is no favourable historical constellation of political and ideological forces. What is more directly implied is the increasing ability for collective investments the more per capita income rises beyond the level of a decent private income and living standard in an open economy. This does, however, not necessarily imply the assumption that a high level of per capita income is always accompanied by a high level of collectively shared welfare. How accumulated wealth is distributed is primarily being determined by historically established institutions, which have been shaped by the major political forces, namely the political representation of classes and status groups, and by the historically established ideas of a good and just society. The latter are being framed in the struggle between the different ideological positions of liberalism, conservatism and socialism. Factors such as union density, labour class political representation, the political representation of Christian social teaching by Christian political parties, and the shaping of public discourse by conservative Christian and socialist ideas are therefore more important for explaining the existence of a high level of collectively shared welfare than the simple factor of economic openness.

What has to be taken into account nevertheless is the pressure exerted on governments by increasing risks of displacing employers and employees from the market as a result of more open borders. Such risks give reasons for pressure groups to call for protection and/or compensation by trade and/or social policy. Strikingly, in the United States protective trade policy has always been more important than social policy, while it has been more markedly the other way round in the European welfare states, at least since the end of the Second World War, as Rieger and Leibfried (2001: 183–249) have demonstrated. There is indeed a functional relationship between an open economy and social protection in democracies. Social protection in terms of strong employment protection and/or high unemployment replacement rates allows for free trade, because it prevents resistance against lowering tariffs. As smaller economies with a strong dependence on export need low tariffs, employers, employees and governments in countries with strong social protection will widely support policies of free trade. Such is indeed the situation in the European welfare states. In the United States, by contrast, there is much less dependence on exports, just because of the sheer size of the domestic market; for internal reasons there is only a weak labour movement and promotion of socialist ideas with correspondingly little employment and unemployment protection. This allows sectors of the economy endangered by international competition to lobby successfully for trade protection. The trade unions join the employers in this respect, because protectionist trade policy compensates for lower social protection. The special right of longer entitlement to unemployment compensation granted to employees of economic sectors exposed to the world market, who can show that they have lost their job because of international competition, does not change the generally protectionist position of the unions, because the unemployment replacement rate covers only a small part of previous income from employment.

The institutions of social policy and the comprehensiveness of collectively shared welfare established in a particular country are, however, not a direct consequence of more or less exposure to international competition. A comparison between the United States and the European welfare states reveals that such exposure can be tackled in different ways. This can be done first of all by a more protectionist trade policy, second by more social protection, and third by more or less acceptance of structural economic change with more rapid destruction of old jobs and creation of new jobs. In as much as we live in one world and the interest of developing and newly industrializing countries in having a share in world trade becomes effectively represented in global politics – including the reality of global terrorism – the third approach, that is coping with free trade, gains in significance. This growing significance of structural change calls for more flexibility of the labour market, which is limited by strong social protection. A new conflict is therefore arising between the need for transnational integration by free trade and the privileges of protection by trade and social policy in the highly developed welfare states. Internal changes in the social structure, namely pluralization and individualization of social life, support this change, because they undermine the support of encompassing governmental protection. In order to understand and explain the social construction and reconstruction of welfare states we therefore have to go beyond their functional link to open markets and take into account the political and ideological forces as well as the structure of solidarity leading to welfare state construction, but also their changes fostering welfare state reconstruction.

A look at social democratic cabinet positions in relation to total cabinet positions and trade union membership on the one hand, and union contract coverage, total tax receipts and social security transfer expenditure as percentage of GDP in a comparison of Sweden, Germany and the United States on the other hand clearly shows that it is the solidaristic, political and ideological background that primarily explains the type and level of collectivistically shared welfare in a country (Table 2.1).

The correlation between the political representation of social democratic and Christian social teaching as well as trade union representation in the production regime and welfare state entrenchment has been comprehensively demonstrated by a historical-comparative study conducted by Evelyne Huber and John D. Stephens (2001). Whatever we take as the dependent variable – employing women with children, spending on non-pensioners, public health employment, decommodification according to Esping-Andersen (1990) with regard to unemployment, sickness and retirement, overall decommodification, active labour market policy or redistribution – is strongly influenced in the positive direction by accumulated left cabinet positions. The other side of this coin is a strong

Table 2.1 Basic features of three welfare states (%)

	United States	Germany	Sweden
Social democratic and other left parties in percentage of total cabinet posts, weighted by days (1960–2007)	0.0	40.1	77.9
Trade union membership (2008)	11.9	19.1	68.8
Bargaining (or union) coverage (2006)	13.1	63.0	92.0
Total tax revenue (2009)	24.0	37.0	46.4
Social expenditure as a percentage of GDP (2007)	16.2	25.2	27.3

Notes
Social democratic and other left parties in percentage of total cabinet posts, weighted by days: Calculations based on Armingeon *et al.* (2009). Bargaining (or union) coverage: ICTWSS (Database on Institutional Characteristics of Trade Unions, Wage Setting, State Intervention and Social Pacts), retrieved 3 March 2011, from www.uva-aias.net/uploaded_files/regular/ICTWSSDatabase212009.xls. Total tax revenue retrieved 13 February 2011, from http://stats.oecd.org/Index.aspx?DataSetCode=REV. Social expenditure as a percentage of GDP retrieved 13 February 2011, from http://stats.oecd.org/Index.aspx?DataSetCode=SOCX_AGG.

negative influence on poverty of single mothers aged 25–59, post-tax and post-transfer inequality of the elderly or overall post-tax and post-transfer inequality. Accumulated Christian Democratic cabinet positions exercise a positive, yet weaker influence on spending on non-pensioners and decommodification, a slight positive effect on post-tax and post-transfer inequality overall and of the elderly, and a negative, but less strong influence on poverty. However, their influence on support for employing women with children, public health employment and active labour market policy is moderately negative, while there is no influence at all on redistribution.

According to Huber and Stephens (2001) the number of veto opportunities offered by the political constitution hinders welfare state expansion. The influence of this variable is in blatant contrast to the influence of accumulated left cabinet positions. In the liberal welfare state of the United States we see a peculiar link of no left cabinet positions and the greatest number of veto opportunities granted by the constitution. The Scandinavian social democratic welfare state represents the opposite model: long-term left governments and little veto opportunities. The German conservative welfare state is characterized by predominantly Christian democratic and/or social democratic coalition governments and a considerable number of veto opportunities resulting from the federal structure established by the constitution. This institutional structure has helped to establish a welfare state that differs from both the liberal and the social democratic regimes. As the greater number of veto positions has limited the expansion of welfare provisions it has also a constraining effect on welfare reform as compared to the Scandinavian welfare state, because veto opportunities can be used for resisting reforms (Huber and Stephens 2001: table 2.2).

Alongside governmental representation of social democratic and/or Christian democratic parties and ideologies a set of institutional structures is important for shaping the welfare state, which can be summarized under the heading of a production regime referring to the interrelation of capital, labour and the state. It can be of a more pluralist or a more corporatist nature. The pluralist regime displays lower union density, coverage of wages by union-employer agreements, corporatist cooperation between unions, employer associations and state, and centralization of wage bargaining. In contrast to this pattern, the corporatist regime features all these qualities to the highest degree. The pluralist production regime is closely linked to the liberal welfare state, the corporatist regime to the social democratic welfare state. Again, the conservative welfare state is characterized by greater similarity to the corporatist social democratic production regime than to the liberal pluralist production regime. It is, however, particularly different to the corporatist social democratic regime in its emphasis on the family as the smallest unit of social integration, which implies special support of the male breadwinner and a lower female employment rate compared to the social democratic and/or the liberal regimes. It is also less committed to an active labour market policy, to wage equality and educational upgrading of the whole population than the social democratic regime, yet more so than the liberal regime (Huber and Stephens 2001: table 4.2).

An approach to explaining the emergence and change of the welfare state in terms of party representation in government and strength of trade union representation in the production regime is surely more adequate and more realistic than an explanation in terms of the functional contribution of the welfare state to protecting the population against the risks of an open economy, or in terms of governments responding to corresponding demands of their constituency. Nevertheless such an explanation is not sufficient by far. It does not address the deeper structure of classes and strata and of solidarity behind political representation of parties in government. It needs complementation by a deeper assessment of the structure of classes, strata and milieus as well as the structure of solidarity to which political parties respond. Changes in these structures have consequences for what is represented by political parties leading to changes in their policy preferences. Public discourse on the ideological definition of the situation is closely linked to this structure of classes, strata, milieus and solidarity. This discourse is on the one hand shaped by the historically established great ideologies, namely liberalism, socialism and Christian social teaching, while on the other hand it is formed by the problems the different ideologies have to address in a historical situation. New problems call for new answers and their implementation in reform policy.

The welfare state embodies a comprehensive solution to the problem of social integration in an industrial society characterized by class conflict and risk production within the confines of the nation state. It rests heavily on national solidarity. In as much as this national solidarity is eroding in the process of external entanglement and internal pluralization as well as individualization, the national welfare state loses its solid ground. Under these new structural conditions it becomes increasingly difficult for the state to integrate a greater plurality of interests and concepts of life by the schematic provision of welfare. Corporatist collaboration is being undermined by processes of pluralization and individualization. The diffusion of neo-liberal rhetoric is therefore not simply a fashion that will draw to an end some time, but hits fertile ground because of the changing structure of social life. Its success in setting the agenda of public debate exerts pressure on the social democratic and Christian democratic ideologies to adjust to the new historical situation and to be able to contribute to the solution of the new social problems.

With regard to social integration it is no longer sufficient to restore national solidarity within the confines of the welfare state. In the face of the transnationalization of deep social conflicts in the emerging world society new solutions have to address social integration in the double sense of national *and* transnational integration. Assessing merely the stability or instability of the welfare state is by far no sustainable solution to the problem of social integration. This is the deeper reason why the Continental European social democratic and conservative welfare states are under greater pressure of reform than the Anglo-Saxon liberal welfare states. Their social integration is far more bound to strong national solidarity and internal homogeneity than is the case for the liberal regime. Strong national solidarity is correlated with weak transnational solidarity and vice versa. This – and not simply the strength of national institutions of solidarity production – is the challenge of the contemporary historical situation.

The dependence of a high level of collectively shared welfare within national boundaries on a specific historical constellation of solidarity structure, political representation and ideological definition of the situation tells us that increasing cross-border economic entanglement is no guarantee for a strong commitment to the underlying institutions of this type of society in the future. If class solidarity, family solidarity, socialist parties, unions, Christian parties, socialism and Christian conservatism are being undermined by processes of globalization, pluralization and individualization, the major pillars of the conservative and the social democratic welfare state are being shaken. In this deeper sense of economic, political, solidaristic and ideological change we might expect globalization, pluralization and individualization to exert increasing pressure of change on the institutions of collectively shared welfare in the direction of a more liberal paradigm of social life.

The question therefore is not whether the welfare state will be able to maintain its institutions of collectively shared welfare or whether it will be forced to do so in order to compensate for increasing employment risks in the future under the condition of globalization. The question is instead whether the institutions of collectively shared welfare are being undermined by the changes of solidarity, political representation and ideological definition of the situation, which come about with increasing globalization accompanied by internal changes towards pluralization and individualization resulting from the increasing educational upgrading of the population. In this sense globalization and educational upgrading are complementary forces of social change. It is this solidaristic, political and ideological change we have to focus on.

The transformation of the welfare state is, however, not directly caused by economic globalization, especially not by profit-seeking capital exercising pressure on the state to leave the country in order to enjoy lower taxation and lower social standards elsewhere. This simplistic assumption is refuted by the fact that this turn away from strong welfare states has not taken place thus far, and by the fact that strong welfare states are still strong in terms of taxation, public social expenditure and high social security, while it is more the strategy of liberal welfare states to become more liberal in the face of economic globalization. The reason for this difference is the shaping of strategies to cope with economic globalization by the prevailing political forces and ideological definitions of the situation. This is why a study conducted by Duane Swank (2002) can arrive at the conclusion that the globalization thesis predicting the shrinking capacity of the state to provide for collectively shared welfare is wrong. According to Swank's study the liberal US welfare state has strengthened its liberal elements to cope with global economic competition, whereas the conservative German welfare state and the social democratic Swedish welfare state have widely maintained their conservative and social democratic character. However, it would also be wrong to extend this relatively short-term performance up to the mid-1990s further into the future. Swank (2002: 286–289) himself is cautious with regard to such an extension. His study suffers particularly from taking into account quantitative data up to 1993 only, since considerable changes have taken place in the meantime.

What a policy-oriented study of this type cannot show us is the deeper transformation of the solidarity structure and of the ideological definition of the situation taking place behind the struggle about policies on the surface of public debate. This transformation is breaking up the collectivistic ties of classes and nations in the interdependent process of globalization, pluralization and individualization of social life. In the long run we might therefore expect less favourable conditions for collectivistic forms of social inclusion and more favourable conditions for individualistic forms of social inclusion, as we will see in the subsequent steps of this study. We have to look at what happens with solidarity structures and ideological definitions of the situation, particularly ideas of social justice in the process of globalization, which is not only economic in character, but also involves increasing collaboration across borders beyond economic exchange. Not only international trade has steadily increased over the past forty years, but also membership in the *General Agreement on Tariffs and Trade* (GATT) and in the *World Trade Organization* (WTO), the ratification of conventions concluded by the *International Labour Organization* (ILO) and the number of *non-governmental organizations* (NGOs) of which a growing part is international in character (Figure 2.2). Such data shows that a more comprehensive change is going on, reaching deeper into the structure of solidarity and the ideological definition of the situation. It creates close links between globalization, pluralization and individualization. This change will be addressed in the following sections. First we have to look into the question as to whether there is indeed a watershed between earlier internationalization of trade and political cooperation of strong nation states and current – and even more so – future globalization accompanied by the pluralization and individualization of nation states.

The hard facts of growing transnational solidarity are not simply streams of capital and trade – though they are surely driving forces – but international labour division, international trade law, the activities of international institutions such as the WTO, IWF, World Bank, UN institutions and international regimes like the ozone and the climate regimes. Its national part is educational upgrading, shift towards an increasingly knowledge-based economy, technological upgrading of work, differentiation of the workforce, individualization of life careers and life conduct and pluralization of interest representation. We expect a significant correlation between these factors of change and a change of the welfare state towards the incorporation of elements replacing the collective provision of welfare by the empowerment of the individual and the focusing of equalization policies on equality of opportunity. This is, however, not a transformation coming about by material pressure. It is a transformation that is being driven forward by the elites of modernization and resisted against not only by the marginalized group of losers, but also by a broad majority of people who cling to the rights and privileges the strong social democratic and conservative welfare states have comprehensively granted thus far. It is therefore political

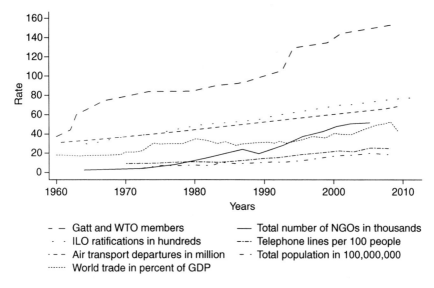

Figure 2.2 Population, transport, communication, world trade, INGOs, ratification of ILO Conventions, GATT and WTO accession, 1960–2010 (source: GATT 1994 retrieved 14 March 2011, from www.wto.org/english/thewto_e/gattmem_e.htm. GATT/WTO 1995 retrieved 14 March 2011, from www.wto.org/english/thewto_e/whatis_e/tif_e/org6_e.htm. From 1994 to 1995 GATT merged into WTO; Czechoslovakia had not joined WTO in 1995. The members that joined WTO in 1995 and were members of GATT before were counted with the year they joined GATT. Lebanon, Liberia, Syria, Taiwan and Yugoslavia quitted GATT in the 1940s and 1950s and were not counted as members. ILO Ratifications retrieved 14 March 2011, from www.ilo.org/public/english/standards/relm/gb/docs/gb277/pdf/lils-2a1.pdf. ILO Ratifications since 2001 retrieved 14 March 2011, from http://webfusion.ilo.org/public/db/standards/normes/appl/appl-lastyearratif.cfm?Lang=EN. Telephone lines retrieved 14 March 2011, from ttp://data.worldbank.org/indicator/IT.MLT.MAIN.P2/countries?display=default. Telephone lines are fixed telephone lines that connect a subscriber's terminal equipment to the public switched telephone network and that have a port on a telephone exchange. Integrated services digital network channels and fixed wireless subscribers are included. Aircraft departure retrieved 14 March 2011, from http://data.worldbank.org/indicator/IS.AIR.DPRT?display=default. Registered carrier departures worldwide are domestic takeoffs and takeoffs abroad of air carriers registered in the country. Total population retrieved 14 March 2011, from http://data.worldbank.org/indicator/SP.POP.TOTL?display=default. Total population is based on the de facto definition of population, which counts all residents regardless of legal status or citizenship – except for refugees not permanently settled in the country of asylum, who are generally considered part of the population of their country of origin. The values shown are midyear estimates. World trade retrieved 14 March 2011, from http://stat.wto.org/StatisticalProgram/WSDBViewData.aspx?Language=E and http://databank.worldbank.org/ddp/home.do?Step=3&id=4. Merchandise trade as a share of GDP is the sum of merchandise exports and imports divided by the value of GDP, all in current US dollars. Own calculations).

struggle that decides on the institutional reforms that are being carried out, as Rieger and Leibfried (2001: 93–104) argue with good reason. And since institutional reform starts on the basis of given institutions, what most likely happens is the incorporation of liberal elements in the framework of social democratic and conservative institutions thus producing institutional hybrids. Nevertheless the incorporation of liberal elements is changing the historically established institutions in the direction of accommodating transnational and national integration in a regime that strengthens the emphasis on network solidarity and justice in terms of achievement, equality of opportunity and fairness. New institutional elements are mostly included in the periphery of institutional programmes and do not immediately affect the paradigmatic core of an institutional code. In terms of Thomas Kuhn's (1962) theory of scientific revolution, new elements can be conceived of as coping with anomalies – that is, for example, inclusion deficits in terms of long-lasting high unemployment rates – with residual categories that are not part of the established paradigm. This is a kind of puzzle solving in times of the regular dominance of a paradigm (liberalism, conservatism, egalitarianism) that might continue to exist for a shorter or longer time without any change in the paradigmatic core. The more such residual categories are being added by way of institutional layering (Thelen 2002; Streeck and Thelen 2005b), the more there is a tension within the paradigm that calls for resolution by way of a more comprehensive paradigmatic change (cf. Hall 1993). Carrying out this change is a matter for new generations and new actors in the field – in our case it is the field of social policy – who are no longer committed to the traditionally reigning paradigm. This is the case, for example, with the increasing dominance of supply-side oriented economists and international NGOs, while legal scholars, social scientists and national welfare organizations are pushed to the edges of the field. In as much as functional deficits and related responses by residual categories accumulate and the field of social policy discourse is being occupied by new actors favourable to market-solutions of social problems and by NGOs representing transnational problems of social integration as against welfare organizations representing national solidarity, there is a chance of more than institutional layering, namely conversion of the core towards new directions (Thelen 2002: 103) or even revolutionary change of the paradigm.

On the one hand, the shocking experience of the Second World War paved the way towards international cooperation. On the other hand, its importance was underlined day by day by the conflict between the Western world and the Communist bloc. The end of this conflict opened up new chances of global economic entanglement and offered new opportunities, but also new necessities and challenges of political cooperation between the states and alliances. Alongside coping with new ethnic conflicts, new nationalism and the safeguarding of peace in view of new nuclear powers, attention is mainly being focused on avoiding a "race to the bottom" and the inherent social, cultural and ecological damages.

In view of the nation states owing their external security, their wealth and their ability to redistribute accumulated wealth in order to increase social integration to the further intensified economic entanglement and inter-state cooperation, the question arises of which reasons are behind the fears of a conversion from the previous "race to the top" towards a "race to the bottom". Why does the previously positively assessed international economic, political, cultural and social entanglement now take a negative quality under the label of "globalization" in public discourse? This question should clearly underline that globalization is a long-term process progressing in phases and with setbacks, which has been a characteristic feature of modernity emerging in Europe right from the start. Trade and division of labour in modern capitalism have always strived beyond traditional boundaries in every sense. The fact is always being underlined that it was not before the middle of the 1970s that world trade once again attained the level that existed between 1880 and 1914. For the period from 1880 to 1914, an average import quota of 13 per cent of the nominal GDP was established for the industrialized countries. Between 1973 and 1987, this quota was 15 per cent. Assessed in real terms, the values amount to 13 and 22 per cent respectively (Seeleib-Kaiser 1997: 79). The two world wars interrupted a development towards a global economy, which was taken up again after the end of the Second World War. A closer glance at the situation shows, however, that the overwhelming part of "global" economic transactions is handled within the group of highly developed industrialized countries and within the big economic areas. As a result, the world economy is mainly a matter of OECD countries, the European single market, the North American Free Trade Association and the ASEAN states. A considerably smaller part of world trade is handled between the big areas, whereas only a fraction of this part covers the developing regions outside these centres (Eurostat 1995: 35, 307–309; Statistisches Bundesamt 1996: 296–299; Hengsbach 1997: 5–6; Held *et al.* 1999: 156–161, 167–183; Dunford 2003). The reality of world society is very much a world of regions under American hegemony (Katzenstein 2005).

Beyond economic entanglement, the system of the European nation states removed smaller political units and integrated practically all regions in the world into the system of colonial rule. The dissolution of this system after the end of the Second World War certainly presented a wealth of new states to the world, but at the same time the institutions of international cooperation grew with the United Nations. European science and technology as well as the European culture of civil and human rights made the affluent society a model for the whole world. Modern Western communication technologies have meanwhile embraced the globe and produced a global society of a Western character (Münch 1991).

Discussing globalization today has least of all to do with the fact that we are suddenly living in a new world, but more with the fact that a long prepared and persistent process has gained new ground after the end of the conflict between East and West thus giving an additional boost to the globalization theme's brimming development. "Globalization" as a new phenomenon is much more a construction of reality produced by the media than a completely new reality. This should not mean that globalization does not exist actually. We should underline, in contrast, that globalization has been progressing for a much longer time than the theme's current boom might suggest.

However, from the fact that the European welfare states owe their affluence to the continually rising cross-border economic linkage and inter-state cooperation, it must not be concluded in a rush that further globalization will continue the existing programme even more comprehensively on a higher level and that, as a result, we are moving strongly towards *the* European welfare state. It is neither a matter of condemnation nor of playing down; instead, a sober analysis of the changes taking place is required. These changes occur to the same extent as globalization exceeds the existing level of linkage of national economies and of the cooperation of nation states and arrives at a new level of European and global division of labour. Here we pass indeed a watershed where the combination of international trade and the cooperation of strong sovereign nation states is being replaced by increasing international labour division and the pluralization and individualization of social life in a multilevel society where the nation state is but one level besides the global, European and subnational levels (cf. Axford 1995; Hirst and Thompson 1996).

Consequences of global labour division for the welfare state: disintegration and structural change

The welfare system of Western societies, which is tailored to far-reaching equality of results, has long benefited from their ability to extend specific locational advantages with regard to short production factors to the entire national economy and thus make them a collective advantage. However, it is precisely this collective property that is broken up by globalization. Production chains expand around the globe and do not remain within national borders. A VW Golf is assembled in Wolfsburg, Germany from parts supplied from all around the world. The local condensation of companies from supply to final production dissolves. Services, too, can be obtained from all imaginable places via worldwide communication networks. Inside the European single market, the job factor becomes more mobile and puts jobs protected so far under pressure, e.g. in the construction sector (Jansen and Turrini 2004; Marin 2006).

Multinational companies can withdraw from the grip of the nation state as far as tax revenues are concerned and can settle at the place that offers them the most favourable tax level (Genschel 2002; Sharman 2006). The workforce has become more heterogeneous and can no longer be represented uniformly by the trade unions (Gaston 2002; Dreher and Gaston 2007). The companies free themselves from the constraints of sectoral wage agreements (Streeck and Höpner 2003; Höpner 2003). Capital becomes more mobile and, from one day to the next, moves to places where better chances for profits are expected. Top staff are sourced worldwide and will commit themselves where they find the best chances of achievement. The business of consultancies has proclaimed "the global war for talents" (Brown and Tannock 2009). The opportunities narrow down, however, for a policy of equal living standards and redistribution within the confines of the nation state (Reich 1991).

Capital and top staff that have been so far traditionally tied to certain regions, cities and communities, can change their locations more quickly and more easily. Below the level of the nation state, regions, cities and communities get involved in a sharpening locational competition. Regions discover their economic importance beyond the boundaries of the nation state and join forces in alliances putting the regional cross-border cooperation into the foreground, while ousting national solidarity into the background. The rich Northern part of Italy feels more closely linked with its Alpine neighbours in Austria and Bavaria than with poor Southern Italy. Bavaria spearheads the struggle against the system of financial redistribution of the German states, which is now regarded as unfair. The reason for this strengthened struggle for regional advantages is the tougher locational competition between regions.

The new politics of location

National solidarity and its conversion into extensive programmes producing inner equality of living standards becomes an obstacle for the economically optimal allocation of resources to preferences. The state is being compelled to take up completely new location policies (Siebert 2006). The old location policies started from a relatively low mobility of the production factors, a relatively long-lasting maintenance of traditional locational advantages and national solidarity as the prerequisite for a policy aiming at the supply of an infrastructure (transportation and communication, legal safety, education), equality of living standards, regulation of the economy and the mitigation of slowly progressing structural change. Today, the production factors capital, labour, knowledge and technology have attained a level of mobility that requires new location policies. These new policies can no longer rest on traditional locational advantages and can no longer rely on national solidarity. They have to provide new stimuli for the mobile production factors to stay or to settle at certain locations and to commit themselves to their locations by raising the chances of profit in worldwide comparison. Investors are being attracted by subsidies and/or favourable conditions of settlement. The immobile production factors have to be fostered, formed, extended and trained in order to gain the commitment of the mobile production factors. Social environment, cultural events and the organization of employees' leisure time must enhance the attractiveness of a location. The marketing of regions becomes a major tool of location policy. The workforce must be trained and further educated to a maximum extent so that they become mobile themselves, can assert themselves on the employment market and are no longer dependent on the solidarity of crowd pullers. A new "culture of entrepreneurs" is being evoked to replace the comprehensive provisionary state (Reich 1991; Thurow 1996; Tiberghien 2007). This is how the new liberal "competition state" is emerging (Cerny 1990, 1997, 2000, 2005, 2010; Hirsch 1995; Hay 2004; Fougner 2006).

In the past, the nation state represented a giant agency charged with the granting of collective solidarity by providing equality of living standards on the basis of existing collective solidarity. Presently, collective solidarity is waning as the nation state takes on the role of an agency whose task is the recruiting of investors and the coaching of its members for increasingly tougher competition. The state acts as an entrepreneur having to advance both area and staff in order to offer them to powerful investors at the most favourable conditions and with an as low as possible tax load. This is the essence of what Wolfgang Streeck (2000) has called the new competitive solidarity. It is also the essence of neo-liberal governmentality as coined by Foucault (2008). Since the investors' locational decisions refer less to the nation and more to the region and local areas, regions, towns and communities have entered into fiercer competition in this field than ever before. Politics' national aspect loses in significance as compared to the regional and local aspects (Aleman *et al*. 1990; Straubhaar 1996).

Locational policy must be undertaken more actively by regions, towns and communities. It is guided by four essential criteria: an attractive social, cultural and ecological environment; low taxation; highly skilled workforce; and synergies resulting from the collaboration of companies, research and educational institutions. Investment bids often have to be accepted at the high price of an intervention into the existing economic and social structures or otherwise they will be realized in the immediate neighbourhood and, from there, threaten one's own location. This is why towns and communities frequently authorize the establishment of hypermarkets, factory outlet centres (FOCs) and leisure resorts in their outskirts, although this endangers the survival of inner city business so that the evolved urban culture consequently is dying. The decision is narrowed down to the balancing of a gain or loss in jobs; in fact, this balancing itself becomes superfluous since the big centres in the immediate neighbourhood absorb the customers from their own inner city anyway. Therefore, frequently a decision has to be made in favour of the big centre on the outskirts although afterwards, less jobs will be available than before, the town centres will be deserted and the city will be invaded by overdimensional concrete buildings and motorway-like feeder roads. This is a large-scale creative destruction as described by Schumpeter (1983, 2004); as compared to the old order the new order is distinguished at best by a larger volume of goods turnover. The question as to whether the new life in the artificial world of the big centres outside the historically evolved cities is better and more beautiful cannot even be asked and even less be answered. Changes may turn out particularly blatantly in small towns located close to a motorway junction, where old half-timbered houses vanish in an ocean of concrete although they were prettily restored only a short while ago. They may only survive as a mosaic of a sunken past in the concrete of the new era.

Globalization means that people come closer to each other and thus enter into fiercer competition with each other, both at a very short and a very large distance. Motorways and mass mobilization by automobiles make the FOC, which is 200 km away, a serious competitor of the retail trade in the town centre and thus a profitable investment for globally acting investors. Telecommunication around the globe makes software specialists in Bangalore enter into direct competition with those in Erlangen; moreover, it transfers capital from one continent to the other within a split second. The same applies to the transport of goods on land, river, sea, and in the air. The worldwide extension and perfection of the ways and means of transportation and communication allows for the just in time delivery of components for final assembly across tremendous distances so that final production becomes independent of warehousing and suppliers located close by. Suppliers enter into competition worldwide and are put under price pressure by the final purchasers (Held *et al*. 1999: 170).

Imbalance as a permanent state of affairs

As long as markets become more open, deflationary crises may be more likely than inflationary ones due to the increasing price pressure (Thurow 1996). Deflation's negative side is depicted by the companies' dwindling readiness to invest into the future, as they do not anticipate their investments paying off. A decline in economic activity and the lack of readiness to maintain and/or create jobs is the consequence. The current situation on the labour market is characterized by the fact that companies do not expect to set off investments into highly paid jobs by higher prices for their products as a result of fiercer competition on the world market. Consequently, it can be assumed that deflationary crises will play a greater role in the future than inflationary ones and that any sticking to a stable currency, which is influenced by the past, no longer lives up to the current situation.

Deflationary crises result from the fact that not all markets respond to the increased price pressure at the same speed. Lower prices in one sector of the economy are not passed on to other sectors immediately. When, for instance, a worker in the car industry earns less, this will certainly make the car more affordable. On the other hand, however, his spending on rent, insurance, education, further education and travels will not decline automatically but only with a great delay, if at all.

From this we can see that a structural change in one sector of the economy is not immediately complemented with a balancing structural change in some other sector. Rather, structural ruptures appear which are problematic in as far as ruptures in one sector are experienced most painfully because of the further existence of the old structures in some other sector. This problem is aggravated by global competition compelling everyone to creative destruction in the sense of the entrepreneurial strategy as described by Schumpeter (1983, 2004) more often, more comprehensively and faster than ever before. Structural change becomes a permanent feature. But as it does not occur in all sectors simultaneously and transferring it from one sector to another takes some time, the balance of demand and supply turns into an ideal state from which the market's reality is far away. The open market will then produce the opposite of the effects predicted by the theory of balance. It accelerates structural change. But as the production factors are not equally mobile everywhere, market liberalization first of all creates imbalances which are, it is true, compensated for after some time but have been replaced by new imbalances in the meantime as a consequence of accelerated structural change.

Balance only occurs in theory but no longer in reality. In contrast, traditionally limited markets were able to maintain their balance over a longer period of time, since supply and demand were harmonized step by step and were not disrupted by permanently offered new chances. We still discuss the question as to whether the growing social problems are attributable to too much or too little liberalization. Yet, the answer to this question must long be that both sides are right, however paradoxical this may appear. Since the well-arranged world of established traditions can never be completely shut off from the outside, the established traditions will always be an obstacle when it comes to the required adjustment to new conditions. Sticking too long to traditions will aggravate structural problems and is responsible for social problems resulting from too hesitant change, e.g. high unemployment figures. The acceleration of structural change by comprehensive liberalization brings about a permanent state of real imbalance and also creates social problems, for instance, precarious, uncertain and badly paid jobs, growing discrepancies between hopes for success and real failures and an increasing trend towards delinquency. The trend towards rising crime rates can only be stopped by strengthening external control. What is lost in social bonds by the economic mobilization of the entire society, the inherent dissolution of historically evolved life-worlds and the growing gap between the quickly rising needs and the actually existing, unequally distributed legitimate means to satisfy them (Merton 1949/1968), must be compensated for by external, technically sophisticated control. Relative deprivation or, in other words, relative exclusion from an affluent society becomes particularly virulent under such conditions. We have increasing opportunities for achievement, yet they call for enormous competitiveness and flexibility such that less competitive people are being marginalized. Taking part in the accelerated race for achievement includes also a greater readiness to apply illegitimate means. The consequences of this situation are at least temporarily rising delinquency rates, as demonstrated by the crime rate in the United States in the decades from 1960 to 1990, when a stagnation and slight decline set in (US Census Bureau 2002: 183). As Foucault (2008) argues, expanding the scope of economic freedom implies a rising demand for setups of security. This is the crucial dilemma of liberal governmentality.

Consequently, safety has become a booming branch of industry in the USA. Private security agencies protect buildings and entire residential areas, shops and entire shopping malls against undesired intruders, society sweeps the streets clean of suspicious persons and offers protection from persistent offenders by filling prisons (Wacquant 1997, 2008). Prisons have become an interesting object for private investors. Within twelve years only – between 1983 and 1994 – the number of private prison beds rose from zero to 43,500 (Donziger 1996: 89). In June 2006, the number of prisoners held in private facilities was 111,975, which was 7.2 per cent of all prisoners (Bureau of Justice Statistics 2011a). The so-called "prison industrial complex" benefits from the increased fear of crime, which is being heated up by the media. The number of finally sentenced prisoners never rose substantially over the mark of 100 per 100,000 inhabitants over a longer period of time between 1860 and 1970. Since 1970, however, it has grown continually to over 350 in 1994. Texas holds the record accounting for a quota of 636. The USA displays the highest imprisonment rate in the Western world by far. It contributes to reducing the unemployment rate (Western and Beckett 1998). In a comparison of the overall imprisonment rate for the years 1992 and 1993, which also covers persons who have not yet been legally convicted, the USA, accounting for 555 prisoners per 100,000 inhabitants, is far ahead of South Africa ranked second with 369 inmates. The figures reveal ninety-three prisoners for Great Britain, eighty-four for France, forty-nine for the Netherlands and thirty-six for Japan (Donziger 1996: 31–43). In 2008 or 2009, the rate was 760 in the USA, 624 in Russia, 329 in South Africa, 153 in the UK, 100 in the Netherlands, ninety-six in France and sixty-three in Japan (OECD 2011a). In the 1970s and 1980s, the crime rate grew from 8.5 to fifteen million offences registered per year. By strengthening external control, the authorities have succeeded in consolidating the rate at the still high level of fourteen million since the beginning of the 1990s (Donziger 1996: 8). With its rigorous safety policy, which removes any suspicious person as quickly as possible from public places, the notorious and dreaded New York has become a model of a safe town. In general we observe an inverse relationship of a rising rate of incarceration and a falling rate of crime in the USA in the 1990s (Pettit and Western 2004; Western and Pettit 2005; Gottschalk 2006). In 2009, the total crime rate was down to 10.6 million offences (Bureau of Justice Statistics 2011b; FBI 2011).

The phenomenon of relative exclusion has, however, in the meantime also affected the European welfare states. Global economic competition and internal educational upgrading have put more emphasis on individual achievement on the market. Placement in the status hierarchy is no longer a self-evident matter of origin and belonging to a class, but a matter of individual educational achievement and its continuation in an occupational career. In this situation there is more comparison of one's achievement with competitors from the outside and from within the nation. This implies necessarily the feeling of relative exclusion in as much as one's achievement falls behind relevant reference groups. Efforts of restoring balance between goals and means are the result of this experience of relative exclusion. Some respond by reducing goals, others seek compensation through drugs, still others with illegal achievement via delinquency. It is not surprising therefore that crime rates have increased in all European welfare states (see Chapter 5, Figure 5.1).

Creative destruction: economic growth and anomie

Structural change is being accelerated by global competition on several levels: capital leaves locations more quickly leaving behind badly qualified staff that cannot be retrained quickly enough to be of interest to new investors from new sectors (Deutschmann 2008). Production processes have to be rationalized and redesigned ever more quickly by means of the latest technological innovations. The job factor once again proves to be too slow when it comes to its adjustment to the new situation. Products have to be permanently renewed technologically, new products must be launched on to the market. Science must be converted into technology, mass production processes and mass products more quickly than before. This also involves permanent changes in the demand for personnel, which meets with a supply that is not tailored to it. The same applies to the constraint of having to conquer new markets worldwide. As foreign competitors penetrate domestic markets, entrepreneurs have to offset their sales losses on their home markets by gains on foreign markets. To be able to operate more profitably there, they have to replace domestic production units with foreign ones. Yet, the remaining staff will only be interesting to new investors after a retraining phase.

The quick migration of capital from one location to another, accelerating process and product innovations, the shortening of product cycles, a faster conversion of scientific findings into production and product technology and the worldwide operation of companies that is required by the world market create increasingly faster changes on the employment market that make unstable jobs a mass phenomenon. The workforce differentiates into a shrinking core of regular staff and an increasing circle of marginal staff. Switching from one job to another, from employment to unemployment, from full-time to part-time work, and from dependent employment to self-employment is seizing a growing part of the working population. This development can be observed in liberal welfare states in particular. It has also hit welfare states – though on a smaller scale – with special emphasis on standard full-time employment like Germany, where we have also noted declining permanent employment and rising temporary employment, a declining number of full-time jobs and a rising number of part-time jobs as well as growing self-employment with no employees since the 1990s.

In countries where the employment market has been opened up much more – such as in the USA, the UK, the Netherlands and Denmark – unemployment figures have dropped, on the one hand, but, on the other hand, the volume of part-time, extremely precarious, uncertain and badly paid jobs has increased. The high unemployment figures recorded for a longer time in a greater number of European welfare states, which boast relatively closed employment markets, are the reverse side of the same coin (Bradley and Stephens 2007). The pressure towards deregulation of the job market, a cutback in wages and social benefits, and a greater dispersion of wages has increased (Cornia 2004); this is underlined by the example of countries that have been most successful so far in lowering their unemployment figures. In the USA, the inequality in incomes and the spreading of wages is far greater than in the European welfare states. The percentile ratios of gross earnings P90/P10 were 2.2 in Sweden, 3.1 in Germany and 4.7 in the USA in 2000 (OECD 2003c). In the mid-2000s, the ratios were 2.79 in Sweden, 3.98 in Germany and 5.91 in the USA (OECD 2009a). Income inequality has risen considerably in the USA over the past thirty years, for example in terms of the Gini ratio (Figure 2.3), but also in terms of wages, both between and within occupations (Agion 2002; Kim and Sakamoto 2008, 2010; Mouw and Kalleberg 2010). Only the upper fifth of the working population accounted for rising incomes over the past twenty-five years, whereas the remaining four-fifths had to accept stagnating or even falling incomes (US Bureau of the Census 1973: 137; 1992: 148; Danziger and Gottschalk 1993; Nelson 1995: 6–12; Thurow 1996; Gottschalk and Danziger 2005; Rosenfeld 2006). This downward trend could be tolerated by many families only by increasing their employment volume. This means, above all, that men's lower income was balanced by additional work on the part of women, which is the reverse side of the further advanced women's emancipation in the USA. It is a consequence of this development that the education of children had to be left to TV more than ever before. Complaints about violence among young people and its spread in schools have become more and more prevalent thus demonstrating the perilous situation encountered by many families due to accelerated economic structural change. The higher speed of structural change must apparently be paid for with growing social problems.

The gap between rich and poor widens, and flourishing centres of upswing are being opposed by centres of decline, violence and destruction. As Table 2.2 – including nineteen OECD countries – shows, the USA not only has the highest percentage of poor, but also of children and elderly people living in poverty. One

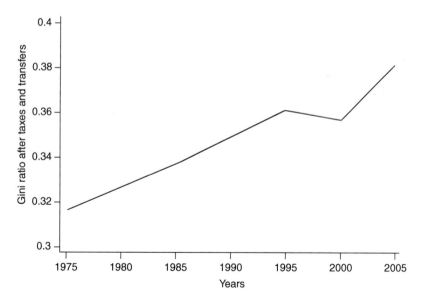

Figure 2.3 Gini ratio, USA (source: OECD 2011e).

Note
Gini coefficient after taxes and transfers. Own calculations.

analysis characterizes American social policy as "a war against the poor" (Gans 1995; Wacquant 2009). There is no doubt that excessive "creative destruction" has its price (Schumpeter 1983, 2004). It is an excellent means of *economic* advancement by permanent product innovation, but also a risk for social order. What accelerates advancement in the economy will easily produce anomie in social life. Creative destruction and anomie are two sides of one and the same coin (Durkheim 1973b; Merton 1949/1968).

From the viewpoint of the neo-liberal economic doctrine, these negative side effects of tougher competition do not appear as a result of market liberalization, but only as an effect of barriers, which prevent this transformation of social life-worlds into functioning markets such as the educational system, which is erroneously geared towards the one-time supply of a basic education instead of promoting lifelong learning. A market of educational programmes would have to cope with this problem from an economic point of view. The same applies to the labour market. For the neo-liberals, the welfare state's closed labour market rewards inflexibility. The deregulation of that market would literally "put the

Table 2.2 Poverty rates in OECD countries

Country	Poverty line (50% of median)[1]		
	Total population	Children	Elderly
United States	17.3	21.2	24.6
Germany	8.5	10.7	8.6
France	7.3	7.9	8.5
Italy	12.1	18.4	11.2
United Kingdom	11.6	14.0	16.3
Canada	13.0	16.8	6.3
Australia	12.2	14.0	22.3
Austria	7.1	7.0	9.4
Belgium	8.1	7.2	15.4
Denmark	5.6	3.9	8.5
Finland	6.5	3.7	10.1
Ireland	13.2	15.8	23.8
Netherlands	6.3	9.1	2.4
New Zealand	10.8	–	–
Norway	7.1	4.9	8.5
Portugal	12.9	–	–
Spain	14.1	17.2	23.4
Sweden	5.6	4.7	6.6
Switzerland	8.0	9.2	15.2

Sources: Luxembourg Income Study (LIS). Retrieved 17 February 2011, from www.lisproject.org/key-figures/kf-workbook.xls); OECD StatExtracts, retrieved 17 February 2011 from http://stats.oecd.org/Index.aspx?DataSetCode=POVERTY.

Note
1 Data is from 2000 for Belgium, France; 2003 for Australia; 2004 for Austria, Canada, Denmark, Finland, Germany, Ireland, Italy, Netherlands, Norway, Spain; Switzerland, United Kingdom, United States; 2005 for Sweden; mid-2000s for New Zealand, Portugal.

working people on their feet" and make them go where investments are made and acquire precisely those skills that are needed. The employee of the future is his/her own entrepreneur, is permanently under way, is at home nowhere and always eager to undergo further education. Moreover, the transformation of the welfare system into a market is also important. The more social security is separated from the individuals' own performance, the more it can be exploited and ruined by free-riders. This is, at least, what neo-liberal welfare theory teaches. Moral hazard, the individual exploitation of the collective, undermines the viability of the welfare system. The beneficiaries of social insurance, the enterprises and the wage contract partners exploit the web of social security to the detriment of those who pay the fees (Berthold 1997: 16–19). The neo-liberal welfare theory hopes to gain a more efficient allocation of resources and needs from a closer coupling of contributions and benefits. The more efficient dealing with welfare funds is to ensure that sufficient money is available for the needy: paying one's own share for medical service; unpaid days instead of the continued payment of wages in the case of illness; the reduction of social insurance and pension schemes to basic security for all; beyond basic security, private insurance is to safeguard a higher standard of living; public assistance only for participation in charitable work; and the transformation of welfare organizations into competing welfare companies, which are to commit the welfare system to a "revolution of efficiency". Forcibly, global competition subjects the welfare systems to market conditions and, in line with neo-liberal theory, sets Hayek's search machinery in motion looking for the evolutionary selection of the most efficient models of social security (Berthold 1997: 44–56). According to Friedrich A. von Hayek's doctrine, the market is not only an adequate tool for the allocation of individual goods to individual preferences, but also for learning about the most efficient collective rules for living together (Hayek 1969). A competitive educational system and lifelong learning now rank high on the agenda of asserting the position of an industrial location (Olssen and Peters 2005; Field 2006; Fejes and Nicoll 2008; Jakobi 2009). The immobility of labour as a production factor has to be removed as the last relict of times gone by so as to be better prepared for the accelerated process of creative destruction and the inherent structural change. The revolution of efficiency in the welfare system is to ensure that the flotsam and jetsam washed on to the edge of society by the waves of creative destruction cause as little cost as possible. To put it in more optimistic terms, it is hoped that the streamlining of the welfare system along with the regained economic development dynamics create the latitude for support of the truly disadvantaged, which the European welfare states have lost as a result of their total provision for the entire population. This is designed to regain the ability for a limited and targeted, first of all efficient, redistribution. From their relatively low mobility in Europe as compared to the USA it is concluded that the achievers are prepared to accept redistribution of this kind. Due to this relative immobility of the highly skilled workforce a certain chance of survival is even seen for local welfare traditions (Berthold 1997: 66–72).

Only "flexible men" fit into a permanently changing world in the eyes of Richard Sennett (1998). The human being seems to be completely reduced to the status of a production factor, while life is narrowed down to the optimum utilization of all production factors. Nevertheless, all that the market-type organization of the educational system, the labour market and the welfare system may attain is to arrive at "American conditions". In that country, education, labour and welfare have always been organized in a market-like way, much more so than in the European welfare states. This has, however, always been accompanied by the frequently described effects of growing disparities, deep structural ruptures, the simultaneity of flourishing and decay, richness and poverty, centres of well-being and centres of violence and crime in close proximity to each other. The life conditions prevalent in the Third World seem to be closer to the future than those to be found in the European welfare states if we follow the sceptical views of the ongoing transformation process (Danziger and Gottschalk 1993; Donziger 1996; Wright 1997; Gottschalk and Danziger 2005; Wacquant 2008).

From the point of view of global integration accelerated structural change is the prize the rich industrial countries have to pay for the inclusion of the developing countries in the world market. The two basic principles of world trade order according to GATT and WTO are non-discrimination and reciprocity (Langer 1995). The reduction of tariffs for allowing better access to one's market should be offered to all partners, and it should be reciprocated on equal terms by those partners in the agreement. The strict implementation of these two basic principles would require above all the reduction of tariffs on agricultural and labour-intensive products in the industrial countries to open their markets to developing countries. Such an agreement would, however, exert even greater pressure of structural change on the industrial countries with corresponding crises of adjustment (Krueger 1995; Bhagwati 1998, 2004; World Bank 2002; Mandle 2003; Stiglitz and Charlton 2005).

From national to transnational solidarity

An open employment market, the permanent renewal of skills and the market-shaped organization of welfare achievements complement and stimulate each other. This means that no one can rest on his/her acquired skills any longer. Better chances are being offered to all those who stand out by their will *and* their ability to achieve in education and vocational training, while chances diminish for all those who are unwilling and/or unable to keep abreast in the general race for certificates (Peters 2005).

This development is underlined by the unemployment rate being by far highest among the least skilled in the highly developed industrialized nations (Berthold 1997: 58). The programme of educational upgrading, which started in the mid-1960s, has certainly increased the number of young people with higher skills, right through to the A-levels and the college certificate. However, it has also considerably lowered the occupational career chances for young people having only the lowest or no skills at all and little or no vocational training.

In Germany, attendants of the ordinary secondary school (*Hauptschule*) are in fact discouraged long before they have entered the labour market. Since the higher-ranked jobs do not grow to the same extent as higher skills in all areas, a competition of displacement is taking place which continually raises the required skills for those who apply for medium-ranked jobs thus making these jobs no longer accessible for ordinary secondary school graduates with or – in the worst case – without additional apprenticeship (Solga 2002). At the same time, wage dispersion of the highly skilled staff is growing. A rising number of them have to accept lower incomes than their more successful competitors (Thurow 1996; Kim and Sakamoto 2008, 2010; Mouw and Kalleberg 2010). We even witness the paradoxical effect that a college education appears too risky and not attractive for young people from the lower classes, although they have more chance than ever before to experience it. The share of working class children at the universities is stagnating at 15 per cent in Germany.

The programme of educational upgrading, which has been going on for thirty years, has certainly increased the chances for young people but, at the same time, has started a competition of displacement that already decides on future career chances in people's early youth. Basically no other effects are to be expected from a programme of further educational upgrading. Competition will attain a higher level and become even harder. This means that even medium-level skills do not offer a reliable basis for job and income. Moreover, acquired skills will quickly fall in value. They have to be renewed, completed and complemented over and again. The struggle for better skills in competition with others has to be fought from the beginning until the end of one's life. People with lower skills will have to find new chances for further training. For those who do not want to or are unable to live up to the rising expectations, the situation will be even more precarious than before. This competition of displacement is smoothened only in as far as the better paid and more respected jobs are growing in numbers so that the level of occupational work and income is increased on a wide basis. It cannot be expected, however, that this process will involve the collective raising of an entire nation towards highly skilled work. The growing international division of labour no longer allows for collective benefits of an entire nation. Instead, the better jobs are being assigned around the globe. To the extent that competition for better jobs is carried out openly worldwide, such jobs will no longer be concentrated on the entire working population of one nation. The result of this race for educational achievement is stagnating or even decreasing returns on educational investment for a growing part of the population (Brown 2000; McNamee and Miller 2004; Brown *et al.* 2010).

The more the workforce has to face worldwide competition, the less those who are successful can care for their less successful fellow citizens, as they have to be mobile and can no longer feel tied to national solidarity. The more they accept solidarity with their fellow citizens the more they will endanger their position in international competition. Their cosmopolitan attitude, which is required by the market, brings them in touch more with their likes around the world than with their fellow citizens in their country of origin. The middle class is shrinking and torn between a globally oriented elite and an increasingly heterogeneous underclass. The collective solidarity of the European welfare state splits up and gives way to a new differentiation of solidarities (Münch 2010). For instance, the semi-annual Eurobarometer polls underline that the population of the EU member countries can, meanwhile, be differentiated into three groups. Only about 10 per cent consider themselves exclusively or primarily as Europeans in the near future; about 47 per cent see themselves mainly as members of their nation though embedded into the European Union; 43 per cent still cling exclusively to their national membership. It is clearly shown here that the inclination towards Europe is growing together with income, education and occupational status, while clinging to national solidarity is generally a matter of the lower strata (Table 2.3). There are also differences with regard to the support given to European integration across strata according to the self-perception as winners or losers (Mau 2005; Gerhards 2007, 2008; Gerhards and Hessel 2008). This differentiation of solidarity is being extended because global competition for the most appropriate location spurs subnational competition between regions, cities and communities (Batey and Friedrich 2000; Bröcker et al. 2003; Cooke et al. 2004; Blonigen and Kolpin 2007; Dembour 2008). Therefore, national solidarity is weakened by the revitalization of regional and local solidarity. The revival of regional and local solidarity is, on the one hand, first and foremost a matter of the strong regions and communities, as they anticipate better opportunities for their strengths when being freed from national solidarity. On the other hand, the weak prefer national solidarity, as they will otherwise feel unprotected in the storm of European and global competition. Whereas strong regions join forces beyond the borders of their home countries, the weak regions cling to the cover of the nation state. Northern Italy gets along better in Europe and the world without Southern Italy, above all in the alliance of the Alpine countries. Southern Italy, on the other hand, needs Rome to secure the support of Northern Italy. However, this tendency is opposed by the share of weak regions in the regional support funds of the European Union, making weak regions favourable to European integration. Because national solidarity is waning anyway, their hopes are pinned on the European integration project.

In the global economy, national solidarity turns into an anachronism. However, the success of the European welfare state is based on precisely this solidarity. It is only a powerful state, which is supported by the mass of the population, that is able to ensure collective supply of living standards and security at the level of the European welfare states. This includes relatively strong internal homogeneity and the sharing of welfare benefits by the entire population. The provisionary state did not only support the poorest, but ensured social security for all and provided services for all such as free education, museums, theatres, operas, symphonic orchestras, the promotion of clubs and subsidies for public transport. The European welfare state could rely on broad support, since the entire population benefited from it. It is not astonishing, therefore, that the volume of the state's activities was extended to a 46.9 per cent share of public spending in the GDP in Germany in 1998. In 2009, the percentage was at 53.3

Table 2.3 To be national/European in the future (% by demographics)

	Occupational status														
	Responsible for ordinary shopping, etc.	Student	Unemployed, temporarily not working	Retired, unable to work	Farmer	Professional (lawyer, etc.)	Owner of a shop, craftsmen, etc.	Business proprietors, etc.	Employed professional (employed doctor, etc.)	General management	Middle management	Employed position, at desk	Employed position, service job	Supervisor	Skilled manual worker	Unskilled manual worker	Total
Q43 European Citizenship Future Feeling																	
(Nationality) only	52.9	30.4	46	53.6	50	24.7	42	33.3	28.5	18.3	25.1	32.6	42.8	38.3	47.4	52	43
(Nationality) and European	39.6	57.2	42.5	38.1	41.1	63	47	51.7	55.8	59.6	65.2	58.2	47.8	50.6	44.3	36,8	47,2
European and (Nationality)	4.3	8.6	7.8	5.6	6.7	7.5	7.3	10.2	10.3	18.3	6.2	5	5.7	6.2	4	5,9	6,2
European only	3.3	3.8	3.7	2.7	2.2	4.8	3.7	4.8	5.5	3.7	3.5	4.2	3.7	4.9	4.3	5,3	3,6
Total	100	100	100	100	100	100	100	100	100	100	100	100	100	100	100	100	100
N	887	654	409	1,846	90	146	219	147	165	109	597	625	600	81	625	323	7,711

Source: Gesis (2011); Eurobarometer, No. 62, 2004. Retrieved 27 March 2011, from www.gesis.org/dienstleistungen/daten/umfragedaten/eurobarometer-data-service/data-access/.

Note
Respondents were asked the following question: Item Q43A – European Citizenship Future Feeling ask for "In the near future, do you see yourself as...?". Data access is restricted for non-registered users. Own calculations.

(OECD 2010h). Tax progression and social security contributions along with the growing incomes have ensured that an average employee may keep hardly more than 60 per cent of his/her gross income for him/herself. This holds true even more in the Scandinavian social democratic welfare states. The increased global competition necessitates the state to release more capital for profitable investments in innovative products so as to keep the economy competitive. The USA's state quota of merely 32.8 per cent in 1998 (share of state expenditure in the GDP) is considered a yardstick for a dynamically growing economy (Murswieck 1997: 238; Rieger and Leibfried 2001: 118). Nevertheless, the percentage had risen to 42.2 in 2009 (OECD 2010g).

Summarizing our theoretical discussion so far, we can conclude that the expanding division of labour calls into question national solidarity and justice in the sense of the collective share of wealth within nations at the cost of sharing wealth across nations. The change is promoted by the elite of well-educated, mobile, transnationally oriented people, while the less educated, less mobile and nationally oriented people cling to the historically established national solidarity and sense of justice. We can derive the following hypotheses:

1 The more global trade grows and the more a country is included in global trade, the more there is support of attributing income and rank according to achievement, and the less there is support for compensating lack of achievement by governmental redistribution and generous social benefits.
2 The higher the status of a person in terms of education, occupation or income, the greater the support of attributing income and rank according to achievement, and the smaller the support for compensating lack of achievement by governmental redistribution and generous social benefits.

Combining both hypotheses we expect an increasingly stronger correlation, as predicted by hypothesis 2, over the past two to three decades leading to a growing bifurcation between the upper and the lower classes with regard to supporting comprehensive and strong national solidarity represented by the strong welfare state. Survey data provides support for our hypotheses. A comparative analysis of survey data from Britain and Germany carried out by Steffen Mau (2003) shows declining commitment to the collectivistic solidarity of the strong welfare state as well as an increasing bifurcation between the upper and the lower classes. According to the International Social Survey Project (ISSP), consent to the government's job of guaranteeing a decent standard of living for the unemployed has declined between 1985 and 2006 in Britain and West Germany, namely from 85.4 per cent to 57.4 per cent and 85.4 per cent to 70.9 per cent respectively (ISSP 1985, 1990, 1996, 2006; Mau 2003: 133). Upper classes, self-employed people and people in work show a considerably smaller support for governmental redistribution and generous social benefits than lower classes, employed people and people out of work both in Britain and Germany (Mau 2003: 133–146; see also Liebig *et al.* 2004; Mau 2004; Mau and Veghte 2007).

According to Allbus surveys, support of differences in rank according to achievement and of financial incentives for achievement has increased slightly between 1984 and 2000 (Figures 2.4 and 2.5). Interpreting the only slight change in the direction of the principle of achievement, we have to take into account that there is always a time lag between a change in the structure of social relations – namely expanding networks beyond national borders – and the change in values and attitudes. This is the hysteresis effect of an enduring habitus after conditions have changed (Bourdieu 2000: 263). The slight change of attitudes that has taken place can be interpreted as a reflection of a deeper, long-term change in the dominating principle of justice.

Further surveys show that a change in the sense of justice is indeed currently under way. For Germany, data reveals a rising sense of justice with regard to achievements between 1977 and 1986 followed by a clear drop until 1997. A survey conducted by Allensbach shows that, in 1977, 38 per cent of those surveyed thought that achievement is not being rewarded, whereas 56 per cent said that achievement pays off. In 1986, only 23 per cent gave a negative assessment, while 61 per cent made a positive comment. In 1997, the opinion of 39 per cent was negative and that of only around 50 per cent was positive. The belief that achievement pays off clearly increases along with education, occupational status and income. From the semi-skilled and skilled worker through to white-collar employees and civil servants from the administrative class right through to top

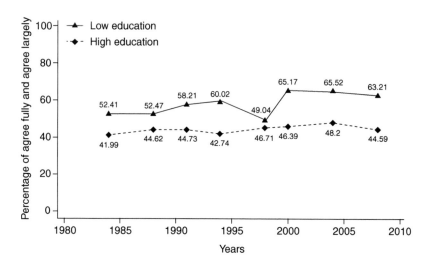

Figure 2.4 Question 1: V153 Status differences are acceptable, by education over time (source: Gesis 2011).

Notes

Years excluded from analysis because of missing data: 1980, 1982, 1986, 1988, 1990, 1992, 1996, 1998, 2002, 2006, 2008. Weighted data; corrected for oversample structure; accounting for sample design. Respondents were asked to indicate their level of agreement with the following statement: "Differences in status between people are acceptable because they basically reflect what people have made of the opportunities they have had." Own calculations.

70 *The change of solidarity*

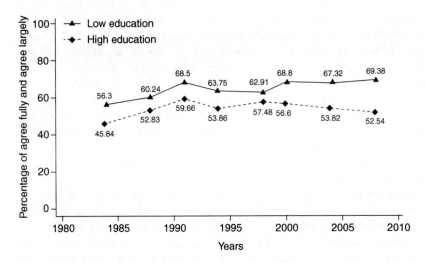

Figure 2.5 Question 2: *V152 Income differences raise motivation, by education over time* (source: Gesis 2011).

Notes
Years excluded from analysis because of missing data: 1980, 1982, 1986, 1988, 1990, 1992, 1996, 1998, 2002, 2006, 2008. Weighted data; corrected for oversample structure; accounting for sample design. Respondents were asked to indicate their level of agreement with the following statement: "Only when differences in income and in social standing are large enough is there an incentive for individual achievement." Own calculations.

executives and civil servants as well as self-employed and freelance professionals, the opinion that achievement is worthwhile ranged from 46, 51 and 52 to 55 per cent in 1997. In contrast, the negative opinion ranged from 55 to 44, 37, 34 and, finally, 29 per cent (Noelle-Neumann and Köcher 1997: 992–993). Further data shows increasing agreement with the statement that performance is very important for advancement in society between 1984 and 2004, from almost 60 to almost 70 per cent. Agreement with the statement that education is important for advancement in society increased among people of low education from 66 per cent in 1984 to 72 per cent in 2000 and then decreased to 70 per cent in 2004. Among people of high education, it increased from 67 per cent in 1984 to nearly 75 per cent in 2000, then decreased to 74 per cent in 2004 (Gesis 2011).

Survey data of this kind clearly reflects the fact that promoting the principle of achievement is, above all, a matter of the competitive strata, whereas the less competitive strata are substantially more sceptical with regard to this principle. The generally shrinking articulation of the opinion that achievement pays off and the discrepancy between the upper and lower classes in this respect may lead to considerable legitimation conflicts in as much as the principle of achievement becomes more important than the principle of a large share in wealth for all. This is also underlined by data gathered from a survey on the extension, the maintenance or the cutting of employers' contributions conducted in 1994. The most blatant conflict is revealed between East and West Germany: 71 per cent of the East Germans wish to extend employers' contributions as against a mere 28 per cent of the West Germans; 28 and 60 per cent respectively wish the current level to be maintained, and 1 and 28 per cent respectively opt for a cutback. In the West, the plea for an extension decreases from the workers via the white-collar employees and civil servants right through to the self-employed, namely from 29 to 25 to 22 to 8 per cent. The vote for maintenance of the current level is almost equal between 62 and 65 per cent. As far as cuts are concerned, however, the percentage rises from 9 to 12, 13 and 29 per cent from the workers to the self-employed (Statistisches Bundesamt 1997: 610; Allbus 1994).

The trend revealed by research on changing values, leading away from obedience, submission and love of order and moving towards free development and self-realization, reflects what is demanded by fiercer economic competition: self-assertion by training and specialization. "Obedience and submission" declined continually as a goal of education in West Germany between 1951 and 1986, namely from 25 to 6 per cent. Ever since, however, it has slightly increased again to 9 per cent. As far as "love of order and hard work" are concerned, a decline from 41 per cent to 33 per cent has been established. The most blatant change could be seen in the goal of "independence and free will", which boasted a rise from 28 to 65 per cent (Klages 1993; Gensicke 1996). Surveys conducted with regard to related goals of education between 1967 and 1996 revealed similar results: "asserting oneself" climbed from 59 to 72 per cent; "conforming" fell from 61 to 40 per cent. Virtues supporting the ability to assert oneself such as "doing one's work orderly and conscientiously", remained at a relatively stable 75 per cent (Noelle-Neumann and Köcher 1997: 119).

While in the 1980s, the trend towards self-realization had been interpreted as liberation from all external constraints and turning away from meritocracy's material criteria for achievement in a naive belief in the continuation of the '68 movement, the signs have clearly changed in the light of the globalization debate and under the dominance of the new efficiency thinking. The idea of self-realization is now in a new way coupled with the principle of achievement and requires everybody to be able to maintain him/herself. In public discourse, this change in significance of self-realization is shown through the cultural elite having to pass on its dominant position within society to the economic elite. Today, it is no longer writers and philosophers who set the tone for society, but consultants, managers and trend researchers. This trend is pushing the belief that self-realization requires, above all, good self-management both as far as occupational work and personal life outside the job are concerned. Job and leisure time are subjugated to the same criteria of efficiency (Voß and Pongratz 1998). Even in his/her search for adventures, the post-industrial person cannot let him/herself go. Driven by the fear to miss something, he/she has to search for as much adventure as possible within the time limit available to him/her (Schulze 1992). Time research has consequently established that time available for leisure has not increased despite the technical perfection of household and job. And, logically, the pressure to use the time available as efficiently as possible grows along with the range of possible alternatives of action (Garhammer 1999: 450–454). The "multi-option society" requires everybody to keep to a strict timetable (Gross 1994).

The market's selective processes dominate man's ability to determine how he/she would like to live with his/her fellow citizens. Along with the market's worldwide triumph over the state and its penetration into all areas of life, people's ability to decide together on how to live in the future is dwindling. What the future will bring about is more and more a consequence of innumerable individual decisions and their interaction, which can only be controlled to a limited extent. Undesired external effects of economically rational individual decisions can only be avoided or amended by political decisions. The more, however, politics has to withdraw under global competitive pressure and the more politics is unable to gain new strength on the supranational and global level, the less this kind of prophylactics and correction is possible. In this respect we observe an increasing weight of economics and a shrinking weight of politics in the process of globalization (Rodrik 2007, 2011; Narr and Schubert 1994; Koch 1995; Münch 1998: 347–414).

According to the principle of achievement, the single individual's success on the market determines his or her income and status in society. This principle is at the core of the liberal welfare state's idea of justice. In contrast to this liberal idea, the conservative welfare state is committed to the principle of justice within an organic whole of occupational status groups with male breadwinners caring for their family. This principle links income to a person's occupational rank. The male breadwinner earns his income according to his occupational status and his obligation of caring for his family. Compensation for a lack of income because of sickness, unemployment or old age tries to maintain the earlier status of the whole family. The social democratic principle of justice is egalitarian and considers the individual as a citizen who should share as much as possible of the collectively produced wealth of society. The liberal principle calls for pre-market equality of opportunity and tolerates post-market inequality of results. The conservative principle respects the inequality of occupational status groups according to the attributed value of their contribution to the functioning of the organic whole of society. Inequality of income and status is justified in as much as it guarantees the functioning of society. The conservative justification of inequality can be represented in a modernized form by the idea of meritocracy. In as much as a once-and-for-all earned status through education and occupational training guarantees a certain level of income and respect, the traditional hierarchy of estates is replaced by a modern hierarchy of occupational status groups. This hierarchy of status groups works as a limitation of open market competition and therefore at least to some extent against the principle of achievement in an open market. Therefore, it is endangered by the expansion of market competition in the globalized economy. This can be observed along the advancing abolishment of privileges pertaining to occupational groups for a long time and their confrontation with stronger market competition. The social democratic principle of justice starts with the assumption that not everybody is equally equipped to achieve on the market, while, however, wealth is the result of collective production and should therefore be shared collectively in terms of far-reaching post-market equality of results on the basis of social citizenship.

The principle of achievement celebrates its final triumph and ousts the principle of equality of results to the background, since the principle of equality is now being tuned to the best possible offer of schooling for everybody with the purpose of creating equal opportunity in the ubiquitous race for jobs. In the system of values, there is a shift from the principle of equality of results to the principle of achievement under equal opportunity (Roemer 1998; Nash 2004; Cogneau and Naudet 2006). Equality is being interpreted less as equality of conditions of life by comprehensive social balance, i.e. less as equality of *results* and more as equality of *opportunities*. "Social balance" as a value is being replaced by "fairness" (Dettling 1998b). It is less important for all to have a maximum share in national affluence – since the latter does not exist any more – than to have equal opportunity and to acquire affluence through their own achievement irrespective of the resulting outcome. Equal opportunities are easily compatible with unequal results. A fair race will also have its winners and its losers. Fairness will merely guarantee that the losers will not start a rebellion. They will not do this for as long as they are ensured that everything went fairly, that they had the same opportunities and will continue to have them if they show a sufficient *readiness* to make their achievement. This is the doctrine of meritocracy (cf. Arrow *et al.* 2000; McNamee and Miller 2004; Alon and Tienda 2007; Goldthorpe and Jackson 2008; Bukodi and Goldthorpe 2009).

Similarly, the conservative principle of justice in the sense of a stable hierarchy of occupational status groups and male breadwinners caring for their families has come under pressure of globalized competition. Acquired status is not an effective guarantee of income and respect once and for all. They rather have to be gained afresh on the market day by day. Historically established privileges of occupational groups are increasingly being removed. Educational status does not guarantee a certain level of income. Earnings dispersion within educational levels is growing. In this respect, the United States has particularly set the pace, while other countries are following at a slower speed (Prasad 2000; Pischke 2005; Kim and Sakamoto 2008; Dustmann *et al.* 2009).

But what will happen with all those people whose *capability* for achievement has reached its limits and makes them losers in the long run? In the framework of fairness, merely a "collective safety net" can be made available to them protecting them from falling below the commonly shared standards of a dignified life. Everything beyond this minimum help in need would mean an unmerited privilege, which is incompatible with the principle of fairness. It would punish all those who have to subsidize such privileges with their achievement. Fairness covers the unadulterated remuneration depending on the achievement made and the granting of equal opportunity to all along with the readiness to support all those who are unable to stand up against competition. Fairness is an idea of justice that is shown in an exemplary way in sports. The rules are to ensure that a victory will only be won due to one's better achievement but not due to force and fraud. The loser should not lose courage and should try again next time. The community of sports(wo)men supports everybody so much that he/she can continue to take part in competition but not beyond that limit, as this would create unequal conditions.

The principles of achievement, fairness, equal opportunity and minimum help in need complement each other and form the core of values of a liberal society (Zajac 1995; Kaplow and Shavell 2003). It seems to be that embodiment of the Enlightenment's big ideas of liberty, equality and fraternity, which corresponds better with the new structural conditions of the emerging world society than the far-reaching compensation of lacking achievement by the equality of results, which was established by the European welfare states in their privileged niche position. The European welfare state was tied to strong internal collective solidarity, which is shrinking as a result of increasing internal differentiation and external entanglement. The liberal concept of fair competition under the terms of equal opportunity and minimum help for the needy makes, in contrast, lower claims to collective solidarity, in its social democratic form of social citizenship or in its conservative form of an organic hierarchy of status groups. It is compatible to a greater extent with the heterogeneity of groups and the pluralism of lifestyles. This greater openness makes the liberal society model a candidate for the formation of the emerging European society and world society, whose outlines become more and more visible for us. The baseline of equal conditions of life, above which the standard of life is determined by achievement, need not necessarily be as low in Europe as in the USA. As far as fairness gains more importance, however, justice will no longer attain the level of equality of results or of status preservation existing so far in the European welfare states. The differences in the collectively guaranteed equality of results or status preservation depend on the ideas of an appropriate, dignified life, which can be agreed upon by all members of society. Since solidarity relationships drift apart, it will hardly be possible to reach an agreement on the current high level of equal conditions of life or status preservation.

In his theory of justice, John Rawls underlined in an exemplary way what justice means in the sense of fairness. It has explicitly been designed as the creed of a liberal society (Rawls 1958, 1971, 1993, 2001). Rawls wonders on what basic principles the members of a society in its original state would decide, if they are surrounded by a veil of ignorance in regards to their future position. Rawls argues that they would opt for the following two basic principles:

1 Everybody should have the same basic liberties.
2 Inequalities should be justified only in as far as they imply advantages for those who are not so well off and as everybody has the same initial chance to reach any position in society.

Rawls regards the human being as a basically rational maximizer of individual benefits. Therefore, the goal shared by all people can only be offering maximum chances for freedom and development to each individual. In Emile Durkheim's

(1964) terms, the negative solidarity of the avoidance of conflicts rules among people in a liberal society, whereas the positive solidarity of sympathy, sharing and the common definition of a good life has shrunk to a minimum that merely ensures that all continue to take part in the game and will not withdraw or mobilize for rebellion. The illusion of being able to achieve has to stay alive, if investments in the race for achievement are to be continued (Bourdieu 1994: 151–153; 2000: 21–22). The two basic principles introduced by Rawls do not say, however, where the limit has to be set beyond which inequalities are no longer a benefit for those who are worse off. People in favour of neo-liberalism might claim that any public assistance beyond the limits of minimum help in need will reduce everybody's readiness to perform, thus involving a lower overall performance. In this way, those who are worse off would receive less of the accumulated wealth available for distribution than if unequal results were corrected only slightly. In turn, people in favour of a comprehensive welfare state might reply that the poor do not profit from the richness of a liberal society and are better off in a less rich but also less unequally distributing society. Both can refer to Rawls. Regarding its basic statement, Rawls' theory of justice tends towards the liberal model of society, as it places the profit-maximizing individual above the collective. This means that the majority of Rawls' individuals would opt for a liberal society rather than for a welfare state as they back the chances for profit linked with the liberal society on the basis of a sufficiently large social network. Only a group of potential losers would opt for the model of a strong welfare state. However, real people will opt for one or the other model due to the values they have internalized and due to their views on the effects of specific models of society, but not due to abstract profit calculations (Andreß and Heien 2001; Arts and Gelissen 2001; Alesina and Angeletos 2005; Jaeger 2009; Sachweh and Olafsdottir 2010). The majority of Americans would prefer the liberal version, while the Swedes would opt for the egalitarian welfare state and the Germans for a more conservative welfare state. The neo-conservative sympathizers of the Republican Party in the USA would choose liberal justice, while the socially oriented sympathizers of the Democratic Party would mainly stand for a welfare state complementation of the liberal model of society (Table 2.4).

But where does development actually go? Our analysis indicates that globalization draws men and women out of national solidarity and makes them self-responsible more than before; collective solidarity is dwindling and is therefore less able than before to correct the unequal results stemming from tougher competition. The more liberal interpretation of justice in the sense of fairness is consequently favoured by the new structural conditions. The scope then narrows for redistribution measures of the welfare state. This is easier in the USA than in Europe as the liberal interpretation of justice in the sense of fairness has always dominated there, whereas this lesson has not been learned yet in Europe. So far, the idea of social balance is preserved although it is gradually being outdated by the factual conditions, whether it is in the form of exorbitantly high long-term unemployment rates or in the form of moving towards the liberal model of society.

Table 2.4 Activities of the state in selected fields of social and economic policy

Country	Agree strongly/agree that government should provide a job for everyone		Agree strongly/agree that government should provide a decent standard of living for the unemployed		Agree strongly/agree that government should reduce income differences rich/poor	
	High income	Low income	High income	Low income	High income	Low income
United States	31	56	44	70	45	68
Great Britain	51	67	50	79	65	81
West Germany	64	72	71	78	73	79
Netherlands	44	60	56	57	50	76
Spain	70	89	90	95	80	90

Source: ISSP (2006). Retrieved 3 March 2011, from http://zacat.gesis.org/webview/index.jsp?object= http://zacat.gesis.org/obj/fStudy/ZA4700.

Though survey data cannot directly represent the deeper change of justice resulting from the expansion of social networks beyond national borders, there is nevertheless some reflection of this change if we take Allbus survey data from West Germany. Two items can be used to indicate support of state responsibility for the individual person's welfare. One of these items enquires as to whether the state should provide for a decent living standard, if one does not earn any income due to sickness, disability, unemployment or old age. The other item asks whether social benefits should be extended, reduced or continued on the same level as before. According to both items there has been a slight shrinking of support for comprehensive social benefits since 1984 (Figures 2.6 and 2.7). It is not wrong to interpret this slight change of attitudes as reflecting a deeper long-term change of justice away from the conservative principle of maintaining status hierarchy or the social democratic principle of equality of results in the case of a person's inability to earn herself/himself a living.

Based on our previous considerations, the analysis therefore focuses on the question of what chances exist at all of retaining the essential elements of the welfare state in global competition on a national level and of spreading them beyond Europe worldwide. Moreover, we have to ask whether a social balance can be achieved on a supranational and global level, which would continue the success of the European welfare states on a higher level (Wildenmann 1991; Archibugi and Held 1995; McGrew 1997; Streeck 2009). A reply to these questions has to start from the fact that the European welfare state rested on a level of national solidarity which is shrinking more and more due to its growing internal differentiation and external entanglement. Nevertheless, heterogeneity is even greater on the level of the European Union and the world society so that the

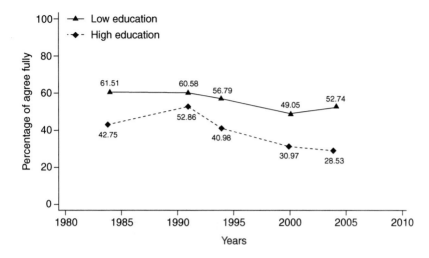

Figure 2.6 Question 3: V169 State is to supply provision in case of illness, hardship, unemployment and old age (source: Gesis 2011).

Notes
Years excluded from analysis because of missing data: 1980, 1982, 1986, 1988, 1990, 1992, 1996, 1998, 2002, 2006, 2008. Weighted data; corrected for oversample structure; accounting for sample design. Respondents were asked to indicate their level of agreement with the following statement: "The state must ensure that people can have a decent income even in illness, hardship, unemployment and old age." Own calculations.

prerequisites for an inclusion of the individual into collectively shared equality of results exist even less and cannot be reached. Even the advancing of institutions of political decision-making and public opinion formation, which exist only in a rudimentary form in the European Union and not at all worldwide, will change nothing of this fact. This is true, above all, since the nation state has attained its inner homogeneity and capacity of social balancing with means that would be rejected on a European and global level as being an illegitimate constraint from above. The European nation state with its monopoly of power emerged from warfare on territorial rule; it has levelled regional differences by way of a uniform official language and a uniform law (Münch 1993a: 15–33). The extension of the welfare system, which in turn contributed to a further consolidation of the nation state, was only possible on the basis of a nation state that is consolidated in itself. The European Union, and even more so the United Nations, could attain this consolidation and capacity to rule only if they continued the nation states' achievement in homogenization on a higher level. Due to the far too great heterogeneity of their members the European Union and the United Nations would, however, require an extent of homogenization that is incompatible with the principles of liberty and democracy (Knieper 1991; Guéhenno 1995).

The European single market established at the end of 1992 has certainly improved the chances for a common growth in welfare according to the law of

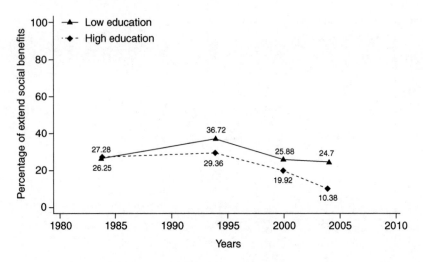

Figure 2.7 Question 4: *V197 Should social benefits be cut in the future or should they be extended* (source: Gesis 2011).

Notes
Years excluded from analysis because of missing data: 1980, 1982, 1986, 1988, 1990, 1992, 1996, 1998, 2002, 2006, 2008. Weighted data; corrected for oversample structure; accounting for sample design. Respondents were asked to indicate their level of agreement with the following statement: "Should social benefits be cut in the future, should things stay as they are, or should social benefits be extended?" Own calculations.

comparative cost advantages by a pan-European division of labour, yet at the same time it has limited the capacity of the individual member states to pursue their own welfare policy. They have entered into a regulatory competition and cannot afford an excessive redistribution of resources according to the principle of equality of results, which is geared towards social balance without provoking the migration of capital to locations that are less regulated by social policy. This limitation on national welfare policies has been strengthened in particular for the member states of the Monetary Union. The reintroduction of comprehensive welfare regulations on a European level has, however, to face tighter limits than the highly developed welfare states due to the European Union's tremendous economic, structural and institutional heterogeneity. The limited ability to enact social policy programmes of a federal system, which grants only little competence in social policy to the Federation due to its heterogeneity, is proven by the USA. In the European Union, the internal heterogeneity prevents a far-reaching transfer of social policy competence to the level of the Union (Münch 1993a: 133–181; 2010).

A country like Portugal recording a per capita GDP of US$24,980 in 2009 cannot afford a social policy to the same extent as Denmark whose per capita GDP amounted to US$37,688 in the same year (OECD Statistics). From a structural point of view, the two countries have established very different welfare systems with particular focal points as far as expenditure is concerned (such as pensions, support in the case of illness, family aid) as well as various forms of financing (tax, employers' contributions, employees' contributions). In institutional terms they have made very different organizations the bearers of their welfare systems. An accommodation of its social budget to the level existing in Denmark would destroy Portugal's economy and make the country dependent on transfer payments from richer countries. An excellent proof of this is supplied by the breakdown of the East German economy in the wake of Germany's reunification. The transfer payments from the West to the East represent a unique tour de force, which cannot be repeated on a European level due to the lack of collective solidarity. The accommodation of the social systems would require a tremendous structural and institutional conversion from those countries whose systems are not adopted (Scharpf 1998: 332–336).

With the extension of the single market, the European Union has limited the scope of its members to choose their own ways in social policy without gaining more scope for social policy itself to compensate for this loss. The frequently deplored democracy deficit on the input side of participation chances is complemented by a democracy deficit on the output side, if we understand lacking social integration achievements as a democracy deficit. The extension of democratic participation and control – such as the increased competence of the European Parliament – cannot remove the output deficit. A legitimation of European policies through the knowledge of experts acting as representatives will be effective only in very limited areas within the convergence of interests but will by no means be so in areas where interests clash and distribution struggles have to be fought out. Social policy is definitely one of these disputed areas (Majone 1994, 1996; Scharpf 1997a, 1998: 322–328, 336–340).

Justice in the sense of fairness can be transferred on to European and global levels more easily than justice in the sense of equal living standards, since it requires less collective solidarity (cf. Albin 2001). The more of what I have achieved I am supposed to share with other people, the closer I must be linked with them. As a rule, this kind of close tie implies a strong demarcation of the community towards the outside world. The out-group morality of non-sharing differs greatly from the in-group morality of sharing. So far, the European welfare states have represented this contrast. High equality standards inside are coupled with low social support for developing countries outside (Bradshaw and Wallace 1996; Jordan 1998: 6–15). The opening of national markets through the establishment of the European single market and of global free trade levels off the difference between in-group and out-group morality along with the corresponding international division of labour (Cogneau and Naudet 2006). The difference between the native and the foreign is levelled. A type of morality is emerging that covers the relationships between people within and across nations in the same way and is gaining global significance (Mau *et al.* 2008; Mau 2010). Nevertheless, this cannot mean the transfer of welfare morality on to global relations, since the structural prerequisites for such strong welfare provisions are lacking.

The change of solidarity

In the genesis of capitalism, the latter's economic ethics have replaced the ethics of brotherhood within particular communities and have subjected all relationships to the same normative standards of loyalty, reliability, legitimacy and fairness beyond all borders between the native and the foreign. This feature of modern capitalism has already been pointed out by Max Weber. It is misleading to consider the rise of modern capitalism only as the formation of an economic system free from any morality and rules and to ignore the replacement of the old particularistic morality with a new, basically universalistic one, which is taking place with that historical development (Schluchter 1979; Habermas 1981; Luhmann 1988). The same misleading interpretation is once again promoted, if global capitalism is conceived of merely in its effect on the dissolution of morality. According to this interpretation, global capitalism makes the moral chains of the welfare state burst in order to establish a worldwide economic system that is completely free from morality and legal rules. The complaints about this development plead for a "renewed embedding" and a renewed "closure" of the market on a higher, first of all European and then global level, after having stripped national markets of their social regulation (Beck 1997; Habermas 1998). In this context, Karl Polanyi's argument of disembedding and re-embedding is being invoked (Polanyi 1944). According to Polanyi, the "great transformation" of the formation of capitalism is a process of disembedding in the sense of liberation from the "moral economy" and the regulations of traditional estate society, to which the welfare state has provided the right answer, namely re-embedding. This pattern of thought is only partly correct; it neglects what matters in a moral respect: the replacement of a fading particularistic morality that applies different rules of conduct depending on whether one is confronted with members of one's own group or with members of other groups and that is differentiated according to estates by a rising universalistic, group-transcending morality. It should be noted that it is not the transformation from a morally regulated condition to a condition without any moral regulation (Münch 1982/1988: 514–520; 1984/1992: 590–615; 1986/1993b: 127–165; 1998: 68–117). Studies interpreting the currently ongoing transformation of the welfare state as a phase of discarding the historically established embeddedness of capitalism in institutions of welfare provision by the triumph of neo-liberal thinking and as a turn to a new disembedding process tell us only half the story. They neglect that this is not simply a disembedding process, but a deeper reaching process of restructuring national and transnational solidarity where disembedding and re-embedding go hand in hand.

This is precisely the situation we are witnessing at the moment. Global capitalism is not simply building up a moral-free world economy, but is linked with a change of solidarity and justice. The welfare state's *historically established* solidarity with its particularistic welfare morality and the differentiation of in-group and out-group morality is giving way to a new type of solidarity and morality stretching beyond all borders existing so far. The new social relations are characterized by border-transcending solidarity and justice, which, however, necessarily lose in substance, depth and density. They rather assume a *formal* character. The individual has to coordinate a far greater number of solidarities and has to live up to a far greater number of claims. This is exactly what justice as fairness means. It tends to regulate the relations among a plurality of people all over the world and not just between those who make part of one particular community. Nevertheless, this also means that the differentiation between people nearby and people far away is levelled off and that my behaviour towards my fellow natives is approaching my behaviour towards people who were foreign before. The result of this moral change is a formal legality and justice as fairness, which are as far away from moral-free capitalism as they are from the profound yet particularistic morality of the welfare state. It is always worthwhile recalling a passage from Max Weber's lecture on economic history, whose importance has rarely ever been recognized adequately:

> Originally, two opposite attitudes towards the pursuit of gain exist in combination. Internally, there is an attachment to tradition and to the pietistic relations of fellow members of tribe, clan, and house-community, with the exclusion of the unrestricted quest of gain within the circle of those bound together by religious ties; externally, there is absolutely unrestricted play of the gain spirit in economic relations, every foreigner being originally an enemy in relation to whom no ethical restrictions apply; that is, the ethics of internal and external relations are categorically distinct. The course of development involves on the one hand the bringing in of calculation into the traditional brotherhood, displacing the old religious relationship. As soon as accountability is established within the family community, and economic relations are no longer strictly communistic, there is an end of the native piety and its repression of the economic impulse. This side of the development is especially characteristic in the west. At the same time there is a tempering of the unrestricted quest of gain with the adoption of the economic principle into the internal economy. The result is a regulated economic life with the economic impulse functioning within bounds.
> (Weber 1927: 356)

We are facing this transformation of morality today in the process of globalization. The institution in charge of the development and accomplishment of the new rules of the game and the corresponding understanding of justice is the World Trade Organization (WTO). It is interested in fair terms of competition, and not in the production of equality standards on the level of the welfare states (Charnovitz 2004; Petersmann 2007). Reciprocity between trade partners and non-discrimination with regard to third parties are the two basic principles of trade according to WTO rules. They are the embodiment of fairness in international trade. The core labour standards stipulated by the International Labour Organization (ILO), which have a chance of effective implementation worldwide, represent likewise abstract and formal minimum standards, which do not possess the same substantial quality of social balance as those of the European welfare states. Contrary to the WTO agreements, the ILO standards cannot be enforced by way of sanctions.

82 The change of solidarity

The overall change of justice within nation states and between nation states is reflected in the shrinking inequality of household incomes between nations, but rising inequality within nations worldwide (Firebaugh 2003; Cornia 2004). This holds particularly true for those nations that are most strongly included in the world market, both developed and developing nations, while the least included nations suffer from an increasing gap between their poverty and the overall growing wealth in the emerging world society (World Bank 2002: 23–51).

With regard to activities aiming at an improvement of fair terms in global free trade and the international division of labour, interesting differences emerge between Europe and the USA. While the Europeans are first and foremost – or at least as an intermediate stage – interested in the establishment of a new exclusive community, namely the European Social Union, the Americans endeavour more to create fair terms in the world economy (Petersmann and Pollack 2003). In fact, we can recognize the contours of an emerging global civil society, when we look at the tremendous growth of international non-governmental organizations (Boli and Thomas 1999; Keane 2003; Amoore and Langley 2004; Scholte 2004; Steffek *et al.* 2007). Humanitarian organizations pursue the accomplishment of fairness in the world economy: these include *Human Rights Watch*, *Global Exchange*, *Clean Clothes* and *Sweatshop Watch*. These organizations pilloried, for instance, the sports goods manufacturer Nike, which employs 16,000 staff but has almost 100 per cent of its sports footwear produced in South-East Asia by a network of suppliers employing more than 100,000 people. It is claimed that Nike's sports footwear is produced in these supplier companies at conditions that contradict human rights. Driven by the pressure that human rights organizations exercise on manufacturers of consumer goods, in particular, several companies have established the initiative *Social Accounting 8000* in cooperation with the consumer organization *Council of Economic Priorities*, which observes the certification and control of supplier companies as far as the respecting of certain minimum equality standards is concerned (Merck 1998; Scherer and Löhr 1999; Conroy 2007; Boiral 2008). In 1995, the US Department of Commerce launched the *Model Business Principles*, a catalogue of standards that recommends American companies to commit themselves voluntarily to social and ecological minimum standards worldwide. This catalogue covers abstract and formal rules, which can be summarized under the principle of fairness. It is recommended to pay attention to health and safety in the work place as well as to fair employment practices, responsible behaviour with regard to protecting the environment, the respecting of American and local laws, and an ethically respectable company culture. American companies should serve as a model for local companies as far as good commercial practices are concerned (Scherer and Smid 1998).

Such behavioural standards are far away from the regulatory depth and density of corresponding welfare state regulations, but they are more than merely worthless paper. In cooperation with active consumer organizations, human rights groups, alarmed consumers, image-conscious companies and the WTO, such recommendations for a voluntary commitment on social and ecological minimum standards work towards the development of worldwide solidarity, justice and attention to environmental protection. And since this does not concern deep interventions into social relations, but rather formal behavioural standards, whose respect is possible in one's own interest, and which do not endanger one's own competitiveness, their accomplishment is feasible without a world state endowed with a monopoly of power. The extension of the understanding of one's own interest may lead towards the readiness to acknowledge the WTO as an arbitrator.

The causes and consequences of global labour division

Since the publication of Adam Smith's study on *The Wealth of Nations* (1776/1937) the utility maximizing effect of free trade on each participating nation has been taken as an economic truth. Referring to David Ricardo's (1817/1977) teaching the growth of international labour division can be explained by the increasing comparative cost advantages resulting for the participating nations. In the world of both classical and neo-classical economics, there are, however, no transaction costs, which make up a crucial part of social reality. This is what Emile Durkheim has emphasized in a particularly clear manner.

In his classic study on the division of labour, Durkheim (1964) clearly recognized the reverse side of the law of comparative cost advantages. In a critical discussion of Herbert Spencer's utilitarianism he pointed out that the division of labour can by no means be explained from people's growing happiness (Durkheim 1964: 233–255; Spencer 1972). Rather, the regions where the division of labour and – with it – civilization have most fully advanced are most strongly plagued by growing problems of social disintegration. For example: urbanization signals increasing and more densely woven labour division, but also growing rates of delinquency, divorce, mental disorders, riots, and other forms of disorganization. The mastering of such problems requires particular efforts whose success cannot be anticipated. He went on to explain that the multiplication of the goods on supply, which results from the division of labour, responds in no way to natural needs whose increasing satisfaction would make people happier. Rather, the increased supply of goods is itself producing a wealth of new needs of which people were not aware before having been drawn into the new world of consumer goods. People who have never seen a mobile phone before will not suffer from not having one. The trouble only starts with the awareness of the existence of mobile phones. But as the world of goods grows faster than the individual's income, it creates more trouble than happiness, namely relative deprivation.

From Durkheim's point of view we can gain a new understanding of the economic doctrine of "global affluence" that grows with the comparative cost advantages of the global division of labour. It explains less what will happen, but rather attributes a meaning and a legitimation to factual events. It assumes the role of religion and offers a theodicy in the classic sense: people may consider events in the world as detrimental, unfair and senseless, but in the long run, they will ensure happiness, justice and meaning for all people in line with the growing "global affluence", i.e. the continually rising supply of goods. This is a theodicy on the most sublime level. The cathedrals of the new religion are the shopping malls and leisure resorts. Its priests are no longer educated at the theological departments of the universities, but within the economic departments. Its bishops can be found in the management teams of the World Bank, the International Monetary Fund (IMF), the World Trade Organization (WTO) and the Organisation for Economic Cooperation and Development (OECD) (Deutschmann 2001; Peet 2003; Barnett and Finnemore 2004; Fourcade 2006; Park and Vetterlein 2010).

The progress of labour division cannot be explained by increasing happiness or usefulness resulting from that process for the people. In contrast, it brings about a wealth of troubles, damages and problems. Nevertheless, it is progressing steadily. What are then the hidden forces that are driving the division of labour forward despite the problems it creates? It is the shrinking distance between people resulting from population growth and, above all, the extension and technological perfecting of the ways and means of transport and communication (Durkheim 1964: 256–282). These changes are raising competition for scarce goods and are compelling people to specialize in precisely those activities that differentiate them from their fellow citizens and protect them from competition. In the wake of progressing specialization, old occupations disappear, while a far greater number of new occupations are being born. The list of occupations grows more and more. The tougher competition becomes, the more subtle differentiation and greater efforts on the part of advertising for demand with continually renewed and extended supply are required to ensure sheer survival. This includes the permanent training of skills challenging people's intellectual capabilities to the highest possible level and leaving little room for survival to all those who are unable to develop such qualities. In this way, people are forced into a vicious circle where they have to outdo each other permanently and have to inundate the world with ever new goods and services in order to maintain their position in competition. At the same time, they are drawn into the world of amassing goods in their role of consumers (Durkheim 1964: 272–275). People have to work harder, more efficiently and more intelligently to be able to afford those goods they have to produce in order to stand up against their competitors.

The advancing division of labour is the means that makes the lethal struggle for survival a peaceful competition for consumers. This peace must, however, be toughly sought after and paid for. Durkheim leaves no doubt about this. And it will only come about to the extent that people's legal and moral relationships will grow beyond the nation state's boundaries along with the division of labour. Otherwise, the division of labour will have an enforced, anomic character and produce deep social crises. It will drive people into specialization without giving them remuneration they would consider a fair compensation. Moreover, it will be accompanied by growing disparities, uncertainty, crises and crime. According to Durkheim the increasing division of labour is replacing the internal mechanical solidarity of segmentary units, which live a life widely separated from each other, by an organic solidarity across previously separated segmentary units. Organic solidarity is growing between the specialized parts of an all-embracing whole. Each part of the whole contributes its specialized service and receives the specialized service of all other parts. The organic whole is composed of specialized parts, which are linked to each other through exchange of special goods and services. Mechanical solidarity exists between people who share the same life and the same qualities within narrow confines, organic solidarity emerges between people of different mutually complementing qualities. We can interpret national solidarity as a kind of mechanical solidarity of the nation as a segmentary unit into which the organic solidarity of labour division within the nation state is embedded. The international division of labour is breaking up the mechanical solidarity of the nation state and is fostering the development of cross-border organic solidarity. Transnational solidarity of this kind does not emerge between nations as collectivities but between individuals across nations. In this way the border-transcending ties between individuals are complemented with the differentiation of the social structure and the pluralization of lifestyles, attitudes and cultures within nations.

The replacement of the mechanical solidarity of the nation as a segmentary unit by the transnational organic solidarity of the division of labour does not automatically result from growing mutual dependence beyond segmentary units. It requires a parallel border-transcending growth of legal security, of a common spirit of cooperation, of a collective consciousness and of a common sense of justice (Durkheim 1964: 276–288, 402–408). Mechanical solidarity ties people together by a strong common spirit. It is immediately visible in the repressive law geared towards retribution of violations of the common moral feeling and the common sense of justice. Organic solidarity is based on mutual dependence and specified cooperation. It is represented by restitutive law, which aims at the compensation for damages and the restitution of a given state of rights. For Durkheim, penal law represents mechanical solidarity, civil law the organic solidarity. With the division of labour, civil law acquires a rising importance compared to penal law.

Referring to the situation of the welfare states, one might say that welfare law and social expenditure are an embodiment of mechanical solidarity, whereas organic solidarity is represented by the volume of market-shaped relationships. The extent to which the individual's living standard is not determined by his/her market performance but rather by social rights guaranteed by the state, could be used as an indicator for mechanical solidarity. According to the welfare study conducted by Esping-Andersen (1990), this concerns the degree of decommodification, i.e. the determination of the living standard irrespective of market achievement in the case of unemployment, sickness and retirement. Assuming a mean value of 27.7, Australia and the USA occupied the extreme positions of the lowest mechanical solidarity in 1980 at 13.0 and 13.8 respectively. Denmark, Norway and Sweden, on the other hand, boasted the highest mechanical solidarity at 38.1, 38.8 and 39.1. France and Germany are exactly in the middle at 27.5 and 27.7. Great Britain featured 23.4 thus tending towards the group of less mechanically integrated countries, whereas the Netherlands tended towards the more strongly integrated countries at 32.4 (Esping-Andersen 1990: 52; cf. Goodin et al. 1999; Room 2000; Holden 2003; Bambra 2006). It is a typical feature of the less mechanically integrated countries like the USA and Great Britain that a plurality of voluntary associations and, in the USA also, the courts carry out more integrative tasks than in other countries. This proves a greater weight of organic solidarity. We can conclude that organic solidarity has developed thus far primarily within the confines of nation states and has stretched much less beyond their borders. It has been embedded into a more or less strong mechanical solidarity of the nation.

In the more than one hundred years since the publication of Durkheim's study on the division of labour in 1893, the European welfare states have solved the integration problem by attributing a rising weight to mechanical solidarity compared to organic solidarity. The USA prefers organic solidarity to the mechanical one. In the European welfare states, the organic solidarity of the division of labour was based on mechanical foundations more than in the USA by processes of their external demarcation and internal homogenization. As we have discovered, it will most probably not be possible to realize the same quality of a mechanically funded organic solidarity on the European and the global level. From this point of view the mechanical solidarity of the European welfare states appears to be a relict from a vanishing epoch which makes adjustment to the new dimensions of the European and global division of labour more difficult.

Nevertheless, the cross-border division of labour frees people from the constraint of collective solidarity of traditionally existing segmentary units; presently they are freed from the collective constraint of the nation state. It is a driving force of individualization. Durkheim (1964: 283–303, 403) also clearly pointed out this feature of labour division. The collective consciousness loses in strength and concretion, it weakens and becomes more abstract. It acquires the quality of abstract values and leaves a wider latitude for development to the individual consciousness. At the same time, dependence among people grows across larger distances. Societal effects result from an almost infinite number of individual actions having an impact on one another across large distances. Emile Durkheim considered this, on the one hand, a chance for the creation of a new quality of "organic" solidarity due to the mutual dependence of different and individualized people, which he distinguishes from the mechanical solidarity of segmentary units. However, he realized the risk that it will not be possible to forge a sense of community to that extent across larger distances from sheer interdependence. He considered such a sense of community indispensable as a non-contractual basis in order to give social relationships that differentiate into a large number of contractual relations a binding, calculable order that will provide social balance. He was convinced that without the simultaneous growth of morality and law the individualism of modernity will drift towards egoism and the struggle of all against all (Hobbes 1651/1966; Durkheim 1964: 3).

Durkheim observed a tendency to an abnormal labour division of which he distinguished three types. Anomic labour division lacks rules for regulating exchange and contract. Enforced labour division occurs under unequal conditions of exchange, where one party is able to impose its will on the other party. Uncoordinated labour division includes individual people insufficiently in the exchange of goods and services because there is lack of demand for the goods and services supplied.

In the preface to the second edition of his study Durkheim expected a major contribution to the control of disintegrative forces of labour division from the organization of labour division through the cooperation of occupational groups with each other and with the government and their participation in political decision-making in a representative body. He envisioned a kind of corporatism, which has been partly accomplished by the system of tripartism in the collaboration of employers' associations, trade unions and the state in the Scandinavian egalitarian as well as the Continental European conservative welfare states. The special achievement of the egalitarian and conservative welfare states is the embedding of the organic solidarity of specialized individuals into a relatively strong mechanical solidarity of the nation. In the egalitarian welfare state the individual shares equal civil, political and social rights immediately with his/her fellow citizens. In the conservative welfare state the individual shares solidarity with his/her family as well as solidarity with his/her occupational group, which links him/her to the solidarity of the broader society. In the egalitarian welfare state the organic whole is composed of equal individual citizens; in the conservative welfare state the organic whole is composed of families and occupational groups. Family, occupational groups and state complement each other in the system of subsidiarity of support for the individual. Support shall be provided on the appropriate level, first of all by the family; then by the occupational group where the family cannot help; and by the state where the occupational group is unable to help. Both models of a strong welfare state can be interpreted as a peculiar embodiment of Durkheim's idea of embedding organic solidarity into a strong mechanical solidarity. His conception of modern society as an organic whole comes however particularly close to the conservative type of welfare state, which is explicitly founded on the idea of an organic whole.

If we try to apply his theory to our subject matter of international labour division we have to recognize that his conception of organic solidarity entails the idea of a demarcated organic whole of the type of the strong welfare state particularly in its conservative form. However, he envisioned indeed the emergence of a nation-transcending European society as a result of growing international labour division with the effect of shrinking differences between nations along with their internal differentiation and pluralization. What we have to recognize, however, is the moving away of labour division from its embeddedness in the confines of nation state mechanical solidarity. The emerging transnational solidarity is characterized by weaker embeddedness in transnational mechanical solidarity. It resembles less an organic whole and more a network with open ends. It is therefore appropriate to distinguish the emerging transnational solidarity as a kind of multilevel network solidarity from the still nationally and mechanically embedded organic solidarity of the welfare states.

Similar to Durkheim, Georg Simmel pointed out that the human being can and has to develop his/her individual character along with the increasing volume and number of social circles in order to stand up in a world where he/she has to mediate between the expectations placed upon him/her from the most different directions (Simmel 1908/1992: 454–511, 791–863). The growing volume and number of circles in which people are included are going to release them from the constraints of their circles of origin; yet this growth of memberships subjugates them to new constraints that arise far beyond their reach and can, therefore, not be controlled by themselves. The conflict between subjective and objective culture is strengthening. On the one hand, man develops an ever more sensitive feeling for his/her unique subjectivity, on the other, he/she has to face an infinitely growing objective material and immaterial culture on whose development he/she has no influence at all. This culture, however, determines the environment within which people develop their subjectivity.

Following Durkheim, we will see that the conflict between the rising individual latitude of action and the simultaneously increasing submission to the uncontrolled effects of far-away actions can only be solved by the fact that morality and law will grow with economic links. In a similar way, Alec Stone Sweet and James A. Caporaso (1998) and Neil Fligstein and Alec Stone Sweet (2002) have empirically demonstrated the process of the mutual pushing of economic and legal integration according to Ernst B. Haas' (1958/1968) neofunctionalist theory of European integration. Free markets are constituted by rules (Vogel 1996).

Yet if we follow Durkheim, transnational or European law necessarily has to be more formal and more abstract than national law. It is then the expression of a formal and abstract collective consciousness. Durkheim explained this by the fact that restitutive law geared towards compensating for damage acquires an increasing volume with the division of labour, while repressive law geared towards punishment will hardly grow. Restitutive law protects the individual's subjective rights from violations and aims at the restitution of the individual's rights in cases of their violation (Durkheim 1964: 105–132). This is why economic law dominates by far on the European level. In a homogeneous community there are concrete commonly shared ideas as to how these rights are made up and how they can be exercised by individuals in mutual respect. "Equal rights for all" may, in this case, signify the farthest reaching share of all in the commonly acquired wealth. The more heterogeneous and comprehensive a society becomes, namely a European or even global society, the less can society influence the individual's willingness to contribute his/her part and the more free-riders have to be expected. The feeling of togetherness will dwindle so that the concrete sharing of accumulated wealth must inevitably produce terrible struggles. "Equal rights for all" can only be agreed upon in a formal and abstract sense saying that the distribution of accumulated wealth should be accomplished according to formal procedures granting everybody exactly that share he/she merits due to his/her individual performance. People who will not be able to live on this share will have a right to support in as far as they are guaranteed a dignified life, which does not undermine any people's readiness to make their contribution to societal life.

In this way, the principle of equal opportunity will gain the upper hand on the principle of social balance, as far as the volume of social units is growing and as far as they become more heterogeneous. Collective consciousness must necessarily be more formal and more abstract, if it is to provide an ordering framework for the new situation. Consequently, globalization promotes a change of values in the direction of formalization and abstraction of morality and law and the predominance of the formal guarantee of subjective rights over the substantial establishment of public welfare into which the exercising of subjective rights has been woven, as well as an interpretation of the ideal of equality as equal opportunity and the narrowing down of the idea of social balance to help in need. The idea of justice covers less the collective provision of the best possible conditions of life for all and more the proportional allocation of compensation depending on achievement from the point of view of its greater or smaller shortage. Justice is increasingly being interpreted as a distribution of goods according to the principle of achievement. This principle has the leading edge over the equality principle, since too little homogeneity and common spirit exist for distributing wealth according to the principle of providing far-reaching equal standards of living for all. This is how increased income inequality within nations coming about with regional and global economic integration finds its legitimation (Beckfield 2006; Neckermann and Torche 2007).

3 Symbolic change
The new cult of the individual

Social change does not take place because of material forces alone. They are reflected in public discourse on appropriate strategies aiming at overcoming functional deficits. This is the subject matter of symbolic struggles on symbolic change in the sense of framing the situation by way of establishing a dominating vocabulary or semantics used to address problems of inclusion. Symbolic change first of all needs a change of the rhetoric used in framing social problems and possible solutions. This is what we can call the rhetoric of social inclusion. It entails basic ideas, concepts and remedies, which different strategies of social inclusion in a variety of problem areas have in common. Beyond rhetoric used in public discourse, basic ideas, concepts and remedies might form a semantics – that is a common language defining situations and problems in the same way – or even a paradigmatic core of social inclusion, which is complemented by special programmes designed for the solution of special problems (employment, sickness, old age, discrimination). While the core of a paradigm is of a relatively enduring character and is protected against change, programmes are of a less enduring kind and are adjusted in as much as changes of the situation call for such adjustment. The core is sacred and untouchable. As a rule, change starts with programmes and might lead to the accumulation of anomalies when new programmes are started to solve problems that could not be solved with the established ones. Regular programmes fit in the paradigmatic core. With a rising amount of anomalies – that is, the inability of established programmes to solve problems – the chance is increasing that new programmes will be introduced that do not fit in the core. They are like residual categories of a foreign kind. They produce tensions in the paradigm and bear the potential of greater change, which affects the paradigm's core, the more they are complemented by further new programmes of a foreign kind (Hall 1993).

It is the intention of this chapter to go through a sample of new strategies of social policy to look for signs of an emerging common meaning with an increasing potential of paradigmatic change of inclusion. Before such change takes place, inclusion regimes will, however, go through a time of aggravated tensions, hybridization and institutional layering (Streeck and Thelen 2005a). It cannot be determined by an analysis of rhetorical change, whether this change will lead to a change of the paradigm of inclusion with the conservative and social democratic welfare states joining the paradigm of the liberal welfare states. What can, however, be predicted with greater certainty is the liberalization of the meaning of conservative and social democratic welfare. More generally, we might speak of changing paradigms of inclusion. Speaking of inclusion instead of welfare, we address a significant aspect of the change under way. Social integration is no longer conceived of primarily as a problem of social policy in the narrower sense, but – in a much broader sense – it includes education, migration, interethnic relations, minority rights, gender equality and removal of discrimination.

For assessing the depth and scope of social change of inclusion we can thus distinguish the following levels:

1 Rhetorical change: New vocabulary of ideas, concepts and remedies invades public discourse on inclusion.
2 Semantic change: The new vocabulary of ideas, concepts and remedies penetrates the whole language of inclusion and leads to a new coherent definition of situation and problems, to a new perspective on inclusion.
3 Programmatic change: Introduction of new programmes aiming at solving inclusion problems in legislation, administration and practical action.
4 Paradigmatic change: New inclusion programmes dominate and precipitate the change of other programmes with the effect that the paradigmatic core can no longer produce a common meaning and coherence of programmes so that a new meaning-producing core is being established.

The assessment of strategies of social policy in this chapter tries to find out whether they share a common meaning of tackling problems of inclusion. What matters is the discovery of rhetorical and programmatic change in as much as strategies are not only discussed in public discourse, but also implemented in legislation, administration and practical action. The further the common meaning of strategies reaches, the more we approach semantic change. The greater the number of programmes sharing this meaning, and the more we find a thoroughgoing restructuring of semantics and programmes, the more we come close to paradigmatic change. How far change will go is, however, a matter of the future; first of all change is most likely on the level of rhetoric, but to some degree also on the level of programmes.

Rhetorical change is a matter of public discourse, which does not, however, take place in a vacuum. It is shaped by four basic factors. First of all, structural conditions determine the effectiveness of inclusion programmes. Second, the cultural horizon establishes what kind of strategy makes sense and appears legitimate in terms of representing basic values. (We have, however, to take into account that values change themselves particularly with the extension of the cultural horizon beyond national and civilizational boundaries.) Third, the power structure of the field of discourse exerts some influence on which group has the best chances to promote ideas, concepts and remedies and to define the situation in a powerful and, in the long run, effective way. Thus it is (1) functional fit; (2) cultural legitimacy; and (3) backing by a powerful carrier group on which the diffusion of new rhetorics and programmes depends. Looking at the symbolic change under scrutiny in this chapter, we can start with the following facts, which are favourable for change in the direction of a new rhetoric of individual empowerment:

1 Solidarity change in the direction of network solidarity across and within nations.
2 Extension of the context of legitimation and expansion of the cultural horizon beyond national borders on to the global level.
3 Replacement of traditional incumbents of power positions in the field of discourse with new challengers: experts of labour and social law, social policy advocates and national welfare organizations are challenged by neo-liberal economists, consultants and international NGOs. This means that the world is less conceived as a house that has to be kept in order by the responsible housekeeper (the state), but rather as a transnational marketplace on which empowered individuals engage in mutually advantageous exchange.

An established rhetoric of social inclusion is promoted by its symbiotic link to favourable structural conditions of solidarity. The rhetoric of collectively shared welfare organized by the nation state has been supported by its symbiotic link to national solidarity in its different variants of a liberal competitive solidarity, a conservative organic solidarity or a social democratic egalitarian solidarity. This symbiosis is increasingly being undermined by the change of solidarity and justice coming about with the globalization, pluralization and individualization of social life. The rhetoric of nationally shared welfare loses solidaristic ground and legitimacy in terms of justice. In the current epoch of transition a new rhetoric is emerging focusing on the empowerment of the individual. This new rhetoric is particularly being promoted by the global diffusion of neo-liberalism. This is, however, only half the story. The other half is the change of structural conditions as well as the internal renewal of the conservative and social democratic ideologies in order to cope with the new situation. Therefore the rhetoric of individual empowerment is no ephemeral fashion sponsored by the wave of neo-liberalism that will fade away some time, but is part of a broader movement fostered by a deeper structural and ideological transformation affecting the change of the conservative and social democratic ideologies, too. What we will do in this chapter is analyse a sample of new strategies of social integration with regard to their fitting in the new structural conditions and with regard to their commonly shared meaning converging in the establishment of the rhetoric of individual empowerment in the context of the rising significance of neo-liberal governmentality (Bröckling 2007; Foucault 2008). Beyond territorial rule by the law and disciplinary techniques applied to govern the population of the nation state, global multilevel governance assumes the form of neo-liberal governmentality (Münch 2010).

The historically established rhetoric of social policy has been directed towards protecting the individual who is incapable of earning his/her own living and to live on his/her own. This is particularly true of the social democratic and conservative ideas of welfare. Social policy has been more important for them than educational policy aiming at the educational upgrading of the population. This has been the other way round for the liberal welfare state. Here educational upgrading has always compensated for the lack of protection of the individual by the state. With their turn to policies of educational upgrading in the 1970s, the conservative and the social democratic welfare states have joined the liberal programme of empowering the individual. Meanwhile, competition in the globalized economy exerts strong pressure on improving skills by education and occupational training in all welfare states across the different types (Crouch et al. 1999). Therefore, the change of structural conditions promotes a change in the understanding of welfare. It is less conceived as a guaranteed protection of the individual against any danger and risk, and more conceived as enabling the individual to stand on his/her own feet in the face of increasing dangers and risks. There is also greater mistrust that comprehensive protection might be misused by moral hazard so that social security as public good is overused and weakened. We therefore observe a trend of replacing the rhetoric of protecting the incapable individual with the rhetoric of empowering or enabling the individual to make himself or herself capable of mastering any kind of danger and risk by himself or herself.

What is taking place in this process of symbolic change is the invigoration of the "cult of the individual" on a new transnationalized level beyond the nation state. Emile Durkheim (1964: 172; 1973a, 1973b, 1973c) saw the cult of the individual as the moral counterpart of the growing social division of labour. What Durkheim means is not the celebration of reckless egotism. It is rather the celebration of the sacred character of the individual's dignity as a moral person who is able to act in an autonomous and responsible way in the universalistic sense (Marske 1987; Vogt 1993; Rothenbuhler 2005). This means exercising individual rights along with respecting the rights of any other person. The modern nation state's constitutional commitment to the basic rights of the individual has put Durkheim's cult of the individual on firm grounds. The national constitutional courts have performed the role of practicing this cult in an exemplary way. Nevertheless, they have been largely bound to protecting the rights of nationals. With the globalization of the discourse on individual rights, both on the basis of expanding the sharing of constitutional rights and on the basis of the United Nations' *Declaration of Human Rights* of 1948, national courts right through to constitutional courts have contributed increasingly to conferring rights to any resident of a national territory beyond nationals alone (Soysal 1994; Joppke 1999; Koenig 2005). In doing so, they have contributed to the transnationalization of the cult of the individual. Beyond national courts, the European Convention on Human Rights and the European Court of Human Rights have put the cult of the individual on the transnational (European) level. Practically, the European Union's European Court of Justice in Luxembourg has become the major pillar of that cult in the context of the judicial construction of the European single market. In the wake of this institutional transnationalization of the cult of the individual, the discourse on the individual's empowerment is a driving force of a symbolic change that puts this cult increasingly on a broader basis (Elliot 2008).

The symbolic change from welfare to inclusion and from the protection to the empowerment of the individual is particularly promoted by the transnationalization of the field of discourse. Monitoring and benchmarking have become prominent forces of policy change. OECD statistical reports and EU procedures according to the Open Method of Coordination (OMK) have become widely used instruments of the international coordination of policies (Heidenreich and Bischoff 2008). They are called "soft" instruments of internationalized governance, leaving real decision-making to the nation states. From an intergovernmentalist view, the nation states remain masters of inclusion policy in general and of labour or social policy in particular. This perspective pays, however, too little attention to the logic and long-term effects of such procedures of international coordination. As a matter of fact, such procedures determine how situations are defined, which types of strategies appear to be well chosen and what kind of inclusion policy or social policy gains legitimacy. It is increasingly difficult for national policies to resist trends of symbolic change taking place in the field of international coordination. Best practice models serve as guidelines for the rhetorical change, which exerts pressure on the practical change of inclusion or social policy programmes. A collective learning process is taking place, which starts with the questioning of practice that is taken for granted and widens the horizon of thought in the face of a broader spectrum of alternative practices. Traditionally established practice is losing legitimacy so that the floor is open for innovation according to best practice models. In this process, the terms of legitimacy of inclusion policy in general, and social policy in particular, are changing so that continuation as well as change of practice has to be justified with explicit reference to best practice models emerging in the transnational field of discourse (Bernhard 2005, 2010). In this sense the nation state is not – and never has been – master of the legitimacy of its policies. From the perspective of the neoinstitutionalist world society approach (Meyer et al. 1997) the nation state is largely a construction of the global diffusion of role models in its constitution, structure and policies. This means that the nation state is largely a construction of world society. It is all the more true, the more international institutions, organizations and coordination procedures promote the practice of global discourse, which exerts legitimatory pressure on nation states to adopt internationally consented models of political practice. The definition of role models might remain on the level of pure rhetoric leaving practical action as it is. That means the role model is nothing but a myth represented in formal structures (of constitutions, for example) or rhetoric, while the activity structure is still deeply entrenched in the traditions of a national society (Meyer and Rowan 1977). This gap between formal structure and activity structure might not be closed for a shorter or longer time. Nevertheless, taking up a role model in national formal structures and rhetorics implants a yardstick against which actual practice can be measured – and is measured indeed – the more national public discourse is linked to transnational discourse particularly by the national and local representation of international NGOs as well as groups of experts. In neoinstitutionalist terms, the organizational or discursive field of inclusion policy or social policy is transnationalized so that the traditional incumbents of power positions in the national field, namely experts of labour and social law and national welfare organizations, lose control of the situation and have to give way to the increasing definitional power of new challengers, namely economists, consultants and international NGOs. External constraint of international labour division, normative pressure of the new transnational elite and the imitation of the best practice models not only help to implant inclusion and social policy innovations in the formal structure and rhetoric of national societies, but also to implement them in the activity structure and in practical action. From this point of view, the diffusion of rhetoric is more than a myth without any practical effects, because it changes the terms of legitimacy of practical action fundamentally.

In the perspective of Bourdieu's (1986, 1994) theory of fields and capital a transnational field of policy-making has emerged that is superimposing itself on the national fields. Social policy in the national field has long been dominated by the social policy committees of parties and parliaments in collaboration with the representatives of the big associations (trade unions, employer federations). Experts of science and managers have long remained in a dominated position, being limited to providing knowledge from theory to improve existing practice. In the newly established transnational field the relation of domination has changed. Parliaments, parties and associations have become marginalized, while the transnational elite of scientific experts and managers occupies the dominant position. While the old elites ruled on the basis of "cultural capital" in the sense of preserving a "sacred" traditional life-world and practice of social policy and "political capital" in the sense of occupying positions of power, the new transnational elites rule on the basis of scientific and managerial knowledge that claims to be universally valid and technically useful in furthering economic advancement and the well-being of humankind (Majone 1989). This is scientific and informational capital (Bernhard 2010). With the superimposition of the transnational field on the national fields, the symbolic capital of cultural practices and traditional authorities in the sense of the power to define the situation loses in importance, while the scientific, technological and informational capital of the new transnational elites gains in value. This is how the new governance of global science tends to replace the old governance of parliaments, parties and associations (Drori et al. 2003). Symbolic power moves from national authorities, parties and associations to transnational elites, networks of experts and think tanks (Figure 3.1).

The global governance of science and its representation by networks of experts and think tanks does not, however, really mean that power politics is replaced with the rule of truth in the literal sense. Politics does not wither away, but reappears in the struggle for explaining the world and advising governments in the zone where producing knowledge and mobilizing power overlap (cf. Lahusen and Jauß 2001;

96 Symbolic change

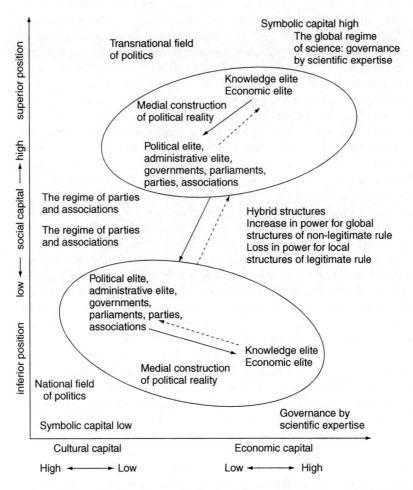

Figure 3.1 The double structure of authority in the national and transnational fields of politics.

Münch *et al.* 2001; Lahusen 2003). This is knowledge production according to mode 2, where truth and power merge to produce paradigms that guide policies in various fields. This kind of knowledge production is different to the older mode 1, which drew a clear distinction between basic research and applied research for practical use (Gibbons *et al.* 1994). Mode 2 of knowledge production implies scientification of politics and politicization of science at the same time (Weingart 2001). In this new world of merging science and politics, the political ideologies and programmes of nationally bound parties are no longer taken for granted. Together with the shrinking number of voters committed to parties, political ideologies and party programmes no longer help sufficiently to reduce the complexity of decision-making in order to produce binding decisions.

Global paradigms and rationality models and their enactment by networks of experts and think tanks indeed reduce the increased complexity in the global context of policy-making. They provide orientation for politicians and voters who have become disoriented, because national traditions and party programmes are no longer self-evident in the globalized discourse on how to explain the world and how to act in a reasonable way.

Paradigms make a distinction between the inner core of principles, which are sacred and protected against falsification, and practical programmes linked to that inner core. This distinction allows for attributing failures to the misinterpretation of the core principles by some programmes, to deal with them as anomalies so that they do not endanger the validity of the core (Kuhn 1962). Strategies of immunization help to keep the sacred core principles untouched by profane struggles about policy programmes. One major strategy of this kind is the explanation of failures by lacking commitment and belief of the practitioners, which are expected to get more schooling in the right application of the paradigm. This is all the same, whether we look at strategies of protecting religious faith against doubts resulting from everyday disappointments, or whether we look at the strategies of protecting policy paradigms against failures in everyday practice. Such strategies help to maintain the capacity of paradigms to reduce complexity against the increased chances of being questioned by new evidence and the discovery of unintended consequences. This is how global networks of experts and think tanks have become much more powerful, while political parties have lost in power. This does not mean, however, that parties do not matter anymore and that expert networks together with think tanks rule without any opposition. Yet, the cleavage structure of policy-making has changed. It is now strongly shaped by the cleavage between globally oriented networks of experts and think tanks and nationally rooted political parties.

In questions of the political governance of society on the national, European and global level, it is economics that has taken a hegemonic position. Being a global profession, economists have displaced the nationally bound legal profession from the dominant position of political consulting (Lebaron 2000; Fourcade 2006, 2009). The hegemony of economics is backed by the hegemony of US science, which is first of all rooted in the world's by far largest, internally densely woven US scientific community and publication market. This market power forms the material basis of the dominant role of US economists in the world, which has been consecrated by the awarding of no less than forty-nine Nobel prizes to economists working in US institutions out of a total of sixty-four laureates in economics since 1969. Of the forty-nine US laureates in economics, ten were teaching at the University of Chicago at the time of receiving the Nobel prize (Lebaron 2006). Forming the academic centre of neo-liberal thinking, and along with the fitting of neo-liberal thought in the historically dominant liberal tradition in the United States, the Chicago economists have created a kind of monopolistic structure for establishing a hegemony in matters of explaining the world and advising governments. This is just like the Catholic Church ruling globally in matters of religious faith without there being a competing confession, a situation similar to the European Middle Ages and the rule of scholastic teaching (Plehwe *et al.* 2006; Mirowski and Plehwe 2009).

On this basis, neo-liberalism has become the dominant paradigm to explain the world and to advise governments. Its hegemony means that the renewal of conservative, social democratic and nationally rooted liberal traditions has to be approved by the standards of neo-liberalism in order to be acknowledged as up to date. Neo-liberalism is in the position of serving as the crucial measure of veridiction (approving the truth) for the lower order political ideologies bound to national traditions (Foucault 2008). The latter do not disappear, but they incorporate the new vocabulary and view of the world and change their meaning in this way (Marttila 2010). Hence, conservative or social democratic orders and programmes survive, though more as a kind of facade that still lends legitimacy to a changed meaning of words and practices. It is therefore not enough to study the convergence or non-convergence of welfare states in the liberal regime in terms of accounting for changes in the social security system and social spending at face value (cf. Brady *et al.* 2005; Mills *et al.* 2008). What is required is studying the change of vocabularies, rhetorics, semantics and paradigms, which are applied to understand, explain and construct the social world.

In the following paragraphs of this chapter, we will deal with a sample of social policy strategies that have gained some significance as models of practical reform. International monitoring and benchmarking have separated them from their original context in particular national traditions of welfare to serve as generally applicable models worth being tried out everywhere. We will discuss the sample of social policy strategies with regard to their contribution to rhetorical change in the direction of the individual's empowerment, their fit in the solidarity structure of international labour division, their potential of attaining legitimacy in the transnationalized cultural horizon, their support by the changed power structure in the transnationalized field of discourse, the preconditions of them working at places other than their place of origin, and their side effects with regard to the character of social integration they promote.

We will discuss the following strategies:

- welfare reform between neo-liberalism, defence of the national welfare state or European Social Union;
- activation of the labour force;
- individualization of the employment relationship;
- decentralization of wage bargaining;
- civic self-organization; and
- social entrepreneurship.

This sample of strategies represents symbolic change in the direction of individual empowerment instead of individual protection. The different strategies originated primarily in the context of liberal welfare regimes, but have spread across all regimes in the meantime. This is why they announce broad symbolic change and convergence. And they fit in the changing structure of solidarity as well as the extended horizon of discursive legitimation. They are promoted by the new transnational elite of economists, consultants and activists of INGOs. This overall supporting structural context – and not simply their superiority in the technical economic sense – helps to disseminate the new strategies across different welfare regimes and to push symbolic change despite the difficult and meaning-transforming transfer of the strategies from their original cultural context to other places. This is how the liberal understanding of society attains a hegemonic position (Gramsci 1971; Laclau and Mouffe 2001; Blyth 2002; Soederberg *et al.* 2005; Cerny 2008).

Neo-liberalism, defence of the national welfare state or European Social Union?

The debate about the appropriate strategy to cope with the challenges of globalization is marked by the following three positions:

1 Scholars in favour of removing trade barriers expect new chances of economic growth from the open world market. Profits shall result from comparative cost advantages as an effect of growing international labour division. Further profit shall arise from state measures of improving the competitiveness of enterprises and both employed and self-employed working people (Berthold 1997; Monopolkommission 1998; Weizsäcker 1999).
2 Scholars in favour of saving the welfare state want to improve the safety net for those who are weaker in competition by way of old and/or new forms of social protection. They also want to remove competitive pressure from the employment market by sharing the same amount of total work by more people, by giving stimuli for temporal retreat from work in the form of sabbaticals and a state guaranteed basic income for every citizen as well as stimuli for voluntary citizen work (Hirsch 1995; Altvater and Mahnkopf 1996; Cattero 1998). The narrative of the powerless state is a myth in this perspective (Weiss 1998).
3 Scholars in favour of the formation of a European Social Union and a socially integrated world society want to raise the level of social integration attained by the welfare states to the level of the European Union and, later on, to the level of the world society (Held 1995; McGrew 1997; Beck 1998: 61–66; Archibugi *et al.* 1998; Habermas 1998; Pauly 1998; Schwengel 1999; Eriksen and Fossum 2000).

All of these strategies include something correct, but are one-sided and need complementation. The strategy of market liberalization neglects or trivializes the anomic consequences of continually accelerated structural change. On the one hand, creative destruction fosters the competitiveness of companies. On the other hand, it makes structural change and thus the release of workforce who are no longer needed a permanent phenomenon (Schumpeter 1983). A balance of supply and demand on the job market can only be attained at the expense of increasing flexibility of the workforce implying high losses in income and the permanent changing of job and place of living with an accompanying destabilization of families and neighbourhoods (Delhousse 1998; Sennett 1998). Social inequality may reach a level that creates whole areas of social breakdown.

Alongside social risks, the strategy of market liberalization neglects any ecological, cultural and political risk. With the international division of labour, the volume and variety of products and the amount of traffic is growing, as is the consumption of resources, waste, pollution and noise, which all have attained a critical level today such as is shown, for instance, by forecasts regarding anticipated climate change. With regard to culture we may expect that the global consumer culture penetrates ever deeper into all areas of life thus leaving ever smaller space for the authentic persistence of cultural traditions without having to "upgrade" them for marketing reasons.

The strategy of saving the welfare state presupposes that enough latitude of action is available to the nation state so that it may withdraw somewhat from the process of ever sharper global competition in a move to build up protective areas. It would make life without the stress of having to improve one's own competitiveness permanently possible to at least part of the population. This strategy would have to put a brake on the increasing integration of the world market or even set it back in some way and would have to stop the growing differentiation of solidarities both upwards and downwards. It would allow getting back to that focusing of the division of labour on one's own national economy and to that collective solidarity that has supported the regulative and redistributive power of the welfare state. Since, however, the development cannot be simply turned back, this strategy is doomed to fail.

The strategy of forming a European Social Union and, in a far away future, a socially integrated world society, must count on the fact that the same depth of social integration can be reached on these levels as in the old welfare states. This is being counteracted by a number of given facts: Both on the European and, even more so, on the global market a far greater heterogeneity of interests must be subjected to a common denominator; the economic levels of achievement are poles apart and solidarities are differentiated so much that only individual interests can be harmonized in formal procedures. No effective regulation of societal life according to uniform substantial standards is possible. For instance, uniform social and environmental standards would strengthen unequal economic achievement of individual countries and would thus increase international inequality even more. For a far-reaching redistribution of incomes between countries, the necessary cross-border collective solidarity is lacking both on a European and a global level. Particularly on the European level it may certainly grow some part along with cross-border division of labour and European political decision-making and opinion formation on the basis of the cross-border integration of political parties, interest groups and publics throughout Europe, but it will never reach the depth of nation state solidarity. This is even more so, since all signs point towards a differentiation of solidarities. Neither a European nor a global solidarity will be able to provide more than a formal frame for the wider differentiation of solidarities, a frame within which the differentiated solidarities can be coordinated, but not "abandoned", in such a way that they are fully subjected to the European or global common good (Delhey 2007; Bach 2008; Münch 2008, 2010).

From a political viewpoint, the nation states' shrinking power of regulation and redistribution cannot be compensated for by a similarly effective political regulation on either a European or a global level, since the interests cannot be focused in the same way on these levels. The growing heterogeneity of interests only allows for establishing the guidelines for the coordination of interests, and this on all levels of politics, from the local and regional, national and European right through to the global levels, and on all stages, from programme formulation and programme formation right through to the implementation of the law and the filing of lawsuits for the selective harmonization of interests. Politics becomes a permanent competition between individual interests and is no longer in a position to create a common good that *integrates* interests. It moves away from the model of a *substantially regulating* European welfare state and is approaching the *conflict moderating* liberal democracy of the United States (cf. Lahusen and Jauß 2001; Pontusson 2005). There the citizens' participation in politics is not *mediated* by strong political parties, long-established associations and representative opinion formation in the media, but occurs in a wealth of larger, smaller and very small interest organizations. All this includes the mobilization of the public by way of the mass media, congress lobbyism, the exertion of influence on political regulation by regulatory agencies and administrative decisions, and even lawsuits. In this case, it is less important that interest conflicts are settled by general law in the interest of the common good, but what counts, rather, is all interests having a fair chance of exercising some influence in political competition (Goldstein 1999).

What seems to be realistic under such conditions is a reasonable combination of the three strategies with a clear view for their limits. The strategy of market liberalization is unavoidable in view of the nevertheless ongoing global competition and is right to the extent that disintegration and anomie can be avoided. The strategy of saving the welfare state is correct in as far as it helps to keep the disintegrating and anomic tendencies of ever tighter competition within socially acceptable limits. The strategy of forming a European Social Union and a socially integrated world society is appropriate, as it is important to give a sustainable order to global competition and the ever growing international division of labour. First and foremost, supranational institution-building will concern fair terms of competition and exchange and the control of negative external, social, ecological and cultural effects of the global flow of capital, goods and services. Social integration will focus on fairness in the sense of equal opportunity – on a national, a European and a worldwide level – but will not be in a position to create equal conditions of life such as those possible within the highly developed welfare states.

The extending and differentiating international division of labour is the tool breaking through the particularistic solidarity of the nation states and allows for the construction of a worldwide network solidarity of cooperation based on the division of labour. It avoids a war of all against all on scarce resources to replace it with the peaceful exchange of ever more differentiated and specialized goods and services. Withdrawing from this growing network by non-participation in the international division of labour requires exclusive commitment to particularistic nation state solidarity. In the worldwide weave of the division of labour such isles of particularism are, however, no longer viable. As the state withdraws some part from the regulation of society, society's ability for self-organization is particularly challenged. The state's exclusive cooperation with well-established and privileged associations in determining the common good, which has prevailed in the welfare states so far, will give way to a more open process of balancing a greater number of interests. In this case, the representative definition of the *common good* will matter less than the fair *balancing of interests*.

Activation of the labour force

How much latitude for programmes of social policy has remained for the nation states in the framework of European and global competition? In order to attract capital, they have to commit themselves – more than ever before – to an active locational policy instead of social policy by redistribution and have to overcome paralysis of economic activity by social policy regulations. Innovations in social policy have to be adjusted to the new situation (Scharpf 2000).

Until the 1980s, we witnessed a co-evolution of economic growth, full employment and high social security including high employment protection, high unemployment compensation and low earnings dispersion. Since the 1990s this linkage has been under pressure. Comparing the development in the United States and in Europe there seems to be an increasing trade-off between economic growth and high employment rates on the one hand and high social security and high unemployment rates on the other hand. The European welfare states have suffered particularly strongly from high enduring rates of unemployment and shrinking rates of transition from unemployment to employment. It seems to be fair to say that their production of greater social security and equality of results has been maintained at the expense of producing an increasing class of outsiders. Certainly people in work are safer with regard to staying in employment in the strongly protecting than in the liberal welfare states. However, people who are out of work – mainly women, youth and the unskilled – have far smaller chances of being included in work (Esping-Andersen 1999: 109, 132–140). Measures of reform are therefore concentrating on solving the dilemma of social security/ equality vs. jobs.

Strategies of activating the labour force have gained increasing significance (Lødemel and Trickey 2000; Berkel and Valkenburg 2007; Serrano Pascual and Magnusson 2007). Such strategies are welfare for work programmes, wage subsidies/negative income tax, employer–employee agreements on sustainable employment, and service sector growth. Originating in particular contexts of welfare practice, they are increasingly taken as models to be practiced everywhere. Their global diffusion is promoted by the transnationalization of the field of social policy discourse through OECD and EU coordination procedures (Heidenreich and Bischoff 2008). They are particularly favoured by the challengers of traditionally established social policy, neo-liberal economists and consultants, who have occupied power positions in policy advising committees, while labour and social law experts representing traditional practice have lost definitional power. The strategies of activating the labour force, however, not only speak the language of the new elite of economists and consultants, but also fit in the changed structure of solidarity in the context of international labour division. The rhetoric common to these strategies is the "empowerment of the individual". Creating human capital in the knowledge society has become the major strategy for meeting global competition (Culpepper 2002; Wolf 2002; Grubb and Lazerson 2004). The OECD (1996, 1999) has put this strategy on its agenda of growth and employment in the knowledge-based economy. The European Union did so in its Lisbon strategy to build the most competitive region in the knowledge-based economy.

Welfare for work programmes

There are two radically opposed positions with regard to solving the problem of enduring high unemployment rates propagated in public discourse. Supply-side policies look for incentives for employers to offer jobs and for unemployed people to seek and take up jobs. Demand-side policies in turn assume that productivity gains and consumer satiation result in an enduring gap between the number of jobs available and the number of employable people. Demand-side policies therefore prefer programmes like job-sharing, part-time work, sabbaticals and early retirement. They wish a greater number of people to share available jobs. The major risk of this strategy is a spiral of economic decline because of shrinking competition with the result of a lack of incentives for innovations. There is an inherent tendency of administering shortage in this model. A further obstacle to the working of this strategy is its dependence on the willingness of people in jobs to share jobs with people without a job, that is to give up something, which is of greatest importance for them particularly in times of high unemployment rates. Such altruism cannot be expected so that the real outcome of a strategy that does not aim at job growth is the persistence of a high unemployment rate. The consequence is the emergence of a marginalized underclass of long-term unemployed.

What remains for solving the problem of inclusion is the supply of a high level of public assistance in order to avoid social disorganization. However, such a strategy would require a high degree of collective solidarity between employed and unemployed people, which is rather unlikely in a situation of shrinking transition from unemployment back to employment. Such shrinking rates of transition result from the concentration of unskilled people in the group of unemployed seeing that it is increasingly difficult for the unskilled to find employment in an economy of rising demands for hard and soft skills. Therefore, we cannot expect long-term solidarity between long-term employed and long-term unemployed people to such an extent that it would avoid tendencies of social disorganization (exclusion, marginalization, poverty, community and family destruction, alienation and withdrawal). In such a situation measures aimed at reducing the level of unemployment compensation and public assistance have to face particularly strong resistance, because unemployment is no longer a temporary phase in a life career but has increasingly become an enduring fate (Alcock et al. 2003).

The supply-side strategy in contrast starts with the assumption that the major means of inclusion in social life is having a job, which does not only provide the money for maintaining a decent standard of living but also social recognition and personal fulfilment and identity. In a society that aims at gender equality work is all the more the central means of inclusion and self-realization for both genders. Neither inclusion nor self-realization exist outside the labour market in such a society. This is why policies of labour-market inclusion have become most important particularly in the liberal as well as the egalitarian welfare states, which share the value of gender equality. Only in the conservative welfare states have strategies of keeping demand for jobs within narrower limits a tradition, namely in the form of the division of labour between male breadwinners and housewives in the family. This tradition has for a long time liberated the state from policies aiming at job growth. The closing of the educational gap between men and women has changed this situation completely. In the face of equal investments in education and a discourse in favour of gender equality there are no longer reasons for unequal participation in employment between both genders. Because of the lack of tradition of furthering employment, ideas of limiting the demand for jobs that conform to the new gender equality have been particularly propagated in the conservative welfare states. Elements of them have been accomplished in the Netherlands with policies of including women through part-time work, but also with higher rates of male part-time work. In Germany, however, this debate has not led to a similar success.

In the liberal as well as the egalitarian welfare states gender equality has been on the agenda for a considerably longer time. They are at least twenty years ahead of the conservative welfare states in this respect. For both types of welfare states work is the centre of inclusion, both regard each individual's contribution through work as the essential prerequisite of a high and still growing level of shared welfare. They only differ in the distribution of collectively produced welfare. In liberal terms, the level of distribution according to achievement must be as high as possible, while the level of distribution according to need independent of achievement must be as low as possible. In the egalitarian welfare states it is the other way round. Their shared dependence on a high employment rate explains why they are both ahead of the conservative welfare states in policies promoting the inclusion of jobless people in employment. Programmes of welfare for work (workfare) are of central importance. Such programmes have become a major battleground in the ideological debate on welfare state reform. They are in line with the neo-liberal paradigm, but are also a choice particularly for the universalistic social democratic welfare state, because of its dependence and emphasis on full employment (Jessop 1993; King 1995; Gilbert and Van Voorhis 2001; Peck 2001; Handler 2003, 2004, 2009; Harrysson and Petersson 2004; McDonald and Marston 2005; Dingeldey 2007; Vis 2007; Dostal 2008; Wacquant 2010).

In the United States rising expenditure on public assistance, particularly according to the programme of Aid to Families with Dependent Children (AFDC), have increasingly called for efforts aiming at bringing back to work unemployed welfare recipients (Backhaus-Maul 1999). Wisconsin has served as a forerunner for such policies since 1986. In 1997, AFDC was replaced by the W-2 programme. Welfare recipients are divided into four categories:

- people with sufficient work experience no longer receive basic public assistance but only support in job placement, childcare and health insurance;
- people with lower occupational skills and job experience are offered a "trial job" and wage subsidies;
- people with insufficient skills and job experience have to learn basic skills in community service jobs; and
- people out of work because of drug addiction or other forms of mental instability have to undergo a therapy, participate in training programmes and take up simple work assignments (Wilke 2002: 210).

Wisconsin's workfare programme resulted in a drop in the number of public assistance cases from 95,000 to 45,000 between 1987 and 1997 (Wilke 2002: 196). In the meantime, AFDC has been replaced by Temporary Assistance to Needy Families (TANF), which is federal law and co-sponsored by the federal and the state governments. It is limited to five years in a person's lifetime and promotes workfare programmes according to Wisconsin's W-2 programme (Wilke 2002: 53–54). The number of participants in the W-2 work programme went up from 12,555 in 1999 to 14,862 in 2004, falling to 9,199 in 2009 and then rising steeply to 17,631 in 2011 in the wake of the financial crisis of 2008 (Wisconsin Department of Children and Families 2011).

Workfare programmes are well-supported by the central belief in work being the major means of inclusion in a society that aims at the continuous growth of welfare. The pressure on job growth has for a longer time been more pronounced in liberal as well as egalitarian welfare states than in conservative welfare states. We may therefore expect that egalitarian welfare states are willing to apply workfare measures more comprehensively and at an earlier time than conservative welfare states as far as they experience longer periods of unemployment beyond the publicly accepted limit. This is how to explain the introduction of such programmes not only in liberal welfare states such as the United States and the United Kingdom, but also in the egalitarian welfare state of Denmark. The Danish government has tightened workfare requirements several times since 1994. Welfare recipients have to participate in mandatory activation programmes including job offers, training and education within the first two years of unemployment (Benner and Bundgaard Vad 2000: 451). The example of Denmark shows that workfare does not necessarily imply the reduction of generosity in employment compensation to the low level of the United States. Though there have been cutbacks this compensation is still much higher than in the United States. What is however similar is the policy counting on work as a means of social inclusion with workfare programmes forming a central part of this strategy. In this respect Denmark teaches us that there are ways to social inclusion through employment even within the framework of a more generous welfare state. What is especially remarkable is the increased emphasis on individual empowerment reflected in the implementation of workfare programmes.

Wage subsidies/negative income tax

Another tool for activating people to participate in work introduced in the United States is the Earned Income Tax Credit (EITC), a means of compensating for badly paid jobs (Meyer and Holtz-Eakin 2001; Hoffman and Seidman 2002; Leigh 2010). According to figures of 2010, a single person or head of household without a child may receive up to $457, if the earned income is not higher than $13,449 per year. For people with one child, the figures are $3,050 and $35,534, for people with two children $5,036 and $40,362 and for people with three children $5,666 and $43,349 respectively (Internal Revenue Service 2009). This programme clearly aims to make low-wage work more attractive than living on public assistance (Seeleib-Kaiser 2001: 322; Wilke 2002: 56). It is perfectly in accordance with the liberal philosophy of achieving social integration through inclusion in work.

Two major objections are being raised to this strategy of inclusion in public debate. The first argues that employers are motivated to keep wages under the limit that would have to be paid otherwise in order to attract labour force. The second says that unproductive labour is being subsidized with the effect of shrinking productivity. Obviously such objections are launched by the trade unions above all in order to preserve higher wage levels. However, the labour market performance of most European welfare states since the early 1990s shows that enduring high unemployment rates have been the other side of this coin. They have become a problem of a lack of social inclusion with further effects of disorganization. Both objections can be doubted. As regards the first objection, it can be argued that without such subsidies there would not be better paid jobs, but no jobs at all. As regards the second objection, it can be argued that the subsidies affect a level of jobs particularly in simple service work, where there is little space for productivity growth anyway. The traditional logic of increasing productivity through technological rationalization under growing wage pressure does not apply in the area of simple service work.

Wage subsidies and/or negative income tax support an employment market for simple production and service work. In this way, the path towards the service society is being furthered and, at the same time, the emergence of a class of working poor can be avoided. To offer a wage level that is attractive enough if compared to public assistance, an employer in Germany today has to pay around

€800 net per month; added to this are €400 of labour costs, which means that he has to spend a total of €1,200. A subsidized wage or a negative income tax would relieve the employer of €400 per month at least (Scharpf 1997b: 9–12). In this income zone, the labour market may be revived. Strategies of this kind aiming at higher employment rates take into account the accelerated structural change making imbalance between supply and demand on the labour market a permanent feature whose removal requires a high level of flexibility, mobility and ability for further training and retraining. This trend fosters competition and correspondingly displacement and marginalization of the less competitive as well as anomie, disorganization and relative deprivation. As a consequence, rising delinquency rates call for targeted efforts of re-establishing social integration. New tools of social integration focus on precarious jobs so that switching between work and non-work is being made easier and long-term unemployment can be avoided. This is why subsidized wage and negative income tax have become increasingly attractive across different types of welfare regimes. Such models are tailored to include disadvantaged people in occupational life. Their advantage is their breaking up of the demarcation line between work and non-work and their aiming at the zone of intersection of these two areas for ensuring participation in working life.

The introduction of a negative income tax creates support for low-wage employment and even self-employment granting only a small income. It keeps people in work with all the side effects of maintaining social relationships and training skills. Further on, the differentiation between collective basic security and private additional insurance relieves the state from the comprehensive supply of collective goods and services for the entire population. The state's focus turns more to the inclusion of the less competitive citizens in society. Deregulation calls for complementation by innovations in social policy whose structure is designed to allow for greater flexibility. What has to be recognized, however, is the move away from comprehensive welfare and towards residual welfare benefits coming about with such a change of social policy. The negative income tax is clearly an instrument of keeping people in employment according to the principles of neo-liberalism.

Employer-employee agreements on sustainable employment

Another area that is important for the inclusion of people in work is the cooperation between employers and employee representatives with or without state moderation in so-called social pacts (Rhodes 2001; Siegel 2005; Acocella and Leoni 2007; Yerkes and Tijdens 2010). Despite its similarity to deregulation policies practiced in the USA and Great Britain, a glance at the new cooperation between capital, work and state in the Netherlands is proving that – at least in part – there is a third way out of the crisis beyond sticking to the established welfare state and neo-liberal policies (Visser and Hemerijck 1998; Pruijt and Dérogée 2010). In contrast to the USA, the changes in the employment situation have not simply been left to the forces of the market in the Netherlands, but have rather been actively formed by a renewal of the cooperation between employers, trade unions and the state and have therefore been directed into different tracks than in the USA. The negotiations between employers and the trade unions have successfully been changed to run away from fighting for victory or defeat with resulting losses on both sides and towards searching for solutions to problems involving benefits for both parties. A zero-sum game has been turned into a win-win situation with a growing sum. In this way, the trend towards growing disparities in income, disorganization and anomie has been kept within closer limits than in the USA and in Great Britain. The Dutch model of corporatism is supported, above all, by the two-party foundation for labour, which was established in 1945, and the three-party council for social and economic policy, which was founded in 1950. Between 1950 and 1962, the corporatist cooperation enjoyed the support of the vast majority of the population and was largely incorporated in political decision-making. Afterwards, however, corporatism turned out to be an obstacle to societal innovations. Societal support decreased; the state was looking for new instruments of regulation outside corporatist cooperation. In 1983, the highest unemployment rate was recorded at almost 14 per cent (Visser and Hemerijck 1998: 22). The rhetoric of crisis sets the imperative for reform (Kuipers 2006). The change towards a new corporatism ready for innovation was started in November 1982 by the agreement attained between the trade union federation and the employers' organization with regard to a new employment policy. Above all, this new approach included a moderate wage policy of the trade unions, a reduction in the average working hours per year from 1,530 hours in 1983 to 1,372 hours in 1996 and an increase in part-time jobs from 6.8 to 16.1 per cent for men and from 22.0 to 38.0 per cent for women. Between 1983 and 1996, employment figures rose on average by 1.6 per cent per year with the figures rising from 69.1 to 76.6 per cent for men and from 34.7 to 55.0 per cent for women. In 2009, the employment rate in percentage terms of the working-age population was at 75.8 in the Netherlands, while it was at only 67.6 in the United States (OECD 2010c). Labour costs rose by 57.5 per cent, whereas they climbed by 102.4 per cent in Germany. The average level of wage costs was at DM 34.87 per hour in 1994, while it reached DM 43.97 in Germany. Based on an index of 100 for Germany, wage costs reached 89 per cent in the Netherlands in 1994 (Visser and Hemerijck 1998: 41–51). In 2009, however, labour compensation per employee was higher in the Netherlands than in Germany; the figures were US$45,290.13 and US$39,980.47 in Purchasing Power Parities (PPP) adjusted (OECD 2011e). In the wake of this development, the unemployment rate dropped to 2.8 per cent in 2002, but returned to 5.1 per cent in 2006 to go down again to 3.4 per cent in 2009 (OECD 2003a; OECD 2011e). Contrary to the USA, the trade union's moderate wage policy did not mainly affect the lowest stratum, but all strata at about equal shares so that the disparities in income rose only marginally. Whereas employment in the USA increased by more than 25 per cent with the disparities in income growing by over 35 per cent at the same time, the Netherlands recorded a growth in employment of about 20 per cent whereas the disparities in income rose by a mere 2 per cent (Visser and

Hemerijck 1998: 64). The decile 9/decile 1 ratio was at 2.8985 in 2000 and at 2.9065 in 2005, while it rose from 4.4875 to 4.8581 in the USA over the same period of time (OECD 2011e). A new model of industrial relations within the company might be the so-called "employability contract". A contract of this type was signed at the Heineken brewery at the beginning of 1997: (1) employment is guaranteed until 2003; (2) minimum wage increase is agreed; (3) examination of capabilities and abilities of the entire staff is to take place; (4) all employees are entitled and obliged to undertake further training (de Lange 1998: 134).

The success of the Dutch model can be located, above all, in the increasing employment figures and the simultaneous drop in the job volume accompanied by an avoidance of the deregulation effects of growing inequality, poverty, disorganization and anomie, all of which can be observed in the USA. The model confirms the advantages of a strategy aiming at the inclusion of the entire working population in paid work and avoiding a considerable part of the working population withdrawing from the labour market and falling into paralysis. However, the darker side of the "Dutch miracle" should not be overlooked. The growth of jobs and employment rate started from a very low level. The greater part of this growth concerns part-time and temporary employment. This implies the risk of poverty after retirement, especially for women (Knijn 2004). Early retirement has contributed considerably to reducing the unemployment rate and postpones problems of financing pensions to the future. About 50 per cent of unemployment is long-term unemployment of over one year (Gorter 2000: 197–203). Finally, it has to be recognized that employer-employee agreements on sustainable employment introduce a liberal element of the direct adjustment of wages to changes in the market so that market performance determines wages more than before (Siegel 2005; Yerkes and Tijdens 2010).

Service sector growth: lousy jobs or marginalization through long-term unemployment?

A major point of controversy of public discourse in the European welfare states is the strategy of promoting private service employment to compensate for the loss of jobs in simple industrial production. There seems to be a trade-off between "lousy jobs" on the one hand, and marginalization through long-term unemployment on the other hand (Esping-Andersen 1999: 107–111). What works in favour of expanding private service work is the significance of labour as a central means of social inclusion. And there are no signs of a real decline of this significance of labour either. Strategies of expanding private service work have, however, to take into account the low level of productivity of this kind of work, which cannot be upgraded in its productivity by technical rationalization in a similar way as industrial production work in the past (see, however, Tripplett and Bosworth 2004). The results are more limited chances of the collective upgrading of wages than in industrial production. Therefore, there is greater pressure of earnings dispersion so that individual achievement determines more than before a person's income and living standard. The promotion of private service employment thus contributes to symbolic change in the direction of the individualization of social inclusion. It makes apparent, on the one hand, that the individual has to acquire special skills to achieve on the basis of opportunities offered. On the other hand, it supports differentiation of inclusion according to individual achievement. This consequence makes strategies aiming at increasing private service employment largely controversial in societies thus far used to more egalitarian inclusion in societal wealth. Nevertheless, the significance of work as a means of social inclusion is in favour of this strategy in the long run. It brings European welfare states one step closer to the reality of the liberal regime represented by the United States.

What appears impossible is attaining national and transnational integration outside labour division and without comprehensive inclusion of the people in occupational work. The attempt at redefining joblessness as a "happy" form of life (Beck 1999) seems to be as futile as the strategy to return to uninterrupted full-time employment as a normal state of affairs. According to the vision of happy unemployment, jobless life should be given a meaning by volunteering and do-it-yourself work just to save people from badly paid production and service jobs. Such jobs would, however, help them make a living due to wage subsidies and negative income tax. The so-called "neo-feudal" society of masters and servants would more or less be replaced by a society that splits itself into achievers and underachievers. This idea ignores the fact that volunteering and do-it-yourself work are almost exclusively done by people who are also extremely strained by their normal occupational work. Non-working people carrying out honorary jobs are mainly the wives of well-to-do managers, doctors, lawyers and civil servants. Therefore, the problem of society's division into active and inactive people cannot be solved by backing non-participation in gainful employment.

The proposal of making joblessness the symbol of a happy life is based on the idea that we live in a homogeneous powerful nation state and in a national welfare organization with a strong collective solidarity. This solidarity alone ensures that achievers pay sufficient taxes and insurance rates to allow the state to organize a happy life for the unemployed. Moreover, the realization of this idea implies that in the long run work is distributed unevenly between the highly developed industrial nations and the developing countries: sophisticated professions on the one hand and "dirty" jobs on the other. This idea, however, is robbed of its basis by the real change in solidarity structures. The network of solidarity relationships goes far beyond the nation state and differentiates itself considerably. Under such conditions there is simply not enough national solidarity available to realize the idea of happy unemployment. It involves a division of society into achievers and underachievers. This division can be prevented if moving between work and non-work with a broad transitional zone is being facilitated in a targeted way by subsidized wage and negative income tax. In this way technical and social skills can be preserved even in insecure conditions. Instead of producing a continued loss of skills by permanent unemployment, it is important to maintain participation in occupational life. Because structural imbalance is going to be a permanent state of affairs, we can no longer expect the return to full employment in "normal" conditions of work for everybody at any time. The achievement of measures aiming at the reduction of unemployment therefore has to be accounted for according to the principle of reducing the duration of joblessness and making unemployment a short-lived transitional, maybe recurring episode in a person's working life.

For the support of the happy unemployed by the elite of achievers, the basis of collective solidarity is missing. This idea neglects the structural change in solidarity, which is strengthening the link between achievement and income in the wake of globalization, pluralization and individualization rather than creating new chances for income not coupled to achievement. These chances are narrowing instead of being widened. Blaming the fostering of simple service jobs for creating a neo-feudal society of masters and servants has the effect that service work will either not grow at all or will be disapproved of where it grows. This disapproval of simple service work is being justified with ideas of "reasonable" work. As a matter of fact, the expansion of the service sector covers, however, a multiplication of jobs that have long been established and become more and more varied. One has to wonder whether hairdressers, sales assistants, messengers, switchboard operators, receptionists, waiters, party service people, pizza drivers, parking wardens, hostesses at fairs, babysitters, household aids, nurses, etc. really do inferior jobs which should rather be foregone just to support an army of happy unemployed people.

In the service sector, we witness the most striking employment deficit of Germany compared to the USA, in particular, but also in comparison with Sweden and Denmark. Whereas, in the 1990s, 41 per cent of the working population between fifteen and sixty-four in the USA, and 39 per cent in Sweden were employed in the local service sector that is not exposed to the world market, this figure is 13 per cent lower, namely 28 per cent, in Germany, Austria, France and Italy. In Germany, this service gap covered six million jobs (Scharpf 1997b: 5). In 2009, civilian employment in services was at 68.4 per cent in Germany, 77.7 per cent in Sweden, 78.8 per cent in Denmark and 80.9 per cent in the USA. Civilian employment in industry was at 29, 20, 19 and 18 per cent respectively (OECD 2011e). If we look at the development between 1967 and 2002 we see a steady decline of employment in the industrial sector. While this decline has become widely compensated for by service sector growth, this did not occur in the German economy, where the growth of the service sector lags considerably behind the decline of the industrial sector and behind growth rates in other OECD countries.

An extension of the service sector might reduce unemployment considerably (Anxo and Sterrie 2002; Fagan *et al.* 2005). In contrast, much less opportunity exists in sectors exposed to global competition, especially as the number of employees in these sectors is much higher in Germany than in the USA, namely 38 as opposed to 30 per cent. This includes all fields open to the world market: agriculture, industry, transport, warehousing, communication, financing, insurance, real estate and economic services (Scharpf 1997b: 3–4). The big difference between Sweden and the USA is that only 17 per cent of people worked in the private service sector in Sweden – about the same number as in Germany – whereas it was 28 per cent in the USA in the 1990s. The overall picture changed slightly up to 2008, with a small increase in public sector employment, but larger growth in private sector employment in Sweden, small public sector reduction and larger private sector growth in Denmark, visible public sector reduction and private sector growth in Germany, and public as well as private sector growth in the USA (ILO 2011). However, the Scandinavian way is hardly practicable under terms of global competition for favourable taxes due to the high tax load and is even abandoned there for some part. This is why an extension of private local services ranks high on the agenda. As these services are under wage pressure due to limited increase in productivity, tax-financed additional incomes – subsidized wage or negative income tax – must be taken especially into account here so as to ensure an income meeting the minimum standards of dignified life.

Service employment not only meets the function of providing income, but also fulfils social and cultural functions and forms the personality. It implies responsibility, recognition and self-assertion, social relationships and social inclusion. It retains social competence and technical skills, serves as a secondary, occasional or transitory job and helps to finance studies and further education. It can be upgraded by training and can be used as a platform for further education.

Those who are expelled completely from the field of occupational work can neither be won for work for public welfare nor for do-it-yourself work. The crisis of the labour society in the global economy cannot be coped with by one part of the people working hard and finding self-realization in occupational work and the other part reaching self-realization outside occupational work while being supported by the working people. One argument against the viability of this type of divided labour society is the nation state's dwindling power of integration; another is the social fact that income, social status and self-realization are searched for worldwide by an increasing number of people more actively; and more and more people expect this realization more comprehensively. In fact, the acquisition of income, status and self-realization by work is done today in worldwide competition. There seems to be no room left for a national pact of solidarity being concluded between the working people and the permanently unemployed, a pact that assumes the dirty work being permanently carried out in the world's underdeveloped regions for the benefit of the rich and those people who are sheltered by the rich in the core of world society.

The competition for scarce resources that has increased with worldwide population growth and the acceleration and global expansion of traffic, transport and communication leave only one way open out of the lethal struggle for survival: work specialization and labour division across borders. The worldwide division of labour offers the material substratum of the worldwide respecting of equal rights for everybody. In this sense, global labour division fuelled by unbounded capitalism and respect for equal rights of every human being on this earth promoted by moral discourse complement each other. There is no social integration outside of the division of labour the further modernization progresses on the global level. Labour division includes the individual in networks of mutual dependence and continual cooperation thus producing an elementary form of solidarity between the people (Durkheim 1964). Whoever remains excluded from this solidarity network of modern society promoted by the division of labour as he/she is unemployed, will lose social esteem and consequently self-respect and will be isolated and therefore have diminished his/her capability for social participation. This has been proven by all empirical studies on unemployment since the classic study by Jahoda *et al.* (1933/1975) on the unemployed from Marienthal. Along with unemployment, not only the occupational life broke down in Marienthal, but consequently also social, family and associational life. It was only the unrelenting optimists who still hoped for a future that can be formed. Those who resigned, were in despair or apathetically abandoned all hopes. A long-term study conducted in East Germany over a five-year period from 1990 to 1995 reveals the same findings. Long-term unemployment creates a loss in orientation, depression and bitterness and undermines self-confidence (Zempel and Frese 1997). Other research confirms these results (Brinkmann 1984; Rosenbladt 1991). It is also a hard fact that comprehensive welfare depends on a very high employment rate as is clearly demonstrated by the Scandinavian egalitarian welfare states. Employment rates are higher in the egalitarian and the liberal welfare states than in the conservative welfare states (Scharpf and Schmidt 2000, Vol. I: 342, table A.5). However, some convergence has taken place in higher employment figures across all welfare regimes in the more recent past. In 2009, the employment rates in percentage terms of the population were 52.96 in Denmark, 52.77 in Sweden, 53.64 in Norway, 50.53 in Finland, 52.40 in Australia, 51.27 in the United Kingdom, 50.63 in the USA, 50.91 in Germany but only 45.81 in France (OECD Statistics). There seems to be no escape from the dilemma of "lousy jobs vs. outsiders" (Esping-Andersen 1999: 107–111) other than furthering private service work and to subsidize that sector by some kind of negative income tax additionally to every effort of improving skills through training programmes.

Individualization of the employment relationship

New labour market strategies aim at the individualization of employment relationships. Collective agreements between employer federations and trade unions are considered as inflexible and responsible for labour market rigidities leading to the polarization between insiders in jobs and jobless outsiders. Because of the internationalization of labour division and the internal fragmentation of capital and labour force, the collective representation of interests has become increasingly difficult for trade unions and employer federations alike. The traditional collective representation of the labour force is therefore eroding and there is little chance to reorganize this type of labour force representation on the European, not to mention the global level. The structural conditions are in favour of the individualization of the employment relationship and its complementation by activated job placement through job agencies as well as strategies of smoothing the increasingly frequent transition from unemployment to employment. This change in the direction of an individualized employment relationship is, on the one hand, being furthered by the changing structure of solidarity and by the changing horizon of legitimating the representation of interests. On the other hand, it is particularly being pushed by employers and employer federations as well as economists and consultants in transnational discourse on labour market reform. It supports rhetorical change directed towards replacing the individual's protection by his/her empowerment.

Much of the literature addressing the consequences of globalization is bound to the national welfare states' particularistic view. Therefore, it describes the globalization process mainly as a threat to the achievements of the welfare state: collective wealth and collective safety guaranteed by powerful trade unions. From this point of view, the national welfare state is succeeded by the national competition state (Jessop 1994; Hirsch 1995; Cerny 1997, 2010). This definition of the situation hinders the formation of an unbiased understanding of the whole process, which allows drawing viable conclusions as regards its regulation (Weizsäcker 1999). The argument reads as follows: The liberalization and deregulation of the European – and beyond it the global – market raises the mobility of capital, whereas labour remains more strongly tied to its location. Capital will then flow unhindered to where it finds the best conditions for its investment. Companies may withdraw from national welfare state regulations by shifting their production venues to places with minimal tax load and labour costs. They play off the states against each other thus triggering a "race to the bottom" between them. The states are forced to lower taxes and social and environmental standards, so that their capacity to regulate shrinks even more. At the same time, the trade unions are losing power; they can no longer meet the employers' negotiation power on an equal standing. It is more difficult to reach a binding agreement in sectoral, industry-wide or society-wide wage negotiations and other regulations. Instead, more space is given to company-specific or even individual agreements in the framework of private contracts. This results in a growing de-solidarization of the workforce and a related spreading of wages and unequal living standards. The state has become too weak to produce social equality by way of redistribution. This description of the situation is indeed supported by the significant correlation between the centralization of wage bargaining and wage equality (cf. Iversen 1999).

Ultimately, the national governments will reap the seeds of their own efforts with regard to the establishment of the European single market and the liberalization of the world market. This move has, so to speak, freed the national governments from legitimation constraints: They can now officially quote their limited ability to regulate and redistribute as an excuse for their inactivity. Launching the argument that international agreements are necessary in order to solve national problems and are difficult to achieve, they find a comfortable excuse for their regulative underperformance and can focus in a targeted way on getting the economic location fit by way of further liberalization and deregulation (Streeck 1998: 17–18). At the same time, the companies can bid farewell to social partnership with the trade unions and turn to social integration by means of human resource management without any trade union cooperation. This is contrary to the previously existing society-wide integration through social partnership; moreover, it is less binding and rather "voluntaristic", namely it can be freely agreed upon, in a company-specific or even individual way and can be changed depending on the situation.

This description of the globalization process from the point of view of the achievements of the welfare state does, however, not imply that sticking to the established institutions of the national welfare state would be a successful strategy of maintaining social integration within the nation state, not to mention social integration beyond its borders. The welfare institutions' ability to order and integrate the national economy signifies in no way that they can preserve this ability also under the terms of open markets and differentiated solidarities in the world economy. On the contrary, their national ties form an obstacle to the order and integration of the European and global markets.

Advocating, for example, the "model Germany" without any change would bypass the realities of international labour division and would hinder the institutional innovations required by those realities (Cattero 1998). In this way, the unrelenting support of the "model Germany" would become an ideology that justifies both the status quo and the corresponding vested interests. The term of the national competition state (Hirsch 1995; Cerny 1997, 2005, 2010) likewise has to be understood as but one element in the more complex multilevel system of solidarities. We cannot assume the continued existence of a national collective solidarity and a national economic and social policy resulting from it. These are dissolving in the global multilevel society and are giving way to a horizontally and vertically differentiated complex of solidarities and politics. Competition will be taking place not only between nation states, but also between regions, local communities, companies and individuals in the future.

Structural heterogeneity and differentiated solidarities do not allow for a simple transfer of the well-known recipes of welfare state integration on to the European and global levels. This does not mean, however, that market order and social integration cannot be attained on these levels. Both the EU and the WTO have created a market order to a large extent with the help of the legal ordering of competition. Therefore, national regulations are not cancelled by a norm-free global economy but rather by higher ranking European and/or international law. The basic norm of this new formation of market order is the idea of fair competition. All efforts to achieve a normative regulation of the market process have to bear this idea in mind, since it forms the common denominator for actors that would otherwise pursue different interests. Of course, this ousts national traditions of market regulation. However, this is the price to be paid for cross-border integration through progressing division of labour. First and foremost, it is necessary here to define rights to act so that they do not interfere with each other, that means to define "negative" solidarity and/or integration. The integration process will certainly not stagnate, since mutual dependence and solidarity will increase along with the division of labour, as will positive solidarity and/or integration.

Together with competition law, labour and social law can grow beyond the borders of the nation state, but will then necessarily undermine the binding nature of existing national regulations (Leibfried and Pierson 1998; Kowalsky 1999; Carr and Massey 1999). One example for this is the EU guideline on European works committees. The guideline grants them the right to information and hearing, but no right to a say similar to that available to German works committees and to the German system of co-determination. Yet this does not affect the national systems of representation of workers' interests on the company level. From the viewpoint of a German trade unionist, the EU guideline is disappointing and can only be considered the beginning of a development, which must ultimately lead to a regulation equalling the German model. The German model starts from the idea of uniform interests of the workforce, which have to be brought to the attention of the management. In the meantime, however, the interests of the workforce have become so strongly differentiated that they can no longer be represented in a uniform manner. Combining human resource management with institutionalized consultation between management and staff and/or parts of the staff in differentiated procedures may allow for balancing the far more heterogeneous interests of the workforce as well as the management, a balance which has to be redefined over and again.

The differentiation of interests of the workforce can no longer be forced into a system of uniform collective representation. In an ever more heterogeneous world of interests, this system appears to be a relic of the past, whose supporting environment is fading away. And this not only concerns the capital-owners' commitment to the nation state, but also the nationwide solidarity of workers. *Both* sides increasingly withdraw from the uniform solidarity of the nation state though to a differing extent, exceed national boundaries and differentiate increasingly on the inside. A more heterogeneous system of interests favours a more flexible process of harmonization of interests and situation-specific integration.

Globalization, pluralization and individualization exert pressure of institutional innovation (Manning and Shaw 2000). The future form of integration seems to be no longer long-established collective organizations, but rather networks, which do not grant security by way of generous representation, but through offering widely branched access to singular ties. In this case, social integration is no longer fostered by inclusion into a particular welfare organization, but by extending chances of access to networks of the most different kind. Over the past thirty years, the structures of work and employment have strongly differentiated and pluralized. The scope of activities and the forms of employment have broadened and multiplied substantially (Statistisches Bundesamt 1999: Fachserie 1, Reihe 4.1.1; OECD 2003c; Heidenreich 2004b). Along with the increasing differentiation of activities, the rising self-responsibility and self-realization of individuals, interests have become more varied and changeable. It has become increasingly difficult to simply represent them under the roof of a large trade union. Nevertheless, some concentration of representation in larger unions – also as a result of mergers – has taken place (Ebbinghaus 2004). Larger associations differentiate internally in a move to serve varying interests.

Moreover, they become service providers having different offers in store for a wealth of interests and are in a position to satisfy the interests of the individual working person. In addition, a rising number of specialized service providers establish themselves to meet particular interests. Both trends, internal differentiation of large associations and the emergence of a growing number of specialized service providers, are changing the representation of interests fundamentally. It is moving away from uniform collective representation and towards servicing particular interests and needs. As far as individual working persons are concerned, they are therefore no longer represented by a powerful trade union in all areas of life, but rather have to find the appropriate service for a special purpose. As interests multiply, the trade unions' monopoly of interest representation is breaking up. Instead, a market of competing service enterprises is emerging, which are specialized in serving specific interests. Traditional trade unions are losing the environment of simply structured interests that can be easily focused, which is indispensable for mobilizing collective power. They are abandoning their traditional identity while, at the same time, asserting their position in competition with a growing number of specialized service providers (Streeck 1987). Their declining membership is clearly mirroring this situation. The same applies to the trade unions' partners in wage agreements, i.e. the employers' associations. They, too, are adjusting to the growing variety of entrepreneurial activities through internal differentiation and pluralization. If we look at unions, we see declining membership nearly everywhere – with the great exception of Scandinavian countries – particularly since the 1980s (Gaston 2002; Rosenfeld 2006; Dreher and Gaston 2007). Increasing membership in the Scandinavian countries is against the general trend and reflects the still powerful position of the unions in the administration of the social democratic welfare state including the administration of special benefits like the *Wage Earner Fund* (WEF) in Sweden. To take part in the all-embracing social democratic welfare state one has to be a member of a trade union.

The relationship between workforce and management no longer concerns a collective, uniform representation of interests, but rather communication, cooperation and harmonization of interests in line with the particular company, job and situation. There is no chance of having a uniform representation of all those aspects. The interest in the partner changes on both sides. In the so-called Fordist regime of mass production and mass consumption, an enterprise was able to secure the purpose-bound commitment of its employees through sector-, industry- and society-wide cooperation with the trade unions and the state by way of generally accepted collective security and wage increases avoiding larger differences. The employees could share in the enterprise's economic achievement and attain continued improvement of their material living standard through their collective representation by the trade unions and the state's legal regulations. In the post-Fordist regime, in contrast, management and workforce are in direct negotiation with each other. The enterprise relies on the personal identification of its employees with their jobs and the business, whereas the employees desire the enterprise's readiness to support their career plans, self-realization and flexible way of living. In a move to win the employees' personal commitment, the enterprise, competing with other enterprises, shows a greater interest in its staff than under the conditions of the Fordist regime. A growing number of working people are currently in this situation, where there is a link between entrepreneurial activities and self-realization beyond mass production in the large enterprise. We can take the flexible labour markets of the "new economy" in information technology as a pioneering model of a general trend. A study on flexible labour markets in Silicon Valley in California offers an insight in this new world of welfare capitalism (Benner 2002).

In as much as trade unions and employee representatives in companies adjust to transnational integration and national differentiation, pluralization and individualization of life careers, loyalties and solidarity networks they cooperate with employers in working out new forms of flexible, performance-dependent and achievement-based agreements on contracts, working time and wages. According to a study on the hundred largest German corporations, conducted by the team of Wolfgang Streeck at the Max Planck Institute for the Study of Society in Cologne, there is clear evidence of the dissolution of the so-called Deutschland AG with the most internationalized companies working as pioneers (Streeck and Höpner 2003; Höpner 2003). The close network of banks and industrial enterprises is losing its strength; long-term bank loans are partly being replaced by capital drawn from the capital market, and hierarchical control of the management by the supervisory board (*Aufsichtsrat*) by market control. This change gives preference to orienting investments to the shareholder value. Under this new regime employee representatives see themselves increasingly compelled to cooperate in agreements, which place greater emphasis on flexibility, performance of the company on the market and individual achievement. Though there is no change of the major institutions of industrial relations (co-determination, works councils), they are nevertheless filled out in a new, more liberalized way. This transformation of the substance of industrial relations within the established forms can however not only be explained by the strengthening of market forces in the global economy. The global forces would not have the same effect, if there wasn't a corresponding change in the national solidarity structure, which moves away from a homogeneous national collective and workforce towards a far more pluralized population with greater individual autonomy and differentiation of life careers. Both trends – globalization and individualization – work together to narrow down the collectively shared part of the labour contract and to increase its individually differentiated part. The labour contract becomes more individualized than before.

Of course not everybody will benefit from this development to the same extent, which more than ever before awards education and permanent further training, but is worsening the chances of all those who do not possess any special skills. In as much as this development cannot be stopped, flexible processes of interest coordination tailored to the individual situation and safety nets for those who are unskilled within and not beyond employment become increasingly significant in view of the growing variety of interests.

The increased dynamics of the labour market and the differentiation of the workforce require the change from the administration of unemployment to the entrepreneurial organization of job placement. This trend is very much in tune with the philosophy of individual empowerment and has spread across all types of welfare states in the meantime. Germany has joined this movement by replacing the federal "authority" of labour with the federal "agency" of labour. It has still not been decided whether this innovation remains on the level of rhetorical change – lip-service to a globally diffusing "myth" – or will indeed be brought down from the level of formal structure to the level of activity structure in the sense of the neoinstitutionalist world society approach of John Meyer's Stanford group (Meyer and Rowan 1977; Meyer et al. 1997). In the ongoing process of international monitoring and benchmarking – which promotes the convergence of policy strategies with the establishment of a transnationalized field of inclusion discourse – pioneers like the Netherlands can serve as role models. They help to precipitate rhetorical change.

In the Netherlands, the activation of job placement beyond the state-run job centres has made an important contribution to the decline in unemployment figures to 2.8 per cent in 2002 (Visser and Hemerijck 1998: 215–232; OECD 2003a). In 2009, the figure was 3.4 per cent (OECD 2011e). Private employment agencies, employment groups and casual labour agencies have introduced a new dynamism into job placement. The state-controlled job centres administer unemployment in a bureaucratic way. Their existence may even seem particularly legitimate in the face of high unemployment figures, as it is often being criticized. In contrast, it is claimed that competition between private job agencies honours quick placement in a job. State-run job administration is being blamed for having no incentives at all to supply a job, whereas private job agencies are assumed to do so, because they earn their living from the premiums paid for job placement. The new philosophy says that it is only if job placement becomes as dynamic as the labour market itself that it will make an efficient contribution to the reduction of unemployment figures. If such an innovation had the effect of lowering the interest of job agencies in the unskilled workforce that is hard to place in employment, this problem is expected to be solved by government premiums for job placement of unskilled and long-term unemployed people. It is assumed that the cost for such incentives would be clearly below that of state-controlled job administration (Dreas 2003).

A special tool for dealing with the increasing uncertainty of the life course is the organization of transitional labour markets to mediate between different phases of the individual's life course (Schmid 2002: 234–322):

- education and employment
- short-term and full-time employment
- unemployment and employment
- private activity and gainful employment
- employment, disablement and retirement.

An area of increasing importance as a transitional labour market is the linking of unpaid and paid work in the third sector alongside state and market. An "activity society" with a vital third sector does not replace gainful employment. It rather establishes a close link to employment. Voluntary commitment is generally based on social capital that has been acquired through the inclusion in employment. The comprehensive organization of volunteering work is a special market, on which a wide variety of state-run and non-state-run welfare and environmental organizations offer corresponding jobs and pay for them. An ever-widening zone of partly paid jobs emerges between paid and unpaid volunteering work (expense allowances), where the market and the "third sector" penetrate each other. Yet, a tool for reducing unemployment can evolve from such innovation to such an extent only that a labour market emerges for volunteering services with a competitive material and symbolic remuneration. Here, symbolic remuneration through respect and self-assurance may to some degree compensate for the far lower material remuneration. This however has always been a reality in the field of social services (Spear *et al.* 2001).

Decentralization of wage bargaining

Decentralization of wage bargaining has occurred nearly everywhere over the past two decades in one form or another. Where sectoral or national bargaining has persisted, at least the margin for company level agreements has been widened. This trend fits in the changing structure of solidarity and the changing horizon of legitimating strategies of inclusion. It is particularly being pushed by employers facing globalized competition, but also by economists and consultants who see markets as tools for solving any kind of problem. Decentralization of wage bargaining reintroduces market forces in the otherwise collectively organized labour market. It is legitimated by the spreading rhetoric of individual empowerment. Decentralization of wage bargaining needs much more empowered individuals than centralized bargaining. It is therefore a major part of the rhetorical change away from protecting and towards empowering the individual.

In the past, centralized systems of coordinated wage bargaining have largely supported the performance of national economies. This advantage seems, however, to have turned to a disadvantage in the meantime.

The success of the Dutch model in coping with the problem of unemployment under the pressure of economic globalization has nevertheless once again demonstrated the comparative advantage of a working system of coordination between trade unions, employers' associations and the state. As comparative studies show, the effective working of this kind of corporatism seems to be a privilege of small countries (Siaroff 1999). The effects of corporatist coordination on economic performance (economic growth, inflation, employment) depend largely on exposure to global economic competition and on the more or less stability-oriented monetary policy of central banks.

According to an analysis by Torben Iversen (1999) non-accommodating stability-oriented monetary policy has no detrimental effects on employment, but implies higher wage dispersion, if wage bargaining is largely decentralized to be carried out on the company level. This is the typical situation of liberal market regimes, though non-accommodating monetary policy is not rigorously applied in most of the countries pertaining to the liberal type. According to Iversen's theoretical assumption and empirical assessment the liberal countries would make employment gains, if they adopted a more rigorous monetary policy. A hard currency policy would exert greater pressure on wage restraint in those countries. In corporatist regimes with highly centralized wage bargaining on the national level a hard currency policy is not compensated for by wage restraint. The leading unions of high productivity industries set high wage levels that weaken the competitiveness of less productive sectors and firms and thus imply the loss of jobs particularly of unskilled workers. This was the case in Denmark between the early 1980s and the mid-1990s, and in Sweden between the early and late 1990s. Both countries have coped with this situation by turning to centrally organized decentralization of wage bargaining leaving concrete wage agreements to the company level within the confines of central frame agreements in the meantime. According to Iversen's study medium centralization of wage bargaining has a positive employment effect under the conditions of non-accommodating monetary policy. The cases for this arrangement are Japan, Switzerland, Germany, the Netherlands and Belgium. The explanation is greater differentiation of wage agreements according to economic competitiveness of sectors.

Germany has, however, been an outlier in this group since the early 1990s because of the greater heterogeneity of productivity since reunification and the deflationary pressure exerted by the ECB. Germany is the only large country where corporatist coordination has been effective for a long time. In contradistinction to largely centralized coordination in the small Scandinavian countries, coordination in Germany is a matter of sectoral bargaining with the metal industry in North Württemberg/North Baden in a pace-making role for all other sectors. It was important that the metal industry was an industrial sector strongly exposed to the world market. This exposure contributed to the adjustment of wage policy to international competition. Wage increase sustained by productivity growth became the guiding line. This type of sectoral coordination worked rather effectively within the German system of "ordo-liberalism" with a strong independent central bank in the 1950s and 1960s. The turn towards Keynesianism occurred rather later, in the 1970s. Its institutionalization in the *Concerted Action* was rather ineffective, because this body was too large and heterogeneous and had no binding influence on sectoral wage bargaining. With the oil crisis the system of sectoral wage bargaining with the metal industry in the lead slipped into a spiral of excessive wage growth and inflation thus producing the phenomenon of stagflation.

In the 1980s, sectoral wage bargaining was brought back to its typical function of not only serving particularistic interests but also assuming public responsibility by taking into account the competitiveness of the German economy in the general macroeconomic situation. A major factor for this recovery was the replacement of

Keynesianism by monetarism with the central bank (*Bundesbank*) assuming the central role of stabilizing price development. Reunification and the European Monetary Union along with the establishment of the European Central Bank (ECB) changed the situation considerably for Germany. The difference in productivity between East and West undermined the conditions needed for sustainable sectoral bargaining. On the one hand, equalization of wages between East and West lowered the competitive strength of the German industry; on the other hand, this decreasing competitive strength led to increasing deviation from sectoral wage agreements by special company agreements. A further disadvantage is the fact that ECB monetary policy is oriented to keeping inflation rates down in countries with no tradition of self-restraint. This restrictive monetary policy has deflationary effects in Germany so that the country suffers from a lack of incentives for economic growth (Traxler 2005). Because of this change of situation the German system of sectoral coordination is no longer working effectively. In comparison to the smaller corporatist countries it lacks central organization of decentralized wage bargaining with a centrally set corridor within which special agreements are concluded at the company level. This decreasing capacity for the coordination of solidaristic wage agreements with economic performance (economic growth, inflation and employment rate) might push Germany – just like other larger countries (France, Italy) – some steps further towards the liberal regime of uncoordinated wage policy, which is characterized by unorganized decentralization under the condition of a more comprehensive central bank policy; like the American Federal Reserve the latter takes overall economic performance into account, not only monetary stability (Iversen 1999: 119–165). This type of unorganized decentralization would entail a growth of wage dispersion as we know from the liberal welfare regimes (Traxler and Kittel 2000; Traxler 2001, 2003a, 2003b; Traxler *et al.* 2001; Dahl *et al.* 2009; Antonczyk *et al.* 2010). This development has indeed taken place in the meantime and has enhanced the competitiveness of the German industry on the world market, as is demonstrated by Germany's surplus in exports as against imports. This competitive advantage is criticized as a kind of neo-mercantilism by governments such as France, which see their economy disadvantaged by such policies.

Because monetary policy has been Europeanized with the establishment of the ECB the conditions for returning to nationally organized decentralization of wage agreements seem to no longer exist for Germany nor for other larger countries. It is therefore the organization of decentralized wage agreements on the European level that is the target of efforts aiming at preserving the social cohesion of societies by combining economic growth with high employment rates and only limited wage dispersion. All attempts at establishing this kind of organized wage bargaining on the European level have, however, failed thus far. Its establishment is hindered by the heterogeneity of economic development, institutional structures and cultural traditions of the member states of the European Union. If it was impossible to institutionalize the central organization of wage bargaining in the large industrial countries it is very unlikely to overcome the even greater obstacles for this type of corporatist coordination on the European level.

Civic self-organization

Both in social science and in public discourse, the activation of civil society has become a kind of sheet anchor of maintaining social integration in the face of shrinking governmental capacity to guarantee comprehensive national welfare (Cohen and Arato 1992; Alexander 2006; Enjolras and Sivesind 2009). This increased significance of civil society is part of a broader rhetorical change. It is part of a shift away from governmental protection of the incapable individual and towards the empowerment of an individual who is made capable of standing on his/her own feet whatever kind of danger or risk he/she has to face. The rhetorical success of arguments for strengthening civil society is, on the one hand, backed up by the retreat of the state from comprehensive provision of welfare and by the shrinking legitimacy of the strong nation state. On the other hand, it is supported by NGO activists who pursue the expansion of civic self-organization.

The social integration of largely globalized, pluralized and individualized social life with only limited state capacity and organization by representative associations depends on civic self-organization by a strong civil society. Civil society, civic commitment, civic self-organization and the "third sector" have attracted growing interest in recent times besides state and market both in political practice and in social research. Theoretical, empirical and comparative research is steadily growing in this field (Cohen and Arato 1992; Gaskin et al. 1996; Anheier et al. 1997; Priller and Zimmer 1997; Salamon and Anheier 1998; Salamon et al. 1999; Enquête-Kommission "Zukunft des Bürgerschaftlichen Engagements" Deutscher Bundestag 2002, 2003a, 2003b; Anheier and Toepler 2003; Lang 2003; Adloff 2005, 2010; Anheier and Leat 2006).

Relating state and civil society we might distinguish four types by cross-classifying strong vs. weak states and strong vs. weak civil societies: German status-centred corporatism and Swedish egalitarian tripartism represent a linking of strong states and strong civil societies; American liberalism a weak state linked with a strong civil society; French etatism a strong state linked with a weak civil society; and Italian parochialism a weak state linked with a weak civil society (Figures 3.2 and 3.3). Obviously, parochialism is the worst case in regard to the production of social integration beyond family and family-based ties. This has been well-documented by research on Italy since the 1960s (Banfield 1958; Putnam et al. 1993). Developing countries represent far more extreme cases of parochialism than Italy, where we see extreme variations between North and South with the North being much more advanced than the South. Etatism needs the state to compensate for weak civic self-organization. According to Salamon and Anheier (1998) Japan is the model case for etatism. However, it has to be taken into account that the family and the big companies fulfil integrative functions in a complementary way in Japan. In our view France still displays features of etatism though the state makes increasing use of voluntary associations for providing services of social integration. The etatist form of this arrangement is reflected in the still dominant role of the state. Corporatism and tripartism are

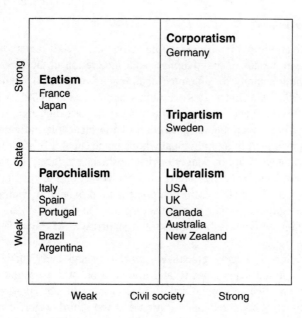

Figure 3.2 State and civil society I.

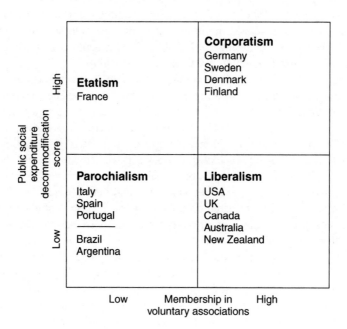

Figure 3.3 State and civil society II.

strong in producing state-led social integration residing on the collaboration of strong civic organizations. Liberalism has to rely on strong civic self-organization to compensate for only limited social integration by the state. The more European societies adopt elements of liberalism they need a concomitant mobilization of civic self-organization. Otherwise they would slip into disintegration.

Whereas in the European welfare states law and state authorities ensure social integration, this is rather a question of the settlement of conflicts and negotiations between interested parties and third parties concerned by the matter in the USA. A varied landscape of public interest groups and public interest science has emerged there ensuring a widespread representation of interests when filtering out public welfare in individual cases. However, this is an endless process of the settlement of conflicts and negotiations in innumerable individual cases, where frequently the grasping of the whole thing is being lost. Where no civic organizations are active, the law of the powerful prevails. Places of a working, well-integrated civil society exist side by side with places of decline, hopelessness and violence.

Social integration by civic organization requires a high level of activity on the part of the citizens and gives privilege to the active as against the inactive. It is empirically corroborated that participation in volunteering grows from the bottom to the top of the class structure in general or of levels of education. According to data gathered in the United States in 2010, only 8.8 per cent of people with an education less than a high school diploma report doing voluntary work, but 42.3 per cent of people with a Bachelor's degree and higher do so (Table 3.1) (cf. Hart *et al.* 2005). The percentage of people doing voluntary work is 27.8 among Whites, 19.4 among Blacks or African Americans, 19.6 among Asians and 14.7 among Hispanics or Latinos. Employed people are engaged in voluntary work at 29.2 per cent, unemployed people at 23.8 per cent (Table 3.2).

Volunteering does not produce the same widespread social integration we know from the European welfare state whose power of integration is being undermined by its external entanglement and its internal differentiation. Integration by civic self-organization would have to replace state integration somewhat, especially since problems have become more varied and can only be coped with

Table 3.1 Volunteering in the USA (I)

Educational attainment	Per cent of adult population doing voluntary work (2010)
Less than a high school diploma	8.8
High school graduates, no college	3.3
Some college or associate degree	29.2
Bachelor's degree and higher	42.3

Source: US Department of Labor, Bureau of Labor Statistics (2011), p. 2, Table A, September 2010. Retrieved 16 February 2011, from www.bls.gov/news.release/pdf/volun.pdf.

Table 3.2 Volunteering in the USA (II)

Race and Hispanic or Latino ethnicity	Per cent of adult population doing voluntary work (2010)
White	27.8
Black or African American	19.4
Asian	19.6
Hispanic or Latino ethnicity	14.7
Employment status	
Civilian labour force	28.7
Employed	29.2
Full time	28.2
Part time	33.2
Unemployed	23.8
Not in the labour force	22.0

Source: U.S. Department of Labor, Bureau of Labor Statistics (2011), p. 2, Table A, September 2010. Retrieved 16 February 2011, from www.bls.gov/news.release/pdf/volun.pdf.

below the level of the nation state through direct negotiations between directly affected people. One example of such direct negotiation is the integration of immigrants in the European welfare states. It cannot be regulated by law alone, but requires implementation by joint committees of natives and immigrants in the cities and communities themselves. Another example is the change in the world of labour. The state can only set a frame for fair negotiations, but will have to abandon generally valid detailed regulations. This creates new latitudes for agreements adjusted to the particular situation in individual regions and communities right through to individual companies. The same applies to wage agreements between the parties in negotiation. They turn away from far-reaching sectoral wage contracts and move towards an agreement on a frame and a set of rules for fair negotiations on the company level for all imaginable sorts of jobs. Employers' organizations and trade unions no longer work out detailed and generally valid agreements, but change into advisors for regional and company-specific agreements from the point of view of fairness. Labour courts see less to the respect of codified law with regard to its contents and more to the respect of the rules of fair negotiations.

According to Tocqueville's (1945) classical study, *Democracy in America*, the United States demonstrates in an exemplary way how a vital world of voluntary associations helps to promote two positive effects for society: Voluntary associations provide a multiplicity of services for their members in particular and for society in general, and they educate their members in the practice of civic virtues to make them good citizens who commit themselves to the good of society as a whole (Edwards *et al.* 2001). The service function can be measured by the employment rate of the non-profit sector. With regard to the service function of voluntary associations it is assumed that the economic liberalization of society calls for a corresponding growth of the third (non-profit) sector in order to meet the new challenges of social integration in a more diversified way than by state-run public administration. There is at least some empirical evidence for this hypothesis insofar as we observe a higher rate of paid and unpaid employment in the non-profit sector on average in liberal welfare states than in conservative and egalitarian welfare states, and a much higher rate than in Middle Eastern European transformation countries, in developing as well as newly industrialized countries. For example, the total rate of paid and unpaid employment in the non-profit sector is 11.9 per cent in the USA and 10.5 per cent in the UK, but 8.0 per cent in Germany, 8.3 per cent in Sweden, 1.6 per cent in Hungary and 2.5 per cent in Brazil. There are also some exceptional cases such as the Netherlands at 18.7 per cent and Belgium at 13.0 per cent (Anheier and Toepler 2003: 31).

Generally, it is claimed that there is a positive correlation between the extension of non-profit service and the extension of public interest advocacy by civic associations. In the United States, for instance, we see a large non-profit sector fulfilling service functions alongside a great number of civic associations devoted to advocating public interest issues. The liberal regime counts on both non-profit service and public interest advocacy, whereas the corporatist and the etatist regimes rely much more on state service and state advocacy of public interest. This is reflected in the relatively high level of voluntary work organized by public administration and of state subsidies for voluntary associations doing public service in Germany. It is also demonstrated in the concentration of voluntary associations on leisure time activities in Sweden leaving service to public administration and public interest advocacy to the collaboration between the state and the large employer federations and trade unions. If we take France as an etatist regime, we see a growing interest of the state in the targeted use of voluntary associations for providing state-subsidized public service. The result is a state-dominated form of corporatism, which is focused on the service function, while the function of public interest advocacy is largely left to the government and to public administration. Public interest advocacy by voluntary associations is therefore less strongly developed. It is generally a matter of the state and of the power struggle of parties in the political arena. In the parochial regime as it still exists to a certain degree in the Mediterranean countries, but much more so in the developing parts of the world, there is a small non-profit service sector as well as a small sector of civic association advocating public interest, which is less compensated by state services and public administration than in the etatist regimes (Anheier and Toepler 2003: 38–41).

Regarding civic virtues as a resource of social life it is assumed that their production is more advanced in societies with a vital world of voluntary associations according to Tocqueville (1945; cf. Münkler 1997). This hypothesis should be reflected on the macro level in positive correlations between the rate of membership in voluntary associations and the number of interpersonal relations on the one hand, and interpersonal trust as well as trust in democracy or trust in political and administrative institutions on the other hand. There is some empirical support for this hypothesis. On the micro level a positive correlation between

128 *Symbolic change*

participation in social and political life and interpersonal trust, the feeling of social and political competence as well as trust in democracy and in political institutions is expected. There is some evidence supporting this hypothesis. A survey on participation in local politics in Germany reveals, for instance, that political participation in local politics is first of all a matter of the upper middle and the upper class and of well-integrated people. Participation grows from bottom to top from 11 to 54 per cent depending on the type of participation such as output-related, party-related or issue-related or civil disobedience. The correlation holds for all forms of participation and for an index of resources as well as an index of social integration (Gabriel 2003). There is also a positive correlation between the various forms of political participation (Gabriel 2003: 135). The survey shows that attitudes of inactive people are fairly well-represented by the active people. And there is indeed a positive correlation between political participation in local politics and trust in democracy as a desirable form of governance in local political institutions as well as the feeling of political competence (Gabriel 2003). It seems to be fair to derive a similar positive effect of participation in voluntary work on social inclusion and the practicing of civic virtues as well as trust in social cooperation from such data on participation in local politics, according to Tocqueville's interpretation of American everyday life.

A growing need of compensating for the loss of the nation state's production of public welfare by the mobilization and reorganization of civil society is widely being articulated in public discourse. For this aspect, too, the USA offers a wealth of examples. In that country, we would find a more varied and more active civil society than in the European welfare states (Table 3.3). In recent times new projects of promoting civic self-organization in local communities have attracted growing interest (Skocpol 1998; Skocpol and Fiorina 1999;

Table 3.3 Volunteering in OECD countries

	Per cent belonging to at least one group (2005)	Per cent belonging to no group (2005)	Per cent doing no unpaid voluntary work (30–49 years old) (1999–2002)
United States	85.9	14.1	29.2
Netherlands	77.1	22.9	51.5
(Western) Germany	67.1	32.9	76.7
Canada	82.1	17.9	46.1
United Kingdom	75.6	24.4	53.6
Italy	61.7	38.3	71.7
France	54.5	45.5	74.6
Mexico	82.7	17.3	63.8
Japan	58.1	41.9	89.1
Spain	38.7	61.3	84.2
OECD average	70.4	29.6	65.5

Source: OECD Family database (2009). Table CO4.1.A and Table CO4.1.C retrieved 16 February 2011, from www.oecd.org/dataoecd/1/25/43200164.pdf.

Sirianni and Friedland 2001; Lang 2003). One example of civil society's self-organization as established in the USA, is the community organizer in charge of mobilizing, coordinating and organizing neighbourhood projects. In England, too, there is the example of the public welfare entrepreneur who advances and focuses civil-societal activities. In the USA, one can, however, recognize the limits of this kind of integration exactly where the weak are left to themselves or are catered to in individual cases only without being included in society in an encompassing way.

In the Continental European welfare state, the law is the tool of state-organized social integration. In law established by the state, the particular interests are harmonized by general law that is consistent in itself and coordinated with other law. The administration's only task is to carry out the law, whereas the courts have to guarantee its validity through correct application. The subjective rights of private citizens are coordinated through objective law. In this way, democracy and the legal state complement each other on the basis of their division of labour. With the state's withdrawal from the integration of rights and interests through general law, the courts are being attributed a new role in the active coordination and integration of clashing subjective rights, both on a national and a supranational level. This development can be observed in the United States, where the accommodation of subjective rights has always been the task of the courts, and where lawyers and law firms are used to struggling toughly for the rights of their clients. This kind of social integration through jurisdiction is shifting the conflict around the definition of opportunities to act some part away from politics and into the legal sphere. Only rights represented by a good and well-paid lawyer will be applicable here. Those who do not possess the necessary means themselves at least have to find access to organizations caring for otherwise neglected people and their problems.

The completeness or incompleteness of social integration is then measured by the variety of active civic organizations devoted to the rights of groups that are endowed with less financial means and are less capable of organizing and articulating themselves. The meaning of this can again be observed in the United States: 82 per cent of Americans say that they are members of a volunteering organization, while it is 68 per cent in Germany, 53 per cent in the UK and only 39 per cent in France. Voluntary unpaid work in volunteering organizations is reported by 60 per cent of those surveyed in the United States, 31 per cent in Germany, 26 per cent in the UK and 35 per cent in France. Voluntary work in volunteering organizations climbed from 26 to 54 per cent of those surveyed in the United States between 1977 and 1995. The volume of donations for welfare purposes rose from US$1.2 billion to US$144.0 billion relative between 1930 and 1995, which is from 10 to 547 per capita. In terms of constant US dollars of 1993, it increased from US$10.4 billion to US$136.8 billion, which means from 88 to 533 per capita. In the decade from 1920 to 1929, a total of 164 foundations occurred, whereas this figure reached 1,620 between 1980 and 1988. As far as high school seniors are concerned, a slight increase of voluntary work was established from 1980 to 1994, namely from 69 to 73 per cent. In 1994, this kind of work was distributed as follows: 3.2 per cent almost every day, 7.6 per cent at least once a week, 17.1 per cent once or twice a month, 44.8 per cent several times a year (Lipset 1996: 278; Murswieck 1998: 712–715).

The number of civic associations endeavouring to cope with tasks in the public interest (*public interest groups*) is higher in the USA than in any other country in the world. They spread like wildfire in the 1960s and the 1970s in the wake of the civil rights movement. Moreover, the Americans' commitment to such associations is far stronger than in comparable countries. There is a *market* of civic commitment, which is quickly and precisely geared to hot spots in whatever form it is needed. For instance, a project may be formed of caring for working homeless people, who do not earn enough to pay for an apartment; another project may look after the labour market integration of people suffering from a particular handicap; a third group may undertake activities to counter discrimination of older women on TV. Major actors in this market are corporations practicing corporate social responsibility (CSR) as part of their branding strategy (Hiß 2006; Curbach 2009). Nevertheless, social integration accomplished in this way will always remain incomplete, and it often fails miserably in the social hot spots of downtown ghettos. As a rule, it requires a certain amount of self-organization of the people in need, since permanent charitable support by caring people cannot be ensured in the long term. Therefore, in the long run it is the strong self-organized people who will win, while the weak unorganized people are among the losers.

In the interaction of civil society and law, the legal accomplishment of subjective rights requires a lot of staying power. The necessary activation of civil society depends on entrepreneurial initiatives. A well-known example of this is Ralph Nader, a lawyer who has succeeded in building up an empire of public interest groups through the successful recruitment of members, who mainly try to improve consumer rights. Frequently, the boundaries between market-type services and civic commitment melt away. In the United States, market and civil society do not form opposing poles, but rather are tightly entangled twins. If we add the state to this, there are even triplets. Market, state and civil society are not spheres that are completely separate from each other, but that interfere and intersect considerably (Rothenberg 1992).

How can the entrepreneurial push necessary for the mobilization of civil society, however, be motivated to a sufficient extent? We are in a field where the necessary measures can rest neither on majorities nor on well-organized interests at first. Neither the majority politics of parties looking for votes nor the interest politics of well-organized groups will help much in many areas of social integration. It is rather a typical problem of the provision of collective goods (Olson 1965). Solving a variety of integration problems would certainly raise public welfare and help not just some single groups, but society as a whole on whatever level. Since, however, the individual can only make a tiny contribution to the solution of the problem, any motive to do so is indeed lacking. But if an individual and/or a small group takes the entrepreneurial role of investing time and money, those who are interested latently can be mobilized more easily, as the probability grows that a relatively large effect will result from their small contribution to the benefit of all.

It is, consequently, important for potential moral entrepreneurs to be offered a sufficient amount of incentives in order to invest time, money and hope so that successful, and in the largest sense profitable, projects can be launched. "Profitable" also means the project paying off and being meaningful. The most fertile ground for such incentives has existed in the United States so far. On the one hand, there is a historically evolved culture of self-employed entrepreneurs, while on the other hand, there is a likewise established culture of philanthropy. Moreover, there is the historically rooted readiness to be inspired and mobilized for new projects. Last but not least, we should not neglect the fact that low taxes create the necessary opportunity for philanthropy while at the same time the possibility to deduct donations and membership fees from taxes offers new stimuli for philanthropic investments. In the societies on the European continent, this culture is less strongly rooted, since the state has taken over a wealth of functions there, which have always been in the hands of private projects in the United States. Therefore, the state's withdrawal in Europe will open large gaps with regard to supply of social integration. The culture of civic entrepreneurship will grow only slowly here, and only if the private existence of the public welfare entrepreneur can be guaranteed through the entanglement of market and civil society with social integrative projects, e.g. private welfare companies. This means that tax incentives would have to create favourable terms for investments in public welfare work.

To promote investments into public welfare work, the European welfare states have taken measures to regulate the third sector in order to break up the existing welfare cartel of privileged associations and to pave the way to market access for new welfare companies. A major driving force of this liberalization of welfare services has been the European competition law (Hammerschmidt and Uhlendorff 2003). The national charity law is expected to support instead of prevent capital formation, and the ban on competition has been removed (Deutscher Bundestag 1998; Bode 2004). Social brokers mediate supply and demand in the field of public welfare work. State authorities are being transformed into agencies and use administrative processes to replace the control of societal life with an *activation* of society by offering incentives for entrepreneurial initiatives in public welfare work (Dettling 1998a). State, market and civil society are no longer separated from each other, but are being networked in a wide zone of mutual penetration (Naschold 1993, 1995; Naschold et al. 1997; Riedel 2003).

The activation of voluntary work has become a major concern of the governments in a growing number of countries. The United States is still ahead in this respect (Lang 2003), however in Europe governments are increasingly engaged in such programmes. According to a recent study, the Netherlands, Britain and Denmark have taken a series of initiatives (Riedel 2003). One example of this is the *Bexley Community Care Scheme* in London's Bexley district. Among other services, it provides information about old-age dementia to the families of people suffering from the disease, helps them to look after their rights to financial support (care allowance), gives them recommendations on competing care services and advice on the combination of professional care and care through family members. At the same time, this communal agency cooperates with a communal self-help group of caring family members (Dettling 1995: 151–154).

With the multiplication of the supply of integration services and the corresponding vitalization of competition in the context of social integration, state and family are relieved of such integrative tasks. The "third sector" is changing its structure. Family, established associations and churches are complemented with a wide variety of associations, organizations, self-help groups and enterprises competing with each other for the provision of integrative services. This means a growth of the third sector. It takes over tasks from the state, but also emancipates itself from traditional and authoritarian kinds of social organization in the form of family and long-established associations. It adopts characteristics of market-type social organization without melting completely in the purely economic market. One example of this integration service is job placement. Its private organization relieves the state from expenditure, yet its acknowledgement as a charitable activity makes a difference with regard to profit-oriented businesses. At the same time, however, it is constantly required to prove its charitable character. The kindergarten is yet another example. It takes childcare away from the family, but has to undergo examinations as to its charitable character, which discerns it from purely economic businesses. A dynamic charity market features precisely the institutional structure that corresponds to the integration of a more open and more dynamic multilevel society.

Without any doubt, the shift of social integration from state and family towards a third sector that is structured in pluralistic, competitive and market-related terms, will change the character of social integration. It will no longer present a far-reaching uniform quality like integration through state authorities (e.g. job centres and social security offices) and will not embody the emotional warmth of integration through the family. In contrast to state integration, the market-type integration by the new third sector can respond more flexibly to quickly changing problems and work more efficiently and effectively. Other than family integration, it can be achieved irrespective of the quality and availability of an inclusion into the family and in favour of liberation from traditional forms of the division of labour within the family. As much as we may appreciate integration through the state and/or family, both are suffering increasingly from deficits in a more dynamic and more open society and seem to require, at least, complementation through market-related restructuring of the third sector.

A growing part of public welfare work is being expected from self-help groups. One example is self-help groups of old-aged people organizing mutual assistance, for instance in the form of service credits as a "new currency" for the welfare state. In this system, each participant may acquire credit points through his/her own assistance being used for the mobilization of help if need be. This is a model created in the United States, which has meanwhile been copied in other countries (Cahn 1990). The networks of nursing family members are another example. They are particularly well-established in the UK and have been united in the *Carer's National Association* since 1988. The *Community Care Reform*, which was introduced in 1990, expressly includes such self-help groups on a local level in the organization of carers' jobs. The target of this project is to ensure the appropriate involvement of helping family members and an optimized mixture of professional and family assistance. It is a clear step away from the model of bureaucratic administration of help organized in a cartel fashion and moves towards a pluralistic system of competing suppliers of assistance and the mutual complementation of professional, family and further non-professional help by volunteers (Dettling 1995: 150).

Self-help groups have become a powerful competitor for established churches, organizations and associations. They contribute a great deal to a change in the understanding of public welfare work. While the traditional honorary post was generally held by the notabilities from club committees and their well-off wives, the new type of welfare work is more strongly marked by the search for meaning, self-realization and also self-interest in the solution of one's own problems (Keupp 2003). For Germany, the data gathered by the Socio-Economical Panel (SOEP) underlines this development: Voluntary work has shifted away from established associations and clubs towards new, smaller initiatives, and from regular to irregular work. Little has changed, however, in the structure of participation. People working full-time are most active in volunteering accounting for a share of 35 per cent, followed by part-time employees at 32 per cent. As far as the unemployed are concerned, their participation rose from 16.5 to 26.5 per cent between 1985 and 1994, which can primarily be ascribed to the rising share of young university graduates among the unemployed. They consider volunteering a good means to maintain or extend their skills (Gaskin *et al.* 1996; Anheier *et al.* 1997; Priller and Zimmer 1997; Berger 1999: 336–339; 351–355; Heinze *et al.* 1999: 193–196).

Of course, self-interest plays a major role in self-help groups. Nevertheless, this should not mean that there is no public benefit involved at all. Self-help groups help to solve the problems of their members and help to integrate them into a network, giving them some support. Especially in a society where family, relatives as well as established associations and churches no longer reach everyone, they fulfil an important integrative function. They reflect the increased variety of integration problems in a more open, more dynamic and more heterogeneous society and form an essential part of the more pluralistic third sector. Polls regarding volunteering might assess work in self-help groups inadequately, since the surveyed people might have a traditional image of volunteering and do not understand their commitment in self-help groups as public welfare work. Accordingly, the actual public welfare work in Germany should have a far higher share than that of approximately 40 per cent of people who report about their voluntary work. This can be guessed above all, when looking at the figures from the United States, where a decline has been registered for participation in the long-established organizations while, at the same time, there has been an obvious increase in more spontaneous volunteering (from 60 to 40 and from 40 to 60 per cent) (Putnam 1995a, 1995b, 2000; Bennet 1998). The United States' advancement over Germany might partly be attributed to the fact that "volunteering" covers more activities in the United States than the "honorary post" in Germany. In 2005, membership in a group was at 67.1 per cent in Germany and 85.9 per cent in the United States; 45.2 per cent in Germany and 62.9 per cent in the United States were active participants in a group, according to the World Values Survey (OECD 2011b).

Self-help groups also introduce an element of competition and market-type structures into civil society. The economic dynamism is being paralleled by the third sector's dynamism. In the multilevel network society of the future, the individual's participation in society is less dependent than before on property, collective guarantees and memberships in exclusive large associations, but much more on the open access to resources (commodities and services) of the most different kind. In this context, the market exchange of goods and services and the organization of solidarities of the third sector approach one another and form an ever widening zone of intersection. The society of the future will be marked less by a divergence, and more by an interference of market, state and civil society (Castells 1996; Rifkin 2000).

Social entrepreneurship

It is the liberal philosophy of an active civil society that provides the legitimatory background for private social entrepreneurship compensating for the lack of public welfare provision. Social entrepreneurship is an important element needed in a liberal society for the mobilization of civic commitment as it is demonstrated in an exemplary way in the United States (Perlmutter 1997). In the trend of international monitoring and benchmarking promoted by international coordination in the hands of organizations like the OECD and the EU, the mobilization of social entrepreneurship according to the American model has entered public discourse. It fits into the rhetorical shift away from the governmental protection of the incapable individual and towards the empowerment of the individual to enable him/her to master all dangers and risks of an uncertain life course. It is being promoted particularly by the entrepreneurial class and complements the increased dynamics of the labour market by a publicly sponsored market of social service (Leadbeater 1997; Thompson 2002; Peredo and McLean 2005; Austin et al. 2006; Thompson and Doherty 2006; Scourfield 2007; Ridley-Duff 2008).

How social entrepreneurship works can be studied in the United States. Booming towns and regions form a fertile ground for social enterprises, since on the one hand, a culture of entrepreneurial spirit is cultivated there, while on the other hand there are enough rich people who can be mobilized to make generous donations and have a good chance of doing so because of the moderate tax load. One example of this is Seattle on the American West Coast, where Boeing and Microsoft are headquartered. Let us take some examples from an inquiry carried out by two journalists in 1999 (Randow 1999; Heuser and Randow 1999; Heuser 1999).

The following sections reflect the situation in 1999, which might have changed in the meantime. All data refers to 1999. Not only do we find Bill Gates in Seattle, but also entrepreneurs like David Guth whose company not only makes profits, but also commits itself to a social integration programme. Having worked as a drug squad officer previously, Guth had observed for a long time how junkies and dealers released from prison carried on precisely what they had done before. He then joined *Pioneer Human Services*, a social enterprise in which he became director later on. The company recorded an annual turnover of US$55 million by producing aircraft parts for Boeing, composing sales packaging and pallets, printing brochures and offering warehousing and logistics services. Pioneer Human Services' social programme covers the employment of around 5,000 "clients" – prisoners, people released from prison and drug addicts – whom it wants to reintegrate into normal working life. After successful training, the clients then receive a normal work contract or find a job in some other firm on the labour market. Almost two thirds make this step, although it is unknown for how long they succeed.

Another example is Jim McClurg. He is the head of *Northwest Center* (NWC), a company employing mentally handicapped people as dishwashers, packers, caretakers and metal punchers or to clear away business documents. NWC accounts for sales of US$15 million per year, e.g. by dealing with apparel and other second-hand articles obtained from donations. *Farestart*, which is presided over by Cheryl Sesmon and Barbara Reed, records annual sales of US$1.5 million. In one restaurant, it educates around 150 homeless people every year; 46 per cent of them pass their exams of whom 90 per cent get a job. The business creates 60 per cent of income itself, added to this are 30 per cent from donations and 10 per cent state subsidies.

Social enterprises of this type are not single cases. In the age of worldwide networking via the web, there is a good chance of them passing on their expertise to others. In Seattle, an infrastructure of consultation for social entrepreneurs has formed. A journal called *Who Cares* reports on practical experience and projects. A prize is being awarded to honour the social entrepreneur of the year. Two universities in Seattle offer courses for social entrepreneurs. An employee of the city council helps in making contacts and in building up an information network.

William Drayton in Virginia demonstates how to promote social entrepreneurial initiatives worldwide. After having studied at Harvard, Oxford, Stanford and at Yale Law School, he worked for McKinsey for ten years and founded *Ashoka* at the beginning of the 1980s. The company is based in the US state of Virginia. Recording donations worth around US$7.5 million per year, *Ashoka* supports people worldwide who in turn work in the social entrepreneurial field and can mobilize hundreds of people for social and ecological projects. One of *Ashoka*'s promotional principles is that the projects have to be self-supporting after an initial phase. Marc Lindenberg, dean of the institute for public administration at the University of Washington, is devoted to the worldwide networking of social entrepreneurial activities in his position as vice-president of the development organization

Care International. He intends to establish a platform for the development of civil society in Seattle, which should be open throughout the world to support mutual learning (all examples taken from Randow 1999). Moreover, Putnam Barber in Seattle offers a special internet service for social entrepreneurs. In his late fifties, he is investing his experience gained on the boards of state-run and partly state-run volunteering organizations in consultation and in the supply of information and management know-how (Heuser and Randow 1999: 26).

In Seattle, various factors come together that favour social entrepreneurship: the American traditions of self-help, entrepreneurship and philanthropy; the state's traditional reserve with regard to the organization of welfare and the corresponding compensation through private welfare organizations; the pioneering spirit of the West Coast, a booming economy with the corresponding promotion of entrepreneurial spirit and the availability of private capital to generate high donations; some crowd-puller companies and the development of a supportive infrastructure as well as the assistance of a member of the city council who is exclusively in charge of this job (Lang 2003).

What flourishes in the United States in cities like Seattle can be found in Europe, particularly in the United Kingdom, in a form that is less organized by private companies. One example of this is Neil Jameson, who established the *Citizen Organising Foundation* in London's poor East End in 1989. Meanwhile, he has built up a network of more than 150 local church communities, schools and clubs paying a membership fee between €1,500 and €3,000 per year. Foundations and private companies grant additional support. Employing fourteen staff in London and other cities, he undertakes lobbying for the poor at coach operators, local authorities and firms. The target of these measures is an activation of the poor in order to enable them to take part in economic acquisition, political decision-making and societal life. The keyword is the meanwhile fashionable term of "empowerment". The establishment of a school for social entrepreneurs in East London proves the fact that social entrepreneurship is being mobilized and modernized in the UK beyond its traditional roots. Over a one-year course, students are taught the construction and management of a social enterprise, from financing, marketing and budget management right through to the handling of law and dealing with authorities (Heuser and Randow 1999: 27).

In Germany projects have emerged as well that work in the field of social entrepreneurship alongside the state and the established welfare associations. One example of this is Christian Presch in Bielefeld. The former social worker founded the joint-stock company, *Bring's & Kauf*, a department store for second-hand products in May 1998. The store, which is housed in a former car shop near Bielefeld's railway station, offers second-hand goods and new bargains on a sales floor of 1,500 square metres. He employs seventeen former long-term unemployed people according to the currently valid standard wage level. During the first five years, the land of North-Rhine Westphalia supported the entrepreneur strongly. In the first year, it paid 80 per cent of the wages. This support was reduced continually until the fifth year, while at the same time, the rental space cost was raised to the local level (Heuser and Randow 1999: 25–27).

Relief circles such as New York's *Womenshare* lead us farther away from social capitalism. In this group, a hundred women help each other with all sorts of craft jobs, advice and childcare (Heuser and Randow 1999: 25). An organization of seniors in the Baden-Württemberg town of Riedlingen in the Swabian Mountains proves that such relief circles also exist in Germany. Around 500 members pay a fee of €30 for single members and €45 for couples. Active members up until the age of seventy provide social services for needy members – from support in dealing with the authorities to assistance in getting ready for bed at night. The majority of members are older than seventy-five and are inactive. Therefore, the group tries to recruit new, younger members in order to reach a balanced relationship between active and inactive members. The senior group in Riedlingen is one example of self-help groups, which are most active in Baden-Württemberg as compared to the rest of Germany. Edith Bode, a voluntary helper of the Red Cross, who established the Ulm table, provides yet another example of social entrepreneurial initiatives. Together with other helpers and assisted by the Red Cross, supermarkets, large bakeries, fruit and vegetables wholesalers, she cooks dinners for unemployed people. The ingredients they cannot use are sold at a cheaper price to people in need in a small shop in the centre of Ulm.

The "exemplary state" in the south of Germany not only holds the leading position in the private economy throughout Germany, but also in social entrepreneurial activities, which underlines and highlights the assumptions made before about the favourable structural conditions of vital social entrepreneurship in Seattle. According to an empirical survey we also see Baden-Württemberg at the top of the individual states (*Bundesländer*) of the German federal republic with 40 per cent reporting voluntary work against an average of 34 per cent. There is also a clear West–East divide with higher rates in the West than in the East (Priller 2002: 47). With the strong entrepreneurial tradition of SMEs, the Pietistic tradition of each individual's social responsibility and Baden-Württemberg's economic wealth, a fertile ground for social entrepreneurial activities is provided. Added to this fertile ground is a targeted boost from the ministry of social affairs in Stuttgart. The then prime minister of Baden-Württemberg, Lothar Späth, came across the idea of citizens networks on a journey to the USA. Back in Germany, he began to establish such networks to help the welfare state with its exorbitant costs. Konrad Hummel, a sociologist who was responsible for the realization of this idea in the ministry, is meanwhile looking after twenty-four model locations and around fifty other projects. Hummel is, so to say, the "spider in the web" of the network of model locations and projects (Heuser 1999: 39).

Here, we recognize yet another condition for the growth of social entrepreneurship: push from the state, which transforms part of its administration into agencies playing an entrepreneurial role themselves and acting as leaders and mediators for a great variety of self-help groups, networks and projects. With the help of the Internet, the projects can communicate with each other, exchange practical experience, support and motivate each other and make others imitate their activities as well as become active themselves. In this way, a powerful social entrepreneurial culture can emerge. One thing, however, turns out clearly in this context: The activation of civil society cannot proceed against the market nor against the private economy, but only in cooperation with them. A powerful market and a powerful private economy coupled with a powerful, traditionally established network of small and medium-sized enterprises form the ground on which a similarly structured social entrepreneurship can prosper. Additional promotion and support comes from the entrepreneurial actions of state agencies.

Nevertheless, it has to be kept in mind that social entrepreneurship can only complement the governmental and public provision of welfare and needs cooperation with governmental authorities. Social entrepreneurship would care for those who can be mobilized to become part of the enterprise, but not for those who cannot be mobilized. What has especially to be recognized in the context of this study is the promotion of rhetorical change by the increased invoking of social entrepreneurship as social policy innovation. This rhetorical change goes clearly in the direction of complementing the dynamics of the labour market with a similar dynamical market of welfare production in the third sector. This change is supported by its being part of the broader movement towards individual empowerment.

Concluding remarks: integration gains as a result of civil society's reorganization?

Global modernity cannot be the modernity of the European welfare state writ large. It will be a different modernity, which complies a little more with the liberal model of society than the welfare state did. It will also be a modernity somewhat liberated from the constraints of the nation state and leaving greater latitude for individuality. In order to keep this latitude of freedom within acceptable social limits, civil society is being invoked in public discourse. The state's withdrawal from society is expected to be compensated for by an activation of civil society. This is the structural basis supporting the ongoing rhetorical change from welfare to inclusion and from protection to empowerment of the individual. Civil society's deficits, however, still need compensation by the state that is responsible for the whole. This is demonstrated by the evidence available in the USA. In that country, the strength and vitality of civil society replace the state's integration services. This principle works well in the neighbourhoods of the middle and upper strata, but not at all in the focal centres of poverty, hopelessness and violence. Nevertheless, the liberal model of the United States is not simply the result of a unique culture, but it is also framed by the structural conditions for social integration in a most heterogeneous and pluralistic society. And in the same way, the European nation states can no longer simply oppose their welfare cultures to the liberal culture of the United States, while ignoring their greater structural convergence with that country at present times, and in the future more than in the past. The outcome of a realistic assessment of the situation does not need to be a copy of the American model of social integration; however, an adjustment of the European welfare cultures to the new structural conditions is under way. This adjustment is moving Europe one step closer towards the United States, whatever efforts the Europeans undertake to remain culturally different. There is neither a determination of the future development by structural constraints and functional requirements alone, nor is there a free choice of unaltered continuation with the established culture (path dependency). Structure and culture interpenetrate in order to produce together the development of the future European society.

The changes in the solidarity structure of the European welfare states, which are caused by globalization, pluralization and individualization, are being converted into a renewal of social integration to the extent that civil society can be successfully reorganized. More than ever before, this programme of civic renewal requires an active citizen working self-responsibly and contributing to the production of common welfare by many small steps (Dettling 1998b; Klages 1998). To carry out this programme, in the hitherto state-dominated European societies, citizens are being motivated in a targeted way to contribute to coping with new social problems, especially by the local political authorities. As a result, the welfare cartel of the cooperation between state and long-established organizations is being broken up and opened to the pluralism of new welfare initiatives (Klug 1995; Evers and Olk 1996). Procedures of cooperative conflict management are replacing administrative state actions by including interested parties and the citizens affected by a particular programme. This applies to so many different areas such as protection of the environment, welfare, youth work, protection of minorities and the integration of immigrants. Civil society's reorganization with the help of the state's support determines how far the nation state's dwindling integration power can be transformed into an integration gain covering all levels, from the local community and the region, the nation and the supranational merger right through to global cooperation. The nation state's shrinking integration power would ensure new integration power being created within the entire multilevel system, from the local community right through to the world society.

The ongoing rhetorical change is not only a short-lived wave promoted by some advocates of neo-liberalism, but also a reflection of a deeper change of solidarity in the wake of international labour division. Both changes in the structure of solidarity and changes in the field of discourse mutually support each other. While the international division of labour promotes the individualization of the life course, the transnationalization of the field of discourse furthers the shift from national welfare to transnational and national inclusion, and from the protection to the empowerment of the individual. The transnationalization of the field of discourse comes along with increasing international monitoring and benchmarking in the wake of the international coordination of inclusion policies. The OECD's monitoring and the EU's Open Method of Coordination are particularly conducive to this transnationalization of public discourse. In this transnationalized field of discourse, the traditional incumbents of national power positions, namely experts of labour and social law and national welfare organizations, are losing ground to new challengers, those being economists, consultants and international NGOs. The shift of power in favour of these challengers promotes rhetorical change towards a broader concept of inclusion and of individual empowerment as well as its spillover to semantic, programmatic and paradigmatic change.

4 Institutional change
Liberal, conservative and egalitarian adjustment to international labour division

In this chapter, we will turn to institutional change. Here path dependency, institutional inertia and vested interests come to the fore. Therefore, change often occurs below the surface of preserving national traditions (Bannink and Hoogenboom 2007), and new policies are adapted to old programmes (Hudson and Kühner 2009). Established institutions are adjusted to the change of solidarity in the context of international labour division. We will look at three examples of path-dependent adjustment to global competition in the context of international labour division according to the typology of welfare regimes introduced by Esping-Andersen (1990): the liberal welfare regime of the United States, the conservative welfare regime of Germany and the social democratic welfare regimes of Sweden and Denmark (cf. Goodin *et al.* 1999; Scruggs and Allan 2006). The focus will be on employment policy. We begin with an outline of the economic performance of these welfare states under globalized competition. Then we look at each case separately. We will start with a description of the structure of solidarity and the idea of justice characteristic of the types of welfare regimes under scrutiny. Then we will cover adjustment to globalized competition in the three types of welfare regime. Finally, we will address a significant convergence between these three types, namely the increasing significance of a new inclusion problem: relative exclusion of a new underclass of unskilled underachievers as a side effect of the individualization of inclusion through educational upgrading. Subsequently, we will submit this new common inclusion problem of the three types of welfare regime to closer scrutiny. The final paragraph rounds off the chapter with an analysis of a further point of convergence in our sample of welfare states, which makes institutional reform particularly controversial and difficult to carry out. This point is the increasing shift of reform processes from compromising corporatist interest coordination between major representative interest organizations and the state towards uncompromising public debate. With this shift veto players multiply and make institutional reform difficult to attain (cf. Swank 2002; Korpi 2003; Ebbinghaus 2004; Taylor-Gooby 2004, 2008; Starke 2006; Daguerre 2007; Clasen and Siegel 2007; Olsen 2008; Viebrock 2009).

Economic performance under the challenge of globalized competition

The internationalization of the division of labour is dissolving the national solidarity of the workforce, and nationally concentrated production chains are being replaced by transnational chains. In this process solidarity is undergoing a fundamental change. A type of network solidarity is emerging across nations and growing within nations, while mechanical solidarity within nations is shrinking. The consequence is more individualization of social life, emancipating the individual from primordial ties and enabling him/her to engage in a greater variety of networks on the local, national, European and global levels. The corresponding cultural transformation is the change away from the equality of results within the nation and the inequality of opportunity and results across nations and towards the equality of opportunity within and across nations. However, as we have noticed in our theoretical outline, this global trend interacts with national cultural traditions, institutions and arrangements of vested interests. It is therefore very unlikely that this global force is producing the same results in each country.

Let us simply take the very common differentiation between liberal, conservative and egalitarian welfare states introduced by Esping-Andersen (1990). These are three internally differentiated families of welfare capitalism. If we look at the United States as an example of liberal welfare states, Germany as an example of conservative welfare states and Denmark and Sweden as examples of egalitarian welfare states, we see first of all more change in the direction of individualization and equality of opportunity in the United States over the past twenty years than in Germany and Sweden. There has been more decline in unionization of the workforce, more deregulation of the labour market, more acceleration of change in investment, in the opening and closing of firms, in the introduction and selling of new technologies, in occupational careers and in employment as well as unemployment in the United States than in Germany and Sweden. That is, the global trend is particularly effective in the United States and less effective in European countries like Germany and Sweden. This difference exists even though the US economy is less open in terms of the slice contributed to the GDP by imports and exports than the German and Swedish economies.

There has been, however, increasing competition from Asian, particularly Japanese, imports on the American market from the 1980s onwards compared to the 1950s to 1970s. Moreover the rise of South-east Asian economies on the world market has become a persistent challenge for both American products at home and abroad. This challenge has become a major argument invoked in public debates and strategies aiming at deregulation, liberalization and the restructuring of companies. According to the deeply rooted belief in the dependence of national welfare on every citizen's individual achievement, economic as well as social policies designed to meet the challenge of global competition have primarily been aimed at improving human capital through education since the early 1980s (Seeleib-Kaiser 2001: 298–302). Investment in human capital is considered an investment in economic wealth and in the inclusion of every citizen in that wealth at the same time. Economic achievement and social integration are conceived as two sides of one and the same coin. Insofar, we observe an earlier rhetoric and programme of reform than in the European conservative and egalitarian welfare states, which is targeted more consequently to the strengthening of market forces and individual achievement in line with the country's deeply rooted belief in the complementarity of individual achievement and social inclusion. In Europe the challenge of global competition collides with welfare regimes and values that are focused far more strongly on national solidarity and equality of results. The same challenge has therefore been met with considerably more reluctance with regard to deregulation and liberalization policies. There is also much less belief in the long-term integrative effects of investments in human capital alone so that there would be no need for further market-correcting measures of social integration.

This difference in responding to a global trend can be explained by the effect of path dependency, namely vested interests, institutional inertia and cultural resistance against change, which contradicts basic beliefs in justice. In Europe it was much easier for Britain to adjust to the global trend through deregulation, because the country was suffering from a deep economic crisis in the 1970s, which paved the way for Mrs Thatcher's "neo-liberal" revolution, and because it was possible to revitalize the historically established cultural tradition of liberalism. This implied state law limiting the space of action for the trade unions, that is, regulation of a formerly law-free area of conventions and voluntary agreements. As a conservative welfare state Germany is lacking such cultural sources, which would back up adjustment to the global trend, and there is the enormous task of reforming a well-established institutional framework. For different reasons the same is true for the egalitarian welfare state in Sweden and Denmark. Let us therefore have a look at the vested interests, the institutional structure and the cultural idea of justice in four countries representing three types of welfare regimes: the USA, Germany, Denmark and Sweden. We will assess these elements against the background of some basic data of economic performance, social integration and labour market performance (Table 4.1).

If we take unemployment replacement rates as a significant reflection of welfare state entrenchment and retrenchment, we will discover expansion everywhere from the 1960s to the 1980s, though to different degrees depending on the different philosophies of liberal, conservative and social democratic welfare states. Since the 1990s, however, at least some cutbacks have occurred across the different types of welfare regimes justified by financial stress in the short run, but also by the rhetoric of strengthening individual responsibility. Thus these cutbacks do not simply reflect adjustment to a changing economic situation, but a turn to a new paradigm of social life across the different welfare regimes (Huber and Stephens 2001: 218, tab. 6.3). What, however, the positive correlation of cutbacks with the unemployment rate tells us is that it apparently needs a deeper employment crisis in order to foster reforms. This is indeed important for explaining the relatively early reforms in the Netherlands and in Denmark. Both countries suffered from especially high unemployment rates in the 1980s. The trend is, however, not confirmed by data in every country. In many countries, there have been cutbacks, some countries have not experienced a change, some have increased entitlements. According to OECD data, benefit entitlements as average gross unemployment benefit replacement rates for two earnings levels, three family situations and three durations of unemployment have changed as follows between 1997 and 2007: Australia from 25 to 20 per cent, Canada from 15 to 12 per cent, the UK from 18 to 15 per cent, the USA from 14 to 14 per cent, Denmark from 62 to 48 per cent, Finland from 34 to 34 per cent, Netherlands from 52 to 34 per cent, Norway from 39 to 34 per cent, Sweden from 27 to 32 per cent, Germany from 26 to 24 per cent, Austria from 32 to 32 per cent, France from 37 to 39 per cent, Italy from 18 to 32 per cent, Switzerland from 34 to 33 per cent (OECD 2011c).

If we take unemployment rates as indicators of a country's achievement in adjusting to intensified competition in the globalized economy, we see best performance of Germany and Sweden in 1980 with a standardized OECD rate of roughly 2 per cent, while the United States and Denmark suffered from an unemployment rate between 7 and 10 per cent in the early 1980s. Germany slipped, however, into an employment crisis from the beginning of the 1980s onwards reaching an unemployment rate of up to 10 per cent, a crisis from which the country has not recovered for a long time. The first signs of recovery were observed only in 2007. Sweden underwent an unemployment crisis in the 1990s with a rate of up to 10 per cent, but has been able to bring it down since the late 1990s to reach about 5.5 per cent, a rate which is, however, still considerably higher than in the 1980s. The United States started with nearly 10 per cent in the early 1980s to come down to rates between 4 and 5 per cent since 1990. Most recently, and fostered by the financial crisis of Autumn 2008, the unemployment rate has risen again. Denmark suffered from an employment crisis with an unemployment rate of more than 8 per cent in the early 1980s. A first success in bringing the rate down to 6 per cent in the mid-1980s was only short-lived, the rate climbing up again to nearly 10 per cent in the early 1990s. It has, however, been reduced to 3–4 per cent since that time (Figure 4.1).

There are two reasons for competition in the globalized economy to exercise pressure in the direction of greater earnings dispersion. On the one hand, top personnel have greater chances of advancement beyond national borders, while, on the other hand, unskilled workers can be more easily replaced by workers from developing and newly industrialized countries. In this situation, top salaries should have higher growth rates than average salaries, while wages at the bottom should go down. However, because wages at the bottom are protected by collective wage agreements and/or minimum wage legislation, while salaries in the top range are not covered by collective bargaining, earnings dispersion in the upper half of the earnings scale should grow faster than earnings dispersion in the lower half. This is exactly what OECD data shows for the countries under scrutiny in this chapter. It also represents the well-known fact that earnings

Table 4.1 GDP growth, public social expenditure and labour market performance of different countries

Country	Public expenditure 2005	Employment rate 2009	Women employment rate 2009	Civilian employment in services 2009	Unemployment rate 2009	Youth unemployment rate 2009	GDP growth 1980–2010	Employment growth 1980–2009	Decile ratios (90/10) of gross earnings 2008
Liberal countries									
Australia	17.11	71.99	66.24	75.63	5.69	11.57	253.57	170.95	3.3385
Canada	16.49	71.54	69.10	77.39	8.37	15.27	209.71	152.96	3.75
Iceland	16.91	78.94	77.22	77.81	7.43	15.96	211.19	158.42	3.2053
Ireland	16.73	62.54	57.80	72.57	12.24	25.90	362.21	167.69	3.7456
New Zealand	18.55	72.88	67.43	72.37	6.31	16.55	214.70	170.64	2.9173
United Kingdom	21.29	70.64	64.24	80.90	7.83	18.86	194.48	113.84	3.6259
United States	15.91	67.62	65.58	75.78	9.38	17.60	227.90	139.92	4.8931
Social Democratic countries									
Denmark	27.08	75.74	73.09	78.78	6.09	11.20	169.35	109.80	2.7313
Finland	26.10	68.39	67.90	71.46	8.39	21.60	191.08	105.00	2.5661
Netherlands	20.88	75.76	70.64	80.88	3.91	7.29	191.04	170.06	–
Norway	21.64	76.47	74.43	77.09	3.21	9.15	221.37	131.50	2.2805
Sweden	29.43	72.18	70.21	77.73	8.46	25.03	178.11	106.31	2.2774
Conservative countries									
Austria	27.20	71.62	66.42	69.65	4.85	9.96	182.23	132.82	3.3196
Belgium	26.40	61.60	55.99	74.85	7.96	21.94	171.11	118.86	–
France	29.17	64.14	60.01	77.43	9.13	22.79	174.22	118.53	–
Germany	26.75	70.38	65.18	68.42	7.83	10.99	–	142.17	3.3209
Luxembourg	23.20	65.19	56.99	77.08	5.16	17.16	349.85	222.95	–
Switzerland	20.26	79.17	73.76	73.42	4.17	8.20	159.85	143.05	2.6909

Southern European familistic countries								
Greece	20.55	61.25	48.94	67.20	9.61	25.78	180.35	135.04	3.2397
Italy	24.98	57.48	46.36	66.68	7.89	25.44	153.14	110.33	2.6912
Portugal	–	66.29	61.58	60.39	10.02	20.02	193.51	125.54	4.2552
Spain	21.24	60.62	53.54	70.99	18.12	37.85	215.91	154.56	3.2846
Eastern European transformation countries								
Czech Republic	19.50	65.36	56.68	58.05	6.75	16.64	–	96.56	3.1496
Hungary	22.54	55.40	49.92	63.87	10.08	26.48	–	–	4.1054
Poland	21.03	59.34	52.75	56.61	8.27	20.65	–	91.55	3.6364
Slovak Republic	16.61	60.16	52.79	64.97	12.09	27.34	–	–	.
Unclassified countries								
Japan	18.58	70.03	59.75	69.45	5.27	9.08	188.69	113.48	3.0193
Korea	6.86	62.94	52.21	68.54	3.82	9.82	612.89	171.79	4.7845
Mexico	7.43	59.45	42.98	61.30	5.35	10.01	192.53	201.22	.
Turkey	13.68	44.26	–	79.32	14.33	25.28	325.84	133.85	.

Source: Public Expenditure retrieved 14 March 2011, from www.oecd-ilibrary.org/sites/factbook-2010-en/10/02/01/index.html?contentType=&itemId=/content/chapter/factbook-2010-75-en&containerItemId=/content/serial/18147364&accessItemIds=&mimeType=text/html and http://dx.doi.org/10.1787/826301580471. Employment rate, Women Employment, Unemployment rate, Youth Unemployment rate retrieved 14 March 2011, from http://stats.oecd.org/Index.aspx?DataSetCode=LFS_SEXAGE_I_R. Civilian Service Employment retrieved 14 March 2011, from http://stats.oecd.org/Index.aspx?DataSetCode=ALFS_SUMTAB. GDP and Employment_Growth 1980–2009 retrieved 14 March 2011, from http://stats.oecd.org/Index.aspx?DataSetCode=ALFS_SUMTAB. Decile ratios retrieved 14 March 2011, from http://stats.oecd.org/Index.aspx?DataSetCode=DEC_I.

Note
Own calculations.

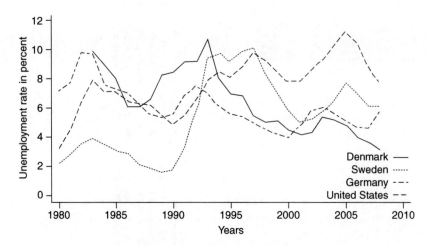

Figure 4.1 Unemployment rates 1980–2008 Germany, Denmark, Sweden, United States (source: OECD 2011f. Unemployment rate retrieved 28 February 2011, from www.oecd.org/document/34/0,3343,en_2649_33927_40917154_1_1_1_1,00. html#box).

Note
Own calculations.

dispersion is highest in the United States and lowest in Denmark and Sweden with Germany in between, but much closer to the Scandinavian countries than to the United States.

Adjustment in the liberal welfare state: the United States

The structure of solidarity and the liberal idea of justice

In the American liberal welfare state the working class has never formed a homogenous, well-organized class in itself in the Marxian sense (Lipset and Marks 2000). Immigration, migration within the country, racial, ethnic and religious plurality, mobility between firms, in employment, job and career and last but not least world leadership in the creation of mass consumption as the basic cultural idea for all people from the bottom to the top have created a nation of individual achievers and consumers in striking contrast to the European class societies (Parsons 2007). The inclusion of people in society has not been primarily a matter of organized class politics, but a far more complex matter of lobbying by a much greater number of interest groups based on occupation, race, ethnicity, religion, immigration, gender, handicap or sexuality; and it was a matter of *individual* achievement on the market. Lobbying is therefore focused on access to the market and access to institutions, which are considered as mediating links to the market (schools, universities, administration, political bodies, media).

Solidarity networks are based not only on class, but also on a number of other, partly cross-cutting memberships. Being an immigration country par excellence the United States has not established stable and clear-cut class lines. The bottom of the social structure has been recurrently filled up by new immigrants. The people who form a comprehensive working class in the European class societies are split into a myriad of groups, some pertaining to the underclass, others pertaining to the middle class and all fragmented according to race and ethnicity. There is not even a uniform underclass, because this is split up in an African American, an Hispanic and a White part. The fragmented character of interest representation is visible in every institutional setting. It is characteristic for industrial relations as well as political participation. Workers are strongly underorganized in terms of union membership; and unions are very much fragmented in comparison to most other industrial countries. Their policy is focused on the wage of their particular clientele on the company level and not on institutional reform. What matters for such "bread-and-butter unions" is serving particular interests and not comprehensive class politics for a united working class (Lipset 1963/1979: 170–204; Lipset and Marks 2000: 88–94). The same is true for political representation. Because of the two-party system there is no working class party. Attempts at establishing such a party have never had enduring success (Lipset and Marks 2000). The Democratic Party represents working class interests only alongside a number of other interests. Influence on decision-making in Congress and Administration is not in the hands of a small number of big representative associations, but scattered across a great many lobbying interest groups. The institutional infrastructure of this type of fragmented interest representation is little legal regulation of employment and the employment relationship. Bargaining is predominantly carried out on the company level and is widely left to the individual relationship between employer and employee. The management of human relations is widely replacing formal collective interest representation of employees in their company.

Corresponding to this fragmented structure of interest representation we have a cultural tradition that attributes much greater significance to equality of opportunity and individual achievement than to equality of results and collective achievement. This is in sharp contrast to the European egalitarian as well as conservative welfare states. Various surveys in the 1980s and 1990s have repeatedly given proof of this statement. There are 88 per cent of those surveyed who believe in individual efforts as effective means of achievement (Lipset 1996, pp. 81ff.). As many as 86.5 per cent of the interviewees have voted for equality of opportunity and as little as 12.5 per cent for equality of results (see Table 4.2). There is only a difference of 85.7 per cent to 80.6 per cent and 13.5 per cent to 17.7 per cent with higher income (US$25,000 or more a year) and lower income earners (up to US$25,000 a year). The difference between Whites and Blacks is 88.4 per cent against 76.6 per cent and 10.6 per cent against 22.2 per cent; the difference between Republicans and Democrats is 91.9 per cent against 85.3 per cent and 7.7 per cent against 13.4 per cent (Davis and Smith 1994). A number of welfare provisions by the state are much more requested in European countries than in the United States. This is true for controlling wages by legislation, reducing working hours to create jobs, controlling prices, provision of healthcare, public spending for old age pensions and reducing differences between high and low income earners. The difference between the USA and Europe is smaller with regard to the public provision of a decent standard of living for the old and the financing of job creation projects (Lipset 1996). The difference is smaller if we compare the USA with her liberal sister Britain (Table 4.3).

It is this structure of interest organization, of institutional interest representation and of cultural beliefs that has produced a welfare state focused on means-tested welfare for the very needy people but restraining from governmental welfare programmes and governmental support of the broad majority of people, particularly the middle class (Moffit 2003). It is only the small number of needy people who are profiting from the welfare state, whereas the great majority of people will not gain anything from welfare programmes and have nothing to lose from the shrinking or more restrictive and more limited granting of help from such programmes. It is therefore unlikely that stronger competition caused by globalization is producing reactions of sticking to or even expanding the welfare state. Below the correlation discovered between the openness of economies in terms of the share of imports and exports in GDP and the strength of social security guaranteed by the welfare state (Rodrik 1996, 1997, 2007; Rieger and Leibfried 2001), there exist significant differences according to the structure of solidarity and the ideas of justice prevailing in a country. The correlation holds for the egalitarian and conservative welfare states but not for the liberal states. The openness of the economy is causing very different reactions with regard to social protection in interaction with the social structure and the basic values of a country. There is no correlation between openness and social protection, if there are no further supporting institutional and cultural preconditions. The related assumption that globalization will cause greater sticking to social security for

Table 4.2 Attitudes towards equality of opportunity and equality of outcome

Group	Equality of opportunity	Equality of outcome
Democrats	85.3	13.4
Republicans	91.9	7.7
Whites	88.4	10.6
Blacks	76.6	22.2
Lower income (up to US$25,000 a year)	80.6	17.7
Higher income (US$25,000 and more)	85.7	13.5
Total	86.5	12.5

Source: Lipset (1996).

Note
Percentages do not add to 100 because some individuals had no opinion or took a middle position.
Question: *"Which do you favour: promoting equal opportunity or promoting equal outcomes?"*

reasons of risk reduction with the populations confronted with greater competition on the world market has therefore to be questioned on a basic level. It does not take into account the dependence of such a uniform preference for risk reduction on a relatively homogeneous workforce. The more there is a differentiation of the workforce into a greater plurality of more or less competing subgroups the less there is a uniform collective preference for high risk reduction through welfare measures. Yet there is a greater differentiation of such preferences in groups preferring more protection and groups opting for less protection such as can be observed with the more pluralistically structured American workforce, as demonstrated by the above-mentioned survey data.

Because of the fragmented character of interest organization and the cultural paradigm of individual achievement it is more likely in a liberal country like the United States that programmes that promote the competitiveness of the economy in general and of firms as well as employees in particular, receive broad support. It is therefore not surprising that the rhetoric of deregulation and liberalization has flourished as have the rhetoric of mobilization for achievement and the rhetoric of advancing equality of opportunity in the face of globalized competition since the 1980s, when particularly Japan's rise to the position of an economic superpower was identified as a challenge to the US economy. The civil rights movement for the abolishment of discrimination of African Americans was the beginning of a wave that included a growing number of ethnically and otherwise discriminated groups to lobby for equality of opportunity up to the lobbying for quotas in jobs, schools and curricula to break white domination. Because the quota system is a kind of equality of results, it is much debated as something that doesn't conform to the basic belief in achievement and equal conditions. What is however most striking with this battle of multiculturalism is its effect on public awareness of inequality, which is predominantly framed in terms of race, ethnicity and gender, but much less in terms of class. This fits very well in the pattern, which is limiting welfare programmes to means-tested support of the very needy

Table 4.3 Attitudes towards activities of the state

Agree/strongly agree government should…	United States	Germany	Great Britain	Norway	Spain
Reduce workweek to create more jobs	35.9	42.8	32.8	28.9	59.7
Control prices	77	78.4	84.7	89.5	91
Provide healthcare	89.7	96.1	99	99.2	97.7
Finance job creation projects	85.3	67.8	75.1	85.9	96.5
Spend more on older age pension	64.5	51.5	74.5	58.9	82.5
Provide a decent standard of living for the old	90	94.3	97.5	98.6	99.5
Reduce differences in income between those with high and low income	52.2	72.1	69.4	74.2	86.3

Source: ISSP (2006). "Role of Government IV", ZA No. 4700, retrieved 3 March 2011, from http://zacat.gesis.org/webview/index.jsp?object=http://zacat.gesis.org/obj/fStudy/ZA4700.

whereas all other people are advised to make use of opportunities to achieve. Offering such opportunities to a greater variety of groups across class lines has been the very programme of civil rights movements including the minority and women movements since the 1960s. Because this type of inclusion process demands well-organized groups and achievement-oriented people it is easy to explain that people who are difficult to mobilize across race, ethnicity and gender lines are being marginalized, that welfare remains limited to means-tested support of the very needy and is not extended to cover a greater number of governmental services for a greater number of people. It is also in line with this type of reaction to enhanced competition that the distance between the achievers and the underachievers has grown and that there has been little or no advancement of the broader middle class.

Adjustment to globalized competition

According to the structure of interest organization, institutional representation of interests, cultural ideas of justice and vested interests the USA has adjusted to globalized competition with a combination of the mobilization of markets and people and the fragmented lobbying for equal access to chances of achievement (Hacker 2002, 2004; Mead 2004; Banting 2005; Sainsbury 2006; Katz 2008). Global competition has been countered with the mobilization of markets and individual achievers. For the United States global competition in the 1980s was in particular the challenge of Japanese products on its domestic market, for instance cars, cameras, TV, video and hi-fi equipment. The result of meeting this enhanced competition through market forces was an extraordinary job growth accompanied by increasing inequality of incomes. Well-paid high-tech and financial service jobs were growing in number as well as low-paid jobs in the private service sector (named "McDonald's" jobs). In this process the industrial sector has been shrinking more than in Europe. Production in the traditional industrial sector, for instance in the car industry, was increasingly being replaced by high-tech production in computer hardware and software and in biotechnology with highly paid specialists as well as by an expanding low-wage service sector. In Germany, in contrast, the industrial sector still holds a bigger part of the economic sectors in terms of GDP as well as workforce employed. The reason for this difference is the different exposure to market forces of the two industries. In the USA, firms are far more dependent on the stock market for financing their investments, whereas firms in Germany can rely much more on long-term credits from house banks with which they are personally linked via mutual representation in the advisory boards. This means that capital moves much faster to new, radically innovative industries with bigger profits in the USA than in Germany (Hall and Soskice 2001: 22–24, 27–29). Further on, US firms are much freer to fire useless labour force and to hire new personnel, or to shut down production plants in order to open new ones at other places. There are few restrictions resulting from interest representation of the firms' employees, which is completely different in Germany with its strong representation of employees on the company level through the works council and through representation in the advisory board as well as a much stronger employment protection by legislation.

Correspondingly, among OECD countries employment turnover – inflow to and outflow from employment and job-to-job movements – is by far highest in the United States. According to various studies referring to the 1980s the amount of annual turnover was 75.9 per cent in the United States, 57.3 per cent in Denmark, 59.6 per cent in France, 43.8 per cent in Germany, 33.5 per cent in the Netherlands and 18.0 per cent in Japan (Gorter 2000: 207). In international comparison we see, however, only a weak negative effect of the strictness of employment protection legislation on the employment rate (Figure 4.2). The effect is slightly stronger with regard to the women's employment rate (cf. Mandel and Semyonov 2006) (Figure 4.3). This liberal element – which is also particularly apparent in Denmark – is obviously in favour of maintaining higher employment rates under sharper competition in the global economy.

Because capital is more fluid it is possible for new entrepreneurs in the USA to create new centres of high-tech development quickly in the neighbourhood of universities, which provide the necessary input from science and technology. The computer industry has emerged from the agglomeration of new enterprises

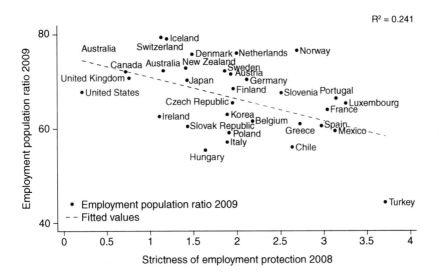

Figure 4.2 Employment protection and employment rate (source: OECD 2011f. Employment population ratio retrieved 28 February 2011, from http://stats.oecd.org/Index.aspx?DatasetCode=LFS_SEXAGE_I_R. Strictness of employment protection retrieved 28 February 2011, from http://stats.oecd.org/Index.aspx?DataSetCode=EPL_OV).

Note
Own calculations.

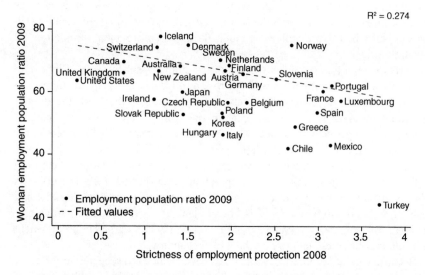

Figure 4.3 Employment protection and women employment rate (source: OECD 2011f. Employment population ratio retrieved 28 February 2011, from http://stats.oecd.org/Index.aspx?DatasetCode=LFS_SEXAGE_I_R. Strictness of employment protection retrieved 28 February 2011, from http://stats.oecd.org/Index.aspx?DataSetCode=EPL_OV).

Note
Own calculations.

around Stanford University in the Silicon Valley, the biotechnological industry from a similar agglomeration around the Massachusetts Institute of Technology (MIT) in the Boston/Cambridge area. The required specialists for this radical industrial innovation are being trained in a system of education, which is focused on the competition for achievement and excellence on a broad basis of general education. This system produces an elite of highly qualified academics, whereas the rest of the students graduate with only moderate skills from general education in high schools and colleges. The educational system feeds innovative industries in microelectronics and biotechnology with top specialists, and the other branches of the economy with generally educated though not specifically and occupationally trained people. This is the other way round in Germany, where the dual system of occupational training is producing exactly such skilled workers on a medium level, who form the basis of the still big industrial production sector in the manufacturing of cars, machine tools and chemicals. According to an analysis by Hall and Soskice (2001: 25–26) they are the specialists who make crucial contributions to the continuous improvement of established products in the manufacturing of cars, machine tools and chemicals. This is the favourable setting for what they call incremental innovation in contrast to the American type of radical innovation in new technology classes and new industries (cf. Estevez-Abe *et al*. 2001).

We also see here the source of greater inequality of income in the USA compared to Germany. The educational system produces highly skilled people for top positions, but also a greater number of relatively unskilled people for "McDonald's" jobs, whereas in Germany the occupationally skilled worker is the stronghold of a well-paid working class in a relatively large industrial sector. There has been far more change towards greater inequality of income in the USA than in Germany over the past thirty years. If we take the share of aggregate income, we see a growth of that share for the highest fifth and the top 5 per cent between 1967 and 2009, while the share of all other income groups has stagnated or declined (Figure 4.4). The 95/50 wage ratio increased from 2.16 to 3.10 for men and from 2.16 to 2.83 for women between 1975 and 2009 (Economic Policy Institute 2011). Inequality of earnings between educational groups has increased significantly (Table 4.4). The same is true for earnings dispersion within educational groups up to the middle ranks at least, which is higher than in Germany, for example (Prasad 2000; Pischke 2005; Dustmann *et al.* 2009; Kim and Sakamoto 2010; Mouw and Kalleberg 2010).

The trend towards greater inequality of income can be explained in particular by the specific American reaction to fiercer competition coming along with globalization through the mobilization of markets and people for achievement on the basis of America's particular structure of interest organization, institutional representation of interests, and cultural tradition of belief in equality of opportunity and achievement as a general framework. Within this framework the observed result has to be explained by the peculiar combination of fluid capital and the control of firms through the market and less through hierarchy in terms

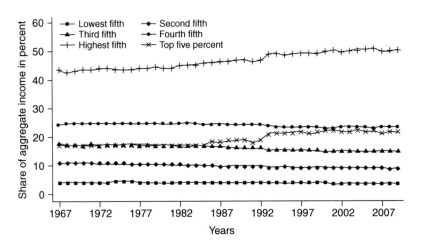

Figure 4.4 Share of aggregate income 1967–2009 (source: US Census Bureau 2009. Retrieved 28 February 2011, from www.census.gov/hhes/www/income/data/historical/household/H02AR_2009.xls).

Note
Own calculations.

Table 4.4 Inequality of income within different groups of education in the USA 1973–2001

	Education*			
	Male (%)		Female (%)	
	High school	College	High school	College
1973	18.2	25.3	20.8	37.7
1979	18.0	20.1	17.6	26.5
1989	18.1	33.9	20.9	41.0
1995	21.0	37.1	23.0	46.7
2000	20.6	42.0	22.8	47.9
2001	21.1	42.7	21.6	47.9

Source: Mishel et al. (2003: 150/151).

Note
* Reference category: no high school graduation. Regression of logarithmized hourly wages to the educational variables represented, to age, squared age, controlled according to colour, ethnicity (Hispanic), marital status and region.

of advisory boards. Further important factors are no control through co-determination and work councils, high-tech agglomerations promoted by the collaboration of fluid capital, science and new entrepreneurs. Part of this arrangement is an educational system that delivers academic top specialists along with a mass of moderately and generally skilled people as well as a considerable number of poorly skilled people graduating from poorly equipped schools in poor neighbourhoods or even dropping out from school before graduation. In addition, lobbying for tax cuts has been particularly successful in Congress over the past thirty years. It has contributed to enormous income growth at the very top of the American class structure (Bartels 2007; Hacker and Pierson 2010).

A special factor contributing to greater inequality of earnings is immigration. It provides a country with a steady influx of people who want to take advantage of the market, because it offers just those opportunities for achievement on any level of the earnings scale that are apparently not available in their home country. Additionally, union membership of immigrants is low. Thus they tend towards accepting distribution of earnings by the market. Correspondingly, natives are more likely to accept immigrants if the market decides on their earnings level (Freeman 1986; Crepaz 2008). In this case natives can calculate that immigrants contribute to the overall growth of societal wealth and do not receive an undeserved share of this wealth. Thus we should expect a higher rate of simple private service employment at low pay and greater earnings dispersion in countries with higher immigration rates. This assumption is corroborated – albeit only weakly – by data, though only in part (Figures 4.5 and 4.6). For the United States we can say that the country's openness to immigration is the other side of its greater reliance on the market as the major device of earnings distribution.

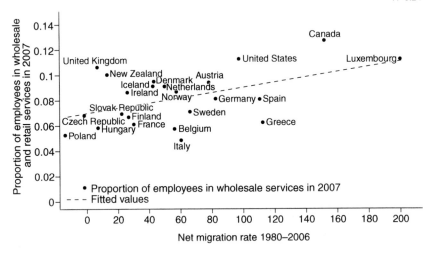

Figure 4.5 Net migration rate – employment ISIC 6 (source: OECD 2010d, 2011e. Proportion of employees in services retrieved 14 March 2011, from http://stats.oecd.org/Index.aspx?DatasetCode=STAN08BIS&lang=en. Net migration rate retrieved 14 March 2011, from www.oecd-ilibrary.org/economics/oecd-factbook-2010/net-migration-rate-table_factbook-2010-table19-en;jsessionid=cky8rkqgewa2.delta).

Note
Proportion of employees as divided total number of employees in services by total population. Own calculations.

The stagnation and even decline of middle-class income since the 1970s has to be explained by a specific change in the inner structure of the middle class. It has differentiated towards the top as well as downward. Top salaries have risen considerably compared to the median. The shrinking number of jobs in the industrial production sector and the rising number of jobs in the private service sector have replaced a well-paid class of production workers with a less well-paid class of service workers. Further on, the remaining production workers have been put under pressure to accept lower wages or no growth in wages because of the crumbling of employee representation. Unions have lost a considerable number of members and are weakened by this development. Firms have shut down unionized production plants and opened up non-unionized new production plants. The decline in union density has contributed to the growth of earnings inequality (Card *et al.* 2004; Rueda and Pontusson 2000). OECD data shows, however, only a small negative effect of union density and earnings dispersion (Figure 4.7).

The threat of competition exerted by Japanese and – today also – South Korean imports has generally supported wage pressure in the manufacturing industry. This is why we can observe a growth in inequality of income, if we

156 *Institutional change*

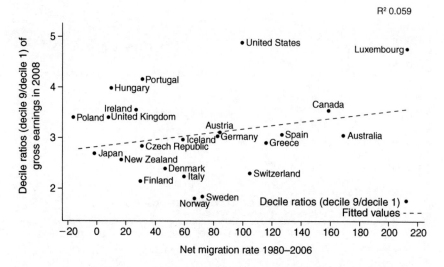

Figure 4.6 Net migration rate – earnings dispersion (source: OECD 2010d, 2011e. Net migration rate retrieved 14 March 2011, from www.oecd-ilibrary.org/economics/oecd-factbook-2010/net-migration-rate-table_factbook-2010-table19-en;jsessionid=cky8rkqgewa2.delta. Decile ratios retrieved 14 March 2011, from http://stats.oecd.org/Index.aspx?DataSetCode=DEC_I).

Note
Net migration rate 1980–2007 as total sum of net migrations rates between 1980 and 2007. Net migration rate defined as the difference between immigration into and emigration from the area during the year (net migration is therefore negative when the number of emigrants exceeds the number of immigrants). Own calculations.

compare the top and the bottom, and a stagnation of income in the middle class in the USA as a result of adjustment to competition originating from globalization. In Germany, in contrast, the still large industrial sector with its occupationally skilled workers is a stronghold of well-paid jobs on the medium level. The other side of this coin is greater job growth in countries with greater inequality of earnings. OECD data gives some support to this assumption (Figure 4.8).

Relative exclusion and disorganization

The predominance of the market as a device for the allocation of resources to preferences has not only been blamed for greater income inequality in the United States as compared to the Continental European welfare states, but also for phenomena of disintegration, namely the disorganization of families, neighbourhoods and local communities. The mobility required from people by rapidly changing markets is being interpreted as contribution to the disruption of families, neighbourhoods and local communities, because they lack the stability necessary for maintaining social cohesion (Sennett 1998). Thus the country has to

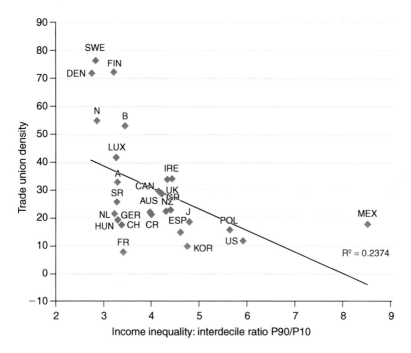

Figure 4.7 Union density and earnings dispersion P90/P10 (source: own calculation based on OECD statistics 2005).

rely much more on external control by police and private security services in order to compensate for a lack of social control provided otherwise by social cohesion. Gated communities are the expression of a lack of social cohesion. This cohesion deficit is further on confronted with special incentives for delinquency. The greater emphasis on individual achievement on the market instead of collective achievement provided by centralized wage bargaining and strong trade unions (Davis and Henrekson 2004; Rosenfeld 2006) as well as by the state's redistribution of income as compared to the Continental European welfare states exerts greater pressure on the single individual to make use of any means of achievement (Sørensen 2006). For the less competitive citizens, however, "meritocracy" turns out to be a myth (McNamee and Miller 2004). Along with strong efforts aiming at achievement by applying legitimate means, we also witness particularly strong efforts aiming at achievement by applying illegitimate means. This is particularly the case in as much as a lack of social cohesion and a lack of social control turn down barriers that would hold down motivation for delinquency as well as access to illegitimate means of achievement. This is the classical constellation described by Robert K. Merton (1949/1968) and, additionally, by Richard Cloward (1959) for the United States' peculiar exposure to higher rates of delinquency. It is Merton's situation of anomie employing a

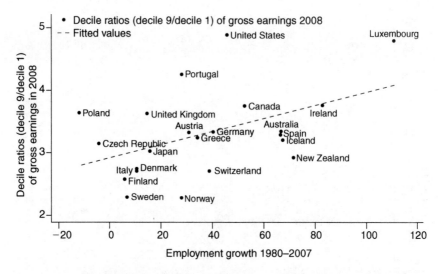

Figure 4.8 P50/P10 percentile ratio of gross earnings and annual job growth (source: OECD 2011e. Decile retrieved 14 March 2011, from ratios http://stats.oecd.org/Index. aspx?DataSetCode=DEC_I. Employment growth retrieved 14 March 2011, from http://stats.oecd.org/Index.aspx?DataSetCode=ALFS_SUMTAB).

Note
Own calculations.

higher rate of innovation both in the legitimate as well as the illegitimate sense. The commonly shared value of individual achievement on the market leads to applying illegitimate means in as much as there is no access to legitimate means, particularly for disadvantaged strata, and in as much as there is lack of social control, which guarantees compliance by the law.

The United States suffered indeed from a considerably rising crime rate from the 1960s to the 1980s. This integration crisis called for an intensive search for remedies. Renewal of family bonds and local communities is one programme aiming at recovery. Another programme is zero tolerance with regard to delinquency. Police control has been intensified, success rates of cleared up crimes have been improved, incarceration has been effected more quickly and for a longer time, punishment has become harder. This zero tolerance policy corresponds to Gary Beckers's (1968) economic theory of crime saying that the criminal calculates whether committing a crime pays enough for the risk of being punished. In as much as the risk of being punished is enhanced by improved success rates of cleared up crimes and harder punishment, crime becomes less attractive. The result of this policy has indeed been a declining crime rate along with a rising incarceration rate (Figures 4.9 and 4.10).

Though the United States has still a considerably higher crime rate than the Continental European welfare states, zero tolerance policy has brought it down

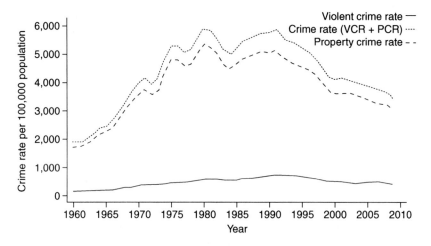

Figure 4.9 Crime rate in the USA (source: Bureau of Justice Statistics 2011a; FBI 2011. Uniform Crime Reporting Statistics as prepared by the National Archive of Criminal Justice Data. Crime rate, violent crime and property crime rate retrieved 28 February 2011, from http://bjs.ojp.usdoj.gov/dataonline/Search/Crime/State/RunCrimeStatebyState.cfm. www.ucrdatatool.gov/Search/Crime/State/RunCrimeStatebyState.cfm).

Note
Own calculations.

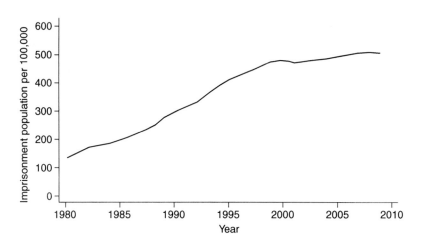

Figure 4.10 Incarceration rate in the USA (source: Bureau of Justice Statistics 2011c).

160 *Institutional change*

to a level that is still above average but nearly the same as in Norway and New Zealand, and below that in Sweden, Iceland, Ireland, the Netherlands, the United Kingdom and Denmark. Along with Portugal and Hungary, the United States turns the correlation between earnings dispersion and the victimization rate to the negative (Figure 4.11). The incarceration rate amounts to about 750 prisoners per 100,000 inhabitants whereas it is below 200 in most other OECD countries (Figure 4.12). Data by the US Bureau of Justice Statistics shows, however, only 500 prisoners per 100,000 population in the USA in 2009, which is nevertheless way above the other countries (Figure 4.10). The differences seem to result from different measures applied by the OECD and the US Bureau of Justice Statistics.

The extraordinarily high incarceration rate is a sign of insufficient inclusion by the institution that is expected to fulfil this function in the liberal welfare state: the market (Pattilo *et al.* 2004; Pettit and Western 2004; Smith 2004; Western and Pettit 2005; Gottschalk 2006; Pager 2007; Wacquant 2009). Liberal policies that are applied to support inclusion by the market aim at bringing about equal opportunity. Access to higher education, fighting discrimination according to race, ethnicity and gender, affirmative action in order to compensate for disadvantage and to provide for equal access to the market are the typical liberal inclusion policies. In as much as they are successful and are broadening access

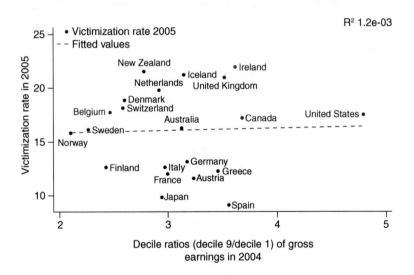

Figure 4.11 Earnings dispersion and property crime (source: OECD 2009c. Retrieved 29 March 2011, from: www.oecd-ilibrary.org/victimisation-by-type-of-crime-and-fear-of-crime_5kmh794czhtb.xls?contentType=/ns/StatisticalPublication,/ns/Table&itemId=/content/table/factbook-2009-table134-en&containerItemId=/content/book/factbook-2009-en&accessItemIds=/content/book/factbook-2009-en&mimeType=application/vnd.ms-excel).

Note
Own calculations.

Institutional change 161

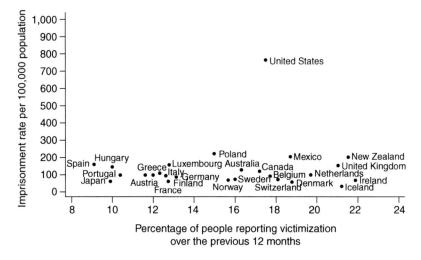

Figure 4.12 Crime and incarceration (source: OECD 2011e. Percentage of people reporting experience over the previous twelve months retrieved 14 March 2011, from http://dx.doi.org/10.1787/550717741440. Prison population rate retrieved 14 March 2011, from www.oecd.org/dataoecd/13/19/43857755.xls).

Note
Own calculations.

to the market, they also enhance competition and striving for achievement. Because the heated race for individual achievement is not only producing winners but also real or at least potential losers, such inclusion policies have also enormous exclusionary effects. In the face of extensive and great achievement little or no achievement is being extremely devaluated. The result is a considerable amount of relative deprivation. Underachievers feel excluded relative to the achievement of the great majority of achievers. Competition for achievement without social balance is producing the deviant milieu of "urban outcasts" (Wacquant 2008). With disorganized families, neighbourhoods and local communities and no sense for the collective organization of improvements of the situation drifting into a criminal career becomes more likely and occurs at a greater frequency than elsewhere.

With the weakness of collective inclusion via family, neighbourhood, local communities and trade unions, which is being enhanced by the preference for the market as a tool of social integration, tightened police control, private security, gated communities, high success rates of cleared up crimes and high incarceration rates as well as hard punishment are left as the only effective means of bringing an otherwise rising crime rate down. Here we recognize the peculiar inclusion dilemma of the liberal welfare state. Inclusion via market mobilization works for the majority of achievers, but it involves considerable effects of relative exclusion, which is producing enormous motivation for delinquency, while

162 *Institutional change*

the market itself undermines the natural means of keeping this motivation for delinquency down, namely stable families, neighbourhoods and local communities. A peculiar part of the lack of means of collective inclusion is the marginalization of class politics by the predominance of race, ethnicity and gender issues in the discourse on discrimination. The achievement of the civil rights movement has contributed its part to the overall displacement of inclusion policies in terms of class. However, the success of the politics of non-discrimination has itself only been possible on the basis of a weak tradition of class politics.

Another consequence of rising inequality in an affluent society has been the increasing use of loans for supporting a lifestyle that is oriented to the upper middle class, promoted by inventions of the finance business. Living beyond one's capacities to earn income has become common practice. The bubble in the US housing market, which triggered the worldwide financial crisis in Autumn 2008, can be explained by this structural feature of a liberal welfare state. We see that inequality in an affluent society is a major cause of the instability of financial markets (Koch 2011).

Adjustment in the conservative welfare state: Germany

The structure of solidarity and the conservative idea of justice

In Germany the prerequisites for adjusting to global economic competition are quite different. Interest organization is much more coordinated by a limited number of big organizations with a long tradition and large membership. These are the unitary, sectorally differentiated trade unions (*Einheitsgewerkschaften*) cooperating under the umbrella of the *Deutsche Gewerkschaftsbund* (DGB) along with the *Deutsche Angestellten Gewerkschaft* (DAG) and the *Deutsche Beamtenbund* (DBB). The service sector unions and the DAG merged to form the new big service sector union *ver.di*. The employer associations are sectorally structured in a similar way under the umbrella of the *Bundesverband Deutscher Arbeitgeberverbände* (BDA) along with the political organization of industrial employer interests in the *Bundesverband der Deutschen Industrie* (BDI). Other big occupational organizations exist for the artisans and for the professions, for instance for physicians, lawyers, architects, engineers, university professors and teachers. Most characteristic of the institutional representation of interests is the cooperation of employer associations and unions within the framework of wage setting autonomy and their close cooperation with the state, with government and administration, to form what can be called the specific model of German corporatism or Rhenanian capitalism (Streeck 1999). It is an institutional arrangement, which mitigates the interest conflict between employers and employees, capital and labour, basically within the legally constructed framework of co-determination (*Mitbestimmung*) and work councils (*Betriebs- and Personalräte*) through a system of mutual acknowledgement, trust and cooperation.

The success of this transformation of "class antagonism" in the Marxian sense into a robust system of cooperation across the employer/employee divide has been a high level of industrial peace in terms of a very low strike rate to the benefit of employers (Table 4.5), and a high level of participation in employee-relevant decision-making and in economic growth in terms of steadily increasing wages as well as extraordinary job security and status-maintaining financial security in cases of unemployment, sickness, disability and retirement to the benefit of employees. What is also typical of the German welfare system is the extent to which it helps to guarantee an acquired income status in the job system beyond employment in cases of unemployment, sickness, disability and old age.

This arrangement is part of the "conservative", status-maintaining system, which particularly rewards occupational achievement in full-time employment. Another part of this system is constituted by status differences between blue-collar workers, white-collar employees and civil servants (*Beamte*), not only in the job, but also in welfare benefits based on that job. A further characteristic feature of this arrangement is the support of the family by generous tax exemptions and by subsidies for children as well as extra pay for married people and for children in the public sector, for instance. The idea behind this arrangement is subsidiarity, which relies on the family as the first instance of social integration and invokes the help of local and national authorities only in a complementary way. A special effect of this institutional setting is the existence of the male breadwinner family to a much higher extent than in the Scandinavian egalitarian welfare state and the Anglo-Saxon liberal one. It is visible in a lower employment rate of women on the one hand and in a lower supply of public and/or private care for children outside the family on the other hand.

Table 4.5 Relative volume of strikes (cross-national)

Country	Days of strike per 1,000 employees		
	Average per year 1971–2006	Highest value	In the year…
Italy	430	1,395	1975
Spain	363	1,562	1979
Canada	413	1,191	1976
Ireland	232	1,273	1979
Finland	282	1,283	1971
Australia	254	1,074	1974
United Kingdom	227	1,138	1984
New Zealand	174	820	1986
United States	125	600	1971
Denmark	150	1,636	1973
Sweden	74	1,085	1980
Norway	66	502	1986
Japan	24	185	1974
Germany	22	218	1984
Netherlands	19	125	1973
Austria	13	347	2003
Switzerland	2	9	2004

Source: Armingeon *et al.* (2009).

164 Institutional change

The roots of this family and status-centred system of welfare can be traced back to Bismarck's social security legislation in the 1880s. It was designed on the background of a still family and status-centred traditional hierarchical society and with the intention of stabilizing the traditional social order in the face of accelerated industrialization and heightened industrial conflict, and also with the intention of countering the revolutionary threat of the labour movement. This conservative welfare legislation was being supported by the Catholic centre party and the Catholic idea of subsidiarity. It was this conservative coalition that inhibited a shaping effect of the labour movement and the Social Democratic Party on the formation of the welfare system in the early days of rapid industrialization. The further development of this system was channelled by the early decisions into the overall framework of securing family and occupationally acquired status. Neither social democratic governments in the Weimar Republic nor the Nazi regime changed this system in a fundamental way. In the Federal Republic the above-described arrangement of interest organization and representation has been formed on the basis of historical roots. The family and status-centred system of welfare was carried on and extended, particularly with Adenauer's pension reform in 1957, which based the pension system on a generation contract with the actually working population paying the pensions of the older population out of work. Further major legislation concerned the system of co-determination and work councils. The social democratic governments, starting with the grand coalition of CDU and SPD from 1966 to 1969, did not change the basic pillars of the system.

The philosophy of this system, that is the cultural idea of justice in its background, is the Christian social philosophy of subsidiarity and the model of the social market economy based on the economic thought of the Catholic economist Adolf Müller-Armack. It was limited in its social dimension by the influence of ordo-liberalism represented by the liberal economists Wilhelm Röpgen and Walter Eucken. Both elements – Christian social philosophy and ordo-liberalism – were amalgamated in practical politics under the leadership of Ludwig Erhard in his position as Adenauer's minister of economic affairs. The basic elements of this model are the following: The market is regarded as the vehicle of economic growth enhancing the nation's wealth in Adam Smith's sense; yet it needs complementation by social policy legislation in order to heal disruptive effects on people and society produced by the market. The human individual is seen in need of being socially embedded. Society is conceived of as a hierarchy of status groups. Occupation of the usually male breadwinner is interpreted as the foundation of the social status of the whole family. This model of a hierarchically differentiated society of families and status groups is the cultural background of a system of welfare that is designed to draw on economic growth produced by the market and to channel this growth into a status hierarchy, which is protected against disruption through market failure by welfare securities.

Status groups in a hierarchical society are not simply income groups produced by the market. They are rooted in institutions other than the market, namely the hierarchically differentiated educational system. Germany still has children enrolled as early as at the age of ten in three different types of secondary schools depending on the level and length of education: the lowest level of the *Hauptschule* (five years), the medium level of the *Realschule* (six years), and the highest level of the *Gymnasium* (nine years being shortened to eight years currently). The system has been largely self-reproductive from generation to generation. In the course of time, besides the exceptional position of some so-called *Gesamtschulen*, ways have been introduced leading from the *Hauptschule* and the *Realschule* to college education (via *Fachoberschule* to the *Fachhochschule* and the university). Degrees earned in the educational system are the decisive gates to occupations that are, on the one hand, paid according to supply and demand, but on the other hand also according to prestige attributed to the occupation, which is based on traditionally shaped beliefs in the functional importance of its contribution to society. This is what we would expect from the functionalist theory of stratification (Davis and Moore 1945). Though the theory has received a lot of criticism from the point of view of conflict theory (Tumin 1953; Huaco 1966), it is still useful, if it is applied with an eye to the specific conditions for its application and with complementation by the conflict paradigm. The hierarchically structured society of well-established status groups seems to display the right conditions for applying the theoretical model. The required complementation would be the acknowledgement that the definition of functional importance is an outcome of symbolic struggles in Bourdieu's (1986, 1994) sense determined by the power and influence of the status groups involved.

The occupation exerts considerable influence on supply because it has substantial say in the legislative establishment of educational requirements for practicing an occupation. This holds true from the top to the bottom. Above the level of the simplest production and service work nearly every job is made an occupation with its specific educational entrance conditions. It is not only the academic professions that have such educational requirements, but also a great many occupations below the academic level in service and production. One needs vocational training in order to be admitted to occupationally defined jobs and in order to earn the income assigned to this job. Wages and salaries are differentiated according to white-collar and blue-collar jobs and are finely graded according to the level of education and vocational training. One is only allowed to offer specific services on the market, to run a corresponding business and to teach apprentices, if one has the master diploma of the relevant occupation. A whole series of occupations are still protected against too much supply by a variety of legal measures. It was not until 2003 that the red-green government of Chancellor Gerhard Schröder drafted a bill to allow craftsmen with a first diploma, but without a master's diploma, to run a business in some occupations. The draft was heavily opposed by the master craftsmen and the CDU opposition.

There are two non-market-related impacts on the income earned in a job, namely limitation of supply through educational and other legally sanctioned barriers, and attribution of functional importance by authorities deciding on wages, salaries and fees. Depending on the strength of these two pre-market forces the income earned in a job is more or less determined by supply and demand on the market. Pre-market forces are stronger, when educational and other legally sanctioned barriers are higher and when authorities that are far away from market achievement are setting wages and salaries. This pertains particularly to the whole public service sector where educational degree and attributed functional importance construct a hierarchy of jobs with authoritatively assigned income. We find this authoritatively established hierarchy of income levels according to educational degree and attributed functional importance also in the private sector economy. The absence of the market in assigning income guarantees the recurrent reproduction of status and income hierarchies for a very long time with little change. The hierarchically differentiated educational system and the authoritative establishing of income levels according to attributed functional importance are the guarantors of the recurrent reproduction of a stable status and income hierarchy, which is being influenced by the market only marginally. It is exactly this income distribution according to procedures other than market competition that also contributes to the lower level of income inequality in Germany in comparison to the USA. The higher inequality in comparison to Sweden can also be explained by the specific effect of education and authoritative income assignment according to attributed functional importance.

In the USA the market works as the most important selective force of income distribution. Because the educational system is generating a mass of relatively equally and generally educated people and only a marginalized group of drop-outs and poorly educated people alongside a small elite of top specialists with academic training in graduate schools (10 per cent only), education alone is not enough to bring forth more finely grained income and status differentiation. This differentiation is therefore much more left to the market. There is also a smaller range of decisions on income assignment for authorities in private and public employment as well, because there is less educational restriction in the access to jobs, and because there is more competition with regard to products and services for both private and public suppliers. In correspondence with this we also have a smaller influence of collective bargaining on salaries and wages and a greater leeway for individual bargaining. This arrangement with the most important influence of market competition is particularly responsible for the greater income inequality in the USA compared to Germany or Sweden. This is the micro-level and more finely grained causal arrangement behind the macro-level correlation between working class representation in governments, union density as well as centralization of wage bargaining and earnings dispersion according to Tilly's (1978) resource dependence theory (Lipset and Marks 2000: 280–283).

The market is an anonymous process that is not in the hands of persons responsible for their decisions. In Marxian terms it is a process that takes place independently of the wishes and moral ideals of the human individual. It is a power that exerts its constraints on the individual, and no individual is in a position to exert control on this power. Such an anonymous process has no inherent stop rule for income inequality beyond explicitly set limits. The income of top managers, top lawyers or top journalists is never being justified in terms of educational achievement or in terms of functional importance for society. It is simply left to the market. If that market pays the chief executive officer (CEO) of a carmaker US$20 million a year – so what! If he makes US$20 million on the market of CEOs, he is worth the US$20 million, because the market is an incorruptible agent of income distribution according to real achievement, if we rely on the philosophy of market liberalism, which is deeply rooted in the American culture. If the US$20 million were too much, the carmaker would fail on the market and wouldn't be able to pay that sum. According to this philosophy of market liberalism nobody would receive from the market what he or she does not deserve because the services are demanded and paid by people who pay by free will. From a viewpoint outside the frame of reference of market liberalism one could, however, ask how the CEO's US$20 million stand against the US$30,000 of the worker in the production line. The market philosophy would simply say that there are many other workers who could replace the worker in the production line, if he doesn't want to work for US$30,000 a year, whereas it apparently needs US$20 million to hire a successful CEO because of a completely different market with a very small number of candidates for such a demanding and risky position.

Income distribution by the market is therefore an anonymous process on the one hand, while on the other hand it is left as it is and is culturally justified because the dominant philosophy of market liberalism is being taken for granted. This is very different in the German conservative welfare state, where income distribution is much more a process of authoritative and representative decision-making on the basis of educational attainment and attributed functional importance against the background of the idea of an integrated hierarchical society within which every status group makes a specific contribution to the functioning of the whole. This philosophy of the functionally integrated hierarchy holds true for the society at large as well as for every individual production or service organization within society. The status groups are cultivating what can be called organic solidarity in the strict sense, meaning that every status group is an organ of the whole with a clear consciousness of everybody that they all form such an organic whole, which needs the contribution of every single part. This collective consciousness of the organic whole gives impetus to everybody of having every part really enabled to contribute its service to the whole and to support every part in the case of inability to contribute so that the whole is not hindered from working. In such a society of organic solidarity the collective consciousness of forming a whole out of different status groups sets tighter limits on income dispersion through market processes than in a society devoted to market achievement. The greater importance of educational status compared to market performance is particularly reflected in the lower inequality of earnings within educational groups in Germany compared to the United States (Prasad 2000; Pischke 2005; Dustmann et al. 2009). The individual earners are members of a status group with representatives who take on responsibility not only for their group but also for the organic whole. There is therefore a sense of belongingness to the same organic whole – firm and society – so that people see their income not as a result of anonymous market processes but as an acknowledgement of services for the whole.

In the frame of reference of this idea of an organic whole income differentiation is functionally required. This is what explains the greater income dispersion in the German conservative welfare state compared to the Swedish egalitarian one. Income differentiation is, however, dysfunctional in this system as soon as it has disruptive effects because it spreads feelings of exploitation and injustice, if earnings reach far beyond imaginable functional importance and far below a decent standard of living. This can be currently observed in the public critique of top salaries of top managers, which have nearer American salaries in the wake of the transnationalization of German companies. The controversy shows that forces of transnationalization run against the traditionally established idea of justice of the organic hierarchy of status groups.

Educational and functional differentiation does not produce the same extent of income inequality as market competition in the American liberal welfare state. Other than market differentiation of income educational and functional differentiation of income occurs by way of collective decision-making. This procedure requires much more consensus within an organic community than the market model, which leaves everything to anonymous processes of market selection. Within such a community toleration of extraordinary deviations from a clear and imaginable income dispersion according to educational achievement and attributed functional importance is more limited than in an individualized market society. There is more organic solidarity with the other parts of the whole so that there is greater willingness to share accumulated wealth, but less willingness to advance far beyond the reach of the others and less tolerance of having parts of the whole drop below a decent standard of living. People living below such a level would blame the organic whole so that everybody feels obliged to help prevent the occurrence of such a poor performance of the whole. Limits on income dispersion and welfare support, which allows everybody in work and out of work a standard of living that is regarded as decent within the collective, is therefore widely consented with simply because of the working of a considerable amount of strict organic solidarity. This consensus within the conservative welfare state is reflected in the still high level of support of governmental responsibility for jobs, decent standards of living and guaranteed basic income across classes as demonstrated by ISSP survey data (Lipset 1996: 76).

The idea of justice pertaining to this organic concept of society does not conform to the liberal combination of rewarding individual achievement under equal opportunity nor to the egalitarian combination of approaching equality of results on the basis of collectively coordinated individual achievement. The conservative idea of organic justice is rewarding the different parts of the organic whole according to entitlement on the basis of education and attributed functional importance and assigns every member of society as much as is required for a standard of living, which is considered deserved by a status group because of functional importance and even for the status groups at the bottom is regarded as decent and respectable in representing the whole of society. The individual attains his or her status not in isolation but as part of an established and acknowledged status group.

The above described conservative model of an organic society resides on a structure of interest organization, which can be called corporatist. Interests are organized by a limited number of historically evolved, well-established and well-organized status groups, which are acknowledged and respected, and which are eager to maintain respect, prestige and the income required for leading a respectable life according to the prestige of the group. They are not simply interest groups but feel as part of an organic whole and therefore also assume public responsibility for the functioning of the whole. They are used to accommodating their interests with the requirements of a functioning whole. The institutional representation of interests occurs in the collaboration of status groups with each other, and with government and administration. The underlying culturally rooted idea of justice is the distribution of rewards according to functional importance within the organic whole. This is the overall framework of the conservative organic model of the welfare state within which more specific institutional elements fulfil specific functions. This holds true for corporate governance, industrial relations, education and interorganizational cooperation in technological advancement. It is the more finely grained micro-level causal arrangement behind the macro-level correlation between Christian democratic parties in government and conservative subsidiarity-centred welfare institutions.

Adjustment to globalized competition

Wolfgang Streeck (1991) speaks of "diversified quality production" to characterize the German industrial production system. For Hall and Soskice the specific nature and institutional framework of incremental innovation is a specific competitive advantage of this German industrial branch, which is of greatest importance for the survival of the German economy in the situation of global competition. Rather than giving in to waves of deregulation invoked by the superficial imitation of the radical innovation strategy of the American "liberal market economy", Germany's "coordinated market economy" should stick to its own strength according to Hall and Soskice (2001: 36–44). Protecting the institutional arrangement that supports incremental innovation is recommended as a more successful strategy of coping with globalization than having this arrangement eroded by approaching the more flexible American model. In doing so Germany would specialize in its specific strength in a global system of labour division. According to this pattern of global labour division it wouldn't make sense to invest in radical innovation and to create its required institutional framework, if this merely destroyed the framework needed for the strength of incremental innovation. One could interpret this specialization in incremental innovation and the maintenance of its institutional framework as competitive solidarity, a term introduced by Wolfgang Streeck (2000). Competitive solidarity is clustering economic activity around industrial branches with special competitive advantage. In Germany, the strongest branches are automobiles, machinery and chemistry. In this perspective "competitive solidarity" would be the answer of a conservative welfare state committed to strict organic solidarity to the challenge of globalization with its advancement of the global division of labour.

The question of special interest here is whether the outlined strategy derived from Hall and Soskice's analysis of innovation regimes and Streeck's notion of competitive solidarity would indeed be effective and would produce the intended effects in the shorter or longer run. If we look at what has really happened in Germany over the past twenty years we observe relatively little change and movement towards the American liberal model of society. Income inequality has increased only slightly as compared to the USA; the major institutions described above as pillars of the regime of incremental innovation are unchallenged and are still in existence. Reforms have for a long time been of a very minor kind in international comparison, if we compare Germany with liberal welfare states like the United States, New Zealand and Great Britain, but also with respect to a conservative welfare state like the Netherlands, and an egalitarian welfare state like Denmark. Only very recently, namely at the beginning of 2005, the strongly opposed Hartz IV labour market reform has brought about a deeper change by limiting status-maintaining unemployment compensation to one year, after which no more than basic income support can be claimed. We should ask why has there been so little change in Germany in particular for such a long time. Can this be explained by the competitive advantage of diversified quality production and incremental innovation or by institutional inertia, vested interests and cultural legitimation? Let us first look at the evidence for the argument of competitive advantage. If this argument was right, there should be no serious problems for the German conservative model of organic solidarity of adjusting to global competition. How can, however, phenomena like the following be interpreted: shrinking employment in particularly those industrial branches that are the stronghold of competitive advantage; high unemployment rates and lower employment rates for a longer time than in most other industrialized countries; and very early retirement resulting in particular from a shrinking number of jobs in the core industrial branches of competitive advantage and causing a deep erosion of the pension system, which needs balance of employment and retirement.

The system is still quite successful in bringing young people into work after having graduated from the educational system. This is mainly an achievement of the special dual system of vocational training at school and in the firm (apprenticeship), which seems to offer a better entrance to the employment system than general education for the mass of young people. Therefore youth unemployment is lower than in most other industrialized countries. However, there is still the unskilled young people who do not participate in this vocational training by school and firm. The other side of the same coin is that their access to employment is hindered by the vocational training of the achievers. Much more than in countries backing a more general and less vocationally oriented training, vocational training forms the major entrance to employment, particularly to well-paid employment. Without such training it will never be possible to achieve in an employment system that is tightly linked with the educational system. Pre-market vocational training is the very precondition for any further advancement on the labour market. A lack of pre-market vocational training cannot be compensated for by training on the job or by further education after having entered the labour market. Such further education and training require a solid basis in previous education and training. It is only logical that inclusion programmes carried out in order to realize equality of opportunity have particularly broadened the access to the educational system, from the bottom of the dual vocational training of workers after having left secondary school, via the medium level of dual vocational training for administrative jobs, up to the level of vocational college graduates (*Fachhochschulen*) and university graduates. Having entered one of these different levels of vocational education it is possible to climb to further levels in further education. Without such a primary basis of vocational training no achievement on the labour market is possible. Achievement is therefore extremely driven by educational degrees and is less strongly driven by training on the job and success in one's job as well as open competition on the job market.

This institutional design has framed class struggle very much as a struggle for vocational education and for the educational upgrading of occupations from the bottom to the top. The results have been rising educational demands for the access to jobs, a race to the top in terms of education. This educational upgrading has contributed a lot to the rise of income for every occupational level, because higher educational qualifications implied an upgrading of jobs in terms of task complexity and the range of responsibility. In a classical study on the end of labour division Horst Kern and Michael Schumann (1984) pointed out this job upgrading in the core industrial branches of manufacturing cars, machine tools and chemicals. Workers who previously carried out a rather simple and limited job in the production line have become technical systems regulators with a complex, extended and more responsible task. On the other side of the upgrading of the technical systems regulators has been the emergence of an underclass of losers who lack the skills for this upgrading process, namely older workers who merely wait for retirement and who are partly forced to retire earlier than expected, as well as unskilled younger workers who are increasingly exposed to unemployment. The formerly relatively homogenous working class has split up into vocationally highly skilled achievers joining the middle class and an unskilled underclass of underachievers and jobless people. For the trade unions it has become increasingly difficult to represent these two completely different clienteles. One has left the trade unions because they have joined the middle class, while the other has avoided joining the trade unions because they do not feel they are members of a broader class, and because the trade unions have become representatives of the typical way of achievement through vocational training and of those who have a job but not of those who don't have a job. The workforce has increasingly been split into insiders and outsiders with the trade unions being committed to support the position of those in jobs in terms of high wages and high job security (Schulze-Cleven 2009). The other side of this coin is the exclusion of the undereducated from the employment system just because this system is focused on a high level of vocational training, a high level of wages and job security for those in jobs of this kind. Between 1975 and 2000 we witnessed a steeply growing unemployment rate on the part of the unskilled, whereas the unemployment rate of people with medium skills increased only slightly, and that of people with high skills nearly not at all. In 1975, the unemployment rate wound up from 2 to 6 per cent according to skills; in 2000 the figures were 2.6, 5.7 and 19.4 per cent respectively in West Germany. In East Germany, we observed a similar development on a much higher level between 1991 and 2000 reaching unemployment according to skills of 4.7, 16.7 and 50.3 per cent in 2000 (IAB 2003). The trade unions have been losing support in this process and have been weakened in their fight for partnership (Fitzenberger *et al.* 2010).

Global competition is strengthening this inherent trend of the German labour market. It favours specialization in diversified quality production, which needs the continuous technical upgrading of jobs. One part of this technical upgrading of jobs is technological rationalization, which implies advancing productivity of the jobs and extending chances of higher wages. Both technical upgrading and high wages exert pressures on the availability of simple production jobs. They are on the one hand replaced by machines, and on the other hand they do not meet the productivity requirements of highly paid work. Shrinking demand for simple production work is therefore the crucial problem of the labour market. It is sharpened by collaboration between the external force of enhanced global competition and the internal force of continuous educational upgrading. The liberal system of the United States is solving this problem by the growth of a low-wage private service sector; the conservative system of the Netherlands by the extensive introduction of part-time work and self-restriction of trade unions in wage policy; the egalitarian system of Denmark by smaller restrictions on displacement from jobs accompanied by relatively high compensation for unemployment and strict policies aiming at bringing unemployed people back to work. Denmark has, however, also an extended public and private service sector, which is able to compensate for job losses in the industrial sector. Germany has the special problem of having maintained a larger industrial sector and having a less developed private service sector. Job losses in the industrial sector have not been countered by job growth in the private service sector for various reasons. One reason is long-term subsidies for the industrial sector, which takes money from the extension of the public and private service sectors. Another reason has been the established high level of wages based on specialization in diversified quality production over a long period of time. In the meantime, several years of wage freeze have changed the situation. A further reason is the still widely consented organic solidarity, which makes toleration of greater income inequality between a high-wage sector of diversified quality production and a low-wage private service sector difficult. There was much resistance against such a change until the coming into effect of the Hartz IV reforms in January 2005. It seems to be more in line with organic solidarity to support a relatively large number of unemployed people than dismissing that solidarity with the introduction of low-wage service work (Cox 2001; Bleses and Seeleib-Kaiser 2004; Clasen 2005; Clegg 2007; Hudson *et al.* 2008).

The existing system of organic solidarity is also supported by conceiving unemployment as effected by the economy and not by the people themselves, and of unemployment compensation as justified by the very contributions of the same people in times of employment. More than in a liberal system jobless people are seen as victims of circumstances outside their control, and people in jobs are regarded as obliged to contribute their share to an organic whole, which would be blamed by people living below a standard of living considered as respectable. People being forced to live below this level would undermine the self-respect of those better-off people who would tolerate this situation. This difference between liberal and conservative welfare regimes is clearly reflected in corresponding attitudes across class lines as demonstrated by ISSP data (Lipset 1996: 76).

Yet another reason for the resistance to change is vested interests. Because the services of organic solidarity of the conservative German welfare state are shared by well-established and well-organized status groups, there is a lot of power and influence that can be mobilized against attempts at reform. The mobilization of all that power and influence against reform is very likely, because every single reform would touch the stakes of at least one, mostly however several, if not all powerful, well-organized and influential status groups. It must also be taken into account that large-scale public and private administrations as well as private administrations in public commission are handling welfare services. There is, for instance, the public administration of unemployment or the semi-public administration of welfare services by the big welfare organizations (*Caritas, Diakonisches Werk, Rotes Kreuz, Paritätischer Wohlfahrtsverband*) or the joint administration of health services by public administration, insurance companies and the association of physicians. They all draw enormous advantages from the system so that reform is working strongly in the direction of leaving untouched the established stakes of the relevant status groups and welfare organizations. It is therefore very likely that technically required solutions of problems are prevented because distributive conflicts interfere and powerful vested interests would be negatively touched. The status groups and organizations are sticking to their stakes in the existing system at the cost of carrying on problems and deficits, which undermine the overall outcome of the system even to the long-term disadvantage of the resisting status groups and organizations. They are locked in what Fritz Scharpf has called the trap of politics entanglement (*Politikverflechtungsfalle*) (Scharpf *et al.* 1976). We are, however, not confronted with a prisoner's dilemma here, because German corporatism provides a sufficient amount of chances of communication between representative players of the game. The greatest obstacle to realizing a technically adequate solution of the problems is the sacrifice one or several groups have to bear in the present for certain, whereas the compensation by better

174 Institutional change

returns in the future is nothing but a very vague promise. In the face of this choice it is very likely that the participants in the game will opt for what they have and will restrain from opting for remedies with rather unpredictable outcomes in a future that is far from now.

Resistance against change due to the unpredictability of its outcomes is further on supported by the dependence of outcome evaluations on the point of view of established knowledge and the definition of the situation by that knowledge. Whether the outcome of a reform is an improvement or not is a question of its perception by the relevant players of the game and their ability to establish their definition of the situation as the right one in public debate. The risk of an outcome from change, which is worse than what the powerful and influential status groups receive from the existing system, is too high so that there is not enough motivation for change. Simple cost/advantage calculation speaks for sticking with the existing system. In other words, transaction costs of change appear higher than costs of no change.

It is this constellation of a broad coalition of vested interests that has led strategies of coping with unemployment in the direction of reducing the supply of workforce by decreasing regular working hours in the industrial sector to thirty-five hours per week and by handing over workers above the age of 55 to the growing group of pensioners. The first result of this strategy was a reduction of the average annual working hours from 1,745 hours in 1979 to 1,535 in 1999 and 1,390 in 2009, while the figures are 1,579 and 1,640 in Switzerland, 1,976 and 1,768 in the USA, 1,643 and 1,610 in Sweden, 1,720 and 1,646 in Great Britain and 1,842 and 1,713 in Japan (OECD 2011e). The second result was the falling in the employment rate of people between fifty-five and sixty-four to a rate as low as 38.3 per cent on average for the years from 1996 to 2000. The corresponding figures are 57.2 in the USA, 70.9 in Switzerland, 51.6 in Denmark and 63.6 in Sweden. The figures for 2009 were 56.1, 60.6, 68.4, 57.7 and 70.1 respectively for these countries (OECD 2011e). The third result was a decreasing number of working people who have to support an increasing number of inactive non-working people, namely the jobless and pensioners. This fact is not being changed by the results of a study carried out at the Institut für Arbeit und Technik (IAT), which demonstrates that the average working hours per year of full-time employed working people was at 1,760 hours in Germany in the early 2000s, which is about average among EU countries. According to this record, annual working hours were lowest in France at 1,689 hours (Süddeutsche Zeitung 2004). In 2009, average weekly hours worked in a main job in full-time employment were 41.2 in Germany and 40.9 in France (OECD 2011e). It can be doubted whether this comparison is better than OECD comparisons including part-time employment. The latter shows indeed how much work is being done to support non-working people, which is not really reflected in the IAT comparison. This is, however, what counts with regard to the viability of a welfare regime. The shift towards a growing number of non-working people in need of support by a shrinking number of working people is being aggravated by demographic change leading to an over-aged society because of the extremely low fertility rate of 1.4 (in 2009) births per female and the growing life expectancy of the population. The consequence of the growing incongruity between the active and inactive parts of the population is the high level of total payments of income tax and social security contributions as a percentage of gross wage earnings at 41.3, as compared to 27.7 in France, 32.7 in Austria, 39.4 in Denmark, 29.2 in Finland, 25.3 in Sweden, 25.3 in the United Kingdom, 22.0 in Australia and 22.4 in the United States (OECD 2011f). Germany has therefore been leading the world in labour costs for a long time until the more recent changes set in (World Bank 2002). This is no problem for highly productive workers in the top ranking industrial sectors of high quality production made in Germany (cars, machines, chemicals), but it is a problem for low-skilled and less productive workers and service employees who can no longer participate in the collective sharing of high wages in the face of increasing international competition. Because Germany has resisted introducing a low-wage sector, the demand for simple work and service has declined to produce a durable unemployment rate of about 10 per cent, which corresponds to 4.4 million people up until 2007. For many of them this has become a long-term status. Up until 2009, the situation has improved slightly, but Germany still lags behind other countries. In 2009, the unemployment rate was at 7.9 per cent in Germany. The unemployment rate for more than six months and less than one year was at 13.5 per cent; the rate for one year and more at 53.4 per cent. The figures in Switzerland were 15.7 and 34.3 per cent, 17.6 and 16.1 per cent in Denmark and 15.3 and 10.6 per cent in the USA (OECD Statistics).

The strategy of combating unemployment by reducing the supply of workforce applied since the mid-1980s has apparently failed in Germany. Countries that did not follow this path have done better over the past two decades. Unemployment has dropped to 3–6 per cent in most OECD countries including all types of welfare regimes. In Wolfgang Streeck's (2004) words, Germany has replaced the labour society with the welfare state and thus has deeply undermined the very basis of a viable welfare state in the long run. In this respect the dream of a society with a shrinking part of work in people's lives has come true, though with the consequence of splitting society into insiders and outsiders and endangering the long-term wealth of society.

If we took this result of our analysis we would conclude that little or no change in the German organic welfare system is not a problem, because this option is simply reflecting the preferences of the status groups and organizations that are shaping political decision-making. However, we have to recognize that we speak of the powerful and influential status groups and organizations that calculate costs according to their definition of the situation and their stakes in the system. Their definition of the situation may be wrong and there may be less powerful and less influential groups for which change would be more profitable than no change. The marginalized underclass of uneducated and/or unemployed people could be such a group. What is better for them is, however, very difficult to say. Is well-supported unemployment worse than low-wage employment? This is exactly the point of controversy; and the position one takes in this controversy depends largely on ideology. For liberals low-wage employment is always better than unemployment because the latter would undermine the work ethic of the whole population and the advancement of society to the disadvantage of everybody including the poor. For many social democrats and conservatives supported unemployment, which allows for a life on the level of a respectable standard of living, is better than low-wage employment below such a standard. For them the working poor are not responsible for their situation, as they are in the liberals' eyes, but rather society which therefore has to care for them in a sufficient way. Nevertheless, the liberal position is receiving increasing support in the face of global competition and institutional comparison with the performance of liberal as well as other conservative and egalitarian welfare states, but also in the face of long-term high unemployment rates and the declined competitiveness of the German economy up until the most recent years.

There has been an increasingly aggressive public controversy going on about how to meet the challenge of globalization over the past twenty years, which is held responsible for the underperformance of the German economy in terms of growth and employment rates. The liberal side votes for the deregulation of the labour market, which is expected to unchain the economy from fetters preventing investment, economic growth and increasing employment. A socialist minority position still starts from the long-dominating premise of limited supply of jobs because of the high level of satiation of markets in the advanced economies and because of the continuous replacement of working people by technology. According to this premise the only feasible strategy for solving the problem is to limit the demand for jobs or the supply of workforce respectively. This can be done in various ways. A very conservative way would strengthen the still existing division of labour between paid work of men and unpaid household work of women; an egalitarian way would extend part-time work equally for men and women; a more flexible way would introduce an account for – let us say – ten years of publicly assisted leave (sabbaticals), which can be chosen during one's occupational life. The widely practiced way has long been the reduction of working hours per week and of the working population by way of a somewhat late entry of younger people from education to the labour market, a well-supported high employment rate and early retirement. This strategy has, however, lost ground because public debate has become focused on the growing gap between a shrinking number of working people who have to support an increasing number of non-working people at working age and particularly beyond working age.

The demographic shift towards a decreasing number of younger people and an increasing number of older people is aggravating this problem, which has recently taken the lead in public discussion. In the light of this rather new definition of the situation strategies, which are reducing the number of working people and working hours, have lost more and more support. The search for solutions is therefore focused on raising the number of working people – both men and women – without creating a new milieu of working poor in this way. This has meanwhile become the majority position shared by conservatives and social democrats.

For conservatives the growing gap between working and non-working people is undermining the model of organic solidarity. If the burden of a decreasing number of working people in terms of tax and social insurance costs is diminishing their immediate return on investments in work, there is a growing danger of resistance to such burdens and thus a decreasing support of people out of work. The result would be shrinking solidarity, because the working people feel exploited by the non-working people, while the non-working people feel neglected by the working people. The breakdown of organic solidarity would create precisely that society of selfish people that is the nightmare of a liberal society.

From the social democratic point of view the gap between working and non-working people is also undermining solidarity, which is, however, interpreted in a more egalitarian sense than the conservative model of organic solidarity. Egalitarian solidarity centres on the idea of equal citizenship, which entails shared civil, political and social rights. According to this model of egalitarian solidarity society is a community of equal citizens, which works on the basis that each citizen makes his or her contribution to the good of the whole, which is equally shared by all citizens. So far we can see that the social democratic egalitarian model of solidarity needs a sufficient employment rate, as does the conservative model of solidarity. This holds true for men and women alike, because both are conceived of as equal citizens. The smallest unit of the conservative model is the family, which implies a strong division of housework including childcare and paid work between men and women. The smallest unit of the social democratic model is the single individual, which implies that men and women are sharing housework, childcare and paid work. In order to make this arrangement feasible a great part of housework and childcare is transmitted to public service (meals in the canteen at work, childcare).

These are the positions taken in the current public debate. As we can see, liberal, conservative and social democratic ideologies are in conflict with each other in shaping the future of the German welfare state. This is not different to the past. It is therefore an exaggeration for the sake of constructing an ideal type to characterize the German welfare state primarily as conservative. Its historical roots are without any doubt conservative. However, this conservative core has been complemented by liberal and social democratic elements in the long history of its further development. Particularly after the Second World War major liberal and social democratic elements have been added to the model in the Federal Republic of Germany. Ludwig Erhard's model of the social market economy is in reality a liberal renewal of Christian subsidiarity and conservative organic solidarity. Co-determination, work councils and the legal regulation of employment with a high level of job security are surely major elements of the social democratic understanding of social citizenship. It is therefore nothing new that the current controversy is focused on the place and meaning of liberal, conservative and social democratic elements in the real system of welfare. The major challenge has been the implanting of more liberal elements in a way that keeps the conservative and the social democratic parts of the model intact. Consensus exists on the search for employment growth. How much deregulation of the labour market is required in order to attain that goal has, however, been the big question. Deregulation of the labour market has particularly been resisted from the social democratic point of view. Another major point of controversy has been how much participation of women in the labour market is required to fill the employment gap. As a continuation of the debate on reducing the demand for jobs the conservative position has seen the special promotion of women's employment as adding pressure on the labour market and as weakening family and childcare. There has been particularly conservative resistance to policies aiming at reducing financial support of the (mostly male) breadwinner family, for instance in terms of the removal of tax exemptions (the so-called spouse-splitting of income tax), while at the same time improving public childcare through day nursery, kindergarten and all-day school. Such policies are in line with the social democratic idea of egalitarian universalism as well as with the liberal idea of individualized universalism, because both ideas are focused on citizenship in terms of equal rights of every individual citizen. This is the universalism they share. It is only the emphasis on civil rights on the one hand and on social rights on the other hand that makes them different.

A central problem of adjustment in the conservative welfare state is its dependence on welfare production by the family, which is traditionally based on the division of labour between male breadwinners and housewives. This model has implied that there is little need of public childcare. In an international comparison only a little more public childcare exists in the German conservative welfare state than in the American liberal one. According to Esping-Andersen (1999: 71, Table 5A) childcare coverage ranges from 1 per cent for the United States, 2 per cent for the United Kingdom, 2 per cent and 3 per cent for Austria, the Netherlands, Germany and Spain to 20 per cent in France, 29 per cent in Sweden and 48 per cent in Denmark. This data reflects the situation in the 1980s. In the meantime, the situation has changed slightly with Germany offering a guaranteed place in the kindergarten for all children from three years on. However, the country lags still far behind Scandinavia with regard to daycare for the under-three-year-olds as well as care after school and all-day schools. In 2007, public spending on family benefits in cash, services and tax measures, as percentage of GDP, was at 3.68 in France, 3.67 in Denmark, 3.56 in the United Kingdom, 3.07 in Sweden, 2.78 in Germany, 1.40 in Switzerland, 1.40 in Canada and 1.17 in the United States (OECD Statistics). In 2006, enrolment rates of children under six in formal care or early education services amounted to 42.9 per cent of those between 0 and two years and 100 per cent of those between three and five years in Germany. In Denmark, the figures were 63.0 and 90.7, in the United Kingdom 39.7 and 90.9, in Germany 13.6 and 89.3, in Sweden 45.3 and 89.6, in the United States 31.4 and 58.4 (OECD 2011d).

The family-related value pattern is now in serious conflict with major changes in the situation. Women are much better educated than before. Gender equality is receiving much more support though it is still in conflict with the family-related value pattern of the conservative welfare state. The result is an especially severe trade-off between childcare and women's employment. It is therefore not surprising that the previously well-established positive correlation between the conservative welfare state's familialism and fertility has completely changed to the opposite. In the 1990s, the Mediterranean countries and Germany clustered around a fertility rate of 1.2–1.4 births per woman, while the Scandinavian and Anglo-Saxon countries along with France clustered around a rate of 1.6–1.8. The French conservative welfare state deviated from the conservative cluster with its fertility rate of 1.6, possibly because of its higher level of public childcare, which was at 20 per cent coverage compared to only 3 per cent in Germany (Esping-Andersen 1999: 71, Table 5A). In 2008, the fertility rate was at 1.4 in Germany and 2.0 in France (World Bank 2011). In 2005, the enrolment rate of children under three in childcare was at 28 per cent in France and 9 per cent in Germany (OECD 2009a). In the conservative welfare state women still have to decide much more between childrearing and an occupational career than in the egalitarian as well as the liberal welfare states. In the egalitarian welfare state public childcare relieves women from that in the household, in the liberal welfare state of the United States very low costs of private childcare help women to combine childrearing and occupational careers. The other side of this coin is the very low wages in service jobs. The liberal system works for middle- to upper-class families but not for lower-class families, because for the latter the relatively low costs of private childcare are still too high to be affordable. Therefore the system produces a milieu of badly cared for lower class children and youth acquiring not enough skills for achievement so that there is a continuous lower class reproduction. In the British liberal regime the American model does not work, because a lack of public childcare is not compensated for by low private service costs. Though not to the same degree there is a similar situation in the conservative German welfare state, where a lack of public childcare implies care deficits for children with double-earner parents particularly in the lower strata. As a result of this situation Germany stands out in the positive correlation between class and literacy according to the much debated PISA assessment (Baumert et al. 2001; OECD 2010a).

Another problematical consequence of the conservative welfare state's changed situation is the still relatively low female employment rate. According to ISSP data Germany differed very strongly from Britain and the United States in 1988 in assigning women the job of household and family attaining a level of 44 per cent, compared to only 29 and 28 per cent in Britain and the United States respectively. Austria scored even higher at 54 per cent in this respect. In 1994, both Germany and Austria had developed more in the direction of Britain and the United States to come very close to these countries in 2002 (Figure 4.13).

It has been argued that the low female employment rate in Germany helps to keep further pressure from the labour market (Ostner 1998). This effect will however be of a temporary nature only, because in the long run a lack of inclusion of women in working life increases the gap between working people and pensioners, which undermines the pension system. Another consequence is the growth of poverty among divorced people, because the turn from the male

180 *Institutional change*

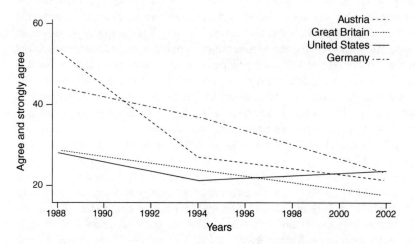

Figure 4.13 Household and family is women's job (source: Gesis 2011).

Notes
Data available for 1988, 1994 and 2002. Percentages agree and strongly agree were summed. Own calculations. Retrieved 28 March 2011, from http://zacat.gesis.org – ZA1700: International Social Survey Programme 1988: Family and Changing Gender Roles I (ISSP 1988). ZA2620: International Social Survey Programme 1994: Family and Changing Gender Roles II (ISSP 1994). ZA3880: International Social Survey Programme 2002: Family and Changing Gender Roles III (ISSP 2002). Question was asked as Q.2: And to what extent do you agree or disagree…? (Please tick one box on each line) Q.2b A man's job is to earn money; a woman's job is to look after the home and family. Own calculations.

breadwinner family to mostly one single-parent household and another single household implies much higher costs than before for both households. Without any job experience and public childcare single mother households are in danger of falling into a milieu of enduring unemployment with a negative effect on children's future achievement.

Lacking public childcare, a strongly felt trade-off between childrearing and occupational career and children as a heavy burden in the case of divorce (which has become very likely with every third marriage being dissolved) has most likely contributed to the extremely reduced fertility rate in the German conservative welfare state, which is at 1.3 births per woman and far below the reproduction rate of 2.1. In international comparison there is, however, no robust evidence for an influence of childcare cost on fertility, while there seems to be a positive effect of enrolment rates of children (0–2 years) in formal care or early education services on the fertility rate (Figures 4.14 and 4.15). Strikingly there is also a positive correlation between female employment and the fertility rate. In Scandinavia and in the United States we find remarkably higher fertility rates of 1.6–2.1 births per woman compared to Italy, Germany and Spain at 1.2–1.4, but also a much higher full-time employment rate of women. Obviously the viability of familistic traditions compels women to make a choice between work and children. In as much as they have invested in education their choice has increasingly been for work. The familistic core value of the conservative welfare state is therefore in a deep crisis. It no longer produces family-based welfare, but destroys its very basis: families and children looking optimistically towards the future. Here we meet a central adjustment problem of the German conservative welfare state. Solving this problem will require the abandoning of the no longer working familistic value pattern. Affordable private childcare furthered by tax subsidies together with public childcare are the widely considered ways out of this crisis.

So far two diverging coalitions have been seen. Conservative, Christian and social democratic positions have been very close to one another in their resistance to deregulating the labour market for a long time. Social democrats, liberals and a mixture of both in the Green Party, all agree in replacing the support of the male breadwinner family with the support of the single individual; equalization of the life career, particularly equal employment of men and women; and daycare of children outside the family home. This means that the two core reform projects of the German welfare state have faced enormous resistance from varying coalitions. Conservatives being centred in the Christian parties but having also support in other parties have been opposing the removal of the conservative pillar of the welfare state, while social democrats and conservatives across party lines have been opposing the removal of the social democratic and conservative protection of employment. This is why there has been a lot of

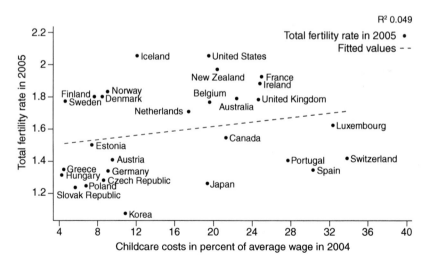

Figure 4.14 Costs of childcare and fertility rate (source: World Bank 2011. Fertility rate, total (births per woman) retrieved 14 March 2011, from http://data.worldbank.org/indicator/SP.DYN.TFRT.IN. Childcare fees in % of average wage retrieved 14 March 2011, from www.oecd.org/dataoecd/44/45/42218978.xls).

Note
Own calculations.

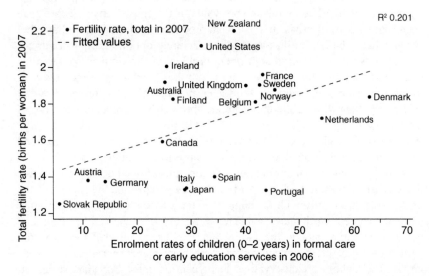

Figure 4.15 Children (0–3 years old) in day care and fertility rate (source: World Bank 2011. Fertility rate, total (births per woman) retrieved 14 March 2011, from http://data.worldbank.org/indicator/SP.DYN.TFRT.IN. Enrolment rates of children (0–2 years) in formal care or early education services retrieved 14 March 2011, from www.oecd.org/dataoecd/55/55/38969007.xls).

Note
Own calculations.

controversy, but not much change for a long time. A more profound change set in when the social democratic/Green government of Chancellor Schröder applied more extensive measures of reform in the face of the country's aggravating economic underperformance in 2003, culminating in the so-called Hartz IV reforms. These reforms have reduced status-maintaining compensation of unemployment to one year. The Schröder government had to pay the price for this major step of reform with its defeat in the elections of September 2005.

Britain and Denmark prove that the existence of different cultural traditions in one country is not only a dangerous source of insoluble conflict, but also an even greater source for experimenting with various strategies of reform. Therefore we have to revise our statement on the peculiar German difficulties of reform referring to the struggle between varying coalitions of the conservative, social democratic and liberal ideologies. The existence of all three ideologies can also be an advantage because of the availability of a broader variety of approaches to reform. Whether this variety hinders consensus formation or instead helps to find ways of innovation depends on the deepness of crisis and the ability of political leaders to form a coalition of reform across party lines. In order to explain the greater difficulties of doing so in Germany compared to more innovative countries like Britain, the Netherlands and Denmark we have to take into account that German governments have been strongly concerned with transmitting the welfare model of the West to the East since 1990, which has drawn attention away from efforts of reforming that model. The breakdown of the economy in the East after reunification is yet another reason for the exceptional underperformance of Germany in comparison to other countries. It is therefore difficult to prove that the German conservative model of the welfare state with its amalgamation with liberal and social democratic elements has as such greater problems of coping with the challenge of global competition. As a comparison of the reform strategies of more successful welfare states over the past two decades shows – such as Britain representing the liberal model; the Netherlands representing the conservative model with a considerable number of social democratic and liberal elements; and Denmark representing the egalitarian model – all three models of welfare states can find strategies of successful adjustment to global competition without having to give up their identity. More recently, Germany has also found a way to reform. It led to a kind of dualization of the labour market, which has been identified by Palier (2010) as a typical adjustment strategy of the Continental European welfare states representing the Bismarckian conservative model. The traditional core of protected employment is surrounded by an increasing periphery of unprotected employment. However, as Rueda (2007) has demonstrated, the tendency of protecting insiders at the expense of outsiders has been typical of social democratic policies, too, for the past thirty years. The social democratic influence has also been effective in Germany during these years. Up until the turn of the millennium the preference for insiders produced unemployment. Since that time, it has created a new category of employed though largely unprotected people.

However, it cannot be denied that there is some convergence in introducing new liberal elements, which is particularly apparent in the new workfare programmes. The common idea behind such models is that of an active society of individual citizens who share civil, political and social rights, and who are obliged to contribute their labour to the wealth of society, which is distributed according to achievement under conditions of equal opportunity on the basis of a smaller or greater amount of shared wealth depending on the relative strength of the liberal or egalitarian idea of citizenship. What is striking in this context is the sharing of the universalistic idea of citizenship of individuals with equal rights by the liberal and egalitarian models of the welfare state. They differ only in the weight ascribed to civil or social rights. The conservative model in contrast conceives of people not primarily as citizens but as members of families and status groups and in fact assigns rights largely according to such membership. Membership in the family is granting public support in terms of taxation; vocational education and training regulates access to the employment system. This special feature of the conservative welfare state raises the question as to whether it has greater problems of adjustment to the challenges of globalization than the other two welfare state models just because of its core structure.

This is the point where we should return to our analysis of the restructuring of solidarity in the process of increasing transnational labour division. If our analysis is correct, transnational labour division is an evolutionary trend, because it extends the opportunities to act for a growing number of people all over the world without facing the Hobbesian war of all against all. The crucial strategy for avoiding this war is the overcoming of a political zero-sum game by an economic game of an increasing sum. The prize to be paid for that progress is establishing the global consumer society and giving more space to the private citizen (*bourgeois*) at the cost of a shrinking space for the public citizen (*citoyen*). Along with this process solidarity relationships are undergoing a fundamental transformation. They are increasingly stretching beyond primordial and historically established boundaries including national boundaries. The other side of this coin is the growing independence of the human individual from primordial ties, his or her growing autonomy and self-responsibility. Progressing individualization is the result of advancing entanglement in social relations beyond the limited ties of family, neighbourhood, status group and nation. If this is right, the organization of solidarity according to the model of an externally demarcated organic whole, which is internally conceived as a hierarchy of status groups, seems to be outdated. External demarcation and the internal composition of traditionally established status groups do not fit into the overall trend of external entanglement and internal pluralization of membership as well as individualization of the conduct of life thus breaking up the boundaries of status groups and nation.

The adequate structure of solidarity seems to be a plurality of networks, with some networks divided according to the local, national, European and global levels of the organization of social life, and other networks stretching across all levels. The nation and the status groups – and with them the national organic whole – have to retreat at least some steps in order to promote the growth of integration in the rising multilevel society through a plurality of networks in more universalistic and individualistic terms on the different levels and across those levels. Networks entail another kind of solidarity to status groups and hierarchically structured organic systems on the level of organizations and national societies. They are externally more open for incoming and outgoing members, have lower entrance barriers, allow multiple loyalties and attract people in a specific role with specific interests, rights and obligations and not as complete persons with diffuse interests, rights and obligations. Status groups and organic systems have clearly demarcated memberships with high entrance barriers and long-term membership. Their members share a common view of the world and a common ethic, which determine responsibilities and obligations. Status groups and organic systems are part of an organic whole within which they carry out responsibilities and obligations to the good of the whole. The commitment of their members to the group or organization is linked with the commitment to the good of the embracing whole (Rubio-Marin 2000).

This is what Emile Durkheim (1964) conceived as organic solidarity. His idea was to overcome the selfishness and class antagonism produced by the capitalist system of the free market competition with the transmission of the idea of the social organization of markets by the medieval corporations to the system of modern capitalism. He expected the occupational groups to organize as corporations, which take responsibility to regulate production, division of labour, trade, contracting and employment on the basis of an occupational ethic. They were expected to cooperate with one another and with the government being represented in a social and economic body on the national level. According to this organization the occupational corporations are the pillars of organic solidarity. What Durkheim had in mind became widely realized in societies with a strong civil society of corporations cooperating with one another and with government and administration in order to organize social life to promote the common good. According to Durkheim the occupational corporations are central to the organization of social life in a society, which is characterized by the increasing division of labour and its effect of replacing territorial politics with economic transactions. For him religion has lost its moral strength in the process of secularization, the family is too small and particularistic to mediate the individual with society, and the state is too far away from the individual's day to day activities. The occupational corporations are however intimately linked with what is of greatest importance and what is always present for the individual, namely his or her work within the organic division of labour. Occupational corporations are intermediary and mediating groups between state and society. The German conservative welfare state comes very close to this idea. It is therefore also called German corporatism (Streeck 1999).

Networks, which are going to replace corporations, are however of a different kind. They are closer to the liberal model of society. They are much greater in number. The individual is a member of a great many networks of which every single one covers but a very small part of the individual. Their relationship to one another is much less based on cooperation, and much more on competition. Their relationship to government and administration is much more in the field of lobbying and much less collaboration in taking responsibility for the whole of society. They have no strong ethic and by far no ethic spelling out responsibilities and obligations as part of an organic whole. Their members are not completely committed to them, and they are not very good at committing their members to contributing to the common good of the society. If at all, the common good is an accidental outcome of a myriad of single acts of networking. In such a system moral hazard, the selfish misuse of guaranteed solidarity to one's own advantage and to the disadvantage of the rest of society is much more likely than in a system in which the individual person is far more committed to status groups and organizations with a strong ethic and social control. This has become a problem of the conservative welfare state in particular because it grants support with the presupposition that individual persons are committed to the good of society via group and organizational membership so that selfishness doesn't come up. However, the strength of social organizations by status groups and occupational corporations is eroding in the face of declining membership of the large corporations, pluralization of associations, shorter times of membership in organizations, faster membership turnover, individualization of job careers and polarization of winners and losers of modernization. With such changes taking place the moral basis of a generous welfare system with few checks with regard to entitlement to social benefits is fading. It seems that liberal and egalitarian systems, which are traditionally less favourable to the self-control of corporations, are also quicker in introducing stricter control of welfare entitlement and special workfare programmes to have jobless people return to employment. It is at least remarkable that Germany has been most reluctant in following this path of liberal as well as egalitarian welfare states. Its welfare system is built on the pillars of vital corporations, which are however losing some of the power required to carry out their traditional obligation to the good of society, if such liberal reforms were introduced. This structural dilemma is responsible for Germany's reluctance with regard to liberal workfare programmes.

Globalization and internal modernization towards the knowledge society are collaborating in changing the solidarity structure of society, which is moving away from organic solidarity and is approaching a new type of the solidarity of a plurality of overlapping networks of private individuals who are no longer exclusively committed to durable groups and organizations (family, status group, private firm, public administration) forming an organic whole. Internal modernization is advancing in terms of (1) the educational upgrading of the great majority of the population; (2) the tertiarization of the economy; and (3) the increasing differentiation of the workforce in terms of skills, job profile and employment situation. These three trends are converging in the pluralization of memberships and social structure and in the individualization of life careers and the conduct of life. Three trends of globalization are strengthening this internal modernization process: (1) Increasing cross-border division of labour is extending loyalties of the pioneers of globalization (managers, scientists, technical specialists, transnationally active members of governmental and non-governmental organizations) beyond national boundaries and is therefore splitting up national solidarity. The elite of globalization is especially advancing the individualization of life careers and lifestyles. (2) The industrialization of peripheral regions of the world economy is establishing a worldwide labour market for labour-intensive production, which makes shifting of labour-intensive production from core countries to peripheral countries increasingly profitable. This trend is supported by the technological advancement of international transport and communication and the facilitated access to peripheral markets resulting from that shift. (3) The removal of barriers for the free movement of capital, goods and services is forcing governments to strengthen the competitive advantages of their economy making locations attractive for capital investment, for instance in terms of capital taxation, labour market regulation, labour costs, skills of the workforce and innovation resulting from investments in the advancement of science and technology and their accelerated transfer to industrial production.

In the advanced industrial countries investment has to focus on innovation, which needs a highly skilled workforce advancing in its habitus well beyond the traditional worker. The highly qualified systems regulator is no longer a member of a comprehensive, collectively organized working class but an increasingly individualized member of a pluralized middle class whose solidarity with the unskilled rest of the workforce is shrinking. For him the displacement of unskilled workers and their replacement by workers in new production plants in peripheral regions of the world economy is an advantage, which is enhancing the competitive strength of his firm and of his own job thus making his job more profitable for his company and for himself. The rising competitive solidarity within firms is therefore not the traditional organic solidarity of people within national or local confines but the new type of network solidarity stretching worldwide beyond local and national production units.

As we see in the three trends – international labour division, a rising global labour market and an increasing focus on innovation for reasons of strengthening global competitiveness – globalization is enhancing the trend of modernization in terms of the pluralization of membership and social structure and the individualization of life careers and lifestyles in the advanced industrial societies. The hierarchically ordered organic solidarity of the conservative welfare state is particularly put under pressure by the outlined trends of modernization and globalization. The trends of pluralization and individualization are shaking off the chains of so far firmly established families, status groups and well-organized corporations, trade unions, employer associations and local firms. These pillars of the conservative welfare state are losing power to organize organic solidarity because of their shrinking membership, the pluralization of associational life and the individualization of life careers and lifestyles. Their position in society is less firmly established, and their influence on people, government and administration is shrinking. They have to share the loyalty of members, government and administration with a greater variety of competing associations.

All this is suggesting a movement away from hierarchically structured and nationally focused organic solidarity and towards pluralized and individualized network solidarity in a rising multilevel society. It may be justified to interpret the stability of institutions of hierarchically structured organic solidarity in the conservative welfare state as a sign of the still effective influence of still powerful corporations, trade unions and employer associations. However, it may also be correct to interpret the crisis of traditional organic solidarity, particularly in terms of a long-term high unemployment rate, as an increasing gap between the number of people in employment and the number of people out of employment, and shrinking technological innovation in international comparison as a sign of the increasing contradiction between the historically rooted institutions of organic solidarity and the evolutionary change that is taking place with the pluralization and individualization of social structure, life careers and lifestyles. If we replace the social structure with the productive forces and the institutional structure with the production relationships we arrive at an example of the contradiction between productive forces and production relationships, which is invoking a time of institutional – not necessarily revolutionary – change in Marxian terms.

In the light of the analysis carried out so far it seems to be unlikely that the German conservative welfare state could stick to its institutional pattern of incremental innovation as a model for the whole economy without long-term

188 Institutional change

economic underperformance with disruptive effects on society. It is more likely that the established pattern can no longer serve as a model for the total economy and needs complementation by patterns allowing for radical innovation and for an expanding service sector and faster turnover of personnel. For the sake of social integration faster change of employment while keeping unemployment at a lower rate and within a closer time limit would have to replace high unemployment protection accompanied by high unemployment rates. Complementing the established pattern with such measures could leave intact that pattern in traditional industrial sectors thus leading to a situation of multiple patterns. It is however more likely that there are at least some repercussions of the introduction of new patterns in new sectors on the pattern in the traditional sector. Whatever is going on under the flag of "approaching more flexibility" is a sign of such a change. New arrangements between management and work councils on the company level – particularly in internationalized firms – are indeed increasing flexibility, for instance in terms of job guarantees in exchange for more flexibility in pay and working hours and variable wage (Kurdelbusch 2002).

We could even argue that the highly skilled workforce in the industrial sector of diversified quality production no longer needs the strong protection of the traditional pattern because it has become more important for them to have a well-paid job in a flexible prospering company than to see their company being shut down because of lost competitiveness caused by inflexibility in the face of more fluid capital. Because the job of a highly skilled worker is safe in a well-performing company it makes sense to agree to variable arrangements with regard to employment, working hours and wages depending upon profits yielded by the company's market performance and upon individual achievement (Zugehör 2003). The increasing number of such arrangements between management and work councils shows that the institutionalized representation of interests is going to survive through a change of policy in the direction of agreements on enhanced flexibility. This is an adjustment of the institutionalized representation of employee interests to the changing solidarity structure in the situation of enhanced global competition. The institution of interest representation through co-determination and work councils is not changing, while the policy of interest representation is. It allows for differentiation with regard to the market performance of the company and with regard to the achievement of the individual employee. This trend, which is set in motion by highly internationalized pioneering companies, is on the way to being recognized on the level of general wage agreements with the increasing use of frame agreements allowing for specification in the company according to market performance (Höpner 2003; Streeck and Höpner 2003; Börsch 2007; Dahl et al. 2009). Another instrument of contracting within firms is social pacts that guarantee jobs for an agreed period of time in exchange for stable wages (Seifert and Massa-Wirth 2005). It is also recognized on the level of legislation in terms of removing restrictions on displacement from jobs, and in terms of acknowledging achievement and not only need of the employee in cases of displacement caused by adjustment to shrinking returns from the market. These are trends that represent without a doubt the

Institutional change 189

transformation of solidarity moving away from broadly shared post-market equality of results across levels of achievement as well as from the solidarity of established status groups as part of an organic whole and towards a more differentiated solidarity with greater emphasis on achievement under the condition of equal opportunity (Streeck 2009). Other realms, where such steps of change towards the liberal idea of welfare can be observed, are the introduction of insurance for the care of disabled people (Lessenich 2003) and the complementation of the public pension system with a private pillar.

Relative exclusion and disorganization

The social cohesion of the conservative welfare state relies on the subsidiarity of family, organized status groups, the inclusionary work of large societal associations assuming public responsibility and the integrative power of the state. All of these are being weakened by processes of globalization, pluralization and individualization. Families have become less stable with every third marriage ending by divorce; status groups are losing in homogeneity because of internal differentiation and diminishing external demarcation; large societal associations like trade unions, employer associations and churches suffer from shrinking membership, the pluralization of interests and lifestyles and from the corresponding pluralization of associational life. The state's capacity for integration is being reduced by the increasing external entanglement and internal pluralization and individualization of social life. All of these collectivistic forms of inclusion have lost some of their power, on the one hand. On the other hand, individualistic forms of social inclusion have gained in importance. These are particularly educational achievements on the basis of broadened access to higher education, individual market performance and active participation in issue-specific networks. These individualistic forms of inclusion imply that individual achievement and individual activity become much more important for the inclusion of the individual in society than simple membership in families and status groups as well as representation by large established societal associations. In this way, the form of social inclusion moves indeed in the direction of the liberal regime and increasingly shares its peculiar dilemma of producing side effects of relative exclusion by way of promoting inclusion through educational and occupational achievement. More responsibility for inclusion is given to the single individual by taking up chances offered by the educational system and the market. Achievement becomes the central value guiding life course and life conduct.

Organic solidarity had a restraining effect on individual striving for achievement and on competition. Its side effect was privileging status groups and limiting access to positions for possible competitors. Family background decided very much about future status via education promoted by the family. Organic solidarity contributed to the high rate of self-reproduction of status groups from generation to generation pertaining to this system of stratification. The working class was incorporated in this system by the dual system of occupational training, which produced the well-situated status group of the German *Facharbeiter* whose high technical training contributed considerably to the production of affluence. According to the principle of organic solidarity it was beyond question that this well-trained status group deserved a respectable part of the collectively produced affluence. Working class inclusion in societal wealth proceeded well along the principle of organic solidarity.

The group of unskilled people was included in organic solidarity as long as there was sufficient demand for simple production work so that this group could be considered part of the broader working class. According to educational status differentiation the group was less respected and received lower pay, nevertheless it was an indispensable and integral part of the system of organic solidarity. Being part of an organic whole meant a guarantee of inclusion for the unskilled. Further on upward mobility was possible in this system particularly via a lifelong career within one's firm. The well-trained working class as well as the well-trained business agents (*Kaufleute*) served as a large pool of talented people whose special talents were discovered and promoted at work after they had left school. Even the less skilled people could see chances of being upgraded simply because their talent was not completely discovered at school. All this means that chances of achievement existed within the system of organic solidarity after school through proven talent, skills and motivation at work. In this way even the highly self-reproductive system of status differentiation according to educational title had its specific channel of upward mobility. Nevertheless, it included the mass of the working class more via collective wage growth than via individual achievement and upward mobility. This formed the institutional basis of the German conservative welfare regime's typical combination of higher educational and lower wage inequality. In contrast, the American liberal welfare regime combines lower educational with higher wage inequality, while the Swedish and Danish social democratic welfare regimes combine lower educational with lower wage inequality. Along with a growing emphasis on equality of opportunity in education, the conservative regime has to find a balance between the liberal and the social democratic model. There has been some change towards decreasing educational inequality and increasing income inequality in the meantime, however without coming really close to the situation in the United States.

This system lost its legitimacy in the 1960s when a public debate about the growing demand for higher education in an advanced industrial society producing and applying technology and about education as a civil right set in. Georg Picht (1964) and Ralf Dahrendorf (1965) travelled through the country to call out for the educational upgrading of coming generations. The political answer was a broad expansion of higher education in the *Gymnasium* and at university. The number of pupils in the Gymnasium rose from 5 per cent to as many as 30–40 per cent of an age cohort, that of students at university from 5 per cent to as many as 30 per cent of an age cohort between 1965 and 2000, depending on the situation in the individual *Bundesländer*. The new *Fachhochschulen* included only the smaller part of the growing number of students. The intended effect of this policy of educational upgrading was broader access of lower class and lower middle-class children to higher education. Because most of this upward mobility was absorbed by expansion in higher occupational positions, it did not imply a corresponding downward mobility. The unintended side effect of this process of educational upgrading was however downward displacement of people with few skills from middle ranges to the lowest ranges. Together with technological rationalization of industrial production this displacement process made the unskilled even drop out of the system of employment. In 2008, 39 per cent of the cohort from thirty to thirty-four years of age attained a high school (upper secondary) diploma and 24 per cent only a main school (lower secondary) diploma. For the cohort from sixty to sixty-four years of age, the percentages were at 19 and 52 respectively (BMBF 2010: 37).

The *Hauptschule* became the reservoir of youth with little expectation for the future in a society in which higher education set the entrance to middle and higher occupational positions. The nexus between family background, educational and occupational achievement was again strengthened after it had been broken up for the lower and lower middle class from the 1960s to the 1980s. After having widely exhausted the pool of talent, willingness and ability, the early selection for higher education is producing a new highly self-reproductive milieu of untrained people, which is no longer an integral and respected part of society. The still existing reliance of the conservative welfare state on the family's inclusionary function adds considerably to this production of a new underclass. Unsurprisingly, in the widely recognized PISA study the differentiated German educational system stood out with an exceptionally strong correlation between family background and reading as well as writing skills (Baumert *et al.* 2001). Whereas the unskilled were formerly part of a broader working class and contributed their indispensable part to the wealth of the organic whole, they have become widely dispensable in a system that offers jobs for skilled people only. The result is disrespect on the part of the well-situated majority and early frustration on the part of the marginalized group of underachievers (Bude 2008).

The conservative welfare state has produced its own type of relative exclusion (Schulze-Cleven 2009). Because respect and inclusion are no longer guaranteed just by being part of a group needed by the organic whole, but only through individual educational and occupational achievement, underachievers fall short of what has become the broadly accepted standard for all. They are shown what is generally attainable day by day, but realize that they themselves fail in attaining what is generally attainable. In comparison to what is attained by the great number of achievers, they feel relative deprivation, which we can also call relative exclusion. This is the situation in which motivation for slipping into careers compensating for relative deprivation grows, thus producing a greater rate of deviation in the widest sense, reaching from compliance without commitment and uninspired life conduct day by day right through to retreat, drug abuse and delinquency. This is the deeper reason behind rising crime rates in the German conservative welfare state since the 1960s, which refer directly to a considerable deficit of social cohesion.

In producing a greater amount of relative exclusion the conservative welfare state is converging with the liberal regime. However, it does so by the interaction

192 Institutional change

of individualization of social inclusion with the established institutional and cultural framework of organic solidarity, particularly the differentiated educational system alongside the weakened inclusionary power of family, status group, societal associations and state. What it would need in particular is compensating for disadvantage resulting from family background by all-day care for children and all-day schools. Another problem to be solved is early selection by the differentiated school system. At least ways to achievement from the *Hauptschule* have to be offered in order to install positive motivation. For all those who nevertheless do not achieve, additional training programmes fulfil the important function of keeping them within a system of respectful treatment by society. In as much as society gives up that kind of activation it openly excludes a group of marginalized people. Even if such programmes do not lead to real success of self-activation, society keeps those people within the confines of respect for the human being. This respect is particularly needed in a society that has turned to individual achievement as the major device of social inclusion, because otherwise it will suffer all the more from disorganization, disintegration and delinquency.

Adjustment in the egalitarian welfare state: Denmark and Sweden

The structure of solidarity and the social democratic idea of justice

Among the egalitarian welfare states Denmark has proved to be rather successful in adjusting to global competition since the mid-1990s, though the country underwent a crisis of economic decline with decreasing growth rates, hourly earnings and employment as well as rising social expenditure and public deficit from the mid-1980s to the mid-1990s. Unemployment had reached 11 per cent by 1993. Denmark adjusted to global competition with cutbacks of social benefits and with higher tax rates. Employment has always been only moderately protected making workforce displacement relatively easy in times of economic decline. Displacement is made acceptable for the workforce by generous state-financed replacement rates of 80–90 per cent of previous earnings for up to five years. Because unemployment benefits are primarily financed by state revenues labour costs for employers are not so much affected by unemployment expenditure. Generous unemployment protection has however been increasingly complemented with workfare programmes aiming at activating the jobless to qualify for return to work. Training, re-education and on-the-job experience have become mandatory. For young people benefits are cut back to 50 per cent after six months. Having introduced such labour market activation policies the country enjoyed a significant reduction of unemployment to 5.3 per cent until 2002 (Benner and Bundgaard Vad 2000: 448–452; Larsen and Mailand 2007). The total tax rate was at 52.2 per cent of GDP in 1996, which is on top in international comparison together with Sweden at 52.0 per cent. It was the basis for a still generous welfare system with public social expenditure of 32.1 per cent of GDP in 1995, which was on top together with Sweden at 33.0 per cent in 1995. Earnings dispersion D5/D1 was 1.44 (in 1993) and – also together with Sweden at 1.34 (in 1993) – lowest in international comparison, but it has been rising slightly in the recent process of adjustment to global competition (Scharpf and Schmidt 2000, Vol. I: 358, 360, 364, tables A.21, A.23, A.27). Denmark has reformed the welfare system in the direction of a liberal state, but has retained its core identity of being an egalitarian welfare state (Anderson 2004; Cox 2004; Etherington and Jones 2004; Martin 2004; Mailand 2006; Campbell and Pedersen 2007a, 2007b; Lindsay and McQuaid 2009). Figures for 2009 show a tax revenue as percentage of GDP at 48.2 per cent in Denmark and 46.4 per cent in Sweden. Public social expenditure was at 26.1 per cent in Denmark and 27.3 per cent in Sweden in 2007. The D5/D1 ratio amounted to 1.57 in Denmark and 1.37 in Sweden in 2008 (OECD 2011e).

Until the late 1980s, Sweden was economically more successful than Denmark in terms of economic growth, public deficit and employment rate. In the early 1990s however, the country suffered from a rapid economic decline with shrinking growth rates, strongly rising public deficit and an enormous drop of employment. Instead of previous growth rates between 2 and 3 per cent annually on average, the GDP declined by 1.1, 1.4 and 2.2 per cent respectively in 1991, 1992 and 1993; public sector deficit reached the record highs of 7.8, 12.3, 10.3 and 7.8 per cent of GDP in the years from 1992 to 1995. The employment rate dropped from 81.3 per cent of the population aged 15 to 64 in 1990 to 68.7 per cent in 1996. Correspondingly, the unemployment rate rose from 1.6 per cent to 8.1 per cent in that period. The country has however been on the way to recovery since 1997. Growth rates of real GDP have been between 1.3 and 3.9 per cent, the public sector deficit has disappeared and the decline of employment has stopped with a slight reduction of the unemployment rate occurring (Scharpf and Schmidt 2000, Vol. I: 339, 341–342, 358–359, tables A.2, A.4, A.5, A.22). Between 2001 and 2006, the growth rates went up from 0.7 to 3.4 per cent in Denmark and from 1.2 to 4.3 per cent in Sweden. The financial crisis of 2008 brought the rate down to –5.2 per cent in Denmark and –5.3 per cent in Sweden in 2009. Denmark recovered to 2.1 per cent, Sweden to 5.5 per cent in 2010 (OECD 2011e). General government financial balances were between +1.9 and +5.0 in Denmark and +0.4 and +3.5 in Sweden between 2004 and 2008 to turn to –2.8 and –4.6 in Denmark and –1.2 and –1.2 in Sweden in 2009 and 2010 (OECD 2010b). The unemployment rate was between 5.6 and 3.4 in Denmark and 7.8 and 5.3 in Sweden in the years between 2002 and 2008. In 2009, the figures were at 6.1 in Denmark and 8.5 in Sweden (OECD 2010e). Sweden has mastered the challenge of global competition though with a time lag and with greater reluctance with regard to cutbacks in social benefits and workfare programmes compared to Denmark. This difference may be explained by the much less challenged governance of the Social Democratic Party in Sweden in close cooperation with the trade unions confederation LO for a long time since the 1930s. However, this has changed as a result of the crisis during the mid-1990s. In Denmark the social democrats have always been forced to receive support from centre to right parties. The earlier willingness to complement the egalitarian social democratic welfare system with liberal elements is a result of this enforced coalition building (Benner and Bundgaard Vad 2000: 429–433).

Adjustments to global competition not only depend on structural features of a specific type of welfare state, but also on more accidental factors like Denmark's crisis in the 1980s and like the Danish social democrats' greater need for compromising with liberal forces. There was for example the tax revolt in the early 1970s in Denmark, which didn't happen in Sweden, though presently the even higher tax load is broadly accepted. It is nevertheless of special interest to our analysis how structural features of the egalitarian welfare state are shaping the adjustment to global competition. We should therefore specify the core features of this type of welfare state and then try to answer the question of their impact on adjustment to global competition.

The egalitarian Scandinavian welfare state has been shaped by the social philosophy of social democracy as an outcome of the labour movement's accommodation with modern capitalism. The social democratic parties discarded the Marxist programme of a revolutionary replacement of capitalism and liberal democracy by communism as a unitary form of government and the organization of production, consumption and distribution. The social democratic "revisionist" programme is aiming at a reconciliation of capitalist economic organization backing the ideal of a dignified life for everybody with a high level of social justice in the sense of the participation of everybody in the accumulated wealth of society. It is assumed that everybody is contributing to the production of wealth according to his or her capacities. In as far as everybody does his or her best, everybody should participate as far as possible in the collectively produced wealth. After having established civil rights and political rights in the process of emancipation, which started in Britain as early as in the seventeenth century and came to its broad completion in the early twentieth century with the realization of universal suffrage for men and women, social democratic policies have been focused on the extension of social rights throughout the twentieth century (Marshall 1964).

The key concept is citizenship, which is shared by the egalitarian and the liberal models of the welfare state and which makes both different to the conservative model. For the egalitarian and liberal models the society is composed of individual citizens who share equal civil, political and social rights. Both models are committed to universalism in terms of granting all citizens equal rights. Beyond citizenship all human individuals share equal human rights. The realization of equal human rights for everybody in the world is therefore a part of the liberal and egalitarian programmes that is reaching beyond the confines of nation states. In contrast to the liberal and social democratic society of individual citizens, the conservative model of the welfare state sees the human individual as a member of a family and of a status group, which are mediators to the broader society. The major difference between the liberal and the egalitarian models of society results from their contrasting views of the state and its role in providing for the citizens' welfare. In liberal terms the state plays only a residual role in helping where civic self-organization doesn't work. The liberal programme believes in the individual citizen's ability to achieve as far as he or she is not hindered by any barrier. It is therefore the duty of the state to remove any kind of such barriers in order to pave the way for the individual's freedom to act. Free markets are conceived as the device par excellence, which helps the individual carry out his or her freedom and which helps coordinate his or her actions to bring about a spontaneously integrated society without imposing constraint.

For the social democratic perspective the liberal programme is creating a society of selfish people in which the strong will carry out their freedom at the cost of the weak. The market in particular would need a strong hand in order to rectify the negative effects resulting from free competition. Particularly the inequality of outcomes of market competition in terms of income dispersion calls for correction through redistribution by the state. The individual citizen's welfare needs a high level of organization by the state, which has to provide for a broad infrastructure of the economy in particular, and for social life in general. It is therefore in line with this social philosophy to see the Scandinavian welfare state providing comprehensive service for society at the highest possible standard, for instance in childcare, kindergarten, education, job training, job placement, industrial policy, labour market policy, social security, health, cultural life, science and technology. Hence, the social democratic organization of society by the state requires much higher public expenditures than the liberal self-organization of society with only a residual role of the state. In this respect the social democratic programme is more compatible with the conservative programme, which also assigns the state a more comprehensive role of organizing social life.

In as much as the conservative programme is relying on the activities of organized status groups, trade unions, employer associations, churches and welfare organizations, it resembles the liberal self-organization of society. The difference is however that they are doing their job as semi-public agents of the state in the conservative model whereas we see a multiplicity of competing voluntary associations doing their job independently of the state in the liberal model. If there is little organization of social life below the state level, we have either an unorganized liberal society, which needs more state activity to correct its tendency to disruption or an unorganized conservative society with a state that is being overcharged in meeting the demands of organizing society (the Mediterranean model). The strong social democratic state is taking more or less advantage by collaborating with major parts of organized society. Cooperation with employer associations and trade unions has been of greatest significance for the success of the social democratic programme. Without this kind of "tripartism" the Swedish success would not have been possible. The coherence of cooperation networks has always been an advantage of the small Scandinavian welfare states in the world market (Katzenstein 1985, 2003, 2006).

When the tripartite cooperation slipped into crisis in Sweden in the 1980s because of a growing divide between the employers' federation (SAF) and the trade union confederation (LO), the state was being greatly weakened and unable to carry out the demanded reforms to cope with global competition. This breakdown of cooperation can be taken as a significant factor for explaining Sweden's sudden economic decline in the early 1990s. Previous cooperation between SAF and LO in offering employment for moderate wage agreements turned into mutual distrust and unwillingness to cooperate on central wage agreements. The established central wage bargaining between SAF and LO broke down and became increasingly replaced by decentralized wage bargaining in the 1980s (Iversen 1999: 125–151; Whyman 2003: 156).

Led by the internationalized firms the employers no longer accepted the strong wage compression promoted by LO in the 1970s. LO resisted moving away from this policy. The leading companies reacted with a steeply increasing capital flight in terms of foreign direct investment (Whyman 2003: 97, tab. 6.1). This left the government with greater pressure of adjusting to the increasing fluidity of capital and the rising competition on favourable conditions for profitable investment, particularly low taxation of capital. The long-established coordination of policies between government, employer federation and trade union confederation didn't work at a time of crisis when it was so badly needed. According to a conceptual distinction made by Vivien Schmidt (2000) the coordinative discourse within the closed circle of trustful partners, who had been familiar with each other for a long time, had to be replaced with a more heated public discourse in which the government was seeking support for reforms including cutbacks in social benefits without success. The government had to pay the prize for its failure of reform in the form of a huge public sector deficit and decreasing public sector employment. The employers reacted with an unprecedented rate of displacements resulting in a steeply growing unemployment rate in the early 1990s (Figure 4.1).

Though further economic decline and growth in unemployment could be stopped in the late 1990s it is still undecided whether the Swedish welfare state will be able to gain in flexibility with regard to the attraction of fluid profit-seeking capital and with regard to a return to full employment, which would require greater wage dispersion in order to promote employment in the private service sector. Full employment has always been a significant pillar of the Swedish egalitarian welfare state. According to the underlying social philosophy everybody has a right to work, because work is the basis of every citizen's standard of living, social status and personal identity. The other side of this coin is the dependence of a generous welfare state with comprehensive services on full employment for the sake of high public revenues from tax and comprehensive public services. Full employment is providing the resources needed for a welfare state with generous social benefits and comprehensive high quality services in the areas of childcare, education, health and help for the handicapped and elderly being available for the whole population.

This type of "institutionalized" comprehensive welfare is quite the opposite of "residual" welfare granted by the liberal state (Titmuss 1958). The whole population enjoys a high standard of living independent of achievement on the market. The commodification of the human individual resulting from the establishing of a free labour market by modern capitalism in Marxian terms is being reversed by a process of decommodification, as Esping-Andersen put it. Taking pensions, sickness benefits and unemployment insurance to set up a decommodification ranking, Sweden, Norway and Denmark rank absolutely highest at a score of 39.1, 38.3 and 38.1 in 1980; the conservative welfare states of Germany and France are ranked on a medium level with a score of 27.7 and 27.5 respectively, while the liberal welfare states of New Zealand, the United States and Australia reach a score of only 17.1, 13.8 and 13.0 respectively, and the moderately liberal welfare states of Ireland and the United Kingdom attain a score of 23.3 and 23.4 respectively (Esping-Andersen 1990: 52; cf. Bambra 2006; Vail 2010). It can be assumed that support of welfare benefits is greater where the number of people who are making use of such benefits is greater. For the egalitarian welfare state this is the whole population and not only a small part of underachievers, as is the case in the liberal welfare state. It is social benefits and jobs in the broadly expanded sector of public service that are attracting broad support for the welfare state. In this way the Scandinavian egalitarian welfare state succeeded in attracting the commitment not only of the working class but also of the middle class, which is far more reluctant to support welfare expenditure in liberal welfare states. This policy of comprehensive inclusion in the welfare state is in line with the very origins of the Swedish welfare state in the red-green coalition forged by the social democrats and the farmers.

Social benefits and employment in public service can however only be provided on the high level reached by the Scandinavian welfare state in as much as the system meets the requirements of the dynamics of capitalist competition, and this is all the more true under the condition of removed barriers for the movement of capital, goods and services across national borders. The Swedish economy with its large industrial sector of internationally active companies met this requirement with great success up to the end of the 1980s. This wouldn't have been possible without a special capacity of innovation and continuously occurring structural change. Sweden achieved in a special way in linking innovation with a wage policy of sectorally equal wages for the workforce. This equalizing policy of innovation is called the Rehn-Meidner model (Whyman 2003: 35–52). The two economists Gøsta Rehn and Rudolf Meidner presented this model for the first time in a report to the LO congress in 1951. It then became the guideline for central wage bargaining between SAF and LO. Agreements on general wage increase were centralized to bargaining between SAF and LO. Negotiations on hourly wages and overtime allowance were carried out between the employers' association and the trade union, which were responsible for a specific sector of the economy. Piecework rates were negotiated on the local level of individual companies. Though the LO policy was generally aiming at keeping local wage drift as low as possible, specific local agreements could amount to up to 50 per cent of total wage increases (Benner and Bundgaard Vad 2000: 403–404).

The Rehn-Meidner model combined an equalizing wage policy in centralized wage bargaining with an active labour market policy of the government. The rationale of the model was the fostering of productivity. The greater the productivity of the company the more it was able to keep the centrally agreed wage increase compatible with profitability, and the more it was capable of reinvesting profits in expanding production, which could imply investment in technology and in jobs. Wage increase should be on a medium level between the least and the most productive companies leaving the best companies more space for investment from profits and expelling the worst companies from the market. The result of this policy was intended to be continuous productivity growth with a corresponding rise of wages as well as a strong limitation of wage dispersion (Benner 1997). This model of productivity fostering and at the same time "solidaristic" wage policy produced comparatively high growth rates of the GDP with worldwide closest to equal share of the whole population up to the late 1980s, when a sudden economic decline set in. Compared to the United States at 100, GDP per capita in purchasing power parities was at 89 in 1982. In Denmark it was at 85.7, in Germany at 81.7, in France at 81.1 and in the UK at 70.5; however it dropped to 77.3 in 1993. In 1997, it was still at 77.2, which was well below Denmark at 83.3, the same as Germany at 77.7 (including East Germany) and above France at 71.7 and the UK at 73.9. The figures for 2008 were 78.0 in Sweden, 78.0 in Denmark, 75.1 in Germany, 70.1 in France, and 75.5 in the UK (OECD 2010d). Earnings dispersion D5/D1 figured between 1.30 and 1.36 in the period from 1980 to 1993, compared to about 1.40 in Denmark, 1.50 in Germany, 1.65 in France, 1.69–1.81 in the UK and 2.05–2.09 in the United States. It is the lowest level worldwide. In 2007, the D5/D1 ratio was at 1.40 in Sweden, 1.55 in Denmark, 1.47 in France, 1.81 in the UK, 1.93 in Germany and 2.11 in the USA (OECD 2011e). A D9/D1 comparison yields similar results. Employment protection and net replacement rates for unemployment rank among the absolutely highest worldwide. Employment protection is much stronger than in Denmark and similar to Germany and the Netherlands; replacement rates are similar to Denmark, Germany, the Netherlands and France (Scharpf and Schmidt 2000, Vol. I: 372, table A.34).

Displacement of workers from their jobs in companies that had to shut down because of underachievement in terms of productivity, was countered by an active labour market policy of the government focusing on further education, re-training and subsidized placement in new jobs. Attempts at an active industrial policy were strictly resisted by the SAF and discarded. All the more governments were focusing on the continuous upgrading of general and vocational education, further education and retraining as well as on investments in research and technological innovation. This special egalitarian innovation policy helped the economy to adjust to global competition by way of increasing productivity through technological rationalization and structural change towards rising industries, particularly in the field of information technology. Sweden is a top scorer in knowledge-based innovation in an international comparison – ahead of other Scandinavian countries and doing as well as or even better than the liberal welfare states of the United States and the United Kingdom.

Adjustment to globalized competition

As Martin Heidenreich (2004b) has pointed out, the Scandinavian countries are combining a worldwide top scoring level of general education of the whole population with a high level of vocational training and a high level of investments in innovations based on science and technology; this results in structural change with a shift away from labour-intensive industries and towards knowledge-based ones (see also Heidenreich 2004a). His study suggests that the Scandinavian welfare states have achieved in combining a high level of equality and social security (decommodification) with a remarkable capacity for radical technological innovation and structural change. This strategy looks like a third way between the liberal regime of radical innovation on the basis of fluid capital, weak and fragmented representation of employee interests, general education and competition for instead of collaboration in innovation on the one hand, and the conservative regime of incremental innovation based on patient capital, strong coordinated representation of employee interests, corporatist cooperation of employers associations, unions and the state, emphasis on dual vocational training and collaboration of firms in technological innovation on the other hand. There seem to be good reasons to question the dichotomy of the two regimes drawn by Hall and Soskice (2001) and to focus interest on the capacity of combining equality and comprehensive welfare with incremental as well as radical innovation and structural change as demonstrated by the Scandinavian egalitarian welfare states. Sweden's leading position in this respect provides at least solid ground for the country's economic recovery after it had slipped into economic decline in the early 1990s. It is also a solid basis for being able to adjust to globalized competition without having to abandon its identity as an egalitarian welfare state. Changes in the direction taken by Denmark in terms of reduced employment protection combined with generous unemployment benefits and strong workfare programmes as well as some increase in wage dispersion to offer better incentives for education, further education and retraining and a better allocation of persons to jobs have improved Sweden's position without it having to abandon the whole model of an egalitarian welfare state (Lindbom 2001; Anderson 2004; Cox 2004; Harrysson and Petersson 2004; Kangas *et al.* 2010).

Decentralization contributed to slightly increasing wage dispersion in the 1980s (Iversen 1999: 128). This trend took place, however, on an unchanged high level of wages, that is, in terms of upward wage drift, so that competitiveness in terms of labour costs could not be improved. The rather unorganized breakdown of central wage bargaining did not produce the wage constraint intended by employers. Hopes were therefore pinned on the establishment of centrally organized decentralization of wage bargaining with a renewal of public responsibility of the bargaining partners setting the confines of wage increases on the central level with an eye on the overall economic situation, and leaving the conclusion of special agreements to the different sectors and to the individual companies (Whyman 2003: 155–158). The success of such a strategy was,

200   Institutional change

however, questioned by sceptical positions arguing that such a system would lead to raising wages above the level of competitiveness of the different economic sectors. The reason for this upward "distortion" of wages is – according to the sceptical view – the interest of trade union representatives in receiving support from their clientele by concluding wage agreements above the centrally agreed level (Björklund 2000: 152). Furthermore, greater wage dispersion was demanded in order to reflect unequal value creation according to skills. Wage compression was being made responsible for a lack of incentives for highly skilled people to seek further education and for the high rate of unemployment of the unskilled. There was also demand for lowering standards of employment protection, for increasing working hours and for promoting non-standard employment (Björklund 2000: 152–155). Only very modest changes have taken place in this direction so that the Swedish welfare state has largely retained its egalitarian character (Björklund 2000: 155–159). Changes in the direction of greater wage dispersion according to value creation have adjusted the welfare state not only to globalized economic competition but also to the modifications in social structure and solidarity in the direction of pluralization and individualization, which have taken place on the way from a heavily industrial society with strong national solidarity towards a post-industrial society with a nation-transcending multilevel solidarity. Sweden has recovered from the crisis along this way. Having reached a level of around 8 per cent in the years from 1993 to 1997, the unemployment rate has dropped to arrive at 5.1 per cent in 2001 (Scharpf and Schmidt 2000, Vol. I: 341, table A.4; Mishel et al. 2003: 429). Afterwards it rose again to 7.8 per cent in 2005 to go down to 6.2 per cent in 2007 and 2008 and to rise to 8.5 per cent in 2009 after the financial crisis of 2008 (OECD 2010, Labour Market Statistics).

Looking at the data gathered in Heidenreich's study (2004b), we will indeed find Sweden, Denmark and Finland on top with regard to a variety of criteria measuring the capacity for high-tech innovation. The Scandinavian countries scored as high as the Anglo-Saxon ones and higher than the Continental European and the Mediterranean countries in the PISA tests with regard to reading literacy, mathematical literacy and scientific literacy. The percentage of the population having at least an upper secondary education is highest in international comparison, namely 89 per cent, compared to 75 per cent in the Anglo-Saxon countries, 77 per cent in Continental Europe and 53 per cent in the Mediterranean countries (OECD 2001b, 2001d). Sweden is not far away from Germany in the enrolment in apprenticeships, but better in reading literacy according to PISA 2000, 2003 and 2006 (Heidenreich 2004a). In 2008, the population of males (age group 25–64) with at least upper secondary education was 83 per cent in Sweden, 79 per cent in Finland, 76 per cent in Denmark, 71 per cent in the UK, 88 per cent in the USA and 88 per cent in Germany (OECD 2010a). The knowledge-intensity of work is highest in Denmark, the Netherlands, Finland and Sweden. These countries are ranking ahead of Austria, France, Great Britain and Germany, and far ahead of Italy, Spain, Ireland, Luxembourg, Portugal and Greece (Heidenreich 2004b).

In accordance with a report published by the European Commission in September 2001, Sweden headed an innovation scale covering the then fifteen EU member states as well as the United States and Japan at that time. The scale is based on an innovation index of seventeen variables. At the top, there are also two other Scandinavian welfare states, namely Finland and Denmark alongside the liberal welfare states of the United States and the United Kingdom, and Japan as the most innovation-fostering conservative welfare state. The conservative welfare states of Germany and France only rank in the middle of the scale. The Mediterranean countries can be found at the bottom of the scale (European Commission 2001, 2001 Innovation scoreboard).

Sweden along with the other Scandinavian countries is outranking Germany and the other conservative Continental European welfare states and is matching the United States and the other liberal welfare states not only with regard to investments in innovation but also in the implementation of innovations in high-tech manufacturing (2.7 per cent in the egalitarian Scandinavian countries with Sweden at the top at 3.5 per cent compared to 2.2 per cent in conservative Continental European and 4.1 per cent in liberal Anglo-Saxon countries), and high-tech industries' trade coverage ratios of exports and imports (1.03 and 1.47 compared to 0.93 and 0.8). The Scandinavian countries have however also a higher trade coverage ratio of exports and imports in medium to low-tech and in low-tech industries. They are below the scores of the other countries in medium technology manufacturing and knowledge-intensive market services (OECD 2001a, 2001c). In 2006, business R&D in the manufacturing sector in high technology as percentage of manufacturing was at 67.3 per cent in the USA, 52.6 per cent in Sweden and 34.3 per cent in Germany (OECD 2009b).

We can say that the Scandinavian egalitarian welfare state has proved capable of adjusting to globalized competition with the crucial strategy of combining incremental as well as radical innovation with maintaining high levels of employment, equality, social benefits and public service for the whole population (Campbell and Pedersen 2007a, 2007b; Huo et al. 2008). Sweden was most successful until the end of the 1980s when it slipped into a rapid economic decline. Denmark was challenged to master economic underperformance earlier than Sweden in the 1980s, but achieved in promoting reforms in the mid-1990s through the combination of low employment protection, generous unemployment compensation and strong workfare programmes as well as the fostering of innovation and the shift to a post-industrial economy. Though the egalitarian programme was enriched with liberal elements and inequality has risen slightly, the country can still be identified as a predominantly egalitarian welfare state (Lindsay and Mailand 2004; Schulze-Cleven 2009).

Sweden has recovered since the late 1990s. The country has managed reforms of the kind undertaken by Denmark to attain a lasting return to full employment and the previous performance in innovation and structural change. A special problem may be that the shift towards a post-industrial economy is concentrated on the expansion of public sector services of welfare. This is in marked difference to the United States, where this shift has included the expansion of private services much more. A glance at the data shows that this private service expansion is including high quality technical services (financial experts, lawyers, housing, medical service, teachers, therapists, counsellors) as well as "McDonald's" jobs in the United States. However, the Swedish government has pushed changes towards an expanding private service sector by way of privatizing welfare services with the so-called choice revolution (Blomqvist 2004). This revolution gives the citizens a choice between competing public and private services, from kindergarten and school right through to care for the elderly. There is no evidence of the thesis that an expanding service sector would produce overwhelmingly McDonald's jobs. However, there is no doubt either that a considerable part of the service sector has to offer such jobs for educational underachievers, if they aren't to be sent into enduring unemployment. Slightly increased wage dispersion seems to be an unavoidable step towards expanding private service. A small step in this direction may possibly be enough, because a merely modest wage dispersion is broadly accepted by the population. Under this cultural condition, a modest wage dispersion produces similar incentives as higher wage dispersion in a country with a liberal tradition. It is remarkable that the United States is better above all in the number of service jobs that offer "fun services", as Esping-Andersen (1990: 204) has noticed for the 1980s. These are the jobs in entertainment, for which the United States claims world leadership, and which are far away from simple McDonald's services. It is a special challenge for the European economies to close up to the leadership of the United States in this respect. Such a movement towards an expanding entertainment economy is still in its infancy in Europe. The same is true for the penetration of information technology into the various areas of the economy, from production to public administration and private life.

The United States is far ahead in this area of innovation. The information society is still in the making in Europe, and lags well behind the leadership of the United States. It is in this area where new jobs are being created. And it is this movement towards a post-industrial economy that is fostering the change in social structure and individual lifestyle towards pluralization, individualization and the multilevel organization of social life. With this change the solidarity structure is being transformed. In as much as the welfare system has been linked to a solidarity structure of a largely homogenous population sharing similar work and employment conditions it is under pressure of change in order to adjust to the more differentiated structure of multilevel solidarity being pluralized within the nation state and stretching beyond the nation state to reach the European and global levels.

The transformation of solidarity is stretching solidarity beyond the established boundaries of nations of full-time employed white males to include both genders and a multiplicity of racial and ethnic groups. It is no accident that the liberal welfare state of the United States has achieved much more in this respect than the European conservative and egalitarian welfare states. The strong solidarity of full-time employed white males and their representation in trade unions, parties and governments have hampered the inclusion of women and racial and ethnic minorities. Though the Scandinavian welfare states have fully included women in the working population, they provide an extremely segregated labour market for women and men. The inclusion of women in employment has taken place almost exclusively in the field of public social service. Women have turned from unpaid caring for children and elderly within the family to paid caring for children and elderly outside the family in public organizations. They send their own children to one kindergarten in order to care for other children in a different kindergarten. Women are extremely underrepresented in industrial, technical and managerial jobs. Leading positions are still an exclusive domain of men. In this respect the Swedish egalitarian welfare state is far away from the achievements of the American liberal welfare state and is not much better than Continental European conservative welfare states (Esping-Andersen 1990: 208–217). However, Sweden has undertaken steps towards a change in this direction (Gorlov 2009).

Relative exclusion and disorganization

In comparison with the liberal and the conservative welfare states the Scandinavian social democratic welfare state has achieved in attaining a high level of skilled labour force, knowledge-based innovation, economic growth, employment and equality of results. Phases of higher unemployment rates were tackled with comparatively good success. In this respect the Scandinavian societies still stand out as being highly cohesive. Nevertheless, it cannot be denied that changes in a more liberal direction have taken place in the face of intensified global competition, increasing FDI of Swedish firms outside the country, unemployment and public deficit. And more change in this direction is being demanded by critics of the social democratic welfare state in order to improve economic performance as well as participation of marginalized groups in economic and social life. The social democratic welfare state has achieved in attaining a very high level of education, nevertheless it has also produced a marginalized group of educational and occupational underachievers. On the one hand, solidarity wage has exerted enormous pressure on enhancing productivity by way of technological rationalization so that unskilled workforce in industrial production has increasingly been sent into joblessness. On the other hand, solidarity wage has advanced minimum wages to such a high level and has compressed earnings so extremely that further education and the upgrading of skills is no profitable goal, particularly for the lowest income group. The growth of employment in public service has offered skilled women an increasing number of jobs in clerical service, healthcare, childcare and education. Unskilled men have not been able to take such jobs, but have instead filled the files of unemployment administration. High minimum wages and high unemployment compensation have neither encouraged employers to offer jobs to unskilled workforce nor jobless people to take a job.

This outcome of educational upgrading together with solidarity wage policy under the pressure of globalized competition has been mainly made responsible for increasing rates of unemployment, particularly of unskilled people. In the midst of an all-inclusive society a group of outsiders has emerged who have no more access to the core of the social democratic welfare state: employment. Though they are in a far better situation than non-working or working poor in the United States, these people nevertheless experience relative exclusion. Without a job they are no longer an integral part of a society dedicated to collectively shared welfare based on full employment. Compared to what is attainable and what is attained by the great majority they might feel being excluded as much as underachievers in the liberal American regime do. Similar to the conservative regime the social democratic welfare state has been pushed a step towards individualized inclusion, because educational achievement has become more important than ever before in order to be an integral part of the collective production of collectively shared welfare. It is therefore quite logical that we see much higher unemployment rates of the unskilled compared to better skilled people particularly in Sweden (see Chapter 5, Figure 5.5). This is also reflected in the comparatively high rate of jobless youths (see Table 4.1). The educational system in Sweden shows exactly the problems arising when inclusion is shifted primarily to the tracks of educational achievement. Sweden has relocated educational responsibility down to the level of local communities with the result of a greater dispersion of the quality of schools. There is a wider variety of schools and a great choice for parents and pupils (Blomqvist 2004). Nevertheless, the social democratic values of comprehensiveness and equality have been maintained as yardsticks of school performance (Helgøy and Homme 2006). Elite schools have differentiated from average establishments. Qualification deficits of the teaching staff, lack of homework assignments and regular evaluation only in the final classes are blamed for having too many pupils with insufficient achievements in at least one subject in class 9 of the regular school. Knowledge in mathematics, natural sciences and a second foreign language after English is claimed to have declined. Because every youngster is expected to go through the final phase of three years of high school preparing for university studies a quite considerable number fail to meet higher standards of theoretical knowledge, but do not receive practical occupational training either, and are thus misqualified for the labour market (Daun 2003; Björklund et al. 2005; Korpi and Tahlin 2008). The country therefore suffers from similar relative exclusion of unskilled or wrongly skilled people as the liberal welfare states (Myrberg and Rosén 2006; Westling 2007; Norberg-Schönfeldt 2008). Denmark is doing a bit better in this respect because of its greater efforts of bringing back people to jobs by combining moderate unemployment protection with high replacement rates of earnings in the case of unemployment and workfare programmes.

As far as our analysis is correct we should expect that increased relative exclusion is being reflected in delinquency rates. This is indeed so. According to World Bank data rates of robberies have risen in Denmark and Sweden since the mid-1980s. The rates are higher in Sweden than in Denmark, but lower than in a number of other countries (see Chapter 5, Figure 5.1). However, victimization data regarding property crimes shows Denmark and Sweden above average and in the neighbourhood of the United States (see Figure 4.11). For explaining this phenomenon of disintegration of the social democratic welfare state, we first have to take into account the trend towards individualized inclusion via educational and occupational achievement, which drives the social democratic welfare state a step towards the liberal regime. Its tendency to produce disintegration is being supported by a number of weaknesses. Though not as important as in the conservative welfare regime the family has lost stability with comparatively very high divorce rates. This destabilization of the family weakens an important factor of social inclusion of the individual and breaks down barriers against compensating relative exclusion in deviant careers.

The Scandinavian model of state care for children from birth on surely makes a child's education largely independent of the family's stability. Nevertheless the coordination of work and family for parents has provoked debates about the complementation of state care by parental leave and even cash benefits for childcare offering parents the choice between work and family as is preferred in the conservative welfare state. Schemes of parental leave have complemented state care in the meantime. Cash benefits for childcare are, however, highly controversial. They were introduced in Sweden by the centre-conservative government in 1994, but withdrawn the following year by the new social democratic government. However, Finland and Norway have implemented such schemes. The controversy about childcare benefit schemes results from their deviation from the model of the double-earner family relying widely on the state's provision for childcare and their tendency to support a return to the conservative model of the male breadwinner family. Though open to fathers and mothers alike, only a small minority of fathers are making use of parental leave and childcare benefits (Leira 2002). The controversy nevertheless reflects the intensified search for means that help to overcome the apparently existing problems of offering children comprehensive integration in a society that has become more open and more competitive in character.

Further on, counteracting institutional forces typical of the social democratic welfare state are apparently not strong enough to keep motivation for deviant careers down. Though inclusive in upgrading the great majority of an age cohort in terms of education schools have only limited capacity in keeping underachievers within conforming confines, though the broad availability of all-day schools is a necessary device for that.

A further element that has to be considered is the reluctance of the social democratic welfare state to apply a deterrence policy of high success rates of cleared up crimes, quick sentencing and hard punishments (see Figure 4.12). The belief in the integrative power of the welfare state does not allow turning to such a liberal policy, which would have to admit that the welfare state is no longer fulfilling all of its assigned functions. There are at least signs telling us such a story. In this respect the social democratic welfare state joins the conservative regime in having evoked forces of disintegration by turning to individualized inclusion according to individual instead of collective achievement. Both have come closer to the liberal regime in this respect and both might be required to go a step towards corresponding liberal remedies, namely deterrence instead of welfare in order to keep delinquency rates down.

However, before following the liberal regime on its track, there is still a reservoir of devices fitting in the conservative as well as the social democratic welfare philosophy, namely making extensive use of programmes of education, training and activation beyond school. Though this strategy might produce a social milieu that is permanently dependent on such help, with a greater part not returning to regular work, even in their failing they have the side effect of keeping this milieu within the boundaries of society and surely under social control. Besides their primary function of activating and reactivating underachievers, such programmes fulfil the important secondary function of demonstrating society's willingness to help and to keep those who are not really activated or reactivated within the boundaries of conformity. Greater investments in these kinds of seemingly "inefficient" social programmes will remain an important demarcation line between a social democratic and/or conservative welfare state and their liberal counterpart. It is the basis on which deterrence and punishment will only be widely considered legitimate within the boundaries of the social democratic and the conservative welfare philosophy. Apart from activation and maintaining conformity, legitimation of punishment is the third function fulfilled by social programmes of activation and reactivation.

Globalized economic competition exerts pressure on welfare states to advance in science, technology and education. There is little space for simple production work. Educational upgrading has therefore become the central strategy of improving competitiveness. This response to globalized competition gives older policies of educational upgrading a special push. These policies originated in the 1970s as programmes of improving equal opportunity in order to overcome the reproduction of class membership from generation to generation. Such policies have been introduced in liberal, conservative and social democratic welfare states in the same way, thus representing a major point of convergence between them. By shifting policies of equalization towards the educational upgrading of the broad majority – at best 100 per cent – of the population, the conservative and the social democratic welfare states have implanted the central strategy of attaining equality of liberal welfare regimes. Attaining pre-market equality of opportunity has gained greater importance so that the conservative idea of inclusion through collective representation by status organizations, as well as the social democratic idea of inclusion through collective representation by trade unions and post-market redistribution, have become less important. The latter have also become less effective because educational upgrading has made men and women capable of leading a responsible life on their own, independently of any kind of organized care.

The consequence of this policy shift is the turning away of social inclusion from collective representation and towards individual achievement on the basis of equal opportunity in the access to education. Inclusion has become individualized. The result of this individualization of inclusion is greater emphasis on individual achievement and shrinking inclusion independently of achievement. Because society offers everybody best chances through educational achievement, there is little reason for comprehensive collective compensation of underachievement and particularly little reason for the collective recognition of underachievers. The latter have to cope with this situation by themselves. Because the collective praise of achievement on the basis of equal opportunity makes underachievement particularly frustrating, underachievers are easily put on the path for a deviant or even delinquent career. This frustrating perspective hits particularly unskilled young men who do not make their way on the paths of educational upgrading (Westgaard-Nielson 2008).

The broadening of access to higher education at first enhanced educational upward mobility from the working class to the middle class. A further effect has, however, been the concentration of inability to achieve educationally within a newly created underclass, from which there is no hope of any upward mobility through educational achievement. In creating such a milieu of a marginalized underclass, both the conservative and the social democratic welfare states have joined the liberal ones. This effect of shifting towards individualized inclusion is additionally aggravated by the transmission of jobs in simple production work from the highly developed industrial societies to developing and newly industrializing societies. If the welfare states do not achieve in compensating for this loss of jobs in simple production by creating new jobs in service work, there are no jobs for the new underclass and no chances of achievement and recognition in a society devoted to individual achievement on the basis of equal opportunity. It is therefore easy to predict increasing rates of delinquency and overrepresentation of the new underclass in acts of delinquency not only in liberal welfare states, but also in conservative and social democratic ones. This trend comes out in a particularly blatant way, the more the special institutions of inclusion typical of the different welfare regimes are weakened. For the liberal welfare regime, it is the flexible labour market with low unemployment rates of unskilled males 15–30 years old and short duration of unemployment. For the conservative welfare state, it is particularly the stable family with a low divorce rate and a low rate of single-parent households. For the social democratic welfare state, it is little earnings dispersion, a low unemployment rate of unskilled males 15–30 years old and broad educational achievement. However, most welfare states have problems in meeting their special requirements of inclusion and suffer additionally from failing to meet the inclusion standards, which are not typical of them but which are nevertheless important as protective shields against increasing disorganization and delinquency rates. Thus high unemployment rates of unskilled males 15–30 years old, long duration of unemployment, high rates of divorce and single-parent households, increasing earnings dispersion and a considerable rate of educational underachievement hit welfare states across liberal, conservative and social democratic regimes.

The politics of adjustment: between compromising interest coordination and uncompromising public debate

The change in solidarity that is taking place in the process of globalization and modernization is calling particularly for reforms in order to re-establish innovative strength to foster the structural change in the conservative and egalitarian welfare states. There is at least some evidence that there is a way for the egalitarian welfare state towards a more open, more rapidly changing, more pluralistic and more individualized society with a differentiated structure of multilevel solidarity, which is joining the liberal welfare states in terms of flexibility, innovation, change and shift to a post-industrial economy, but which is retaining the core features of egalitarianism in a revised form. The revision that is taking place is producing a form of egalitarianism that offers a larger space for individual differentiation than the egalitarianism of the past. This is demonstrated, for example, by the significance the concept of the entrepreneur has attained as a crucial force of innovation not only in the realm of the economy, but in any other field of society, too, in Swedish public discourse (Marttila 2010).

The ability to find and implement identity-preserving reforms successfully depends on the existing structure of the welfare state, and on how far this structure allows for adjustments to new challenges without slipping into an identity crisis. It is most easy for the liberal welfare state to revitalize its liberal tradition in order to cope with globalized competition, nation transcending and internally differentiating solidarity, the pluralization of social structure and the individualization of lifestyles. This underlines our finding that states with a liberal tradition were the forerunners of reform under the label of "neo-liberalism". In as much as such liberal traditions exist and are being revitalized in a predominantly egalitarian or conservative welfare state, there is a good chance that reforms aiming at including liberal elements receive some support and are succeeding in political struggles. This constellation can be held responsible for the liberal reforms in the Danish and Swedish egalitarian welfare states. In a similar way, it was possible for the Netherlands to recover from a deep economic crisis with an extraordinary unemployment rate of up to 14 per cent in the 1980s, beginning with a revitalization of corporatist consensus formation between employers and unions in 1982. Moderate wage increases, the fostering of part-time work and an active labour market policy reduced the unemployment rate to 3.5 per cent in the late 1990s, and have considerably raised the previously very low employment rate of women.

What the Netherlands and Denmark have in common on their road towards recovery is the deep economic crisis they underwent in the 1980s, and which paved the way for a willingness to new cooperation aiming at reform of the major political forces and the capacity to find a way to interest coordination in coordinative discourse, though no such discourse had existed before for a long time. Sweden experienced a similar crisis in the early 1990s and followed Denmark and the Netherlands on the way to recovery. In coordinative discourse the major political forces are trying to find a line of consensus that is to the good of the whole of society. Coordinative discourse has to be distinguished from public discourse according to an analysis carried out by Vivien Schmidt (2000). Coordinative discourse is drawing their attention to the good of society and somewhat away from their particular short-term interests so that the blocking of reforms by negatively affected short-term particularistic interests can be overcome. Politics is enabled to escape the traps of mingling distributive conflicts between short-term interests and technical problem solutions to the good of society and the entire population. It is being rescued from the trap of politics entanglement (*Politikverflechtungsfalle*) in Fritz Scharpf's terms (Scharpf et al. 1976).

Coordinative discourse between political actors who are willing to trust and to cooperate is an important corrective of public discourse, which tends to fuel uncompromising confrontation because it is taking place in an arena in which representative speakers have to speak up unrelentingly for the interests of their clientele in order to have assured their support and loyalty and to prevent opponents from defining the situation in their own particular interest. They also have to avoid making concessions without being sure of being rewarded by concessions of the other side.

The more politics is slipping into public discourse without a footing in coordinative discourse the more its capacity for reform affecting short-term particularistic interests is shrinking. It is striking to note that the two especially successful welfare states – the Netherlands and Denmark representing the conservative and egalitarian models – were able to find a way to reform because they achieved in establishing an effective coordinative discourse. The Netherlands revitalized the cooperation between the employers' federation and the trade unions' confederation in a special agreement in 1982. Denmark overcame a long-lasting inability to form stable political coalitions by stepping away from public ideological confrontation and moving towards situationally formed pragmatic alliances in the solution of practical problems. It is also striking to see that Sweden was enormously weakened by the breakdown of SAF-LO cooperation and the transfer of the search for practical problem solutions to the arena of uncompromising public debate. This explains the country lagging behind Denmark in recovering through effective reforms.

The increasing domination of uncompromising public discourse over compromising coordinative discourse is an important factor when it comes to explaining Germany's failure to overcome its economic crisis with effective reforms for a rather long time. Moreover, the country's economic crisis was not as deep as in the Netherlands and in Denmark during the 1980s, and added to this there is the special handicap of reunification. This explains at least in part the special German problems of mastering economic decline. However, the increasing domination of public discourse over coordinative discourse as the main arena of political problem solving has to be taken into account in order to give an appropriate explanation of Germany's special adjustment problems.

Though the structure of the conservative welfare state displays features that hinder reform there are nevertheless vital liberal and egalitarian traditions that would help to find a way of modernizing the welfare system to overcome its peculiar problems in terms of flexibility and gender equality, as demonstrated by the Dutch conservative welfare state. This draws our attention all the more to the political structure of society, which appears as the crucial barrier to reform. Presently, it seems to foster the blocking of reforms by affected short-term interests more than is the case in the political structure of the Netherlands and Denmark.

210 *Institutional change*

This has not always been like that in the past. The country's success in economic growth, technological rationalization and social integration was particularly favoured by the establishment of a special consensus model, which entailed far-reaching cooperation between employers and unions as well as between all political forces in coordinative discourse. Consensus formation in coordinative discourse implied, however, also the establishment of a relatively closed policy community, some kind of a cartel, which solved problems at the expense of unrepresented interests, particularly unemployed people, women, immigrants and upcoming younger generations.

The cartel dominating coordinative discourse became insensitive to the problems arising outside of its confines and ran the country in its current crisis. Its inability to solve the problems created by itself led to an increasing withdrawal of political forces from coordinative talk and to a turn to public discourse. Employers began to campaign for improving the competitiveness of the economy (the "Standort Deutschland"). The trade unions answered by emphasizing the competitive strength of peaceful working conditions. Discourse left the arena of compromising coordination and entered that of uncompromising public debate. This trend can be observed in a variety of policy fields where major political actors turn from coordinative talk to heated public debate and do not find a way back to compromising coordination. Reform is demanded in taxation, the pension system, employment and medical service. All this has been publicly debated for a long time, and it has taken a while to make the appropriate steps towards successful reforms.

With the turn of policy-making to public debate a special feature of the German political structure is increasingly weakening the government's capacity to rule. It is the federal system, which entails the splitting up of governmental power between the federal government (*Bund*) and the individual states of the federation (*Länder*). In the current situation of heated public struggle for reform the governments of the individual states are increasingly using their power to resist legislation by the federal government on the basis of the federal parliament's (*Bundestag*) majority. The state chamber (*Bundesrat*) has been increasingly used by the state governments, which are of a different political colour than the federal government, to get a second chance of opposition in party-political terms. If the majority in the state chamber is of a different colour than the majority in the federal parliament, legislation is being paralysed. Proposals disapproved by the state chamber have to undergo mediation by a special committee of representative members of both chambers. Because federal, state and local elections are not coordinated, there is a trend towards permanent campaigning of the political parties. As soon as one campaign has stopped on election day, the campaign for the next election starts already.

This turn from coordinative talk to public debate and permanent campaigning is accompanied by a change in political representation. Because of the pluralization of the social structure and the individualization of life careers and lifestyles political parties and interest associations are losing their power of integrating a greater variety of interests. The number of loyal voters is shrinking, and the number of floating voters is rising. This calls for greater investments in campaigning in order to achieve in elections. Trade unions, employers' associations and churches are suffering from shrinking membership, while new associations and churches are emerging, making for a more pluralized civil society. This trend represents the pluralization of social structure and interests. The representation of interests is being made increasingly complicated. The coordination of interests by the well-established associations is being unmasked as a cartel, which needs to be demolished in order to grant access to political decision-making to a greater variety of interests. The so-called revolution in political participation in the 1970s, which had been preceded by the students' movement in the second half of the 1960s, consisted, in particular, of addressing the public by way of attracting the attention of the media to spectacular actions including civil disobedience. The inability of the established cartel to incorporate new interests was handing over the promotion of these interests to public discourse. This was the way of the Green movement, which eventually led to the establishment and regular parliamentary as well as governmental representation of the Green Party. The result was a fundamental change in the system of political parties. It was an inclusion of a so far excluded interest into the party system caused by the inability of the established parties to incorporate the new movement and by the representative voting system, which allows small parties to be represented in parliament (as far as they obtain at least 5 per cent of the votes).

The inclusion of the Green Party can be called a successful transformation of the party system to represent a greater variety of interests. The process was however part of a transformation of interest representation, which ended with the demise of the established cartel of parties and representative associations, and which shifted political decision-making away from compromising coordinative discourse and towards uncompromising public debate. The legends of unsuccessful reform committees of experts who did their work but have never seen their proposals put into legislation give a lively expression of this transformation of politics. Their number has grown enormously as has the number of their meetings; yet the number of non-implementations of committee reports has also increased enormously. To have a tiny step of reform implemented mountains of papers and reports have to be produced. This is what we can call an inflation of power, which is caused by the new discourse (Münch 1995). The power of the government is undergoing a devaluation process because its majority increasingly needs mountains of reports from experts to bring about increasingly smaller steps of reform.

This shift of political decision-making from coordinative discourse to public debate has also been described as a process of medialization of politics (Münch 1991). It is a process to be observed everywhere, the consequence of which is increasing participation in the form of public attention, but decreasing governmental capacity for effective legislation. Federal systems seem to be especially affected by this transformation of politics, as is demonstrated by the United States and Germany as well. Though the United States was able to adjust most quickly to the globalization of economic competition by revitalizing its liberal tradition through deregulation, it is also clear that the US government lacks the power needed to control the disruptive effects of deregulated markets in order to achieve in social integration. In this respect we can also speak of the enormous adjustment deficits of the United States. In Germany it is the other way round. For a long time, German governments have lacked the power to adjust to globalized competition by way of effective reform with the effect of enduring economic underperformance and social disintegration. Lacking power has prevented the US government from including new egalitarian elements in its liberal welfare regime. Lacking power prevented the German government from including new liberal and egalitarian elements in its conservative welfare regime until the recent reforms.

The lesson we should learn from this result of our analysis can be summarized in the following statement: Liberal, conservative and egalitarian welfare states are all under pressure to adjust to globalizing competition and to the transformation of social structure, life careers, lifestyles and solidarity. Their history of institution building sets the frame within which adjustment takes place. Every primary frame entails secondary aspects of other frames, which can serve as elements facilitating reform. According to path dependency, past history and established frames are the starting conditions of reform, but they do not prevent reform in principle. Past achievement within specific frames is no guarantee of continued achievement, particularly under changed external and internal conditions. Change in such conditions requires changes in the frame in order to re-establish a balance between supply of and demand for institutional performance. Countries representing the three types of welfare states have achieved in adjusting to the new conditions.

The achievements of the liberal welfare states are accompanied by their underperformance in terms of social integration. The Netherlands represents achievements of the conservative type of welfare state; Denmark and Sweden stand for achievements of a social-democratic egalitarian type of welfare state. Germany may be taken as representing the specific adjustment problems of a conservative welfare state. There is some truth in this interpretation. However, it should also be taken into account that Germany's delay in undertaking reforms was caused not only by path dependency and misfit of the conservative type of welfare state with the pluralization of the social structure, the individualization of life careers and lifestyles, and the fostering of a post-industrial economy. It has to be explained also by the transformation of democracy with a shift from the cartel of interest coordination to the domination of uncompromising public debate in the media.

5 Relative exclusion and disintegration

Convergence in the liberal competition state?

Drawing on anomie theory as established by Emile Durkheim and Robert K. Merton, this chapter attempts to show that relative exclusion is an essential cause of disintegrative phenomena such as delinquency rising beyond the limits conceived as "normal" in society and has become a widespread phenomenon in contemporary welfare states. It has long been a characteristic feature of the American society, which represents the liberal welfare regime. More recently, it has also considerably hit the European societies representing the conservative and social democratic types of welfare regimes. It is a point of convergence and challenge of societies pertaining to different families of welfare regimes in the paradigm of liberal governmentality in the new competition state (Cerny 1997, 2010; Foucault 2008).

This chapter deals with this new integration problem of the emerging liberal competition state in five steps. The first step gives an outline of the causal relationship between relative exclusion, disintegration and delinquency. The second step points out the convergence of liberal, conservative and social democratic egalitarian welfare states in the increased significance of relative exclusion, disintegration and delinquency. The third step identifies trends of post-industrialization and globalization as major causes of the increased significance of relative exclusion and disintegration. They imply a turn from collective inclusion to individualized inclusion as explained in the fourth step. In the fifth step the theoretical argument is spelled out in a set of hypotheses that are tested by a multiple regression analysis. The test gives support to the main thesis that increasing individualization of inclusion leads to increased chances of disintegration reflected by higher delinquency rates and that liberal strategies of inclusion turn out increasingly to be more effective than conservative and social democratic ones, though they do so in their typical form with side effects that counteract a deeper rootage of social integration.

Relative exclusion, disintegration and deviance

Relative deprivation is experienced by people who live in a state of unfulfilled aspirations. It occurs in a double sense: on the one hand with regard to the individual's or the group's own level of aspirations and, on the other hand, with regard to the standard of living of a reference group (possibly of the vast majority of the population). In the highly developed welfare states, the level of aspiration of almost all people is high since a high level of consumption has become a commonly shared standard of living. Those who stay back behind this level compared to their aspirations and to the achievement of others will feel relative deprivation. The latter will become particularly virulent, as the comprehensive realization of a high level of wealth gives the impression that everyone is capable of achievement (Merton 1949/1968).

The type of levelled middle-class society that Helmut Schelsky (1965) described in the 1950s, features the majority of the population on a medium to upper level of affluence. The latter appears attainable for all so that exclusion from middle-class wealth seems even more depriving. When many are able to achieve, exclusion is an even more painful experience for the few who do not. As long as a low standard of living is shared with a greater part of the population, there is little reason for deprivation. Since a higher standard of living appears to be out of reach anyway everyone shares his/her own fate with the majority of people on his/her level. Most people compare themselves with the majority of people on this level, but not with the better-off strata and leading groups. Marginalized groups in the affluent society compare themselves with the majority of people. However, as compared to the majority, marginalized people live in the shadow of affluence and are suffering from a high degree of relative deprivation in the sense of being far away from the level of the majority in their standard of living. The income gap is smaller between people excluded and the majority in a middle-class society than between the majority and the upper class in a strongly differentiated class society. Nevertheless, the feeling of relative exclusion is stronger in the first case than in the second. Alongside the discrepancy between the individual's actual standard of living and his or her desired standard of living, this discrepancy between his or her own standard of living and the standard of the great majority of people forms the second dimension of relative deprivation. The first dimension can be called "unfulfilled aspirations", the second "relative exclusion". Both are frustrating for the individual.

According to Durkheim (1952), both the individual and the society are in a state of imbalance in the situation of relative deprivation. This triggers efforts to restore the balance, whether these may be successful or not. For the individual, relative deprivation is hard to bear in the long run. Society suffers from the disintegrative phenomena triggered by relative deprivation, in the form of an increasing number of violations to rules, political alienation, a lack of commitment and conflicts. According to Durkheim, the individual on his/her own is not in a position to create the corresponding balance when society does not provide the necessary assistance. Since human needs are basically unlimited, the human being is determined to experience frustration caused by relative deprivation. Therefore, it is a matter of societal order to ensure a sufficient balance of resources and needs. In this regard, the modern capitalist society, with its strong economic ups and downs, is faced with particular challenges, which it will recurrently fail to meet. The level of aspiration goes far beyond the standard of living that is really attained in periods of strong economic upswing, or the standard of living drops as compared to the level achieved before a recession. Whereas the traditional estate society defined a specific standard of living for each estate, which nobody strove to go beyond and which remained stable for an unlimited time, the principles of civil liberty and equality before the law apply to the modern market society so that now everybody may strive for everything if they only can. This is the root of relative deprivation recurring again and again in the modern market society. It largely leaves the balancing of the level of aspiration and the actual standard of living to the laws of the market. Consequently, those who do not achieve and suffer from relative deprivation have to seek a new balancing of resources and needs on their own account, since society does not provide any assistance. This also implies the frequent use of illegitimate ways of smoothing out tensions. For example, an "illegitimate way" is committing suicide, if the frustrations experienced seem to be unbearable. In fact, Durkheim (1952) established a relationship between economic upswings and downturns and suicide rates rising in both cases. He also discovered that those strata whose situation of living depends most strongly on their individual achievement on the market – such as businesspeople and entrepreneurs – are affected by suicide at an above-average rate. He would have made similar findings if he had researched into crime rates, frequency of strikes, political extremism and political alienation. In Durkheim's eyes, such phenomena will introduce a state of anomie, if the validity of societal norms is doubted in view of a substantial volume of deviating behaviour and if the sanctioning of deviance neither derives from a legitimating consensus nor involves a far-reaching confirmation of the norms.

Robert K. Merton (1949/1968) adapted Durkheim's theory of anomie to specific features of the American society (Featherstone and Deflem 2003; Marwah and Deflem 2006). Drawing on Durkheim, Messner and Rosenfeld (1994/2007) have advanced a theory of institutional anomie and have gathered quantitative evidence in support of that theory. In Merton's eyes, American society has made a life in affluence a generally shared model of culture more than any other society. At the same time, it made individual achievement on the market the essential tool for realizing this model, based on the assumption that everybody will be able to advance if they only want to. A person might indeed succeed in making their way from being a dishwasher up to becoming a millionaire. The actually attained mass affluence of the broad middle class stretching from well-earning blue-collar workers to white-collar executives, has transformed this assumption into a social fact. Measured by this yardstick, the exclusion of the underclass represents a deprivation that is felt even more strongly (African Americans and Hispanic Americans are overproportionately affected here). We can speak of relative exclusion as a special case of relative deprivation here. The efforts to reduce deprivation are therefore reflected in the frequent choice of illegitimate ways in the form of delinquency, since they too, are to a substantial degree left to spontaneous self-organization. In contrast, the collective organization of the reduction in deprivation – by trade unions, welfare associations and political parties, for instance – is, in fact, not available for a larger part of the underclass. Greater relative exclusion and individualized tension reduction explains to a great extent why African Americans are four to five times more frequently involved in property and violent crimes than Caucasians (US Department of Justice 2003; see also Bruce 2000).

According to Merton's typology, we have to distinguish five types of adaptation: (1) Deviation from the institutionalized norms represents a strategy of balancing between the means available and the cultural model of affluence on the way to a higher level of consumption. It is the type of *innovation* without which there would be no social change in a society but which is, at the same time, the source of anomie. There is anomie in a double sense: as strain of the individual to bridge the gap between means and goals and as de-institutionalization of means of achievement (Featherstone and Deflem 2003). (2) If the legitimate means are being applied, although the cultural model is neither reached nor considered attainable, Merton speaks of *ritualism*, which characterizes, for instance, the lower middle stratum of civil servants and white-collar staff. (3) If both the legitimate means of achievement on the market and the model of high-level consumption are abandoned, this is, according to Merton, a *withdrawal* from society, such as in the form of a rural commune or a religious sect. (4) Merton calls the rejection of legitimate means and of the cultural model occurring along with the simultaneous supporting of new means and models a *rebellion*. This aims at a change of society. (5) If both sides exist – i.e. the access to legitimate means and the pursuit of the cultural model – this is, in Merton's typology, the type of *conformity*. For Merton, the type of innovation characterized by high crime rates is typical of the American society, since it has made mass affluence the generally shared cultural model far more than the European societies. It leaves inclusion in mass affluence largely to the individual's achievement on the market and holds collective inclusion by trade unions, political representation and government on a relatively low level. The unequal access to legitimate means goes hand in hand with the unequal share of social strata in crime: the less access there is to legitimate means, the higher is the crime rate. Consequently, it is hardly surprising that the excluded underclass is overproportionately affected by crime. In this context, it should also be pointed out that the underclass includes an overproportionate number of African Americans and Hispanics. As a result, entire subcultures of delinquency come into existence with their own models and laws. This applies, above all, to the African American and Hispanic downtown ghettos, which are not only producing delinquency at an overproportionately high rate, but which are also suffering from delinquency and from the fear of delinquency (Wilson 1990; Murswieck 1998: 669–674). This is the social milieu where we see social disorganization concentrated in the sense of instability of the family and the local community in terms of single-parent families and little participation in community work (voluntary associations). According to the classical study of Shaw and McKay (1942) and a more recent study by Sampson and Groves (1989) this is what nurtures delinquency as an enduring and widespread phenomenon. It is also the milieu of great social strain, which is conducive to crime according to Agnew's (1999) strain theory (Warham et al. 2005). This provides access to illegitimate means (Cloward 1959) and contacts to learn deviant behaviour (Sutherland 1939) as opportunity structure (Marwah and Deflem 2006).

According to the typology elaborated by Esping-Andersen (1990), the United States represents the model of a liberal welfare regime. This regime is focused on the universalistic guarantee of a very modest, means-tested, basic security for all in the case of proven neediness; predominantly, it supports the inclusionary effect of open markets and pre-market equal opportunity. Consequently, the individual's standard of living above modest basic security depends, to a very large extent, on individual achievement on the market. Opposed to this type are the models of the conservative Christian democratic and the egalitarian social democratic welfare regime. The conservative regime – of a corporatist nature in Germany and of an etatist type in France – primarily relies on the family's power of integration. It aims at securing the established hierarchy of status and proceeds according to the principle of subsidiarity. It ties social payments above subsistence level to the family's main breadwinner, which is, as a rule, the husband working full time. Moreover, it attains a certain equality of results in the wake of post-market redistribution and does so more extensively than the liberal welfare regime. The egalitarian, social democratic regime in Scandinavia goes one step further. It grants a universalistic basic security for all on a very high level, which is financed by correspondingly high taxes resulting from the high employment level of both men and women. The three types of welfare regimes represent different conceptions of social justice (Lessenich and Ostner 1998; Goodin *et al.* 1999; Merkel 2002).

The reason for the lower crime rates of the European welfare states was, above all, their having remained class societies for a long time – contrary to the United States – while the individual's participation in the accumulated affluence was organized collectively by political parties and trade unions in cooperation with the employers and the state and was not a matter of individual market achievement as in the United States. This difference in including the individual in a society's accumulated affluence can be measured by the decommodification index introduced by Esping-Andersen (1990). This index determines the extent to which an individual's standard of living is independent of his or her achievement on the market in the case of unemployment, illness or retirement. Whereas the liberal welfare state of the United States reaches a value of 13.8 in this ranking, it is at 27.7 in the conservative welfare state of Germany and at 39.1 in the egalitarian-social democratic welfare state of Sweden (Esping-Andersen 1990: 52, table 2.2). The commodification index for 1998/99 was 14.0 for the USA, 27.7 for Germany and 34.7 for Sweden (Bambra 2006). Similar differences can be established as far as the distribution of income or public social expenditure is concerned. The gini-coefficient was at 0.375 in the USA in 1997, at 0.3 in Germany in 1994 and at 0.22 in Sweden in 1995 (Smeeding and Grodner 2000: 213). In the mid-2000s, the figures were 0.38 for the USA, 0.3 for Germany and 0.23 for Sweden (OECD 2011e). It is apparent in this context that the interaction of a high inequality of incomes and a relatively strong economic growth involves particularly high scores of relative deprivation, which, in turn, result in correspondingly high crime rates. In an international comparison, the interaction of a high inequality of incomes and strong economic growth correlates with higher crime rates. This was demonstrated up to the late 1980s, for instance, by a comparison between liberal welfare states on the one hand and conservative and/or egalitarian welfare states on the other hand, but also between the rapidly developing nations in Latin America and South-East Asia (for evidence see Gartner 1990; Messner and Rosenfeld 1997; Bruce 2000; Entorf and Spengler 2000, 2002; Phillips 2002; Wilkinson and Pickett 2007; Bernburg *et al*. 2009).

A high inequality of incomes in a static, traditional estate society does not produce any relative deprivation by itself since mass affluence is not a generally shared cultural model aspired by all strata. A growing economy, together with the cultural model of mass affluence, will not produce over-average relative deprivation with rising rates of deviant behaviour if a moderate inequality of incomes ensures a wide range of participation in mass affluence. Post-market redistribution will dampen the competition for better positions in the market. The accomplishment of the cultural model "mass affluence" is not exclusively a matter of the individual, but also a matter of collective organization and redistribution as a result of the cooperation between the state, the employer associations and the trade unions. Consequently, there is only little pressure to balance the lack of achievement on one's legitimate path of occupational career through illegitimate means. The individuals are more strongly relieved from the pressure of having to achieve, according to the cultural model, in order to be acknowledged by themselves and the others. This fact should be mirrored by lower crime rates, less psychic disturbances, less disturbances of private partnerships, e.g. lower divorce rates, political alienation and political extremism.

A comparison between liberal welfare states on the one hand and conservative and egalitarian welfare states on the other reveals that this deduction from theoretical assumptions is not consistently confirmed in empirical terms. If we take a look at the conservative and egalitarian welfare states, we notice that, there too, the rate of delinquency, psychic and partnership disturbances has risen blatantly over the past thirty years as has, for some time at least, the level of political alienation and political extremism. It should be taken into account in this context that political extremism makes itself seen in different forms depending on the political institutions. The political system of the United States is very open for lobbyism and features two parties that are very heterogeneous internally and are relatively weakly organized. This turns extremist positions fairly easily into daily lobbying work and into the two parties. This is shown, for instance, by the influence of Protestant fundamentalism in the Republican Party. The more limited openness to lobbyism and the stronger ideological and organizational unity of the European party systems, instead, is compelling extremist positions down to the streets and to politically motivated violence as well as to the collective organization of movements and new parties.

If we take property crime, we actually see no correlation with earnings dispersion (see Figure 4.11 in Chapter 4). With respect to robberies there is a similar situation; while the rate declined in the United States during the 1990s, it has risen in some European countries (Figure 5.1).

The United States was in a position to lower the crime rate through tighter police control and higher imprisonment figures during the 1990s (Pastore and Maguire 2003: 189). The crime rate has dropped as the incarceration rate has risen (Figure 5.2). However, the United States' clearly higher level of imprisonment as compared to the European welfare regimes still refers to a high level of relative deprivation, which can obviously not be balanced out without applying physical constraint. The rate of imprisonment is in the meantime six times higher than in most other OECD countries, particularly because of a more rigorous application of the law (Donziger 1996; Western and Beckett 1998; Pettit and Western 2004; Gottschalk 2006; Wacquant 2009).

The clearly grown signs of disintegration – measured by delinquency, psychic disturbances, divorce rates, xenophobia, political extremism and political alienation – in the conservative and egalitarian welfare regimes require a particular explanation. If we look at the two factors of inequality in incomes and economic growth, we will establish that both displayed a stronger increase in the liberal welfare regimes during the 1980s and the 1990s than in the conservative and egalitarian regimes. In the United States, income inequality rose by 7 per cent to 15 per cent in the 1980s and 1990s, in France and Germany only by 1 per cent to 7 per cent (Smeeding and Grodner 2000). There was no change in the Scandinavian countries.

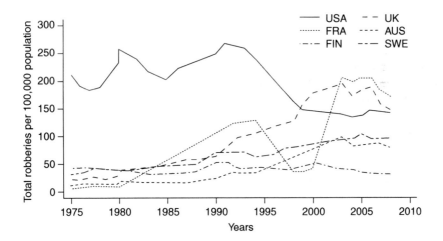

Figure 5.1 Total robberies (1975–2008) in selected OECD countries (source: United Nations 2011. Surveys on Crime Trends and the Operations of Criminal Justice Systems (CTS) 1975–2008. Total robberies retrieved 29 March 2011, from www.unodc.org/documents/data-and-analysis/Crime-statistics/Robbery2.xls and www.unodc.org/unodc/en/data-and-analysis/United-Nations-Surveys-on-Crime-Trends-and-the-Operations-of-Criminal-Justice-Systems.html).

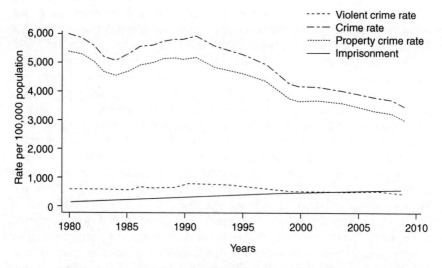

Figure 5.2 Incarceration rate and crime rate in the USA (source: Bureau of Justice Statistics 2011c; FBI 2011: Uniform Crime Reporting Statistics as prepared by the National Archive of Criminal Justice Data. Imprisonment rate retrieved 28 February 2011, from http://bjs.ojp.usdoj.gov/content/glance/sheets/incrt.csv. Crime rates retrieved 28 February 2011, from http://bjs.ojp.usdoj.gov/dataonline/Search/Crime/State/RunCrimeStatebyState.cfm).

Note
Own calculations.

The same goes for accompanying features such as the frequency of changes in job, place of residence, partner and church membership and the change in the support of parties in elections. It appears that despite the discussion about the destructive consequences of globalization, living conditions have retained a level of stability in the conservative and egalitarian European welfare states that ensures sufficient balancing of the attained standard of living and the level of aspiration, i.e. an attenuation of relative deprivation. Nevertheless, according to our initial hypotheses, living conditions have changed in such a way that relative deprivation – and above all the special case of relative exclusion – is emerging to an increasing and stronger extent. A first sign of this phenomenon is the permanent high unemployment rate in the greater part of the European welfare states since the 1980s. While doing better than the United States in the 1970s and 1980s, the situation turned around in the 1990s with the United States outranking most European welfare states in terms of economic growth and employment (OECD 2003a). On its own, however, the unemployment rate can hardly be used as an explanatory factor as long as it is compensated for by a high level of income stabilization outside the job, which was the case in the past, in fact, in the conservative and egalitarian welfare states.

Another factor that might more readily be used as an explanation is youth unemployment, which varies, however, greatly across the European welfare states.

It is, for instance, particularly high in Italy (2000: 32.1 per cent), but also in the UK, the USA, the Czech Republic, Ireland, Norway, Spain, Australia, Portugal and New Zealand (OECD 2003b). This development promotes the emergence of subcultures of delinquency in those countries, especially in the suburbs that are affected particularly strongly by this phenomenon (Dubet and Lapeyronnie 1994; Kronauer and Neef 1997; Heitmeyer and Anhut 2000). In fact, the often lasting lack of perspectives rather than the youth unemployment rate leads to the disorganization of society in the form of delinquent subcultures. Unemployed youth may certainly share this lack of perspectives with the employed youth who have a low expectation of gaining a comprehensive share of mass affluence due to their low skills – this applies above all to the group of young people without an occupational training (Solga 2002, 2003). Despite a lower spreading of incomes as compared to the liberal welfare state this segment of the population considers itself exposed to a strong relative exclusion. It remains excluded from the affluence that the mass of the population is enjoying before their very eyes. What is tangible is at the same time very distant, and is thus producing a very high degree of relative deprivation. As compared to the majority of the population and their own level of aspiration, these people live on a low level, for which there is no sufficient legitimation. This lack of legitimation can be explained by the failing of the legitimatory idea of participation in affluence as a result of one's own efforts. Such efforts do not involve achievement, and people among one's own peers who achieve in a legitimate way are shrinking in number. In most OECD countries people with low skills are hit up to four times more by unemployment than people with high skills (OECD 2003a). The conservative and egalitarian welfare regimes seem to have lost the power of controlling the dynamics of structural change and its effects of displacement in such a way that relative deprivation can be kept within close limits. Therefore, deviations cannot be sanctioned in a way that is both legitimate and lives up to the norms. The new marginalized groups do not see any mechanisms of status selection that they would consider fair. Since the number of people among their own peers who are achieving in a legitimate way is decreasing, there is no driving force and legitimatory proof of the existing order of an individualized participation in society.

Here we get one step closer to a satisfactory explanation of the phenomena of disintegration, which are found in the conservative and egalitarian welfare regimes, too. Specific reasons for this disintegration may be new trends of marginalization of low skilled and unskilled youth (Solga 2002, 2003). Weaknesses of inclusion become visible in this context. The established welfare institutions are obviously not sufficiently armed to overcome these weaknesses.

Causes of relative exclusion and disintegration: trends of de-industrialization and globalization

For a long time, the Scandinavian social democratic welfare regime has demonstrated a particularly strong capacity of social integration based on collective inclusion in terms of social citizenship. The conservative welfare regime as represented by Continental European countries like Germany, France and Austria has not lagged far behind. These countries also have attained a high capacity of social integration based on the collective inclusion of the individual in society through membership in family and status group. Characteristically, phenomena of exclusion and disintegration have been attributed exclusively to the liberal regime as represented by the United States thus far. However, the situation seems to have changed in the meantime. Obviously, both the social democratic and the conservative welfare states suffer from the same phenomena of exclusion and disintegration that have been observed in the United States for decades. Is this assessment of the situation correct? How can we explain this "convergence" of different types of welfare states in the liberal regime? We will try to find an answer. In doing so, our emphasis will be on the exclusionary effects of two developmental trends of the past thirty years: de-industrialization in the knowledge-based economy and globalization. Since the 1970s, trends of de-industrialization and globalization have changed the structural conditions on which the conservative and social democratic welfare states depended in their higher capacity of social integration compared to the liberal model of the welfare state.

Trends of de-industrialization include:

1   The inclusion of an increasing number of people in higher education right through to post-secondary education at college or university.
2   The increasing differentiation of the workforce according to skills, profile, job and employment situation.
3   The expansion of the economy's service sector.

Trends of globalization include:

4   The inclusion of so far peripheral regions in the world market and the increasing supply of workforce for simple labour-intensive production work.
5   The growing cross-border division of labour according to the principle of comparative cost advantages.
6   The tightened locational competition in the open world economy, which forces welfare states to subject social policy to locational policy.

All these factors work towards intensified competition on individual achievement, towards growing pluralization of group memberships, towards differentiation of the conditions of living and towards individualization of personal fates and ways of living (OECD 2002, 2003d). In this way, the structural changes tend to bring the conservative and social democratic welfare states one step closer to the liberal model.

Skill formation has become the battleground of keeping advanced economies and their workforce internationally competitive (Crouch et al. 1999; Allmendinger and Leibfried 2003; Mayer and Solga 2008). The new paradigm of lifelong learning in the knowledge society subjects the individual to competition for educational achievement for his/her whole life (Olssen and Peters 2005; Field 2006; Mitchell 2006; Fejes and Nicoll 2008). The increasing number of people in higher education has displaced less skilled people by better skilled people from the middle and higher positions and from the internal upward mobility in their company (cf. Oesch 2010). As far as the younger cohorts are concerned, their educational achievement determines far more their occupational chances than was the case for the older age groups. Advancement from apprenticeship to a management position, which was still possible for Werner Niefer (the managing director of Mercedes-Benz in the 1980s), is impossible today and will be so in the future. Secondary school graduates and drop-outs without any occupational training (apprenticeship) are most affected, because for them, the way to the top is once and forever obstructed by better skilled competitors. Surveys confirm that the share of less skilled people – and even more so of those lacking occupational training – in middle and higher positions has dropped continually for the age cohorts from 1930 to 1960. Vice versa, the share of better skilled people in lower positions has increased, though not to the same extent (Solga 2002). In the 1990s, the unemployment rate of unskilled people increased steeply in Germany attaining 19.8 per cent in the West and 49.1 per cent in the East in 2002 as compared to the average of 8.3 per cent and 18.5 per cent, respectively. Since 2005, the rates have, however, gone down (Figures 5.3 and 5.4).

There is also clear evidence that in liberal, conservative and egalitarian welfare states the unemployment rate of people with the lowest skills is up to four times higher than the unemployment rate of people with highest skills, namely roughly 8

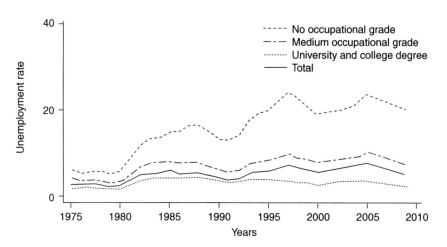

Figure 5.3 Unemployment rate and qualification, West Germany/West Berlin (source: IAB 2011. Unemployment rate retrieved 14 February 2011, from http://doku.iab.de/zfibel/06_03_01.xls).

Note
Own calculations.

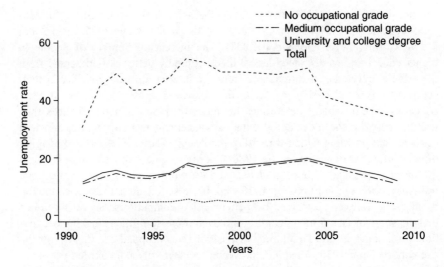

Figure 5.4 Unemployment rate and qualification, East Germany/East Berlin (source: IAB 2011. Unemployment rate retrieved 14 February 2011, from http://doku.iab.de/zfibel/06_03_01.xls).

Note
Own calculations.

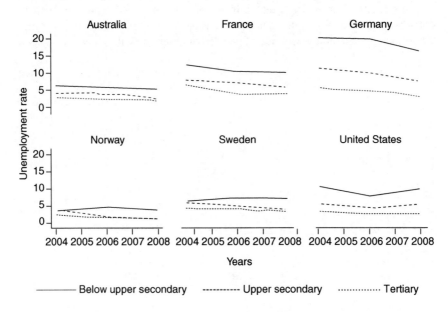

Figure 5.5 Educational attainment and unemployment (source: OECD 2006, 2008, 2010b).

Note
Own calculations.

per cent as opposed to 2 per cent (Schmid 2002: 52/54, tables 1.3 and 1.4). OECD data shows this correlation for countries representing different welfare regimes (Figure 5.5). This is the price that has apparently to be paid for the advancement from the industrial to the knowledge society (Brown and Hesketh 2004).

The classical era of the workforce's organization in trade unions was marked by full-time male production workers (Armingeon 1988). A class in itself (*an sich*) developed to form a class for itself (*für sich*) in Marx's sense, which was characterized by the homogeneity of the situation of living and of interests and by a high level of solidarity. Within the working class, the differentiation of education and job profile has in the meantime produced a polarization into highly skilled systems regulators and simple unskilled workers, as has already been proven by the study on the "End of the Division of Labour" by Kern and Schumann (1984; Helfert 1992). There is no longer a homogeneous group of a working class population with a common class-consciousness. Instead, the middle class is absorbing the highly skilled systems regulators, whereas the unskilled workers form a new underclass. They form a marginalized group without any leadership since the leadership of the working class was in the hands of the skilled workers before. This dissolution of the working class is strengthened by the fact that marginalized unskilled workers are splitting up internally into native workers on the one hand and a large number of foreign workers of a most different origin on the other hand. This segment is weakly organized, far away from the trade unions and therefore unable to undertake collective action. The marginalized groups experience their situation as an individual fate the change of which would not be a collective matter but a purely individual one (Hondrich and Koch-Arzberger 1992).

As before, the highly skilled workers form the majority of the workforce organized in trade unions. Accordingly, the trade union's policy is marked first and foremost by the interests of the highly skilled, full-time working male workforce. As before, it is geared towards the securing of standard full-time employment, even at the cost of marginalizing the less skilled groups for whom the securities and the wage structure of the standard employment relationship act as an obstacle to employment. Since the highly skilled workers are more oriented to the middle class, they lack the feeling of solidarity that is necessary for them to participate in the inclusion of the less skilled groups by making concessions for themselves regarding flexibility. The securing of their position and the participation of the less skilled groups in employment are two completely different things, which can no longer be handled under one roof. The high employment protection attained by the labour movement in the Continental European welfare states has produced a sharp borderline between highly skilled insiders and lowly skilled, particularly young, jobless outsiders (Esping-Andersen 2000). This trend forms the background to declining union density across most OECD countries (Visser 2006; Fitzenberger *et al.* 2010). The Scandinavian countries are the only exception here, which is mainly due to their linking of social benefits and union membership (Figure 5.6). Wage inequality tends to increase along with de-unionization (Addison *et al.* 2007; Dahl *et al.* 2009).

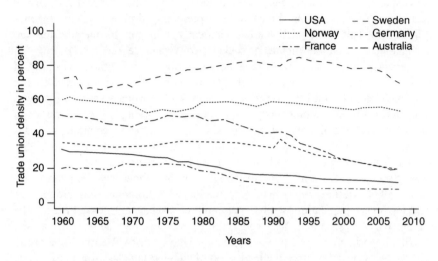

Figure 5.6 Trade union density (source: OECD 2011e. Retrieved 28 February 2011, from http://stats.oecd.org/Index.aspx?DatasetCode=LFS#. Trade union density retrieved 28 February 2011, from http://stats.oecd.org/Index.aspx?DataSetCode=UN_DEN).

Note
Own calculations.

The expansion of the economy's service sector has, meanwhile, advanced a great deal in all industrial countries, even if there are differences and the liberal welfare regimes, in particular, have proceeded farthest (Figure 5.7). Moreover, there are special cases such as Germany, which boasts a long tradition of lower support to private services (Fuchs and Schettkat 2000: 216, table 8.3). The shrinking of the sector of industrial production also means a decline in the collective organization of participation in society's wealth through the corporatist cooperation of state, employers' associations and trade unions. This decline is compensated for to a limited extent only by the strong organization of the civil servants and employees in the public sector. France, above all, excels in this sector due to particular historical conditions of a traditionally low level of organization in trade unions on the part of the industrial workforce as opposed to a stronger organization of the workforce in the public sector. Accordingly, this well organized segment of the workforce is pursuing primarily its own interests (income, security in the public sector), even at the expense of a high tax load and disadvantaging the workforce in other sectors of the economy. There is no room for an overall strategy on the level of cooperation between the state, the employers' associations and the trade unions.

Developments in Germany point in a similar direction – though less strongly marked – with clearly more power on the part of the highly skilled production workers organized in trade unions. The trade unions and associations of the

Relative exclusion and disintegration 227

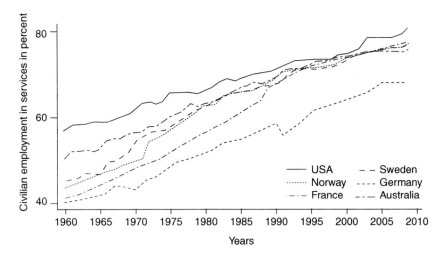

Figure 5.7 The rise of service sector employment (source: OECD 2011e. Annual labour force statistics. Retrieved 28 February 2011, from http://stats.oecd.org/index.aspx).

Note
Own calculations.

service sector are mainly concentrated on civil service (such as ÖTV, DAG and Beamtenbund in former times, and ver.di and Beamtenbund today). The large industrial trade unions and the corresponding employers' associations form a cartel representing mainly the interest of full-time working employees in having a secure job. They are, therefore, less open to new strategies aiming at the inclusion of the new marginalized groups, especially because these do not form the core of their clientele. This split-up of the workforce is aggravated by the female workforce. They hold a large part of the jobs in the civil and private service sector and are generally less inclined to organize in trade unions than their male counterparts. This correlation can also be interpreted the other way round, namely because services – which are provided by women to an above-average extent – resist organization in trade unions in the classical sense. This is because they are not carried out collectively in the factory, but instead in extremely individually separated jobs boasting individual relationships between the service provider and the client or customer. As far as the service sector is concerned, there are no large production units organized according to the division of labour, which are glued together by solidarity. Services take place in a scattered way across administration, sales floors, offices and field service with only little chance of experiencing a common feeling and solidarity. In a large industrial plant, the qualified production worker and the unskilled worker formed a production unit in the factory, whereas the bank clerk and the employee at McDonald's do not. This comparison must be drawn in order to attain similar dimensions of organizable workforce. As a result, large parts of the service jobs hinder the emergence of an encompassing solidarity due to their structure, and therefore make the collective organization of participation in affluence difficult. The structural prerequisites rather guide the organization of interests towards the favouring of specific, better organized segments such as civil servants and towards job-specific representation of interests.

In this context, however, we have to distinguish between private and public services. Our arguments hold much more with regard to private service than to public service, if we look at the empirical evidence of unionization in the different sectors of employment. Whereas union density is particularly low in the private service sector it is relatively high and stable in the public service sector. Therefore, we see a greater decline of unionization where the private service sector has outgrown the public service sector. This holds true for the United States in particular. It is the other way round in the European welfare states of the conservative and egalitarian types. Contrary to the general trend we even realize a growth of unionization to the record highs of 89 per cent in Sweden and 78.8 per cent in Finland in 1996 (OECD 2003c). This can be explained by the growing inclusion of women in the labour market since the 1960s and the linking of some social benefits to union membership. The exceptional situation in the Scandinavian welfare states should, however, not draw our attention away from the general decline of union membership resulting from the expansion of the service sector at least in the private part of the economy. The data for 2008 shows a decline of trade union density in Sweden to 68.3 per cent and to 67.5 per cent in Finland, too (OECD Statistics).

Less skilled people are not only ousted from jobs by better skilled domestic competitors, and it is not only these rivals who block their way to the top. Additionally, they are exposed to competition with workforce in peripheral developing and newly industrialized countries, who are newly integrated into the world market, and who do the same job for a fraction of their wages (Choi 2006). This means that labour-intensive production is being shifted from the highly developed industrialized nations to developing and newly industrialized countries, as shown by rising foreign direct investments (Figure 5.8). The range of jobs available in production is being reduced to jobs requiring a high level of technical expertise (Held et al. 1999: 236–282).

Unskilled people in the highly developed countries feel robbed of formerly available opportunities of achievement. They face displacement by internal and external competitors, and they experience the decline of available opportunities as relative exclusion. It should be borne in mind here that this change concerns jobs that contributed to the attainment of high productivity brought about by production based on the division of labour. Moreover, with their participation in the production of affluence by the national labour division, they also boasted a comparably high proportion in the collectively generated profit in the form of a solidarity wage.

The increasing cross-border division of labour not only involves the transfer of simple production jobs to developing and newly industrialized countries, but

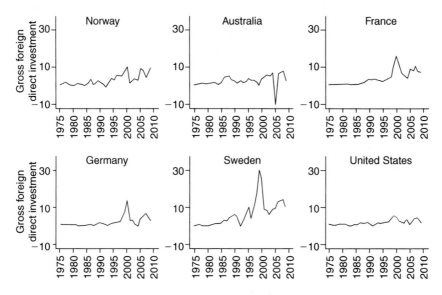

Figure 5.8 Gross foreign direct investment (% of GDP) (source: World Bank 2011. Foreign direct investment, net outflows (% of GDP) retrieved 14 March 2011, from http://data.worldbank.org/indicator/BM.KLT.DINV.GD.ZS. Foreign direct investment, net outflows (% of GDP) retrieved 14 March 2011, from http://data.worldbank.org/indicator/BX.KLT.DINV.CD.WD/countries).

Notes
Gross foreign direct investment is the sum of the absolute values of inflows and outflows of foreign direct investment recorded in the balance of payments financial account. It includes equity capital, reinvestment of earnings, other long-term capital, and short-term capital. This indicator differs from the standard measure of foreign direct investment, which captures only inward investment. The indicator is calculated as a ratio to GDP in US dollars. Own calculations.

also the ever more widely branched cross-border entanglement of production so that workforce from most different regions around the world participate in the production of a product, whose wages differ greatly in accordance with the situation of the market. In OECD countries real labour costs have increased steadily, yet not in developing countries. Whereas the average wage was US$31.88 for industrial production in Germany in 1995, it only attained US$0.25 in India, according to World Bank data (World Bank 2002: 45). According to OECD data, Germany was still on top in 2006 (Figure 5.9). Both data differ somewhat, however, due to different measurement techniques. In 2006, the figures were US$35.8 for Germany and US$0.91 for India (Sincavage *et al.* 2010). The workforce participating in a chain of production no longer forms a single unit of solidarity with one single voice of representation and a corresponding collective power of negotiation. As a result, the entire production chain has ceased to raise all the participating workforce to the top with its achievement, while there is only a moderate spreading of wages, such as was the case within the national borders (Scharpf 2000: 73). Worldwide production chains allow for the use of wage differences in line with the supply of workforce and other locational advantages such as available human resources and thus are bursting the solidarity of national production chains. As a consequence highly skilled people are no longer able and willing to lift those who are less skilled to the top to the same extent as before. The solidarity they have practiced so far is breaking. Therefore, wage dispersion is increasing (Alderson *et al.* 2005; Dickens *et al.* 2007; Kim and Sakamoto 2008, 2010; Antonczyk *et al.* 2010; Mouw and Kalleberg 2010).

Markets have become more open as a result of the establishing of the European single market, the liberalization of capital flows and of world trade through the agreements of the GATT and the World Trade Organization (which resulted from the GATT in 1994), improved ways of transport and new transport and communication technologies. This change has multiplied the options of companies considerably to transfer production venues to those locations that give them the best conditions. Increasing options are tightening competition. The pressure on every single company that is not protected against competition on the world market, is rising. Production plants have to be located from the viewpoint of labour costs, social security costs, tax load and infrastructure. Synergies with cooperating companies and research units, skills of the workforce, work culture, social peace and legal security are also especially important.

Simple production jobs are most easily transferred to countries having lower labour and social security costs, meaning the supply of such jobs in the highly

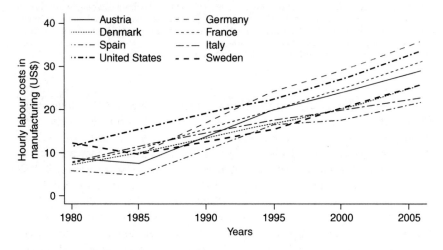

Figure 5.9 Hourly labour costs in manufacturing (US$) 1980–1995 (source: Stalker 2000; OECD 2011e. Hourly labour costs in manufacturing retrieved 14 March 2011, from http://stats.oecd.org/index.aspx?, Unit labour costs – Annual indicators).

Notes
Data for Austria 1980, 1985; Germany 1980, 1985; Spain 1980, 1985; Netherlands 1980, 1985; Sweden 1980, 1985; Australia 1980, 1985 out of Table 3.1 in Stalker (2000).

developed industrial countries is dropping. This development will also drive a wedge between the workforce, since the highly skilled workforce will be favoured by its benefits. This is because such measures are being designed to consolidate their company's position on the market and thus secure their own jobs (Figure 5.10).

The open world economy is restructuring the relation between national and transnational solidarity. The highly skilled workforce in industrial countries are now forming a unit of solidarity with the workforce outside the country and are now forced to terminate their solidarity with the less skilled workers at their own location. The new unit of solidarity on the transnational level, in contrast, unites workforce across very large distances, each having a local organization. Their ties rely, first and foremost, on the complementarity of interests and less on a feeling of being members of the same community. A highly paid specialist at a venue of a rich and highly developed country will benefit from the low wage of the simple worker in a developing, newly industrialized or transforming country. In Durkheim's (1964) terms, there is an organic solidarity between them in terms of payment depending on the shortage of the workforce supply rather than a mechanical solidarity of a less differentiated participation in payment by the company. Going beyond Durkheim's ideas, we can describe this type of solidarity as network solidarity. While organic solidarity still assumes there is a whole with clear-cut boundaries, which differentiates into organically cooperating parts, network solidarity is a sample of interrelated knots with open ends.

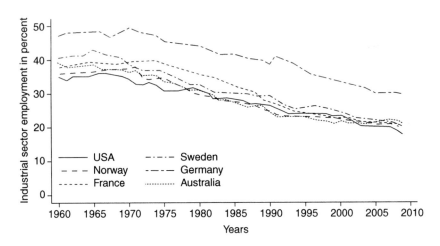

Figure 5.10 The decline of industrial sector employment (source: OECD 2011e. Annual labour force statistics. Retrieved 28 February 2011, from http://stats.oecd.org/index.aspx).

Note
Own calculations.

From collective inclusion through membership to individualized inclusion through educational achievement

The trends of de-industrialization and globalization are undermining the solidarity structure from which the conservative and egalitarian welfare regimes have taken their power of inclusion stretching right into all areas of society right to its margins. The occupational profiles and activities, the employment relationships and the organizational structures of work are differentiated across borders. They lose exactly that uniformity and homogeneity that helped to guarantee the collective, corporatistically organized participation in accumulated affluence. The relatively equal collective participation in national wealth is increasingly being replaced by participation in a more and more transnationally produced wealth, which is differentiated according to the individual level of skills and individual competitiveness.

The basically collective provision of social inclusion on the basis of nationally concentrated division of labour, a relatively homogeneous workforce and a majority of people with low or medium skills has become undermined by changes giving greater emphasis to individualized inclusion on the basis of skills and market performance. This change has brought the conservative and egalitarian welfare regimes one step closer to the liberal model. The dominant position taken by education and vocational training as means of social inclusion clearly bears witness to this change. Acquired and steadily improved skills are individualized means of inclusion per se. They have gained their current importance as a consequence of the trends of de-industrialization and globalization under scrutiny in this study. Each one of them requires advances in education and vocational training in order to be included in society. The broadened access to higher education, the upgrading and differentiation of jobs according to skills in the so-called knowledge society, expansion of the service sector, global supply of labour, international labour division and global locational competition all require a highly skilled workforce in the advanced welfare states, which are transformed into competition states in this process (Cerny 1997, 2010). The competition state represents liberal governmentality (Foucault 2008). The education and training of the young, including the supervision of parenting, is the foremost task of the competition state in order to raise competitive individuals (Gillies 2005). The education and training of the young is seen as most important to meet the challenges of competition and specialization in an open economy as well as the standards of leading a self-responsible and autonomous life that have become binding for everybody, men and women, without any difference. Despite the further existence of institutions of collective inclusion based on family, class, status group and citizenship, education and further education have acquired such prominence that their unavoidable effect of individualizing inclusion has indeed increasingly weakened the effectiveness of the historically established institutions of collective inclusion. In a certain way, the effect of broadening the access to higher education and occupational training in the knowledge society is paradoxical in nature, as empirical studies have demonstrated for Germany (Solga

2002, 2003). The rate of people with the lowest educational level (*Hauptschulabschluss*) or no education at all has dropped steadily since the 1960s. In 1965, 60 per cent of the age group left school with a grade level from the lowest school (*Hauptschule*); in the meantime their number now stands at 26 per cent. The number of those not graduating from school has dropped to a mere 10 per cent. And those 10 per cent attend school for longer than their parents, namely until the age of 16.6 years. This means that they are offered extensive chances of completing school. Having left school without success they enter a career that fluctuates between special training programmes and temporary jobs. In taking their first job lasting for at least six months they have reached the median age of 20.6.

We see the improvement of the inclusion of more people in education and vocational training, working successfully in raising skills, job profile, income and standard of living of a growing percentage of every younger age cohort. This achievement has, however, also produced the paradoxical side effect of marginalizing a special group of people who cannot be included in this programme. This group is the victim of the exclusionary effects of an otherwise successful though individualized inclusion programme. If we take into account that more young men than young women, namely 12 per cent versus 7 per cent (Solga 2003: 20), leave school uncompleted, and if we also take into account that starting careers of delinquency is overwhelmingly young, unskilled males without a chance of a promising occupational career, we can understand what this paradoxical effect of inclusion through education means for the social integration of contemporary welfare states. In a society that did not require high skills from the majority of the people, having low or even no skills at all was no reason for exclusion. This is because people with low or no skills were included in the great majority of people. There was a place for low skilled and unskilled men and women in the occupational system, and they had their share in the collectively produced wealth. For low skilled and unskilled women there was also a place in the family, living on the earnings of the male breadwinner. This type of society is now a thing of the past. In the advanced post-industrial "knowledge-based" economy and knowledge society, there is no room for people with low or no skills. As they have nothing in common with the majority of people, who succeed in finding their place in the occupational system, there is no bond of solidarity that would bind them together. The consequence is the emergence of a new underclass of enduringly marginalized people suffering from extreme relative exclusion, because achievement seems so easily attainable, as is demonstrated by the vast majority of achievers (Kronauer 2002).

We might assume that relative exclusion is even greater, the more easily achievement seems to be attainable, as taught by the majority of achieving people. The more opportunities of educational achievement are offered and the greater the number of people of an age cohort who complete education with success, the more deeply is relative exclusion experienced by those people who do not achieve. This form of relative exclusion is further on intensified by earnings inequality. The farther the earnings of the lowest percentile are away from the median earnings, the greater its relative exclusion. With increasing relative exclusion illegal means of achievement become more attractive. According to a study carried out in Boston, in 1980 31 per cent of youths said they could make more money in irregular ways than in regular activities, and the corresponding number was 63 per cent in 1989 (Freeman 1996).

Besides creating the motivation to replace legitimate by illegitimate means, relative exclusion is also responsible for a greater part of social disorganization in terms of instability of job, residence and marriage, generally affecting the marginalized group of unskilled people. Relative exclusion directly produces motives of looking for illegal means of achievement and indirectly undermines the social networks of family, firm and residence that keep people within the boundaries of legal life. Without such inclusion in legal networks, the relatively excluded individual is much more likely to join illegal networks giving him or her an opportunity of illegal achievement and approval.

Hypotheses

On the basis of our theoretical reasoning outlined thus far we develop a number of hypotheses (Figure 5.11). The dependent variable is the rate of delinquency intimately linked to relative exclusion. Both the total number of robberies recorded per 100,000 inhabitants and the number of people declaring themselves victims of robberies in a survey might serve as dependent variables. For reasons of availability over a longer period of observation, we choose the first one provided by the World Bank.

We start with the assumption that trends of de-industrialization and globalization in the knowledge society give individualized inclusion through educational and occupational achievement greater significance compared to collective inclusion through representative parties, trade unions, occupational groups and family. For de-industrialization, we may take participation of age cohorts in post-secondary education as an indicator. With greater emphasis on educational achievement, social inclusion is individualized automatically. For globalization, we include income inequality, namely P90/P10 earnings dispersion. A significant effect of globalization is the enlargement of markets, which implies tougher competition as well as greater chances for widespread labour division. Fiercer competition exerts pressure in the direction of greater earnings dispersion according to achievement. Under this condition social inclusion is predominantly determined by the individual's market performance, it is an individualized type of social inclusion. Thus we have one indicator measuring individualized inclusion in the post-industrial economy, and one indicator measuring individualized inclusion in the globalized economy.

As we assume, the individualization of inclusion involves greater chances of relative exclusion in the sense of an individual's underachievement with regard to his/her aspiration based on what is predominantly considered the appropriate level of achievement in a society (see classically, Merton 1949/1968; Durkheim 1952). In the two senses of Merton's anomie theory, this is a situation of strain

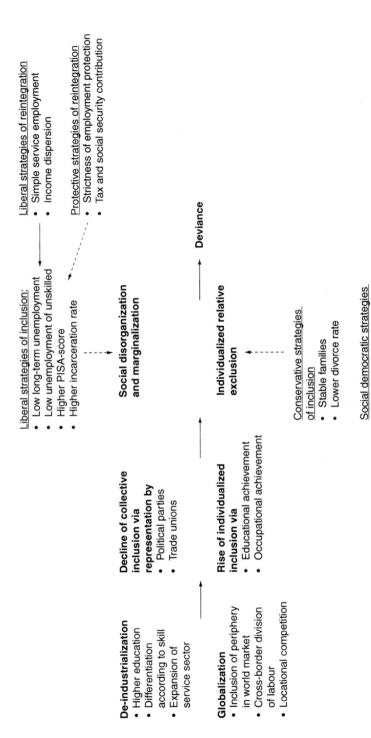

Figure 5.11 De-industrialization, globalization, relative exclusion and deviance.

for the individual and it is a situation of de-institutionalization of means for achievement (Featherstone and Deflem 2003). There is also a particular opportunity structure (Marwah and Deflem 2006) that opens the door to delinquency. This is the dominance of individualized inclusion through educational and occupational achievement at the cost of collectivist forms of inclusion. This situation is also close to institutional anomie (Messner and Rosenfeld 1994/2007; Bernburg 2002; Bernburg *et al.* 2009) as well as disorganization (Shaw and McKay 1942; Sampson and Groves 1989). As inclusion is individualized, so is exclusion. It is not the experience of a group that may organize collective action to bring about political change. It is rather the experience of single individuals who have to find ways of resolving the contradiction between aspiration and real achievement. Because of the individualized nature of this kind of relative exclusion, there is a greater chance for choosing individual forms of resolving the contradiction. Besides resignation and retreat from participation in society there is delinquency, which helps to resolve the contradiction. In terms of Merton's (1949/1968) theory of anomie it is innovation that is the choice of illegitimate means to attain a societally appraised goal (achievement). Based on this line of reasoning we expect higher rates of delinquency (that is the application of illegitimate means for attaining societally approved goals) from greater chances of relative exclusion. For reasons of available data we take robberies as one form of delinquency. As a kind of property crime it may be regarded as closely linked to the feeling of exclusion in an affluent society. Summing up, we postulate greater frequency of robberies under the following conditions:

1 With greater participation of age cohorts in post-secondary education.
2 With greater income inequality (Gini coefficient; P90/P10 earnings dispersion).

These are the two major causes of relative exclusion leading to delinquency that have been promoted over the past thirty years, with the liberal welfare regime of the United States in the lead and other countries with liberal, conservative and social democratic traditions following more or less closely behind. Consequently, over the past thirty years higher delinquency rates should have occurred in the United States than in most other countries, but also a closing-up of those other countries narrowing their distance to the United States. In this respect, we expect a weakening of the institutional barriers of conservative and social democratic welfare states against crime (robberies) over the development of the past thirty years. Convergence of European welfare states with the United States in the dependent variable should be caused by their moving towards the liberal programme of individualized inclusion with greater emphasis on inclusion through educational and occupational achievement on the market implying greater income inequality. A further reason for increased relative exclusion in conservative and social democratic welfare states is the increasing production of exclusionary effects of their typical strategies of collective inclusion in the de-industrialized and globalized economy. This trend can be observed, for example, in the growing split between insiders and outsiders of thoroughly regulated labour markets.

The general delinquency producing effect of relative exclusion is, however, counteracted by institutional countermeasures specific to a certain welfare regime. Liberal philosophy relies particularly on matching demand for jobs and supply of jobs on the labour market. Whatever helps clearing the market is welcome. The success of such strategies is reflected in low rates of unemployment, particularly low rates of long-term unemployment. Because young unskilled males commit by far the greatest part of delinquent acts, a low unemployment rate of young males should contribute a great deal to keeping the delinquency rate down. Along this line of argumentation, liberal philosophy expects lower delinquency rates under the following condition:

3   Lower long-term unemployment.

First of all, the liberal strategy of inclusion counts on incentives for participating in the production of societal wealth on the market. It conceives of society as composed of single individuals maximizing utility for whom society only has to provide the right incentives in order to turn their personal utility maximization into the production of societal wealth. The right device for that is an undistorted market. Nevertheless, there will always be individuals who do not follow the incentives of the market with legitimate means. Because they endanger the working of a society composed of free individuals, they have to be kept on the path of conformity to the rules of the game. From the liberal point of view, the incentives for cooperation have to be complemented by negative sanctions for deviance at this point. Delinquency has to be made risky to the delinquent by the threat of being captured and punished so that conformity turns out to be more gainful than deviance. Thus, deterrence has to complement incentive, as pointed out by Gary Becker's (1968) economic theory of crime along the line of liberal philosophy. The latter, therefore, assumes a lower rate of delinquency under the following conditions:

4   Effective deterrence through high clearing up rates of crime and strong punishment as reflected in higher incarceration rates.

The conservative philosophy invests particularly in the inclusionary power of the family. Support of the family is therefore of primary importance. Along with this emphasis on the family, there is the special support of the male breadwinner and the division of labour between husband and wife with regard to gainful employment, on the one hand, and organizing the household and educating the children, on the other hand. The German model of tax splitting between husband and wife is typical of this conservative support of the family, which saves couples with only one (usually male) breadwinner a considerable amount of income tax. A further element of the conservative inclusion model is its aiming at maintaining the status of the breadwinner in the case of unemployment, illness and retirement in order to stabilize his family. This objective implies compensation payments corresponding to earlier earnings in the case of unemployment, sickness or retirement, which contribute to the continuous reproduction of the vertically differentiated system of status groups. Searching for indicators of family-centred conservative inclusion strategies, we might take a lower (full-time) employment rate of women and a lower divorce rate as indicators. Thus, conservative inclusion strategies expect lower delinquency rates under the following conditions:

5   A lower female employment rate.
6   A lower divorce rate.

The social democratic philosophy is focused on the idea of social citizenship. It conceives of society as a community of citizens sharing the production and consumption of societal wealth on equal terms. Equality is largely conceived as equality of results. This system rests on three main pillars: a high level of governmental activity in the provision of collective goods (kindergarten, school, college, university, hospital, care for the elderly); inclusion of the citizens in organizing solidarity through membership in trade unions; and a comprehensive social security system, which includes the non-working population in the sharing of accumulated societal wealth. Referring to this nature of social democratic strategies of inclusion, we include three indicators that should stand for promoting inclusion and avoiding exclusion and should therefore be correlated with lower delinquency rates:

7   High union density.
8   High public social expenditure.
9   Higher score of decommodification, that is, independence of living standard from market achievement.

Certainly lowering unemployment rates of unskilled males 15–24 years old as well as tackling long-term unemployment have also become objectives of conservative and social democratic welfare policies. Educational training programmes, aiming e.g. at higher PISA scores, have become widely favoured strategies. It has, however, to be taken into account that such programmes move one step closer towards the liberal philosophy of inclusion through individual empowerment, which implies by necessity further individualization of inclusion with the effect of producing greater chances of relative exclusion. Due to the trend towards individualizing inclusion in all countries representing different welfare regimes, we should expect increasing effectiveness of liberal countermeasures against delinquency as well as decreasing effectiveness of conservative and social democratic countermeasures.

We have to use aggregated data on the macro level, because there is too little micro data available, and because it is justified by itself. We have to understand our hypotheses as macro-level hypotheses. That means that the indicators reflect structural features on the macro level, which are assumed to exert a direct effect on delinquency rates on the macro level, too. For example, greater participation of age cohorts in post-secondary education and greater income inequality according to hypotheses 1 and 2 are interpreted as qualities of the macro structure of a society reflecting greater chances for relative exclusion, which should produce a higher rate of delinquency, also as a quality of a society on the macro level. There should be a greater number of people suffering from relative exclusion in such a society or at a time t_1, than in a society or at time t_0 with a lower level of post-secondary education and inequality. Because of the intensified competition on scarce resources in such a society or at such a time, relative exclusion can occur on different educational and income levels, not only on the lowest level. We do not have to postulate that only low individual education and income produce delinquency directly. However, it can be assumed that relative exclusion is greater and more frequent on the lowest levels of education and income so that delinquency rates are highest in this group. Nevertheless, there is the general delinquency producing effect of relative exclusion resulting from intensified competition in a society or at a time with higher participation in post-secondary education and higher income inequality across classes.

The same is true for the other hypotheses. They refer to structural qualities of a society or a time t_0 that reduce competition for scarce resources or exert crime-reducing social control. The effect of such macro structures should be lower delinquency rates, also as a macro-structural feature. Besides this direct macro-level effect on delinquency rates, there should also be a micro-level effect: individuals are affected directly by the structural qualities of a society. Irrespective of that, however, there is the macro-level effect that justifies regression analyses with aggregated data. A recent study using data from Iceland proves that Durkheim's basic assumptions on the social production of deviance are corroborated as far as direct macro effects as well as individual effects on deviance are concerned (Thorlindson and Bernburg 2004). Thus there are a number of good reasons for carrying out macro analysis as such and not only using it as the second best solution.

Findings

A regression analysis has been carried out to verify the hypotheses formulated before (cf. Frerichs *et al.* 2008), whose crucial results will be mirrored in the following paragraphs. Robberies from the data set of the UN Survey of Crime Trends were used as dependent variable. In addition to this, the regressions were carried out using "homicide" as dependent variable. This data has been taken from the data set of the World Health Organization (WHO). The independent variables originate from the OECD statistics and, in single cases, from the World Development Indicators (WDI) of the World Bank (GNP per capita), the data set of the World Institute for Development Economics Research of the UN University (UNU-WIDER) and the Comparative Welfare Entitlements Dataset (decommodification). The period covered by the data stretches from 1970 to 2004. Detailed explanations on data, methods, approaches, testing for interrelations between the independent variables and on the descriptive statistics can be found in Frerichs *et al.* (2008).

Income inequality was measured alternatively with the P90/P10 income distribution (upper tenth versus lower tenth) and the GINI coefficient. To do so, OECD data was used alongside data from the World Institute for Development Economics of the UN University (UNU-WIDER). Multi-collinearity within and between regime-typical integration strategies was tested by way of bivariate correlations and could be widely excluded. Moreover, the dependent variable was estimated time-lapsed in its endogenous context according to the Generalized Method of Moments (GMM). For robberies, the results inch closer to the postulated hypotheses than for homicides. This can be explained by the fact that the quota of robberies in a country is more closely related with relative exclusion than the quota of homicides. The latter cover a great extent of violence within intimate relationships, which is linked with relative exclusion only indirectly and only to a certain extent. Therefore, we restrict our analysis to robberies here.

In detail, robberies show a very close endogenous connection of the time-lapsed dependent variable. As regards income inequality, a significant positive effect on robberies can be established for the WIDER-GINI coefficient only. When using the P90/P10 income distribution, even a significant negative effect has been discovered both for the OECD data and the WIDER data. This mixed result fits in the general indecisiveness of the state of research. The deeper reason behind this indecisiveness is most probably the fact that relative exclusion does not co-vary directly with income inequality, no matter how it is measured. Hence, in an affluent egalitarian welfare state it is possible for young males without any success in education and professional life, whose number has declined due to various activating measures and who are still absorbed by the social network, to feel just as excluded when compared to the vast majority of peers than their fellow sufferers in a liberal welfare state with a high income inequality. This development can even be anticipated as a result of the shift from collective to individual inclusion via education, which occurs in all welfare states. Hence, the heterogenous effects of income inequality are but a falsification of the hypothesis postulating growing delinquency as a result of rising relative exclusion. Different to income inequality, the quota of tertiary education has a significant positive effect on the quota of robberies throughout. This suggests that the quota of tertiary education reflects the shift to individualized inclusion far more directly than income inequality, as it is accompanied by an increased trend towards relative exclusion.

Among the *conservative* inclusion strategies, the female employment quota proves to be generally non-significant, while the divorce rate has a generally significant positive effect. The effect of the divorce rate seems to consolidate the conservative strategy, though not the effect of the female employment quota.

As far as the *social democratic* inclusion strategies are concerned, the level of public social spending proves to be significantly negative, as has been aimed for. Hence, this integration strategy seems to be still effective. Nevertheless, the same cannot be said for the level of trade union organization. The level of decommodification is significantly positive in two models, which does not confirm the social democratic integration strategy.

The *liberal* inclusion strategies feature a fairly successful trend. This goes only in part for long-term unemployment, but it is overwhelmingly the case for the incarceration rate as a liberal strategy of deterrence.

The proportion of males aged between fifteen and twenty-nine in the overall population has also been used as a first control variable. As expected, this variable proved to have a significant positive effect throughout. The second control variable – GNP per capita – is significantly negative throughout. This could be interpreted as an additional indirect confirmation of the liberal inclusion strategy, namely as relying on the production of wealth, from which everybody may benefit, even the individually less successful citizens.

Altogether, the results confirm the hypotheses at least in part. The effect of relative exclusion with increased delinquency rates as a result of the shift to inclusion through education – measured by the quota of tertiary education – is clearly recognizable. Income inequality, in contrast, does not seem to be a reliable indicator of relative exclusion. Among the conservative strategies, it is at least the stability of marriage and family that proves to be an efficient weapon against delinquency. Women's restraining from employment, in contrast, is not applicable in this context. The social democratic strategy of high public social spending fits rather well, yet this does not apply for the strategy of a high level of trade union organization and comprehensive decommodification of the living standard (Tables 5.1 and 5.2).

Conclusions

The peculiar message of this study is a special form of convergence thesis regarding welfare regimes, a particular explanation why convergence occurs and a particular demonstration how the consequences of this convergence limit options for strengthening social integration across all types of welfare regime (cf. Esping-Andersen 1990, 1999; Lessenich and Ostner 1998; Goodin *et al.* 1999; Hall and Soskice 2001). The study contributes primarily theory and empirical evidence to comparative welfare state research. It does so by linking theoretically anomie theory to forms of social inclusion pertaining to different types of welfare regimes and by linking comparative welfare state research to criminological studies, taking delinquency rates as an indicator of disintegration. Our results provide evidence for convergence in the liberal regime. Further on they contribute evidence on the level of cross-national research to studies on the community level explaining higher delinquency rates by institutional anomie (Messner and Rosenfeld 1994/2007, 1997; Batton and Jensen 2002; Messner *et al.* 2004, 2008); and by community disorganization (Shaw and McKay 1942; Sampson and Groves 1989; Kawachi *et al.* 1999; Sampson and Raudenbush 1999; Veysey and Messner 1999; Lowenkamp *et al.* 2003; Patchin *et al.* 2006). The results of studies on the effects of income inequality on crime are mixed (Bursik and Grasmick 1993; Bruce 2000; Entorf and Spengler 2000; Imrohoroğlu

Table 5.1 Robberies: detailed results for measuring inequality according to OECD

	Robberies (natural logs)											
	OECD Gini coefficient						OECD P90 P10 ratio					
	(1)	(2)	(3)	(4)	(5)	(5a)	(1)	(2)	(3)	(4)	(5)	
Robberies (time-lapsed)	0.891***	0.888***	0.891***	0.875***	0.847***	0.923***	0.911***	0.906***	0.927***	0.913***	0.933***	
	(0.000)	(0.000)	(0.000)	(0.000)	(0.000)	(0.000)	(0.000)	(0.000)	(0.000)	(0.000)	(0.000)	
Income inequality (alternative measurements)	−0.002	−0.002	−0.001	0.003	0.006	−0.000	−0.098***	−0.102***	−0.079***	−0.062**	−0.051**	
	(0.716)	(0.638)	(0.911)	(0.533)	(0.214)	(0.935)	(0.000)	(0.000)	(0.003)	(0.012)	(0.047)	
Tertiary education	0.002***	0.002***	0.002***	0.001*	0.002***	0.000	0.002**	0.002***	0.002***	0.001	0.002*	
	(0.003)	(0.002)	(0.005)	(0.061)	(0.020)	(0.814)	(0.033)	(0.009)	(0.007)	(0.121)	(0.085)	
Decommodification		0.004						0.010***				
		(0.270)						(0.003)				
Female employment quota			0.001		0.004*	−0.002			−0.000		−0.003	
			(0.577)		(0.051)	(0.150)			(0.801)		(0.198)	
Divorces				0.026	0.021	0.061**				0.059***	0.069***	
				(0.238)	(0.371)	(0.013)				(0.003)	(0.001)	
Level of trade union organization			0.161		0.039	0.055			0.356**		0.242*	
			(0.199)		(0.750)	(0.614)			(0.013)		(0.079)	

	(1)	(2)	(3)	(4)	(5)	(5a)	(1)	(2)	(3)	(4)	(5a)
Public social spending	0.009***			−0.003	−0.001	0.001				−0.008***	−0.008***
	(0.008)			(0.226)	(0.717)	(0.818)				(0.003)	(0.004)
Long-term unemployment		0.010***	0.000		0.001	−0.000			−0.001		−0.001
		(0.006)	(0.999)		(0.272)	(0.829)			(0.435)		(0.368)
Incarcerations (time-lapsed)			−0.000***	−0.000***	−0.000***	−0.000**				−0.000	−0.000
			(0.000)	(0.000)	(0.000)	(0.039)				(0.101)	(0.313)
Males aged between 15–29	0.009***	0.010***	0.010**	0.009**	0.012***	−0.002	0.008**	0.008**	0.007*	0.010***	0.007*
	(0.008)	(0.006)	(0.012)	(0.011)	(0.003)	(0.789)	(0.018)	(0.016)	(0.074)	(0.004)	(0.061)
GNP per capita	−0.340***	−0.374	−0.341***	−0.340***	−0.375***	−0.076	−0.421***	−0.537***	−0.369***	−0.464***	−0.380***
	(0.000)	(0.000)	(0.002)	(0.001)	(0.000)	(0.215)	(0.000)	(0.000)	(0.001)	(0.000)	(0.001)
Number of observations	401	401	401	401	401	417	390	390	390	390	390
Number of countries	16	16	16	16	16	16	15	15	15	15	15
Sargan test (Pr > chi2 =)	0.575	0.601	0.587	1.000	1.000		0.174	0.266	0.311	1.000	1.000
AB sequence of test series 1 (Pr > z =)	0.000	0.000	0.000	0.000	0.000		0.000	0.000	0.000	0.000	0.000
AB sequence of test series 2 (Pr > z =)	0.401	0.376	0.409	0.348	0.374		0.188	0.199	0.196	0.107	0.099

Source: Frerichs *et al.* (2008).

Notes

* Significant for *p* < 0.1; ** *p* < 0.05; *** *p* < 0.01; standard errors in parenthesis; (1)–(5) GMM difference; (5a) GMM system

Remark: For the OECD Gini coefficient, Belgium, Korea, Spain and Switzerland have not been taken into account. For the OECD P90/P10 ratio, Austria, Finland, Korea, Norway and Spain have not been taken into account.

Table 5.2 Robberies: detailed results of WIDER measurements of inequality

	Robberies (natural logs)											
	WIDER Gini coefficient						WIDER P90 P10 ratio					
	(1)	(2)	(3)	(4)	(5)	(5a)	(1)	(2)	(3)	(4)	(5)	(5a)
Robberies (time-lapsed)	0.907***	0.904***	0.927***	0.909***	0.921***	0.931***	0.915***	0.912***	0.934***	0.909***	0.914***	0.933***
	(0.000)	(0.000)	(0.000)	(0.000)	(0.000)	(0.000)	(0.000)	(0.000)	(0.000)	(0.000)	(0.000)	(0.000)
Income inequality (alternative measurements)	0.005**	0.004**	0.005**	0.004**	0.004**	0.007**	−0.012**	−0.012**	−0.013**	−0.007	−0.009*	−0.005
	(0.013)	(0.012)	(0.086)	(0.010)	(0.022)	(0.004)	(0.365)	(0.325)	(0.545)	(0.058)	(0.072)	(0.749)
Tertiary education	0.002***	0.003***	0.002***	0.001*	0.001	−0.000	0.003***	0.003***	0.003***	0.002**	0.002**	0.001
	(0.013)	(0.016)	(0.006)	(0.018)	(0.015)	(0.024)	(0.015)	(0.015)	(0.017)	(0.140)	(0.088)	(0.389)
Decommodification	(0.001)	0.007**	(0.001)	(0.067)	(0.126)	(0.936)	(0.000)	0.005	(0.000)	(0.010)	(0.036)	(0.680)
		(0.033)						(0.148)				
Female employment quota			0.001		0.000	−0.001			−0.001		−0.000	−0.000
			(0.744)		(0.816)	(0.683)			(0.622)		(0.805)	(0.809)
Divorces				0.063***	0.070***	0.064***				0.041**	0.047**	0.066***
				(0.001)	(0.001)	(0.001)				(0.043)	(0.028)	(0.002)
Level of trade union organization			0.381***		0.180	0.239*			0.234		0.004	0.089
			(0.002)		(0.136)	(0.071)			(0.153)		(0.981)	(0.418)
Public social spending				−0.007**	−0.006**	−0.003				−0.007***	−0.006**	−0.004
				(0.010)	(0.021)	(0.514)				(0.007)	(0.030)	(0.383)
Long-term unemployment			−0.001		−0.000	−0.001			−0.001*		−0.001	−0.001
			(0.470)		(0.448)	(0.450)			(0.054)		(0.208)	(0.181)
Incarcerations (time-lapsed)				−0.000***	−0.000***	−0.000***				−0.000**	−0.000*	−0.000**
				(0.006)	(0.048)	(0.004)				(0.032)	(0.080)	(0.021)
Males aged between 15–29	0.008**	0.008**	0.007*	0.008**	0.008**	−0.000	0.003	0.004	0.002	0.006*	0.007*	−0.002
	(0.013)	(0.012)	(0.086)	(0.010)	(0.022)	(0.970)	(0.365)	(0.325)	(0.545)	(0.058)	(0.072)	(0.749)
GNP per capita	−0.208**	−0.284***	−0.179	−0.290***	−0.283***	−0.101*	−0.400***	−0.455***	−0.428***	−0.460***	−0.483***	−0.289**
	(0.032)	(0.006)	(0.107)	(0.004)	(0.008)	(0.087)	(0.000)	(0.000)	(0.001)	(0.000)	(0.000)	(0.019)
Number of observations	447	447	447	447	447	461	403	403	403	403	403	415
Number of countries	18	18	18	18	18	18	16	16	16	16	16	16
Sargan test (Pr > chi2 =)	0.001	0.002	0.007	1.000	1.000		0.263	0.310	0.441	1.000	1.000	
AB sequence of test series 1 (Pr > z =)	0.000	0.000	0.000	0.000	0.000		0.000	0.000	0.000	0.000	0.000	
AB sequence of test series 2 (Pr > z =)	0.496	0.446	0.483	0.346	0.328		0.544	0.508	0.527	0.434	0.425	

Source: Frerichs et al. (2008).

Notes
* Significant for p < .1, ** p < .05, *** p < .01; standard errors in parenthesis; (1)–(5) GMM difference; (5a) GMM system.
Remark: For the WIDER Gini coefficient, Korea and Spain have not been taken into account; for the WIDER P90/P10 ratio, Japan, Korea, New Zealand and Spain have not been taken into account.

et al. 2000; Kelly 2000; Savolainen 2000; Morenoff *et al.* 2001; Antony and Entorf 2003; Jacobs and Richardson 2008). This is reflected by the findings of this study. Our study shows also evidence for incarceration bringing down the delinquency producing effects of individualized inclusion in the liberal welfare regime. This demonstrates the liberal dilemma of having to turn to deterrence in the face of lacking collectivist forms of social inclusion. This result contributes a specific element from the point of view of comparative welfare state research to the literature on incarceration in the United States. There is indeed a tendency towards replacing social security with police control (Davey 1995; Beckett 1997; Beckett and Western 2001; Garland 2002; Pettit and Western 2004). While most studies are focused on comparing communities or states in the US federal system, our cross-national comparison helps to understand development over time and differences between nations pertaining to different welfare regimes (cf. La Free and Drass 2002; Neumayer 2003; Chamlin and Cochran 2005; La Free 2005; Wilkinson and Pickett 2007).

It has been demonstrated in this chapter that relative exclusion, disintegration and delinquency are no longer exclusively phenomena of the liberal type of welfare regime as it is paradigmatically represented by the United States. Societies pertaining to the conservative and social democratic egalitarian types have meanwhile been affected by the same problem. Their turn from collective to individualized inclusion due to the greater significance of educational and occupational achievement has been identified as a major cause of this convergence of conservative and social democratic welfare states. It has resulted from trends of post-industrialization and globalization. As is demonstrated by the empirical test of the set of hypotheses spelled out according to the theoretical argument, under this condition of individualized inclusion characteristic of the liberal welfare regime, the typically liberal strategies aiming at keeping disintegration and delinquency within closer limits turn out progressively to be more effective than the typically conservative and social democratic strategies. Welfare states of all types seem to run with the same dilemma. Across all types of welfare states individualized inclusion through educational and occupational achievement has increased while collectivist forms of inclusion have eroded and have lost effectiveness. Therefore, all types of welfare states are increasingly compelled to cope with relative exclusion and anomie coming about with increasing inclusion through schools and labour markets. Lack of collective bonds has to be compensated by deterrence in as far as incentives do not work, as taught by the economic theory of crime (Becker 1968). Crime rates have to be kept down by increasing incarceration rates. The only way out of this dilemma seems to be the strengthening of cooperation between governments and the new plurality of voluntary associations. This could be a new form of pluralistic corporatism that is a mixture of liberal pluralism and social democratic as well as conservative corporatism. Answering this question needs, however, further comparative research.

Conclusion
The interdependent change of economy, solidarity, politics and justice

In conclusion, I want to emphasize two results of our investigation. On the one hand, there is the increased openness, dynamics and tendency to crises of the societal order on its way towards the global hegemony of the liberal model of society. On the other hand, there is the dialectic of growing global inclusion and the accompanying new forms of exclusion in the national welfare states.

There are, obviously, signs pointing to an enforced change of coordinated market economies towards the liberal type. Indeed, since the 1980s, the OECD countries have been seized by a far-reaching wave of liberalization and privatization reaching from the privatization of public enterprises right through to the deregulation of labour markets. This liberalization wave has won over Mancur Olson's thesis (1982) saying that nations are paralysed increasingly by distribution coalitions on the part of organized interests and are, hence, prone to economic downfall the longer they are ruled by a democratic government. So far, no satisfying explanation has been found to demonstrate why this liberalization wave has spread worldwide. Martin Höpner (2007) shows that liberalization has grown most where the countries were liberalized least at the beginning of the assessment. The openness of the national economy and the EU membership, however, do not supply a sufficient explanation. This does not mean that international competition does not play a role at all. It seems to urge the OECD countries on to the path of the radical innovation regime, since they face increasing competition from the developing and newly industrialized countries as regards standardized mass production. The expansion of education and the extension of the service sector have, in addition, made the collective solidarity of the workforce in mass production shrink in as far as its significance for societal cohesion is concerned. Hence, the coordinated market economy is put under pressure from two sides: the transformation to radical innovation and the declining collective organization of the workforce. This transformation of the production regime opens the doors to strategies seeking remedy by competition, markets, dynamic change and private initiatives (cf. Fromm 2004). This kind of reform strategy has become a binding guideline in the framework of the OECD agenda on "Employment and Growth in the Knowledge-Based Economy". The EU's Lisbon strategy has implemented this guideline in its programme designed to make the EU the world's most dynamic knowledge-based economic area. In the procedures of the Open Method of Coordination (OMC), the member states are subject to constant benchmarking and monitoring, which is to bring the EU closer to its envisaged goal. In Germany, the reform agenda 2010 launched by the former Red-Green government can be understood as a translation of this strategy (cf. Bernhard 2005, 2008; Schäfer 2005).

The OECD and EU agendas lend international competition a programmatic frame within which society is interpreted as a project to be geared to competition, markets and dynamic change. From this viewpoint, traditions of the coordinated market economy lose their legitimacy, while programmes of liberalization appear increasingly legitimate as such, since the world is seen in these categories. Productive forces, production relationships and superstructure will then be increasingly entwined so as to generate a trend towards a liberal form of society with all its side effects, even though they may appear problematic from the standpoint of a coordinated market economy (cf. Jessop 2008: 178–224). This reform movement spreads irrespective of whether a country possesses a more or less open national economy, and whether or not it is an EU member. In this sense, the global wave of liberalization follows the diffusion model of neo-institutionalism, as it has been promoted by John Meyer (1997) and his research team. Nevertheless, the liberal model's impact cannot be explained exclusively with the establishing of OECD experts as acknowledged advisors (cultural others). This is the superstructure. The power of change results also from the support given to the OECD advisors by the basis of fiercer global competition and its translation into increasing international labour division (Durkheim 1964), where the OECD countries are ascribed the role of radical innovators. At the same time, this implies a shift of power away from national coalitions of parties and associations and towards transnational expert teams. The emerging multi-level governance is, at the same time, a de-democratized and scientificated form of governance (Majone 1996). Transnationalization fuels the scientification of governance and the disempowerment of parties and associations so that Olson's forecast of an institutional sclerosis is being refuted. Friedrich von Hayek predicted this effect of the removal of trade barriers in an essay published as early as in 1939, as Martin Höpner has pointed out (Hayek 1948: 258, 261; cf. Höpner 2007: 338, footnote 32).

Seen from Bourdieu's field perspective, the transnationalization of the political field (Bourdieu 1986, 1994) means that parties and associations lose in capital, while the transnational expert teams gain in capital. Political capital is losing, informational capital is gaining in value (Bernhard 2010). Along with Foucault (2008), we can understand the global wave of liberalization as an increasing complementation of governance via territorially anchored laws and state disciplinary power by a liberal art of governing, which is verified by the market and restricted by the interaction of market and civil law and sets an as wide as possible scope of freedom for individual action. In the EU's structure, the European Court of Justice is the consecration body of this liberal order (Münch 2008). Since both losers and winners of globalized competition have to use the same principles in order to claim their rights, we can speak of a hegemonic liberalization project in this context (Gramsci 1971; Laclau and Mouffe 2001).

Global free trade fuels economic growth. In this way, it helps to avoid struggles of distribution and to extend the scope for social benefits. On this general level, global free trade does not generate a race to the bottom. The same goes for the relationship between industrialized and developing countries. To be able to exploit the growth opportunities offered by global free trade, a structural change of social integration and a paradigmatic change of justice is, however, needed. National and international integration come closer to each other. Financial resources are being shifted from unproductive to productive forms of social integration.

As far as the relationship between industrialized and developing countries is concerned, we should point out, first of all, that both groups of countries compete in a very restricted market segment only: the production of and trade with simple mass-produced goods (agricultural products, textiles, toys, iron and steel products). All these market segments have been protected by the industrialized countries up until the present time through tariff barriers or subsidies in order to fend off competition from developing countries. Accordingly, the developing countries were refused the opportunities of development, while the industrialized countries were offered a chance to delay economic structural change. Hence, the developing countries were also robbed of their opportunities to improve their social standards, to raise their social budgets and to invest in educational capital. In contrast, the industrialized countries were enabled to pursue a social policy aimed at administrating the most different types of unemployment: artificial maintenance of cost-driving expensive jobs at the expense of consumers; unemployment and social assistance as a permanent condition instead of retraining; early retirement instead of reasonable employment at an older age; youth unemployment due to the lack of educational capital and lack of new jobs in growth markets; and insufficient school and university education due to bad mentoring ratios resulting in a high risk of unemployment and lengthy study periods. High social standards could be retained in administrating unemployment. All this resulted in a misallocation of financial resources. Financing the extensive system of non-work consumed precisely those resources that would have been needed for investments in education and innovation dynamics. Older citizens impaired the future prospects of the younger generation and strained them with the high burden of financing an extremely long retirement life.

This uneven distribution of loads has put the allocation system of the "generation contract" under pressure. Hence, the result is a stepwise conversion to a funding principle with a simultaneous shift of the retirement age to a later date and an additional levelling of the transition period. A substantial part of financial resources is being taken from the administration of non-work and invested in the development of educational capital and the promotion of innovation dynamics so as to create new opportunities of employment that will offer future prospects to the young generation.

The distribution conflict between industrialized and developing countries leaves no other choice to the industrialized countries than to proceed along this path of structural change. It allows them to open their markets to the developing countries and offer them those chances of development that enable them to cope with their inner social tensions and, hence, the risk of religious fundamentalism, civil war and terrorism. Recent research teaches us that, along with the market opening, the industrialized countries can make a more effective and more significant contribution to the development of developing countries and international social balance than with the previously ruling system of development aid and lending by the International Monetary Fund and the World Bank. These aids have not been very effective so far, as they are granted to countries that invest the money in development projects whose success is being prevented mainly by protectionism on the part of those countries, in particular, which act as financiers and lenders. As a result, the developing countries struggle regularly with a debt overload that prevents investments in the future for many years to come. The interaction of market opening and economic structural change in the industrialized and developing countries, in contrast, is a policy that does not trigger a race to the bottom, but offers better economic *and* social compensation for both sides providing them with better future prospects and a higher capacity to pay social benefits. It is shown that it is not simply "higher" or "lower" social standards that are at stake here, but rather the most intelligent allocation of financial resources, which results in a comprehensive higher capacity of social compensation.

The previously ruling system of market closure privileges the group of older citizens in the industrialized countries and disadvantages both the younger citizens in these countries and the entire population in the developing nations. So far, high social standards in the industrialized countries have implied a one-sided brotherly in-group morality of the older citizens, coupled with an unbrotherly out-group morality towards the younger generation and the developing countries. The policy of market opening with a simultaneous economic structural change means an adjustment of in-group and out-group morality and a simultaneous conversion to greater emphasis on justice of achievement and fairness to all parts, which should replace brotherly solidarity with one's neighbours at the expense of those farther away. Resources are given, more than ever before, to places where they are not simply used, but transformed into achievements with an increase of these resources in mind, so as to open up more future prospects than before. The social system invests more in the productive use of resources and less in their unproductive use for mere consumption. Social-political efforts focus on securing external and internal equal opportunities. Since the policy of equal opportunity works necessarily towards an individualization of social inclusion, the specific social problem of the highly developed industrialized countries is the social integration of the group of the population, which has been pushed to the margin in the competition for educational qualifications and the resulting jobs, through targeted measures aimed at a transparent structuring of the educational system. Moreover, job growth in the service sector and the subsidization of low incomes with negative income tax must be taken into account.

Replacing brotherliness with fairness means that the borderline between one's own group and the foreign group is removed on the world level; that each individual is given the same opportunities for participating in societal activities (in wealth, to put it in economic terms); that unequal starting conditions are corrected over and again; that those who have been marginalized by competition are supported to an extent that requires their motivation to participate in societal life; and that those who are able to achieve are obliged to contribute to the production of collective goods unless their readiness to achieve is impaired. A conversion from welfare state brotherliness to global fairness need not necessarily involve a cut of social standards in the highly developed welfare states. The intelligent solution to new social problems would, instead, raise its integrative strength and thus replace old rather disintegrative social benefits with new integrative ones. It is not "higher" or "lower" social standards that matter, but social standards that combine inner and outer integration more than before and that understand integration as a dynamic production process changing the structures instead of seeing it as an unproductive maintenance of structure at any cost. It is a paradigmatic change of the social order. The accompanying change of social integration approaches the European welfare states to the United States insofar as they face the same integration problems: the integration of marginalized groups. Nevertheless, they need not necessarily follow the liberal model of society in all its detail. They will not be more successful in solving the new integration problems with the old European welfare state model than the United States, but will only be able to counteract these problems with targeted and profound investments in new integration programmes (cf. Kaufmann 1997; Nullmeier 2000; Mau 2003).

The afore-described change of the social order brings both the mainly conservative and the mainly social democratic welfare states some part closer to the liberal regime. They all converge in the individualization of the inclusion in society, since individual educational success and the corresponding achievement on the market decide far more about participation in wealth than was the case in clearly more conservative or social democratic regimes. Far more importance is attributed to education as human capital; empowerment; and the entrepreneurial self (Bröckling 2007) in order to assert one's position in the competition for participation in wealth than to the protection against this competition. Also, equality of opportunity prior to entry into the labour market is more significant than equality of results after market competition. The essential trigger of this change is the transnationalization – and along with it national differentiation – of solidarity. According to Esping-Andersen (1990), the coalition of the working class with the farmers in the starting years and with the middle class during the years of maturation formed the crucial social foundation of the comprehensively compensating and caring welfare state. In the party system, this has shown its effects in the emergence of the big political parties, which formed a wide centre stretching both to the right and to the left. In this context, the conservative parties developed a comprehensive system of social security geared towards status maintenance and family support, while the big social democratic parties generated a likewise comprehensive system of social citizenship. Depending on the term of office of more conservative or more social democratic governments, the basic trend is more conservative or more egalitarian. In both cases, however, it has been geared towards comprehensive social security. In the context of the globalization of economy and solidarity, the coalition between the working class and the middle class has lost in strength. First of all, the middle class has grown so much that it stretched right up to the top and down to the lower end of the class structure. Large parts of the working class have become part of the middle class in education, living standard, lifestyle and awareness. What remained at the bottom end of the class structure is a lower class of lowly skilled people who can no longer expect the unrestrained solidarity of the skilled workforce. At the top of the class structure, a global elite or upper class goes ahead to detach itself from the bonds of national solidarity that have become too narrow. In this way, the class structure has been given new, sharper cleavages. It is no longer determined by a middle class stretching far into the top and the bottom end and thus embracing the whole society. The middle class has shrunk substantially and now serves as a point of friction for the fundamental conflict between the global elite geared towards transnationalism and the new lower class, whose national part has been left alone and thus forced to flee into a reactionary nationalism (cf. Bude 2008). The ethnically heterogeneous formation of the lower class prevents, however, its uniform political organization. In line with a study carried out by the German Institute for Economic Research, the middle class included around 64 per cent of the population in Germany in the 1980s, while it has shrunk to approximately 54 per cent today. At the top, the upper class of top incomes has grown, as has the lower class of low incomes and welfare recipients at the bottom. While, in 1986, a total of 16.5 per cent of all households achieved a net income of more than 150 per cent of the median, their number had risen to 20.5 per cent by 2006. The lowest income group earning less than 50 per cent of the median comprised of 6.3 per cent in 1986, while it had increased to 11.4 per cent by 2006 (DIW 2008).

In the party system, this development can be observed when looking at the shrinkage of the big political parties and the growth of parties that serve the interests and moods of groups released from the wide middle class in a targeted way. In Germany, the two big parties, *Christlich Demokratische Union/Christlich Soziale Union* (CDU/CSU) and *Sozialdemokratische Partei Deutschlands* (SPD), lost a substantial amount of members, supporters and voters. They represent the reduced stock of the middle class. The *Freie Demokratische Partei* (FDP), in contrast, has become a representative of the global upper class, while the *Left* has been able to win the lower class that is no longer being reached by the social democrats. After all, the *Left* has to share its clientele with right-wing extremist parties like the *Nationaldemokratische Partei Deutschlands* (NPD) and the *Deutsche Volksunion* (DVU) that enjoy varying success.

The fragmented party system is the political expression of the more fiercely accentuated class structure consisting of a shrunk middle class that is no longer representative of the societal whole; an upper class breaking out of the national solidarity community; and a lower class that feels no longer cared for in the national community and, hence, tends towards political extremism and xenophobia. Amid this scattered party landscape, the *Greens* represent an alternative intelligentsia that constitutes the global upper class's ecological conscience. Its global way of thinking shows as little understanding for the traditional forms of social partnership and the corresponding national solidarity pact as the global upper class consisting of managers, scientists and engineers.

The Hessian state elections of January 2009 point out the new political relationship of power in a way that has been exaggerated by the particular situation. After an initial phase of consolidation in the immediate post-war period from 1946 to 1954, where the FDP gained up to 31.8 per cent of the votes (1950), Hessen was firmly in the hands of the two big parties CDU and SPD who formed the governments in alternation. They held 80 to almost 90 per cent of the votes in the Wiesbaden state parliament. In 1999, their common share of votes amounted to 82.8 per cent. Ever since, however, they have been exposed to a process of shrinkage that culminated at 60.9 per cent, i.e. a decline of 21.9 per cent, at the elections of January 2009. On the other hand, the FDP from 1958 on and the Greens from 1982 on won merely 5–10 per cent of the votes (apart from one election where the Greens received 11.2 per cent). In 2009, the Left added to the party spectrum. All three parties together accounted for no less than 35.3 per cent of the votes. While the CDU reached a still rather respectable result of 37.2 per cent, the SPD arrived at a historical low of 23.7 per cent. The FDP, in contrast, rocketed from 9.4 per cent in 2008 to 16.7 per cent; the Greens went up from 7.5 to 13.7 per cent, and the Left entered the Hessian state parliament for the first time ever accounting for 5.4 per cent of the votes (Wikipedia 2009). Only part of this shift of power can be explained with the then prevailing political mood and the awkward manoeuvres of the SPD leaders with regard to an initially rejected and then failed coalition with the Left. In January 2009, a representative survey regarding elections for the German federal parliament produced an even worse result for the two big political parties together: CDU 34 per cent; SPD 23 per cent; FDP 18 per cent; Left 11 per cent; Greens 10 per cent (Blechschmidt 2009). Another survey, however, saw the FDP at 13 per cent only, while the CDU was ranked at 38 per cent (Süddeutsche Zeitung 2009). A substantial part of this change originates from the transformations of the class structure, which are reflected by the new party landscape. Figures C.1 and C.2 represent the changes of the class structure and the political power structure that have occurred between the 1980s and more recent times. The percentages below the party names show the results of the Hessian state elections of 1983 and 2009. Of course, there is no identical relationship between party votes and the outlined groups in the class structure. Nevertheless, the parties recruit their voters mainly from these strata (Figures C.1 and C.2).

The translation of the new class structure into the party system is shown directly when looking at the relationship between educational level and voting behaviour at the Hessian state elections in 2009. As far as university graduates are concerned, more people voted for the FDP and the Greens than for the CDU and SPD put together; 23 per cent of them voted for the FDP; 25 per cent for the Greens; 29 per cent for the CDU; and only 16 per cent for the SPD and 6 per cent for the Left. Among the voters having a university entrance diploma, 35 per cent opted for the CDU; 21 per cent for the SPD; 16 per cent for the FDP; 18 per cent for the Greens

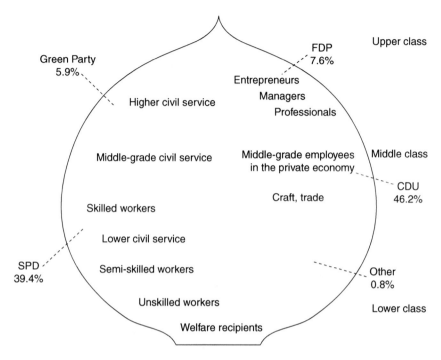

Figure C.1 Class structure and results of the Hessian state elections of 25 September 1983.

and 6 per cent for the Left. The by far biggest potential of voters for both big parties is formed by people with a lower secondary diploma of whom 43 per cent voted for the CDU and 30 per cent for the SPD; 15 per cent voted for the FDP; 6 per cent for the Greens; and 4 per cent for the Left (Süddeutsche Zeitung 2009). We can clearly see that the FDP and the Greens reached the largest potential of voters in the global upper class, with the economic elite and the technical intelligentsia on the one hand, and the creative intelligentsia on the other. The fact that a mere 4 per cent of lower secondary school graduates voted for the Left, but 6 per cent each of high-school and university graduates is not contradictory to the claim that the Left is rooted mainly in the new lower class. This claim must be understood in such a way that the emergence of the new lower class supplies potential voters and legitimatory reasons for both extreme right-wing and extreme left-wing parties. Part of the voters from the higher groups of education and income may then support parties – more or less as trustees – that raise their voices for the lower class that is marginalized in international competition (Figure C3).

The new class structure is mirrored not only by the party landscape, but also by the replacement of the old social partnership between trade unions and enterprises with Corporate Social Responsibility (CSR) (Hiß 2006; Bluhm 2008;

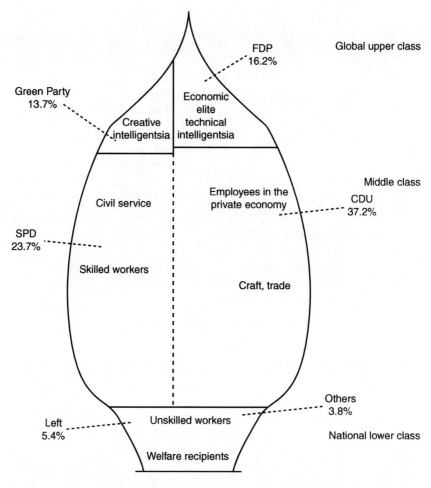

Figure C.2 Class structure and results of the Hessian state elections of 18 January 2009.

Curbach 2009). Multinational companies breaking free from national social partnership can present themselves as moral pioneers of the world society thanks to their strategic use of CSR and effective agreements such as the *Global Compact*. Their main topics are the global ecological balance and the fundamental rights of the workforce in developing countries. For them, the latter are given preference over the social obligations of the national community. Intelligent public relations measures help the companies to present themselves to the public as moral pioneers and to push the national public to the historical holding track. National outrage in the case of comprehensive dismissals and company closures are mitigated in the transnational context, where they are not considered a political power to be taken seriously. For instance, the mobile phone manufacturer,

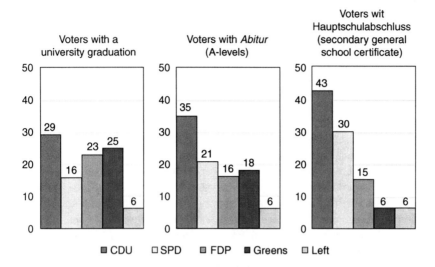

Figure C.3 Education and voting behaviour at the Hessian state elections on 18 January 2009 (source: Süddeutsche Zeitung 2009; Forschungsgruppe Wahlen).

Nokia, could easily counteract the protests raised against the closure of its Bochum plant by referring to the benefits emerging for the workforce at the newly built plant in Romania. The global ecological and humanitarian movements are the new dialogue partners of the multinational companies. They are in the same boat and have thus become part of the global upper class – though only part of the non-ruling group.

Representing this movement in the party scenery, the Greens form the counterpart to the FDP. Both parties stand for the global upper class with the FDP acting for the economic elite and the technocratic part of the knowledge elite and the Greens representing the part of the knowledge elite that displays a marked ecological awareness. Along with the humanitarian and ecological International Non-Governmental Organizations (INGOs), the multinational companies form a global social movement that works towards a transnationalization of solidarity whose construction goes hand in hand with the dismantling of national solidarity (Curbach 2009). This national disintegration that proceeds alongside transnational integration is shown by the accentuation of a new class structure in social-structural terms as well as by the split-up of the party system in political terms.

The fragmented party system finds it more difficult to reach a consensus about a comprehensive system of social security that includes the entire population. The agenda is put up by the global economic and knowledge elite. The latter builds on empowerment by the formation of human capital in the process of life-long learning, i.e. on the entrepreneurial self of every member of society. From the viewpoint of this paradigm, the old welfare state security systems are obstacles to the individual's self-responsible assertion in competition and its self-realization. Hence, they should be removed as much as possible in the interest of the individual itself. Instead, there is even greater need for good schools and colleges and for the related formation of human capital right through to the mobilization of even the last talent pools. Any kind of post-market social compensation can then be restricted to supporting those citizens who are unable to take part in working life for a more or less long period of time.

The traditional welfare regimes may still differ when it comes to implementing the new paradigm. A strictly liberal regime will try to guide as many talented young people as possible to the top of the stratified tertiary education by way of grants. Those citizens who have dropped out of competition will receive nothing but minimum support depending on their needs.

A liberalized conservative regime will, according to its own creed, aim at leading different talents to their appropriate position in the educational process; in doing so, it will continue to use the family as a stabilizing factor and safety net. Nevertheless, under the global regime of liberalism it will approach the outlines of a liberal order. Further elements of the global process of liberalization will contribute to this development. The EU-driven cut of professional protective mechanisms raises competitive pressure and, hence, the need for individual empowerment. The adjustment of the educational level between the genders suggests women become independent of their husbands by securing their own income. Hence, the model of the comprehensive and lasting social security of the mail breadwinner becomes obsolete. The change of unemployment benefits called "Hartz IV reforms" was fiercely debated in Germany. The old scheme guaranteed status-maintaining benefits for jobless people according to their last income for thirty-two months. This generous scheme was intended to support the whole family of a jobless male breadwinner. The new scheme has limited this generosity to twelve months of unemployment. This implies moving away from the model of the male breadwinner. It could, however, overcome all mobilized objections, since the old conservative model of status maintenance of the family breadwinner had lost its firm foundations due to the equal treatment of genders in education. In that way, Hartz IV was able to become a milestone in the turn away from the conservative welfare regime and the turn towards a liberal regime.

When implementing the Hartz IV reforms, it was crucial to unhinge union interests in the federal government's Hartz commission. After the Alliance for Jobs pursued in a cooperation between top governmental officials; employer associations; and trade unions according to the old model of corporatism had failed, the Schröder government manned the Hartz commission mainly with experts. These included second-tier experts from the employer federations and the trade unions, too, and not only top officials. In this way, the globally dominant economic doctrine could trigger necessary reforms directed at deregulation; liberalization; and residual instead of comprehensive welfare on the national level and finally overcome the long years of reluctance to reform. The breakthrough can be explained by a shift of power from the national party and association officials towards global experts in the wake of the transnationalization of the governance of economy and society. While, on the national level, party and association officials had been the top dogs for a long time, while the experts played only a subordinate serving role, the latter have gained the upper hand in the transnational context of benchmarking and monitoring through OECD reports and the EU's Open Method of Coordination (OMC). Under the regime of experts, global doctrines such as the liberalization programme of the OECD agenda of employment and growth in the knowledge-based economy or the Lisbon strategy regarding the EU's creation of the most competitive knowledge-based global economic area can make their way more easily when compared to national traditions of thought, institutional strongholds and interests.

We can observe the influence of experts in direct interaction with economic interests and against all party and association coalitions when taking the transformation of the American and German shareholder rights as an example. Philipp Klages (2010) has carried out an enlightening study on this topic. In the USA, the idea of company managements being first and foremost obliged to their shareholders (owners) ruled the understanding of stock corporations until the big Depression of the 1930s. In the following period, however, the idea was established that a company is a unit sui generis whose long-term stock must be secured by the managers, possibly even against short-term interests on the part of the shareholders. The rule of managers in the enterprises resulted from this institutionalist viewpoint. In the course of the growing significance of institutional investors – above all pension funds – a process of rethinking set in during the 1970s. Activated by the interests of the principal shareholders, the theory emerged in financial economics that enterprises are not a unit sui generis, but merely a complex of contracts. The contractual relationship between shareholders and company management formed the particular focus of interest here. From this new contractarian viewpoint, shareholder rights assumed far greater importance than had been the case from the former institutionalist viewpoint. Hence, the shareholder value has become the guideline of company management. It has been linked with the understanding of the control of company management as a market. The facilitation of hostile takeovers has created a market for company managements. When company managements have generated operative results below the actually feasible level of their companies, they run the risk of a hostile takeover, since investors can easily take over the underrated companies on the stock market by launching teasers for the existing shareholders and can, if necessary, sell them again after a time at a profit.

This transformation of economic thought has been followed by jurisprudence in the form of the economic analysis of law that has been influenced mainly by Richard Posner. In line with this theory, questions of law shall no longer be decided upon according to the independent legal criterion right vs. wrong, but instead according to the economic criterion of efficiency vs. inefficiency. The economic law has to provide efficient solutions for the regulations of the economy – in this case the stock corporation. Hence, the orientation of the stock corporation to the shareholder value has been justified by the legal contractual theory as an efficient formation of the relationship between the company and its shareholders. In the USA, an institutionalist countermovement came into being in the 1980s, however, which limited the further extension of shareholder rights.

In Germany, reforms first of all strengthened shareholder rights according to the American model in the 1990s, and even went much further later on than had been possible in the USA in the wake of the aforementioned institutionalist countermovement. Nevertheless, the spectacular hostile takeover of Mannesmann by Vodafone attributed more significance to counterforces, which contributed to a moderate regulation in the takeover law of 2002 that, after all, goes beyond the takeover possibilities existing in the USA.

The above example proves how the coalition of economic interests, economic thought and legal thought has fuelled the strengthening of shareholder rights to companies and other stakeholders such as the employees, at first in the USA and then, a good twenty years later, in Germany. In this process, old coalitions of parties, associations and the related experts were pushed aside. Due to the hegemonic position of the American financial economics and the American law firms in international contracting, American shareholder law has become a global model that serves as a basis of orientation for European reforms, too. Along with the interests of the institutional investors, the transnational knowledge elite has been able, in this way, to unhinge the resistance of national coalitions of parties and associations and their experts.

The social democratic welfare states in Scandinavia have also made substantial steps towards backing empowerment through lifelong learning and the individual's entrepreneurial activity. The term entrepreneur has been detached from the economic context and has spread in all functional parts of society. The social democratic feature of this programme, which aims at stimulating entrepreneurial thought among all citizens, is that the state makes more comprehensive investments in the provision of opportunities for learning and offers more generous support of all those citizens who are not sufficiently employable in spite of all efforts, than would have been the case in a strictly liberal regime (Marttila 2010).

Altogether, a clear movement of conservative and social democratic welfare states has taken place towards a liberal order. It would be too easy to ascribe this development to "inevitable" financial restrictions only. It is certainly true that political rhetoric is determined by such justifications, nevertheless they are unable to explain why such a profound societal change is not stopped with more resistance. The deeper reasons for this lack of far-reaching resistance are rooted in the fact that the comprehensive and institutional welfare state (Titmuss 1958) has lost the social-structural foundation of support by a middle class that stretches right through to the top and the bottom end of the class structure. Instead, the residual welfare state, which is merely interested in giving minimum support according to needs to weakest groups, is gaining in significance. This development can be attributed to the transnationalization of solidarity and the inherent disintegration of national societies. The societal change is additionally supported by processes of the tertiarization of the economy; the expansion of education; and the equal treatment of genders.

Figure C.4 summarizes the crucial causal factors, pathways and stations of the identified societal change. Following Durkheim's (1964) ideas, we can see the shrinking distances in the wake of the global demographic growth and the acceleration of transport and communication as the essential trigger of this change. It enhances international competition for scarce resources. Several adjustment strategies serve the assertion in the fiercer competition: migration, crime, war and specialization. The latter involves international division of labour to the extent where the transnationalization of the economic constitution provides the necessary legal order. The more the international labour division advances, the more it advances a structural change of solidarity, a structural change of the economy and a paradigmatic change of justice, which intensify each other. The change in solidarity leads to a new class structure and the resulting antagonism of globalism and nationalism in the party system. In the OECD countries, the economic change is increasingly replacing incremental innovations with radical ones and implies a destabilization of economy and society with trends towards anomie. The change in justice aims at removing discrimination of any kind within the transnational horizon of moral discourses; at removing in-group and out-group morality; and, ultimately, at establishing the change of collectivistic forms of inclusion in society into the individual inclusion by human capital formation. The trends towards anomie that accompany this change support, on the one hand, rebellion as the radicalization of political struggles and, on the other hand, relative exclusion and delinquency as the radicalization of the individual's striving for achievement.

The causal factors, paths and stations of societal change as they are summarized in Figure C.4 along with their interdependencies turn the focus of interest to social change. It is these forces that work towards change. The change is, however, continually opposed by factors of inertia and path dependency: thinking in national traditions; institutional consolidation and complementarities; powerful interests in the status quo; and transaction costs. They can delay change for a long time and gear it in a specific national direction. This process creates hybrids with their particular unique consequences (Thelen 2002). The risks of globalization may support political coalitions working towards the protection of the affected workforce and clinging to welfare state securities that would otherwise fall prey to political reforms. Arguments claiming that globalization requires the protection of the welfare state due to the accompanying risks on the labour market to be able to advance any further (Rodrik 1997; Rieger and Leibfried 2001) support the welfare state's forces of persistence. Nevertheless, we cannot deny that a societal change towards a more liberal regime, and away from the institutional towards the residual welfare state in Titmuss's (1958) sense is taking place indeed, even though it is path dependent and does not occur in the same form and at the same speed everywhere (Pierson 2004; Beyer 2006). This fact needs an explanation.

The common explanatory tools are not sufficient to understand the deeper causes of change. This applies, for instance, to the search for variables, which is common practice in political science, such as the number of years conservative

260 Conclusion

or social democratic parties have been in government; the number of veto players; or fiscal crises (Iversen 1999; Huber and Stephens 2001; Swank 2002; Tsebelis 2002). Such explanations are too superficial. They are unable to explain the deeper societal change we can observe everywhere. Nor do functionalist explanations, which interpret the welfare state or – alternatively – trade protectionism as an insurance against the risks of globalization, supply an explanation of the fact that welfare state securities have been transformed towards a liberal regime all around. The additional support of this explanation with the dependence of democratically elected governments on a risk-averse majority of voters (Rieger and Leibfried 2001) does not help either to uncover the reasons and the

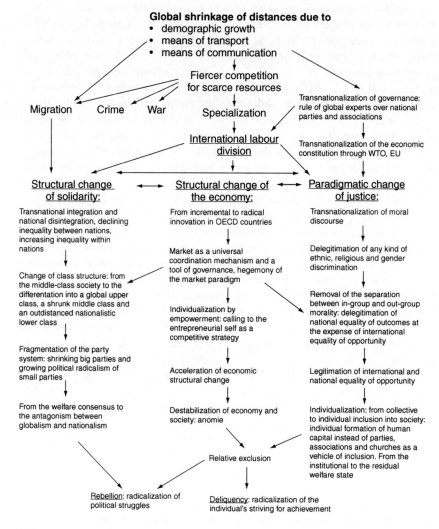

Figure C.4 Causal factors, pathways and stations of societal change.

direction of change. A reference to the political implementation of neo-liberalism by the World Bank, the International Monetary Fund, American think tanks and the neo-conservative governments of Ronald Reagan and Margaret Thatcher are just as insufficient (Dezalay and Garth 1998; Fourcade 2006). Added to this is the fact that contractual law is essentially marked by American law firms according to the liberal American legal thought in international economic transactions. In Europe, there was a substantial amount of political headwind both from traditionally conservative and traditionally social democratic parties. It has delayed change for a certain time, but could not avoid it completely. It is not sufficient either to blame the oil crises of 1973 and 1979; the economic stagflation of the 1970s; the following restrictive monetary policy of central banks; and the crisis of Keynesianism for the global spreading of the new supply-side policy of neo-liberalism (Traxler 2005). Historical events of this kind can explain why neo-liberalism's supply-side policy witnessed a boom at that time and kicked at open doors; yet they do not show why such a profound structural change of the entire societal order has proceeded towards a liberalization of all welfare regimes. Structural change cannot be explained by single historical events. It requires an explanation by preceding and accompanying structural shifts. The global spreading of neo-liberalism mirrors these underlying structural shifts. They support neo-liberalism which, in its turn, strengthens and retroacts upon them by providing them with a meaning and embedding them in a paradigm of the societal order. The identified structural change requires a structure-theoretical explanation.

The explanation outlined here anchors the structural change from the institutional to the residual and from the consumptive to the productive welfare state and the competition state as well as from collective inclusion by parties, associations and churches to individual inclusion by the formation of human capital essentially in three interdependent structural shifts. These structural shifts are supported by the global shortening of distances; the fiercer competition for scarce resources; the thus enforced specialization; and its transfer into international labour division under the terms of the transnationalization of the economic constitution. The first of the aforementioned three interdependent structural shifts concerns the economic change of the OECD countries from incremental to radical innovation and the thus triggered acceleration of economic and structural change. This change should be interpreted as a *functional adjustment* of the OECD countries to fiercer competition both among each other and with the developing countries, which they try to cope with through an increasing turn towards radical innovations. A functional alternative to this situation would be a strengthened protectionism, which is, however, increasingly robbed of its legitimacy in a global discourse headed by the World Trade Organization (WTO). This shows the interdependence between the economic structural change and the change of justice. The second structural shift occurs in the class structure and the resulting shift of power relationships in the political space in general and the field of social policy in particular. It refers to the loss in power of the big parties and the gain in power of small, more radical parties. As a result, the old welfare consensus is replaced with a new antagonism between globalism and nationalism. The third structural shift happens in the discourse on justice, which is detached from the national horizon of thought and subjected to a global horizon. Consequently, in-group and out-group morality are being removed and justice is being interpreted as internal and external equal opportunity for all. This change of justice supports the individualization of inclusion into society.

By focusing on the three identified structural shifts and their interdependencies, we combine a functionalistic explanatory approach concentrating on the adjustment of the OECD countries' economy to international competition with a class- and field-theoretical approach centred on the change of the class structure and – in homology – of the party spectrum, and also with a discourse-theoretical approach focused on the paradigmatic change of justice in the wake of the transnationalization of the political field. A fourth, institutionalist explanatory approach, complements the explanatory programme: the identified paradigmatic change of justice is interpreted as the transfer of a global model to nation states aimed at the acquisition of legitimacy in the context of international benchmarking (supported by rankings); moreover, the change along national developmental paths is regarded as the inertia of existing institutions (Meyer and Rowan 1977; DiMaggio and Powell 1983; Hall and Taylor 1996; Immergut 1998). Since the discursive construction of transnational justice retroacts on the structural change of economy and solidarity in a reifying way, substantial forces of social construction are also involved in the overall societal change (Berger and Luckmann 1969/1977). We can see, therefore, that various explanatory tools need to be combined in order to reach a deeper understanding and a more thorough explanation of the ongoing societal change. We have to bear in mind, however, that the description of this change is an ideal-typical exaggeration, but not a representation of the more varied, more fragmented and more brittle empirical reality. The advantage of such an exaggeration is that it highlights a deeper structural change of society, which would otherwise remain concealed behind the complexity of Yes and No, of change and continuity, of divergence and convergence.

To sum up, the identified societal change is fuelled in its core by four processes that strengthen each other. *Economic globalization* implies a radicalization of innovations that, in its turn, involves an acceleration of the economic structural change. It is related with an intensified *societal stratification*, the accentuation of the class structure, and the end to the middle-class society. Added to this is the *political fragmentation* in the global multilevel system of governance involving a fragmentation of the party system and an end to the welfare state coalition of the big parties. The legitimation of this change results from processes of *cultural universalization* with the transnationalization of justice and the removal of in-group and out-group morality (Figure C.5).

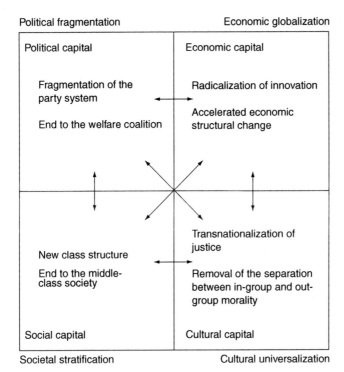

Figure C.5 Interdependent processes of societal change.

References

Acocella, N. and Leoni, R. (eds) (2007) *Social Pacts, Employment and Growth. A Reappraisal of Ezio Tarantelli's Thought*, Heidelberg: Physica Verlag.
Addison, J.T., Bailey, R.W. and Siebert, W.S. (2007) "The Impact of Deunionization on Earnings Dispersion Revisited", in: S.W. Polachek and O. Bargain (eds) *Aspects of Worker Well-Being* (*Research in Labor Economics*, Vol. 26), Bingley, UK: Emerald Group Publishing Limited, 337–363.
Adloff, F. (2010) *Philanthropisches Handeln. Eine historische Soziologie des Stiftens in Deutschland und den USA*, Frankfurt/New York: Campus.
Adloff, F. (2005) *Zivilgesellschaft. Theorie und politische Praxis*, Frankfurt/New York: Campus.
Agell, J. (1999) "On the Benefits from Rigid Labour Markets: Norms, Market Failures, and Social Insurance", *The Economic Journal*, 109 (February): F143–F164.
Agion, P. (2002) "Schumpeterian Growth Theory and the Dynamics of Income Inequality", *Econometrica*, 70 (3): 855–882.
Agnew, R. (1999) "A General Strain Theory of Community Differences in Crime Rates", *Journal of Research in Crime and Delinquency*, 36 (1): 123–155.
Alber, J. (2006) "Das europäische Sozialmodell und die USA", *Leviathan* 34 (2): 208–241.
Albert, M. (1992) *Kapitalismus contra Kapitalismus*. Frankfurt/New York: Campus.
Albin, C. (2001) *Justice and Fairness in International Negotiation*, Cambridge: Cambridge University Press.
Alcock, P., Beatty, C., Fothergill, S., Macmillan, R. and Yeandle. S. (2003) *Work to Welfare. How Men Become Detached from the Labour Market*, Cambridge: Cambridge University Press.
Alderson, A.S., Beckfield, J. and Nielsen, F. (2005) "Exactly How Has Income Inequality Changed? Patterns of Distributional Change in Core Societies", *International Journal of Comparative Sociology*, 46 (5–6): 405–423.
Alemann, U. von, Heinze, R.G. and Hombach, B. (eds) (1990) *Die Kraft der Region: Nordrhein-Westfalen in Europa*, Bonn: Dietz.
Alesina, A. and Angeletos, G.-M. (2005) "Fairness and Redistribution", *American Economic Review*, 95 (4): 960–980.
Alexander, J.C. (2006) *The Civil Sphere*, Oxford: Oxford University Press.
Allbus (1994) *Zentralarchiv für empirische Sozialforschung*, ZA 1795. Cologne.
Allmendinger, J. and Leibfried, S. (2003) "Education and the Welfare State: The Four Worlds of Competence Production", *Journal of European Social Policy*, 13 (1): 63–81.
Alon, S. and Tienda, M. (2007) "Diversity, Opportunity, and the Shifting Meritocracy in Higher Education", *American Sociological Review*, 72 (4): 487–511.

Altvater, E. and Mahnkopf, B. (1996) *Grenzen der Globalisierung. Ökonomie, Ökologie und Politik in der Weltgesellschaft*, Münster: Westfälisches Dampfboot.

Amoore, L. and Langley, P. (2004) "Ambiguities of Global Civil Society", *Review of International Studies*, 30 (1): 89–110.

Anderson, B. (1988) *Die Erfindung der Nation*, Frankfurt a.M./New York: Campus.

Anderson, K.M. (2004) "Pension Politics in Three Small States: Denmark, Sweden and the Netherlands", *Canadian Journal of Sociology*, 29 (2): 289–312.

Andreß, H.-J. and Heien, T. (2001) "Four Worlds of Welfare States Attitudes? A Comparison of Germany, Norway, and the United States", *European Sociological Review*, 17 (4): 337–356.

Anheier, H.K. and Leat, D. (2006) *Creative Philanthropy*, London: Routledge.

Anheier, H.K. and Toepler, S. (2003) "Bürgerschaftliches Engagement zur Stärkung der Zivilgesellschaft im internationalen Vergleich", in: Enquête-Kommission "Zukunft des bürgerschaftlichen Engagements" Deutscher Bundestag (ed.), *Bürgerschaftliches Engagement im internationalen Vergleich*, Opladen: Leske + Budrich, 13–55.

Anheier, H.K., Priller, E., Seibel, W. and Zimmer, A. (eds) (1997) *Der Dritte Sektor in Deutschland. Organisationen zwischen Markt und Staat im gesellschaftlichen Wandel*, Berlin: edition sigma.

Antonczyk, D., Fitzenberger, B. and Sommerfeld, K. (2010) "Rising Wage Inequality, the Decline of Collective Bargaining, and the Gender Wage Gap", *Labour Economics*, 17 (5): 835–847.

Antony, J. and Entorf, H. (2003) "Zur Gültigkeit der Abschreckung im Sinne der ökonomischen Theorie der Kriminalität: Grundzüge einer Meta-Studie", in: H.J. Albrecht and H. Entorf (eds) *Kriminalität, Ökonomie und Europäischer Sozialstaat*, Heidelberg: Physica-Verlag, 167–185.

Anxo, D. and Sterrie, D. (2002) "The Job Creation Potential of the Service Sector in Europe", Transfer: *European Review of Labour and Research*, 8 (3): 377–391.

Archibugi, D. and Held, D. (eds) (1995) *Cosmopolitan Democracy*, Cambridge: Polity Press.

Archibugi, D., Held, D. and Köhler, M. (eds) (1998) *Re-imagining Political Community*, Cambridge: Polity Press.

Armingeon, K. (2005) "Die Ausbreitung der Aktiengesellschaft und der Wandel des Wohlfahrtsstaates und der Arbeitsbeziehungen", in: P. Windolf (ed.) *Finanzmarkt-Kapitalismus. Analysen zum Wandel von Produktionsregimen. Sonderheft 45 der Kölner Zeitschrift für Soziologie und Sozialpsychologie*, Wiesbaden: VS Verlag für Sozialwissenschaften, 441–459.

Armingeon, K. (1988) "Gewerkschaftliche Entwicklung und ökonomischer, beschäftigungsstruktureller und politischer Wandel. Das Beispiel der Gewerkschaften in der BRD", *Soziale Welt*, 39: 459–485.

Armingeon, K., Potolidis, P., Gerber, M. and Leimgruber, P. (2009) Comparative Political Data Set I 1960–2007. Trade union membership. Online. Available at: http://stats.oecd.org/Index.aspx?DatasetCode=U_D_D (accessed 13 February 2011).

Arrow, K., Bowles, S. and Durlauf, S. (eds) (2000) *Meritocracy and Economic Inequality*, Princeton: Princeton University Press.

Arts, W. and Gelissen, J. (2001) "Welfare States, Solidarity and Justice Principles: Does the Type Really Matter?" *Acta Sociologica*, 44 (4): 283–299.

Austin, J., Stevenson, H. and Wei-Skillern, J. (2006) "Social and Commercial Entrepreneurship: Same, Different, or Both?", *Entrepreneurship Theory and Practice*, 30 (1): 1–22.

Axford, B. (1995) *The Global System. Economics, Politics and Culture*, Cambridge: Polity Press.

References

Bach, M. (2008) *Europa ohne Gesellschaft. Politische Soziologie der europäischen Integration*, Wiesbaden: VS Verlag.
Backhaus-Maul, H. (1999) *Von der Sozialhilfe in die Erwerbsarbeit. Die Welfare Reform in den USA als Vorbild?*, Frankfurt/New York: Campus.
Bambra, C. (2006) "Decommodification and the Worlds of Welfare Revisited", *Journal of European Social Policy*, 16 (1): 73–80.
Banfield, E.C. (1958) *The Moral Basis of a Backward Society*, New York: Free Press.
Bannink, D. and Hoogenboom, M. (2007) "Hidden Change: Disaggregation of Welfare State Regimes for Greater Insight into Welfare State Change", *Journal of European Social Policy*, 17 (1): 19–32.
Banting, K.G. (2005) "The Multicultural Welfare State: International Experience and North American Narratives", *Social Policy & Administration*, 39 (2): 98–115.
Barnett, M. and Finnemoore, M. (2004) *Rules for the World: International Organizations in Global Politics*, Ithaca, NY: Cornell University Press.
Bartels, L.M. (2007) *Unequal Democracy. The Political Economy of the New Gilded Age*. Princeton: Princeton University Press.
Batey, P.W.J. and Friedrich, P. (eds) (2000) *Regional Competition*, Berlin, Heidelberg, New York: Springer.
Batton, C. and Jensen, G. (2002) "Decommodification and Homicide Rates in the 20th Century United States", *Homicide Studies*, 6 (1): 6–38.
Baumert, J., Klieme, E., Neubrand, M., Prenzel, M., Schiefele, U., Schneider, W., Stanat, P., Tillmann, K.-J. and Weiß, M. (eds) (2001) *PISA 2000. Basiskompetenzen von Schülerinnen und Schülern im internationalen Vergleich*, Opladen: Leske + Budrich.
Beck, U. (1999) *Schöne neue Arbeitswelt*, Opladen: Leske + Budrich, 7–66.
Beck, U. (1998) "Wie wird Demokratie im Zeitalter der Globalisierung möglich? – Eine Einleitung", in: U. Beck (ed.) *Politik der Globalisierung*, Frankfurt a.M.: Suhrkamp.
Beck, U. (1997) *Was ist Globalisierung?* Frankfurt a.M.: Suhrkamp.
Becker, G.S. (1968) "Crime and Punishment: An Economic Approach", *Journal of Political Economy*, 76: 169–217.
Beckert, J. (2010a) "How do Fields Change? The Interrelations of Institutions, Networks, and Cognition in the Dynamics of Markets", *Organization Studies*, 31 (5): 605–627.
Beckert, J. (2010b) "Institutional Isomorphism Revisited: Convergence and Divergence in Institutional Change", *Sociological Theory*, 28: 150–166.
Beckert, J. (2009a) "The Social Order of Markets", *Theory and Society*, 38 (3): 245–269.
Beckert, J. (2009b) "Wirtschaftssoziologie als Gesellschaftstheorie", *Zeitschrift für Soziologie*, 38 (3): 182–197.
Beckett, K. (1997) *Making Crime Pay: Law and Order in Contemporary American Politics*, New York: Oxford University Press.
Beckett, K. and Western, B. (2001) "Governing Social Marginality: Welfare, Incarceration, and the Transformation of State Policy", *Punishment & Society*, 3 (1): 43–59.
Beckfield, J. (2006) "European Integration and Income Inequality", *American Sociological Review*, 71 (6): 964–985.
Benner, C. (2002) *Work in the New Economy. Flexible Labour Markets in Silicon Valley*, Oxford: Blackwell.
Benner, M. (1997) *The Politics of Growth*, Lund: Arkiv.
Benner, M. and Bundgaard Vad, T. (2000) "Sweden and Denmark: Defending the Welfare State", in: F.W. Scharpf and V.A. Schmidt (eds) *Welfare and Work in the Open Economy, Vol. II*, Oxford: Oxford University Press, 399–466.

Bennet, W.L. (1998) "The Uncivic Culture: Communication, Identity, and the Rise of Lifestyle Politics", *Political Science and Politics*, 31: 741–761.
Berger, J. (2009) *Der diskrete Charme des Marktes. Zur sozialen Problematik der Marktwirtschaft*, Wiesbaden: VS Verlag.
Berger, P.L. and Luckmann, T. (1969/1977) *Die gesellschaftliche Konstruktion der Wirklichkeit*. Frankfurt a.M.: Fischer.
Berger, R. (1999) *Der Umbau des Sozialstaates*, Opladen: Westdeutscher Verlag.
Berger, S. and Dore, R. (eds) (1996) *National Diversity and Global Capitalism*, Ithaca, NY: Cornell University Press.
Berkel, R. van and Hornemann Møller, I. (eds) (2002) *Active Social Policies in the EU. Inclusion through Participation?* Bristol: The Policy Press.
Berkel, R. van and Valkenburg, B. (eds) (2007) *Making it Personal. Individualizing Activation Services in the EU*, Bristol: The Policy Press.
Bernburg, J.G. (2002) "Anomie, Social Change and Crime. A Theoretical Examination of Institutional-Anomie Theory", *British Journal of Criminology*, 42 (4): 729–742.
Bernburg, J.G., Thorlindson, T. and Sigfusdottir, I.D. (2009) "Relative Deprivation and Adolescent Outcomes in Iceland: A Multilevel Test", *Social Forces*, 87 (3): 1223–1250.
Bernhard, S. (2010) *Die Konstruktion von Inklusion. Europäische Sozialpolitik aus soziologischer Perspektive*, Frankfurt/New York: Campus.
Bernhard, S. (2005) *Sozialpolitik im Mehrebenensystem. Die Bekämpfung von Armut und sozialer Ausgrenzung im Rahmen der Offenen Methode der Koordinierung*, Berlin: Wissenschaftlicher Verlag Berlin.
Berthold, N. (1997) *Der Sozialstaat im Zeitalter der Globalisierung*, Tübingen: Mohr Siebeck.
Beyer, J. (2006) *Pfadabhängigkeit. Über institutionelle Kontinuität, anfällige Stabilität und funktionalen Wandel*, Frankfurt/New York: Campus.
Bhagwati, J.N. (2004) *In Defense of Globalization*, Oxford: Oxford University Press.
Bhagwati, J.N. (1998) *A Stream of Windows: Unsettling Reflections on Trade, Immigration, and Democracy*, Cambridge, MA and London: MIT Press.
Björklund, A. (2000) "Going Different Ways: Labour Market Policy in Denmark and Sweden", in: G. Esping-Andersen and M. Regini (eds) *Why Deregulate Labour Markets?* Oxford: Oxford University Press, 148–180.
Björklund, A., Clarke, M.A., Edin, P.A., Fredriksson, P. and Krueger, A.B. (2005) *The Market Comes to Education in Sweden*, New York: Russel Sage Foundation.
Blechschmidt, P. (2009) "Westerwelles Höhenflug. FDP liegt laut Meinungsumfrage bei 18 Prozent – nur noch fünf Punkte hinter der SPD", in: *Süddeutsche Zeitung* 65, No. 35, 12 February 2009, 5.
Bleses, P. and Seeleib-Kaiser, M. (2004) *The Dual Transformation of the German Welfare State*, Houndmills, Basingstoke: Palgrave Macmillan.
Blomqvist, P. (2004) "The Choice Revolution: Privatization of Swedish Welfare Services in the 1990s", *Social Policy & Administration*, 38 (2): 139–155.
Blonigen, B.A. and Kolpin, V. (2007) "Technology, Agglomeration, and Regional Competition for Investment", *Canadian Journal of Economics*, 40 (4): 1149–1167.
Bluhm, K. (2008) "Corporate Social Responsibility – Zur Moralisierung von Unternehmen aus soziologischer Perspektive", in: A. Maurer and U. Schimank (eds) *Die Gesellschaft der Unternehmen – Die Unternehmen der Gesellschaft*, Wiesbaden: VS Verlag für Sozialwissenschaften, 144–162.
Blyth, M. (2002) *Great Transformations. Economic Ideas and Institutional Change in the Twentieth Century*, Cambridge: Cambridge University Press.

BMBF (2010) *Bildung in Deutschland*. Online. Available at: www.bmbf.de/pubRD/ bildung_in_deutschland_2010.pdf (accessed 18 March 2011).
Bode, I. (2004) *Disorganisierter Wohlfahrtskapitalismus. Die Reorganisation des Sozialsektors in Deutschland, Frankreich und Großbritannien*, Wiesbaden: VS Verlag.
Boiral, O. (2008) "The Certificate of Corporate Conduct: Issues and Prospect", *International Labour Review*, 142 (3): 317–340.
Boli, J. and Thomas, G.M. (eds) (1999) *Constructing World Culture. International Nongovernmental Organizations Since 1875*, Stanford: Stanford University Press.
Bornschier, V. (2005) "Varianten des Kapitalismus in reichen Demokratien beim Übergang in das neue Gesellschaftsmodell", in: P. Windolf (ed.). *Finanzmarkt-Kapitalismus. Analysen zum Wandel von Produktionsregimen. Sonderheft 45 der Kölner Zeitschrift für Soziologie und Sozialpsychologie*, Wiesbaden: VS Verlag für Sozialwissenschaften, 331–371.
Börsch, A. (2007) *Global Pressure, National System. How German Corporate Governance is Changing*, Ithaca, NY: Cornell University Press.
Bourdieu, P. (2000) *Les structures sociales de l'économie*, Paris: Seuil.
Bourdieu, P. (1998) *Practical Reason. On the Theory of Action*, Cambridge: Polity Press.
Bourdieu, P. (1994) *Raisons pratiques. Sur la théorie de l'action*, Paris: Seuil.
Bourdieu, P. (1986) "The Forms of Capital", in: J.G. Richardson (ed.). *Handbook of Theory and Research for the Sociology of Education*. New York: Greenwood, 241–258.
Bradley, D.H. and Stephens, J.D. (2007) "Employment Performance in OECD Countries. A Test of Neoliberal and Institutionalist Hypotheses", *Comparative Political Studies*, 40 (12): 1486–1510.
Bradshaw, Y.W. and Wallace, M. (1996) *Global Inequalities*, Thousand Oaks, CA: Pine Forge Press.
Brady, D., Beckfield, J. and Seeleib-Kaiser, M. (2005) "Economic Globalization and the Welfare State in Affluent Democracies, 1975–2001", in: *American Sociological Review* 70, 921–948.
Brinkmann, C. (1984) "Die individuellen Folgen langfristiger Arbeitslosigkeit. Ergebnisse einer repräsentativen Längsschnittuntersuchung", *Mitteilungen aus der Arbeitsmarkt- und Berufsforschung*, 4: 454–473.
Bröcker, J., Dohse, D. and Soltwedel, R. (eds) (2003) *Innovation Clusters and Interregional Competition*, Berlin, Heidelberg, New York: Springer.
Bröckling, U. (2007) *Das unternehmerische Selbst. Soziologie einer Subjektivierungsform*, Frankfurt a.M.: Suhrkamp.
Brown, P. (2000) "The Globalization of Positional Competition?", *Sociology*, 34 (4): 633–653.
Brown, P. and Hesketh, A. (2004) *The Mismanagement of Talent. Employability and Jobs in the Knowledge Economy*, Oxford: Oxford University Press.
Brown, P. and Tannock, S. (2009) "Education, Meritocracy and the Global War for Talent", *Journal of Education Policy*, 24 (4): 377–392.
Brown, P., Lauder, H. and Ashton, D. (2010) *The Broken Promises of Education, Jobs and Incomes*, Oxford: Oxford University Press.
Brubaker, W.R. (1992) *Citizenship and Nationhood in France and Germany*, Cambridge, MA: Harvard University Press.
Bruce, M.A. (2000) "Inequality and Delinquency: Sorting out Some Class and Race Effects", *Race & Society*, 2 (2): 133–148.
Brunkhorst, H. (2002) *Solidarität. Von der Bürgerfreundschaft zur globalen Rechtsgenossenschaft*, Frankfurt a.M.: Suhrkamp.

Bude, H. (2008) *Die Ausgeschlossenen. Das Ende vom Traum einer gerechten Gesellschaft*, München: Carl Hanser Verlag.
Bukodi, E. and Goldthorpe, J.H. (2009) "Market versus Meritocracy: Hungary as a Critical Case", *European Sociological Review*, 26 (6): 655–674.
Bureau of Justice Statistics (2011a) *Prison and Jail Inmates at Midyear 2006*. Online. Available at: http://bjs.ojp.usdoj.gov/content/pub/pdf/pjim06.pdf (accessed 9 March 2011).
Bureau of Justice Statistics (2011b) *Uniform Crime Reporting Statistics*. Online. Available at: www.ucrdatatool.gov/Search/Crime/State/RunCrimeStatebyState.cfm (accessed 9 March 2011).
Bureau of Justice Statistics (2011c) *Correctional Populations in the United States 2009 and Prisoners in 2009*. Online. Available at: http://bjs.ojp.usdoj.gov/content/glance/sheets/incrt.csv (accessed 28 February 2011),
Bursik, R.J. and Grasmick, H.G. (1993) "Economic Deprivation and Neighborhood Crime Rates, 1960–1980", *Law and Society Review*, 27 (2): 263–284.
Cahn, E.S. (1990) "Service Credits: Eine neue Währung für den Wohlfahrtsstaat", in: R.G. Heinze and C. Offe (eds) *Formen der Eigenarbeit*, Opladen: Westdeutscher Verlag, 125–146.
Campbell, J.L. and Pedersen, O.K. (2007a) "Institutional Competitiveness in the Global Economy: Denmark, the United States and the Varieties of Capitalism", *Regulation & Governance*, 1 (3): 230–246.
Campbell, J.L. and Pedersen, O.K. (2007b) "The Varieties of Capitalism and Hybrid Success. Denmark in the Global Economy", *Comparative Political Studies*, 40 (3): 307–332.
Card, D., Lemieux, T. and Riddell, W.C. (2004) "Unions and Wage Inequality", *Journal of Labor Research* 25 (4): 519–559.
Carr, F. and Massey, A. (1999) *Public Policy in the New Europe*, Cheltenham: Edward Elgar.
Casper, S. (2001) "The Legal Framework of Corporate Governance: The Influence of Contract Law on Company Strategies in Germany and the United States", in: P.A. Hall and D. Soskice (eds) *Varieties of Capitalism. The Institutional Foundations of Comparative Advantage*, Oxford: Oxford University Press, 387–416.
Castells, M. (1996) *The Rise of the Network Society*, Malden/Oxford: Blackwell.
Cattero, B. (ed.) (1998) *Modell Deutschland – Modell Europa*, Opladen: Leske + Budrich.
Cerny, P.G. (2010) "The Competition State Today: From Raison d'Etat to Raison du Monde", *Policy Studies*, 4 (1): 1–17.
Cerny, P.G. (2008) "Embedded Neoliberalism: The Evolution of a Hegemonic Paradigm", *The Journal of International Trade and Diplomacy*, 2 (1): 1–46.
Cerny, P.G. (2005) "Political Globalization and the Competition State", in: R. Stubbs and G.R.D. Underhill (eds) *The Political Economy of the Changing Global Order*, 3rd edn, Oxford: Oxford University Press, 376–386.
Cerny, P.G. (2000) "Globalization and the Restructuring of the Political arena: Paradoxes of the Competition State", in: R. Germain (ed.) *Globalization and its Critics*, London: Macmillan: 117–138.
Cerny, P.G. (1997) "Paradoxes of the Competition State: The Dynamics of Globalization", *Government and Opposition*, 32 (2): 251–274.
Cerny, P.G. (1990) *The Changing Architecture of Politics: Structure, Agency and the Future of the State*, London: Sage.

Chamlin, M.B. and Cochran, J.K. (2005) "Ascribed Economic Inequality and Homicide Among Modern Societies", *Homicide Studies*, 9 (1): 3–29.

Charnovitz, S. (2004) "The WTO and Cosmopolitics", *Economics & Law*, 7 (3): 675–682.

Choi, M. (2006) "Threat Effects of Capital Mobility on Wage Bargaining", in: B. Pranab, S. Bowles and M. Wallerstein (eds) *Globalization and Egalitarian Redistribution*, New York: Russel Sage Foundation, 64–86.

Clasen, J. (2005) *Reforming European Welfare States. Germany and the United Kingdom Compared*, Oxford: Oxford University Press.

Clasen, J. and Siegel, N.A. (2007) *Investigating Welfare State Change. The 'Dependent Variable Problem' in Comparative Analysis*. Cheltenham: Edward Elgar.

Clegg, D. (2007) "Continental Drift: On Unemployment Policy Change in Bismarckian Welfare States", *Social Policy & Administration*, 41 (4): 597–617.

Cloward, R.A. (1959) "Illegitimate Means, Anomie, and Deviant Behavior", *American Sociological Review*, 24: 64–176.

Cogneau, D. and Naudet, J.-D. (2006) "Who Deserves Aid? Equality of Opportunity, International Aid, and Poverty Reduction", *World Development* 35 (1): 104–120.

Cohen, J. and Arato, A. (1992) *Civil Society and Political Theory*. Cambridge, MA: MIT Press.

Conroy, M.E. (2007) *Branded! How the 'Certification Revolution' is Transforming Global Corporations*, Gabvriola Island, BC: New Society Publishers.

Cooke, P., Heidenreich, M. and Braczyk, H.-J. (eds) (2004) *Regional Innovation Systems. The Role of Governance in a Globalized World*, 2nd edn. London: Routledge.

Cornia, G.A. (2004) *Inequality, Growth, and the Poverty in an Era of Liberalization and Globalization*, Oxford: Oxford University Press.

Cox, R.H. (2004) "The Path-dependency of an Idea: Why Scandinavian Welfare States Remain Distinct", *Social Policy & Administration*, 38 (2): 204–219.

Cox, R.H. (2001) "The Social Construction of an Imperative: Why Welfare Reform Happened in Denmark and the Netherlands but Not in Germany", *World Politics*, 53 (3): 463–498.

Crepaz, M. (2008) *Trust Beyond Borders. Immigration, the Welfare State, and Identity in Modern Societies*, Ann Arbor: University of Michigan Press.

Crouch, C., Finegold, D. and Sako, M. (1999) *Are Skills the Answer? The Political Economy of Skill Creation in Advanced Industrial Countries*, Oxford: Oxford University Press.

Culpepper, P.D. (2002) *Creating Cooperation. How States Develop Human Capital in Europe*, Ithaca, NY: Cornell University Press.

Curbach, J. (2009) *Die Corporate-Social-Responsibility-Bewegung*, Wiesbaden: VS Verlag.

Cusack, T.R., Iversen, T. and Soskice, D. (2007) "Economic Interests and the Origins of Electoral Systems", *American Political Science Review*, 202 (3): 373–391.

Daguerre, A. (2007) *Active Labour Market Policies and Welfare Reform: Europe and the US in Comparative Perspective*, London: Palgrave.

Dahl, C.M., Le Maire, D. and Münch, J.R. (2009) "Wage Dispersion and Decentralization of Wage Bargaining", *Discussion Papers*, Department of Economics, University of Copenhagen No. 09–15.

Dahrendorf, R. (1965) *Bildung ist Bürgerrecht: Plädoyer für eine aktive Bildungspolitik*, Bramsche/Osnabrück: Nannen-Verlag.

Danziger, S. and Gottschalk, P. (eds) (1993) *Uneven Tides. Rising Inequality in America*, New York: Russel Sage Foundation.

Daun, H. (2003) "Market Forces and Decentralization in Sweden: Impetus for School Development or Threat to Comprehensiveness and Equality?", in: D.N. Planc and G. Sykes (eds) *Choosing Choice. School Choice in International Perspective*, New York: Columbia University Press, 92–111.

Davey, J.D. (1995) *The New Social Contract: America's Journey from Welfare State to Police State*, Westport, CT: Praeger.

Davis, J.A. and Smith, T.W. (1994) *General Social Surveys, 1972–1994* (machine-readable data file), Chicago: National Opinion Research Center.

Davis, K. and Moore, W.E. (1945) "Some Principles of Stratification", *American Sociological Review*, 10 (2): 242–249.

Davis, S.J. and Henrekson, M. (2004) "Wage-Setting Institutions as Industrial Policy", *Labour Economics* 12 (3): 345–377.

Dean, M. (1999) *Governmentality: Power and Rule in Modern Society*, London: Sage.

Dehousse, R. (1998) *The European Court of Justice*, Houndsmills, Basingstoke: Macmillan.

Delhey, J. (2007) "Do Enlargements Make the European Union Less Cohesive? An Analysis of Trust Between EU Nationalities", *Journal of Common Market Studies*, 45 (2): 253–289.

Dembour, C. (2008) "Competition for Business Location: A Survey", *Journal of Industry, Competition and Trade*, 8 (2): 89–111.

Dettling, W. (1998a) "Bürgergesellschaft. Möglichkeiten, Voraussetzungen und Grenzen", *Aus Politik und Zeitgeschichte*, B 38: 22–28.

Dettling, W. (1998b) "Fairneß braucht das Land", *Die Zeit*, No. 8, 12 February 1998, 6.

Dettling, W. (1995) *Politik und Lebenswelt. Vom Wohlfahrtsstaat zur Wohlfahrtsgesellschaft*, Gütersloh: Bertelsmann.

Deutsch, K.W. (1953/1966) *Nationalism and Social Communication*, Cambridge, MA: MIT Press.

Deutscher Bundestag (1998) *Zwölftes Hauptgutachten der Monopolkommission 1996/1997*, Bundestags-Drucksache 13/11291, Bonn, 18 July 1998.

Deutschmann, C. (2008) *Kapitalistische Dynamik. Eine gesellschaftstheoretische Perspektive*, Wiesbaden: VS Verlag.

Deutschmann, C. (2001) *Die Verheißung des absoluten Reichtums. Zur religiösen Natur des Kapitalismus*, Frankfurt/New York: Campus.

Dezalay, Y. and Garth, B.G. (1998) "Le 'Washington Consensus'. Contribution à une sociologie de l'hégémonie du libéralisme", in: *Actes de la Recherche en Sciences Sociales*, 121–122: 3–22.

Dickens, W.T., Goette, L., Groshen, E.L., Holden, S., Messina, J., Schweitzer, M.E., Turunen, J. and Ward, M.E. (2007) "How Wages Change: Micro Evidence from the International Wage Flexibility Project", *The Journal of Economic Perspectives*, 21 (2): 195–214.

DiMaggio, P.J. and Powell, W.W. (1983) "The Iron Cage Revisited: Institutional Isomorphism and Collective Rationality in Organizational Fields", *American Sociological Review*, 48: 147–160.

Dingeldey, I. (2007) "Between Workfare and Enablement – The Different Paths to Transformation of the Welfare State: A Comparative Analysis of Activating Labour Market Policies", *European Journal of Political Research*, 46 (86): 823–851.

DIW (Deutsches Institut für Wirtschaftsforschung) (2008) "Schrumpfende Mittelschicht – Anzeichen einer dauerhaften Polarisierung der verfügbaren Einkommen?", in: DIW Wochenbericht, 75th Vol. No 10/2008, 5 March 2008, 101–108. Online. Available at:

www.diw.de/documents/publikationen/73/79586/08–10–1.pdf (accessed 19 January 2009).

Donziger, S.R. (ed.) (1996) *The Real War on Crime. The Report of the National Criminal Justice Commission*, New York: Harper Perennial.

Dörre, K. and Brinkmann, U. (2005) "Finanzmarkt-Kapitalismus: Triebkraft eines flexiblen Produktionsmodells?", in: P. Windolf (ed.). *Finanzmarkt-Kapitalismus. Analysen zum Wandel von Produktionsregimen. Sonderheft 45 der Kölner Zeitschrift für Soziologie und Sozialpsychologie*, Wiesbaden: VS Verlag für Sozialwissenschaften, 85–116.

Dörre, K., Lessenich, S. and Rosa, H. (2009) *Soziologie, Kapitalismus, Kritik. Eine Debatte*, Frankfurt a.M.: Suhrkamp.

Dostal, J.M. (2008) "The Workfare Illusion: Re-examining the Concept and the British Case", *Social Policy & Administration*, 42 (1): 19–42.

Dreas, S.A. (2003) *Private Arbeitsvermittlungsagenturen zur Reintegration von Langzeitarbeitslosen*, Munich and Mering: Rainer Hampp Verlag.

Dreher, A. and Gaston, N. (2007) "Has Globalization Really had no Effect on Unions?", *Kyklas*, 60 (2): 165–186.

Drori, G.S., Meyer, J.W., Ramirez, F.O. and Schofer, E. (2003) *Science in the Modern World Polity. Institutionalization and Globalization*, Stanford: Stanford University Press.

DSI (2010) *DSI Statistical Compendium* – OECD Selection Edition 02-2010. Rheinberg.

Dubet, F. and Lapeyronnie, D. (1994) *Im Aus der Vorstädte*, Stuttgart: Klett-Cotta.

Dunford, M. (2003) "Theorizing Regional Economic Performance and the Changing Territorial Division of Labour", *Regional Studies*, 37 (8): 829–854.

Dunne, T. and Wheeler, N.J. (eds) (1999) *Human Rights in Global Politics*, Cambridge, MA: Cambridge University Press.

Durkheim, E. (1973a) "Individualism and the Intellectuals", in: R.N. Bellah (ed.) *On Morality and Society*, Chicago: University of Chicago Press, 43–57.

Durkheim, E. (1973b) "The Principles of 1789 and Sociology", in: R.N. Bellah (ed.), *On Morality and Society*. Chicago: University of Chicago Press, 34–42.

Durkheim, E. (1973c) *Erziehung, Moral und Gesellschaft*. Neuwied/Berlin: Luchterhand (French original 1925/1974).

Durkheim, E. (1964) *The Division of Labour in Society*, trans. G. Simpson, New York: Free Press.

Durkheim, E. (1952) *Suicide*, trans. J.A. Spaulding and G. Simpson, London: Routledge.

Dustmann, C., Ludsteck, J. and Schönberg, U. (2009) "Revisiting the German Wage Structure", *The Quarterly Journal of Economics*, 124 (2): 843–881.

Ebbinghaus, B. (2004) "The Changing Union and Bargaining Landscape: Union Concentration and Collective Bargaining Trends", *Industrial Relations Journal*, 35 (6): 574–587.

Economic Policy Institute (2011) *Wage Inequality is not Slowing Down. The State of Working America*. Washington DC: Economic Policy Institute. Online. Available at: www.stateofworkingamerica.org/Files/files/3M_95_50_inequal.xlsx (accessed 17 February 2011).

Edwards, B., Foley, M.W. and Diani, M. (eds) (2001) *Beyond Tocqueville. Civil Society and the Social Capital Debate in Comparative Perspective*, Hanover, NH: Tufts University Press.

EFI (Expertenkommission Forschung und Innovation) (ed.) (2008) *Gutachten zu Forschung, Innovation und technologischer Leistungsfähigkeit*. EFI Berlin.

Elias, N. (1976) *Über den Prozess der Zivilisation*, 2 vols, Frankfurt a.M: Suhrkamp.

Elliot, M.A. (2008) *A Cult of the Individual for a Global Society: The Development and Worldwide Expansion of Human Rights Ideology*, Dissertation Emery University. Online. Available at: http://gradworks.umi.com/33/32/3332320.html.

Enjolras, B. and Sivesind, K.H (eds) (2000) *Civil Society in Comparative Perspective (Comparative Social Research*, Volume 26). Bingley: Emerald Group.

Enquête-Kommission "Zukunft des Bürgerschaftlichen Engagements" Deutscher Bundestag (ed.) (2003a) *Bürgerschaftliches Engagement in den Kommunen*, Opladen: Leske + Budrich.

Enquête-Kommission "Zukunft des Bürgerschaftlichen Engagements" Deutscher Bundestag (ed.) (2003b) *Bürgerschaftliches Engagement im internationalen Vergleich*, Opladen: Leske + Budrich.

Enquête-Kommission "Zukunft des Bürgerschaftlichen Engagements" Deutscher Bundestag (ed.) (2002) *Bürgerschaftliches Engagement und Zivilgesellschaft*, Opladen: Leske + Budrich.

Entorf, H. and Spengler, H. (2002) *Crime in Europe: Causes and Consequences*, Heidelberg: Springer Verlag.

Entorf, H. and Spengler, H. (2000) "Criminality, Social Cohesion and Economic Performance", *ZEW Discussion Paper*, No. 00–27, Mannheim.

Eriksen, E.O. and Fossum, J.E. (eds) (2000) *Democracy in the European Union. Integration through Deliberation?*, London and New York: Routledge.

Esping-Andersen, G. (2000) "Who is Harmed by Labour Market Regulations? Quantitative Evidence", in: G. Esping-Andersen and M. Regini (eds) *Why Deregulate Labour Markets?*, Oxford: Oxford University Press, 66–98.

Esping-Andersen, G. (1999) *The Social Foundations of Postindustrial Economics*, Oxford: Oxford University Press.

Esping-Andersen, G. (1990) *The Three Worlds of Welfare Capitalism*, Cambridge: Polity Press.

Estevez-Abe, M., Iversen, T. and Soskice, D. (2001) "Social Protection and the Formation of Skills: A Reinterpretation of the Welfare State", in: P.A. Hall and D. Soskice (eds) *Varieties of Capitalism*, Oxford: Oxford University Press, 145–183.

Etherington, D. and Jones, M. (2004) "Welfare-Through-Work and the Re-Regulation of Labour Markets in Denmark", *Capital & Class*, 28 (1): 19–45.

European Commission (2001) *2001 Innovation Scoreboard*, Brussels.

Eurostat (1995) *Statistische Grundzahlen der Europäischen Union*, Luxembourg.

Evers, A. and Olk, T. (eds) (1996) *Wohlfahrtspluralismus. Vom Wohlfahrtsstaat zur Wohlfahrtsgesellschaft*, Opladen: Westdeutscher Verlag.

Fagan, C., Halpin, B. and O'Reilly, J. (2005) "Service Sector Employment in Germany and the UK", *Schmollers Jahrbuch*, 125 (1): 97–107.

FBI (2011) *Crime Statistics*. Online. Available at: www.fbi.gov/stats-services/crimestats (accessed 9 March 2011).

Featherstone, R. and Deflem, M. (2003) "Anomie and Strain: Context and Consequences of Merton's Two Theories", *Sociological Inquiry*, 73: 471–489.

Fejes, A. and Nicoll, K. (eds) (2008) *Foucault and Lifelong Learning. Governing the Subject*, London: Routledge.

Field, J. (2006) *Lifelong Learning and the New Educational Order*, London: Trentham Books.

Fiöretos, O. (2001) "The Domestic Sources of Multilateral Preferences: Varieties of Capitalism in the European Community", in: P. Hall and D. Soskice (eds). *Varieties of Capitalism*. Oxford: Oxford University Press, 213–244.

Firebaugh, G. (2003) *The New Geography of Global Income Inequality*, Cambridge, MA: Harvard University Press.

Fitzenberger, B., Kolm, K. and Wang, Q. (2010) "The Erosion of Union Membership in Germany: Determinants, Densities, Decompositions", *Journal of Population Economics*, 24 (1): 141–165.

Fligstein, N. (2001) *The Architecture of Markets*, Princeton, NJ: Princeton University Press.

Fligstein, N. and Stone Sweet, A. (2002) "Constructing Polities and Markets: An Institutionalist Account of European Integration", *American Journal of Sociology*, 107: 1206–1243.

Foucault, M. (2008) *The Birth of Biopolitics. Lectures at the Collège de France 1978–1979*, Houndmills, Basingstoke: Palgrave Macmillan.

Foucault, M. (2007) *Security, Territory, Population. Lectures at the Collège de France 1977–1978*, Houndmills, Basingstoke: Palgrave Macmillan.

Fougner, T. (2006) "The State, International Competitiveness and Neoliberal Globalization: Is there a Future Beyond the 'Competition State'?", *Review of International Studies*, 32 (1): 165–185.

Fourcade, M. (2009) *Economists and Societies*. Princeton: Princeton University Press.

Fourcade, M. (2006) "The Construction of a Global Profession: The Transnationalization of Economics", in: *American Journal of Sociology* 112 (1), 145–194.

Freeman, G.P. (1986) "Migration and the Political Economy of the Welfare State", *Annals of the American Academy of Political and Social Science*, 485: 51–63.

Freeman, R.B. (1996) "Why so Many Young American Men Commit Crimes and What Might We Do About It", *Journal of Economic Perspectives*, 10 (1): 25–42.

Frerichs, S., Münch, R. and Sander, M. (2008) "Anomic Crime in Post-Welfarist Societies. Cult of the Individual, Integration Patterns and Delinquency", *International Journal of Conflict and Violence*, 2 (2): 194–214.

Frietsch, R., Schmoch, U., Neuhäusler, P. and Rothengatter, O. (2011) "Patent Applications – Structures, Trends and Recent Developments", *Studien zum deutschen Innovationssystem* No. 9–2011, Hannover: Niedersächsisches Institut für Wirtschaftsforschung.

Fromm, S. (2004) *Formierung und Fluktuation*. Berlin: Wissenschaftlicher Verlag Berlin.

Fuchs, S. and Schettkat, R. (2000) "Germany: A Regulated Flexibility", in: G. Esping-Andersen and M. Regini (eds) *Why Deregulate Labour Markets?*, Oxford: Oxford University Press, 211–244.

Gabriel, O.W. (2003) "Bürgerbeteiligung an der Kommunalpolitik", in: Enquête-Kommission "Zukunft des Bürgerschaftlichen Engagements" Deutscher Bundestag (ed.). *Bürgerschaftliches Engagement im internationalen Vergleich*, Opladen: Leske + Budrich, 121–160.

Gans, H.J. (1995) *The War against the Poor*, New York: Basic Books.

Garhammer, M. (1999) *Wie Europäer ihre Zeit nutzen*, Berlin: edition sigma.

Garland, D. (2002) *The Culture of Control: Crime and Social Order in Contemporary Society*, Chicago: University of Chicago Press.

Gartner, R. (1990) "The Victims of Homicide: A Temporal and Cross-National Comparison", *American Sociological Review*, 55: 92–106.

Gaskin, K., Smith, J.D., Paulwitz, I. et al. (1996) *Ein neues bürgerschaftliches Europa. Eine Untersuchung zur Verbreitung und Rolle von Volunteering in zehn Ländern*, Freiburg i.Br.: Lampertus.

Gaston, N. (2002) "The Effects of Globalization on Unions and the Nature of Collective Bargaining", *Journal of Economic Integration*, 17 (2): 377–396.

Gellner, E. (1991) *Nationalismus und Moderne*, Berlin: Rotbuch.
Genschel, P. (2002) *Steuerharmonisierung und Steuerwettbewerb in der Europäischen Union*, Frankfurt/New York: Campus.
Gensicke, T. (1996) "Sozialer Wandel durch Modernisierung, Individualisierung und Wertewandel", *Aus Politik und Zeitgeschichte*, B 42: 3–17.
Gerhards, J. (2008) "Free to Move? The Acceptance of Free Movement of Labour and Non Discrimination Among Citizens of Europe", *European Societies* 10 (1): 121–140.
Gerhards, J. (2007) *Cultural Overstretch? Differences Between Old and New Member States of the EU and Turkey*, London: Routledge.
Gerhards, J. and Hessel, P. (2008) "Das Globalisierungsskript der Europäischen Union und seine Unterstützung bei den Bürgerinnen und Bürgern in 15 Mitgliedsländern der EU", *Berliner Journal für Soziologie*, 18 (4): 596–622.
Gesis (2011) Leibniz-Institute for the Social Sciences. Allbus data cumulation 1980–2008. Online. Available at: www.gesis.org/dienstleistungen/daten/umfragedaten/allbus/datenzugang/ (accessed 9 March 2011).
Gibbons, M., Limoges, C., Nowotny, H., Schwartzmann, S., Scott, P. and Trow, M. (1994) *The New Production of Knowledge*, London: Sage.
Giddens, A. (1998) *The Third Way: The Renewal of Social Democracy*, Cambridge: Polity Press.
Gilbert, N. and Gilbert, B. (1989) *The Enabling State: Modern Welfare Capitalism in America*, New York: Oxford University Press.
Gilbert, N. and Van Voorhis, R.A. (eds) (2001) *Activating the Unemployed. A Comparative Analysis of Work-Oriented Policies*, New Jersey: Transaction Publishers.
Gillies, V. (2005) "Raising the 'Meritocracy'. Parenting and the Individualization of Social Class", *Sociology*, 39 (5): 835–853.
Goff, P.M. (2006) *Limits to Liberalization. Local Culture in a Global Marketplace*, Ithaca, NY: Cornell University Press.
Goldstein, K.M. (1999) *Interest Groups, Lobbying, and Participation in America*, Cambridge: Cambridge University Press.
Goldthorpe, J. and Jackson, M. (2008) "Education-Based Meritocracy: The Barriers to Its Realization", in: A. Lareau and D. Conley (eds) *Social Class. How Does it Work?*, New York: Russel Sage Foundation, 93–117.
Goodin, R.E., Headey, B., Muffels, R. and Dirven, H.-J. (1999) *The Real Worlds of Welfare Capitalism*, Cambridge: Cambridge University Press.
Gordon, M.M. (1964) *Assimilation in American Life. The Role of Race, Religion, and National Origins*, New York: Oxford University Press.
Gorlov, V. (2009) *Warum gibt es kaum Ingenieurinnen? Gründe für eine geschlechts(un)spezifische Berufswahl. Deutschland und Schweden im Vergleich*, Bamberg: University of Bamberg Press.
Gorter, C. (2000) "The Dutch Miracle?" in: G. Esping-Andersen and M. Regini (eds) *Why Deregulate Labour Markets?*, Oxford: Oxford University Press, 181–210.
Gottschalk, M. (2006) *The Prison and the Gallows. The Politics of Mass Incarceration in America*, Cambridge: Cambridge University Press.
Gottschalk, P. and Danziger, S. (2005) "Inequality of Wage Rates, Earnings and Family Income in the United States, 1975–2002", *Review of Income and Wealth*, 51 (2): 231–254.
Gramsci, A. (1971) *Selections from Prison Notebooks*, ed. Q. Hoare and G. Nowell-Smith, London: Lawrence & Wishart.
Gross, P. (1994) *Die Multioptionsgesellschaft*, Frankfurt a.M.: Suhrkamp.

Grubb, W.N. and Lazerson, M. (2004) *The Education Gospel: The Economic Power of Schooling*, Cambridge, MA: Harvard University Press.
Guéhenno, J.-M. (1995) *The End of the Nation State*, Minneapolis: University of Minnesota Press.
Guenther, T. (2007) *Struktur- und Kulturwandel international tätiger deutscher Unternehmen: Das Beispiel des Bayer-Konzerns*. Wiesbaden: Deutscher Universitätsverlag.
Haas, E.B. (1958/1968) *The Uniting of Europe*, Stanford: Stanford University Press.
Habermas, J. (1998) *Die postnationale Konstellation*, Frankfurt a.M.: Suhrkamp.
Habermas, J. (1992) *Faktizität und Geltung*, Frankfurt a.M.: Suhrkamp.
Habermas, J. (1981) *Theorie des kommunikativen Handelns*, 2 vols, Frankfurt a.M.: Suhrkamp.
Hacker, J.S. (2004) "Privatizing Risk without Privatizing the Welfare State: The Hidden Politics of Social Policy Retrenchment in the United States", *American Political Science Review* 98 (2): 243–260.
Hacker, J.S. (2002) *The Divided Welfare State. The Battle over Public and Private Social Benefits in the United States*, Cambridge: Cambridge University Press.
Hacker, J.S. and Pierson, P. (2010) *Winner-Take-All Politics. How Washington Made the Rich Richer – And Turned its Back on the Middle Class*. New York: Simon and Schuster.
Hall, P.A. (1993) "Policy Paradigms, Social Learning, and the State. The Case of Economic Policymaking in Britain", *Comparative Politics* 25 (3): 275–296.
Hall, P.A. and Soskice, D. (2001) *Varieties of Capitalism. The Institutional Foundations of Comparative Advantage*, Oxford: Oxford University Press.
Hall, P.A. and Taylor, R.C.R. (1996) "Political Science and the Three Institutionalisms", *Political Studies*, 44: 936–957.
Hall, P.A. and Thelen K. (2009) "Institutional Change in Varieties of Capitalism", *Socio-Economic Review* 7 (1): 7–34.
Hammerschmidt, P. and Uhlendorff, U. (eds) (2003) *Wohlfahrtsverbände zwischen Subsidiarität und EU-Wettbewerbsrecht*, Kassel: Kassel University Press.
Handler, J.F. (2009) "Welfare, Workfare, and Citizenship in the Developed World", *Annual Review of Law and Social Science*, 5: 71–90.
Handler, J.F. (2004) *Social Citizenship and Workfare in the United States and Western Europe. The Paradox of Inclusion*, Cambridge: Cambridge University Press.
Handler, J.F. (2003) "Social Citizenship and Workfare in the US and Western Europe: From Status to Contract", *Journal of European Social Policy*, 13 (3): 229–243.
Harrysson, L. and Petersson, J. (2004) "Revealing the Traits of Workfare: The Swedish Example", in: P. Littlewood, I. Glorieux and I. Jönson (eds) *The Future of Work in Europe*, Aldershot: Ashgate, 83–102.
Hart, D., Donelly, T.M., Youniss, J. and Atkins, R. (2005) "High School Community Service as a Predictor of Adult Voting and Volunteering", *American Educational Research Journal*, 44 (1): 197–219.
Hay, C. (2004) "Re-Stating Politics, Re-Politicizing the State: Neo-liberalism, Economic Imperatives and the Rise of the Competition State", *The Political Quarterly*, 75 (s1): 38–50.
Hayek, F.A. von. (1969) "Die Ergebnisse menschlichen Handelns, aber nicht menschlichen Entwurfs", in: F.A. von Hayek, *Freiburger Studien. Gesammelte Aufsätze*, Tübingen: Mohr Siebeck, 97–107.
Hayek, F.A. von. (1948) "The Economic Conditions of Interstate Federalism", in: F.A. von Hayek, *Individualism and Economic Order*, Chicago: University of Chicago Press, 255–272.

Heidenreich, M. (2004a) "Beschäftigungsordnungen zwischen Exklusion und Inklusion. Arbeitsmarktregenerierende Institutionen im internationalen Vergleich", *Zeitschrift für Soziologie*, 33 (3): 206–227.

Heidenreich, M. (2004b) "Innovation und sozial Sicherung im internationalen Vergleich", *Soziale Welt*, 2/2004: 125–144.

Heidenreich, M. and Bischoff, G. (2008) "The Open Method of Coordination: A Way to the Europeanization of Social and Employment Policies?", *Journal of Common Market Studies*, 46 (3): 497–532.

Heinze, R.G., Schmid, J. and Strünck, C. (1999) *Vom Wohlfahrtsstaat zum Wettbewerbsstaat. Arbeitsmarkt- und Sozialpolitik in den 90er Jahren*, Opladen: Leske + Budrich: 193–196.

Heinze, T. (2001) "Transformation des deutschen Unternehmenskontroll-Systems?", in: *Kölner Zeitschrift für Soziologie und Sozialpsychologie* 53, 641–675.

Heitmeyer, W. and Anhut, R. (eds) (2000) *Bedrohte Stadtgesellschaft. Soziale Desintegrationsprozesse und ethnisch-kulturelle Konfliktkonstellationen*, Weinheim and Munich: Juventa.

Held, D. (1995) *Democracy and the Global Order. From the Modern State to Cosmopolitan Governance*, Cambridge: Polity Press.

Held, D., McGrew, A., Goldblatt, D. and Perraton, J. (1999) *Global Transformations. Politics, Economics, and Culture*, Cambridge: Polity Press.

Helfert, M. (1992) "Segmentierung, soziale Ungleichheit und Qualifizierung von An- und Ungelernten", *WSI Mitteilungen*, 356–364.

Helgøy, I. and Homme, A. (2006) "Policy Tools and Institutional Change: Comparing Education Policies in Norway, Sweden and England", *Journal of Public Policy*, 26 (2): 141–165.

Hengsbach, F. (1997) "'Globalisierung' aus wirtschaftsethischer Sicht", *Aus Politik und Zeitgeschichte*, B, 21: 3–12.

Heuser, U.J. (1999) "Vorbilder aus der Provinz", *Die Zeit*, No. 16, 15 April 1999, 39.

Heuser, U.J. and Randow, G. von (1999) "Das Soziale, neu erfunden." *Die Zeit*, No. 13, 25 March 1999, 25–27.

Hirsch, J. (1995) *Der nationale Wettbewerbsstaat. Staat, Demokratie und Politik im globalen Kapitalismus*, Berlin/Paris: Ed. ID-Archiv.

Hirst, P. and Thompson, G. (1996) *Globalization in Question. The International Economy and the Possibilities of Governance*, Cambridge: Polity Press.

Hiß, S. (2006) *Warum übernehmen Unternehmen gesellschaftliche Verantwortung?*, Frankfurt/New York: Campus.

Hobbes, T. (1651/1966) "Leviathan", in: *Collected English Works of Thomas Hobbes*, ed. W. Molesworth, Vol. III, Aalen: Scientia.

Hobsbawm, E.J. (1991) *Nationen und Nationalismus. Mythos und Realität seit 1780*, Frankfurt a.M./New York: Campus-Verlag.

Höffe, O. (1999) *Demokratie im Zeitalter der Globalisierung*, Munich: C.H. Beck.

Hoffman, S.D. and Seidman, L.S. (2002) *Helping Working Families. The Earned Income Tax Credit*, Kalamazoo, MI: W.E. Upjohn Institute for Employment Research.

Holden, C. (2003) "Decommodification and the Welfare State", *Political Studies Review*, 1 (3): 303–316.

Hondrich, K.O. and Koch-Arzberger, C. (1992) *Solidarität in der modernen Gesellschaft*, Frankfurt a.M.: Fischer Taschenbuch Verlag.

Höpner, M. (2007) "Ist Politik gegen Verbände möglich? 25 Jahre Mancur Olsons 'The Rise and Decline of Nations'", *Leviathan* 35 (3), 310–347.

Höpner, M. (2003) *Wer beherrscht die Unternehmen. Shareholder Value, Managerherrschaft und Mitbestimmung in Deutschland*, Frankfurt/New York: Campus.
Höpner, M. and Jackson, G. (2003) "Entsteht ein Markt für Unternehmenskontrolle? Der Fall Mannesmann", in: W. Streeck and M. Höpner (eds) *Alle Macht dem Markt? Fallstudien zur Abwicklung der Deutschland AG*, Frankfurt a.M.: Campus, 147–168.
Höpner, M. and Krempel, L. (2003) "The Politics of the German Company Network", *MPIfG Working Paper 2003/9*, Cologne: Max-Planck-Institut für Gesellschaftsforschung.
Huaco, G. (1966) "The Functionalist Theory of Stratification: Two Decades of Controversy", *Inquiry*, 9: 215–240.
Huber, E. and Stephens, J.D. (2001) *Development and Crisis of the Welfare State. Parties and Policies in Global Markets*, Chicago: University of Chicago Press.
Hudson, J. and Kühner, S. (2009) "Towards Productive Welfare? A Comparative Analysis of 23 OECD Countries", *Journal of European Social Policy*, 19 (1): 34–46.
Hudson, J., Hwang, G.-H. and Kühner, S. (2008) "Between Ideas, Institutions and Interest: Analyzing Third Way Welfare Reform Programmes in Germany and the United Kingdom", *Journal of Social Policy*, 37 (2): 207–230.
Huo, J., Nelson, M. and Stephens, J.D. (2008) "Decommodification and Activation in Social Democratic Policy: Resolving the Paradox", *Journal of European Social Policy*, 18 (1): 5–10.
IAB (2003) "Geringqualifizierte: In der Krise verdrängt, sogar im Boom vergessen. Entwicklung der qualifikationsspezifischen Arbeitslosenquoten im Konjunkturverlauf bis 2002", *IAB-Kurzbericht* No. 19/2003, Nuremberg: Institut für Arbeitsmarkt- und Berufsforschung.
ILO (2011) *Laborsta Internet. Employment.* Online. Available at: http://laborsta.ilo.org/ STP/guest: Germany; Denmark; Sweden (accessed 17 March 2011).
Immergut, E. (1998) "The Theoretical Core of the New Institutionalism", *Politics & Society*, 26 (1): 5–34.
Imrohoroğlu, A., Merlo, A. and Rupert, P. (2000) "On the Political Economy of Income Redistribution and Crime", *International Economic Review*, 41 (1): 1–25.
Internal Revenue Service (2009) *Earned Income Credit (EIC)*, Publication 596, Cat. No. 15173A, Washington, DC: Department of the Treasury.
ISSP (1985, 1990, 1996, 2006) *International Social Survey Programme.* Gesis: Mannhein.
Iversen, T. (2005) *Capitalism, Democracy, and Welfare.* Cambridge: Cambridge University Press.
Iversen, T. (1999) *Contested Economic Institutions: The Politics of Macroeconomics and Wage Bargaining in Advanced Democracies*, Cambridge: Cambridge University Press.
Iversen, T. and Soskice, D. (2006) "Electoral Institutions and the Politics of Coalition: Why Some Democracies Redistribute More Than Others", *American Political Science Review*, 100 (2): 165–181.
Iversen, T. and Stephens, J.D. (2008) "Partisan Politics, the Welfare State, and Three Worlds of Human Capital Formation", *Comparative Political Studies*, 41 (4–5): 600–637.
Jachtenfuchs, M. (1998) "Entgrenzung und politische Steuerung", in: B. Kohler-Koch (ed.) *Regieren in entgrenzten Räumen*, Opladen: Westdeutscher Verlag, 235–245.
Jacobs, D. and Richardson, A.M. (2008) "Economic Inequality and Homicide in the Developed Nations from 1975 to 1995", *Homicide Studies*, 12 (1): 28–45.
Jaeger, M.M. (2009) "United But Divided: Welfare Regimes and the Level and Variance in Public Support for Redistribution", *European Sociological Review*, 25 (6): 723–737.

Jahoda, M., Lazarsfeld, P. and Zeisel, H. (1933/1975) *Die Arbeitslosen von Marienthal*, Frankfurt a.M.: Suhrkamp.
Jakobi, A.P. (2009) *International Organizations and Lifelong Learning: From Global Agendas to Policy Diffusion*, Houndmills, Basingstoke: Palgrave.
Jakobi, A.P. (2007) "The Knowledge Society and Global Dynamics in Education Politics", *European Educational Research Journal*, 6 (1): 39–51.
Jansen, M. and Turrini, A. (2004) "Job Creation, Job Destruction, and the International Division of Labour", *Review of International Economics*, 12 (3): 476–494.
Jessop, B. (2008) *State Power: A Strategic Relational Approach*, Cambridge: Polity Press.
Jessop, B. (2006) "From Micro-Powers to Governmentality: Foucault's Work on Statehood, State Formation, Statecraft and State Power", *Political Geography*, 26 (1): 34–40.
Jessop, B. (1994) "The Transition to Post-Fordism and the Schumpeterian Workfare State", in: R. Burrows and B. Loader (eds) *Towards a Post-Fordist Welfare State?*, London: Routledge, 13–37.
Jessop, B. (1993) "Toward a Schumpeterian Workfare State? Preliminary Remarks on Post-Fordist Political Economy", *Studies in Political Economy*, 40 (Spring): 7–39.
Joppke, C. (1999) *Immigration and the Nation-state. The United States, Germany and Great Britain*, Oxford: Oxford University Press.
Jordan, B. (1998) *The New Politics of Welfare*, London: Sage.
Kangas, O., Lundberg, U. and Plong, N. (eds) (2010) "Three Routes to Pension Reform: Politics and Institutions in Reforming Pensions in Denmark, Finland and Sweden", *Social Policy & Administration*, 44 (3): 265–284.
Kant, I. (1956) "Die Metaphysik der Sitten (1797)", *Werke in sechs Bänden*, Vol. IV, ed. W. Weischedel, Frankfurt a.M.: Insel Verlag.
Kaplow, L. and Shavell, S. (2003) *Fairness versus Welfare*, Cambridge, MA: National Bureau of Economic Research.
Katz, M.B. (2008) *The Prize of Citizenship. Redefining the American Welfare State*, Updated Edition, Philadelphia: University of Pennsylvania Press.
Katzenstein, P.J. (2006) "Epilogue: Denmark and Small States", in: J.L. Campbell, J.A. Hall and O.K. Pedersen (eds) *National Identity and the Varieties of Capitalism: The Danish Experience*, Montreal: McGill-Queens University Press, 431–440.
Katzenstein, P.J. (2005) *A World of Regions. Asia and Europe in the American Imperium*, Ithaca, NY: Cornell University Press.
Katzenstein, P.J. (2003) "Small States and Small States Revisited", *New Political Economy*, 8 (1): 9–30.
Katzenstein, P.J. (1985) *Small States in World Markets: Industrial Policy in Europe*, Ithaca, NY: Cornell University Press.
Kaufmann, F.-X. (1997) *Herausforderungen des Sozialstaats*, Frankfurt a.M.: Suhrkamp.
Kawachi, I., Kennedy, B.P. and Wilkinson, R.G. (1999) *The Society and Population Health Reader. Income Inequality and Health*. New Press: W.W. Norton.
Keane, J. (2003) *Global Civil Society?*, Cambridge: Cambridge University Press.
Kelly, M. (2000) "Inequality and Crime", *Review of Economics and Statistics*, 82: 530–539.
Kern, H. and Schumann, M. (1984) *Das Ende der Arbeitsteilung? Rationalisierung in der industriellen Produktion. Bestandsaufnahme, Trendbestimmung*, München: Beck.
Keupp, H. (2003) "Lokale Einrichtungen zur Förderung bürgerschaftlichen Engagements: Freiwilligenagenturen, Selbsthilfekontaktstellen, Seniorenbüros u.Ä. – Chancen und Restriktionen", in: Enquête-Kommission "Zukunft des Bürgerschaftlichen Engagements"

Deutscher Bundestag (ed.) *Bürgerschaftliches Engagement im internationalen Vergleich*, Opladen: Leske + Budrich: 13–51.

Kim, C.H. and Sakamoto, A. (2010) "Assessing the Consequences of Declining Unionization and Public-Sector Employment. A Density-Function Decomposition of Rising Inequality from 1983 to 2005", *Work and Occupations*, 37 (2): 119–161.

Kim, C.H. and Sakamoto, A. (2008) "The Rise of Intra-Occupational Wage Inequality in the United States, 1983 to 2002", *American Sociological Review*, 73 (1): 129–157.

King, D. (1995) *Actively Seeking Work? The Politics of Unemployment and Welfare Policy in the United States and Great Britain*, Chicago and London: University of Chicag o Press.

Klages, H. (1998) "Engagement und Engagementpotential in Deutschland", *Aus Politik und Zeitgeschichte*, B 38: 29–38.

Klages, H. (1993) *Traditionsbruch als Herausforderung. Perspektiven der Wertewandelsgesellschaft*, Frankfurt a.M.: Campus.

Klages, P. (2010) *Wirtschaftliche Interessen und juristische Ideen. Die Entwicklung des Aktienrechts in Deutschland und den USA*, Frankfurt/New York: Campus.

Klug, W. (1995) "Mehr Markt in die Freie Wohlfahrt?", *Aus Politik und Zeitgeschichte*, B 25: 34–43.

Knieper, R. (1991) *Nationale Souveränität*, Frankfurt a.M.: Fischer.

Knijn, T. (2004) "Challenges and Risks of Individualization in The Netherlands", *Social Policy and Society*, 3 (1): 57–65.

Koch, C. (1995) *Die Gier des Marktes. Die Ohnmacht des Staates im Kampf der Weltwirtschaft*, Munich and Vienna: Hanser.

Koch, M. (2011) "Gefährliche Kluft. Die wachsende soziale Ungleichheit legt die Saat für neue Krisen", *Süddeutsche Zeitung* 67, No. 58, 11 March 2011, 17.

Koenig, M. (2005) "Weltgesellschaft, Menschenrechte und der Formwandel des Nationalstaats", in: B. Heintz, R. Münch and H. Tyrell (eds) *Weltgesellschaft*, Special Issue of *Zeitschrift für Soziologie*, Stuttgart: Lucius & Lucius, 374–393.

Korpi, T. and Tahlin, M. (2008) "Educational Mismatch, Wages, and Wage Growth: Overeducation in Sweden, 1974–2000", *Labour Economics*, 16 (2): 183–193.

Korpi, W. (2003) "Welfare-State Regress in Western Europe: Politics, Institutions, Globalization, and Europeanization", *Annual Review of Sociology* 29: 589–609.

Kowalsky, W. (1999) *Europäische Sozialpolitik. Ausgangsbedingungen, Antriebskräfte und Entwicklungspotentiale*, Opladen: Leske + Budrich, 352–368.

Kronauer, M. (2002) *Exklusion. Die Gefährdung des Sozialen im hoch entwickelten Kapitalismus*, Frankfurt/New York: Campus.

Kronauer, M. and Neef, R. (1997) "'Exclusion' und 'soziale Ausgrenzung': Neue soziale Spaltungen in Frankreich und Deutschland", in: Deutsch-Französisches Institut (ed.) *Frankreich-Jahrbuch 1996. Politik, Wirtschaft, Gesellschaft, Geschichte, Kultur*, Opladen: Leske + Budrich, 35–58.

Krueger, A.O. (1995) *Trade Policies and Developing Nations*, Washington: Brookings Institution.

Kuhn, T.S. (1962) *The Structure of Scientific Revolutions*, Chicago: University of Chicago Press.

Kuipers, S. (2006) *The Crisis Imperative. Crisis Rhetoric and Welfare State Reform in Belgium and the Netherlands in the Early 1990s*, Amsterdam: Amsterdam University Press.

Kurdelbusch, A. (2002) "Multinationals and the Rise of Variable Pay in Germany", *European Journal of Industrial Relations*, 8 (3): 325–349.

La Free, G. (2005) "Evidence for Elite Convergence in Cross-National Homicide Victimization Trends, 1956 to 2000", *The Sociological Quarterly*, 46 (1): 191–211.
La Free, G. and Drass, K.A. (2002) "Counting Crime Booms among Nations: Evidence for Homicide Victimization Rates 1956 to 1998", *Criminology*, 40 (4): 769.
Laclau, E. and Mouffe, C. (2001) *Hegemony and Socialist Strategy. Towards a Radical Democratic Politics*, London: Verso.
Lahusen, C. (2003) *Kontraktuelle Politik*. Weilerswist: Velbrück.
Lahusen, C. and Jauß, C. (2001) *Lobbying als Beruf: Interessengruppen in der Europäischen Union*, Baden-Baden: Nomos.
Lang, S. (2003) "Die Förderung von bürgerschaftlichem Engagement in US-amerikanischen Städten und Kommunen", in: Enquête Kommission "Zukunft des bürgerschaftlichen Engagements", Deutscher Bundestag (ed.) Schriftenreihe Band 11, *Bürgerschaftliches Engagement im Internationalen Vergleich*, Opladen: Leske + Budrich, 57–90.
Lange, W. de. (1998) "Flexibilisierung im holländischen Modell", in: H.G. Zillian and J. Flecker (eds) *Flexibilisierung – Problem oder Lösung?*, Berlin: edition sigma: 121–135.
Langer, S. (1995) *Grundlagen einer internationalen Wirtschaftsverfassung*, Munich: C.H. Beck.
Larsen, F. and Mailand, M. (2007) "Danish Activation Policy: The Role of the Normative Foundation, the Institutional Set-up and Other Drivers", in: A.S. Pascual and L. Magnusson (eds) *Reshaping Welfare States and Activation Regimes in Europe*, Brussels: P.I.E. Peter Lang S.A.
Leadbeater, C. (1997) *The Rise of the Social Entrepreneur*, London: Demos.
Lebaron, F. (2006) "'Nobel' Economists as Public Intellectuals: The Circulation of Symbolic Capital", *International Journal of Contemporary Sociology*, 43 (1): 88–101.
Lebaron, F. (2000) *La croyance économique: les économistes entre les sciences et politique*, Paris: Seuil.
Legler, H. (2004) "Forschungs- und Entwicklungsaktivitäten", in: *Studien zum deutschen Innovationssystem*, No. 12–2004. Hannover: Niedersächsisches Institut für Wirtschaftsforschung.
Legler, H. and Krawczyk, O. (2009): "FuE-Aktivitäten von Wirtschaft und Staat im internationalen Vergleich", *Studien zum deutschen Innovationssystem*, No. 1–2009, Hannover: Niedersächsisches Institut für Wirtschaftsforschung.
Legler, H. and Krawczyk, O. (2007) "Forschungs- und Entwicklungsaktivitäten von Wirtschaft und Staat im internationalen Vergleich", in: *Studien zum deutschen Innovationssystem*, No. 8–2007, Hannover: Niedersächsisches Institut für Wirtschaftsforschung.
Legler, H., Gehrke, B. and Krawczyk, O. (2005) "Deutschlands forschungs- und wissensintensive Wirtschaftszweige: Spezialisierung, Wachstum, Beschäftigung und Qualifikationserfordernisse", in: *Studien zum deutschen Innovationssystem* No. 14–2005. Hannover: Niedersächsisches Institut für Wirtschaftsforschung.
Leibfried, S. and Pierson, P. (1998) "Wohlfahrtsstaaten: Der Sozialstaat in der Europäischen Mehrebenenpolitik", in: S. Leibfried and P. Pierson (eds) *Standort Europa. Europäische Sozialpolitik*, Frankfurt a.M.: Suhrkamp, 58–99.
Leigh, A. (2010) "Who Benefits from the Earned Income Tax Credit? Incidence among Recipients, Coworkers and Firms", *The B.E. Journal of Economic Analysis & Policy*, 10 (1), *Advances*, Article 45.
Leira, A. (2002) *Working Parents and the Welfare State. Family Change and Policy Reform in Scandinavia*, Cambridge: Cambridge University Press.

Lemke, T. (1997) *Eine Kritik der politischen Vernunft: Foucaults Analysen der modernen Gouvernmentalität*, Berlin: Argument Verlag.

Lessenich, S. (2003) *Dynamischer Immobilismus. Kontinuität und Wandel im deutschen Sozialmodell*, Frankfurt/New York: Campus.

Lessenich, S. and Ostner, I. (eds) (1998) *Welten des Wohlfahrtskapitalismus*, Frankfurt/New York: Campus.

Liebig, S. (1997) *Soziale Gerechtigkeitsforschung und Gerechtigkeit im Unternehmen*, Munich: Hampp.

Liebig, S., Lengfeld, H. and Mau, S. (eds) (2004) *Verteilungsprobleme und Gerechtigkeit in modernen Gesellschaften*, Frankfurt/New York: Campus.

Lindbom, A. (2001) "Dismantling the Social Democratic Welfare Model? Has the Swedish Welfare State Lost its Defining Characteristics?", *Scandinavian Political Studies*, 24 (3): 171–193.

Lindsay, C. and Mailand, M. (2004) "Different Routes, Common Directions? Activation Policies for Young People in Denmark and the UK", *International Journal of Social Welfare*, 13 (3): 195–207.

Lindsay, C. and McQuaid, R.W. (2009) "New Governance and the Case of Activation Policies: Comparing Experiences in Denmark and the Netherlands", *Social Policy & Administration*, 43 (5): 445–463.

Lipset, S.M. (1996) *American Exceptionalism: A Double-Edged Sword*, New York: W.W. Norton & Company.

Lipset, S.M. (1963/1979) *The First New Nation. The United States in Historical and Comparative Perspective*, New York: Basic Books.

Lipset, S.M. and Marks, G. (2000) *It Didn't Happen Here. Why Socialism Failed in the United States*, New York and London: W.W. Norton & Company.

Lødemel, I. and Trickey, H. (eds) (2000) *An Offer you can't Refuse. Workfare in International Perspective*, Bristol: The Policy Press.

Lowenkamp, C.T., Cullen, F.T. and Pratt, T.C. (2003) "Replicating Sampson and Groves's Test of Social Disorganization Theory: Revisiting a Criminological Classic", *Journal of Research in Crime and Delinquency*, 40 (4): 351–373.

Luhmann, N. (1988) *Die Wirtschaft der Gesellschaft*, Frankfurt a.M.: Suhrkamp.

McDonald, C. and Marston, G. (2005) "Workfare as Welfare: Governing Unemployment in the Advanced Liberal State", *Critical Social Policy*, 25 (3): 374–401.

McGrew, A. (1997) *The Transformation of Democracy*, Cambridge: Polity Press.

Mackert, J. and Müller, H.P. (eds) (2007) *Moderne (Staats)Bürgerschaft*, Wiesbaden: VS Verlag für Sozialwissenschaften.

McNamee, S.J. and Miller, R.K. (2004) *The Meritocracy Myth*, Lanham, MD: Rowman & Littlefield.

Maguire, K. and Pastore, A.L. (eds) (2003) *Sourcebook of Criminal Justice Statistics 2001*, Washington, DC: US Dept. of Justice, Bureau of Justice Statistics.

Mahoney, J. and Rueschemeyer, D. (eds) (2003) *Comparative Historical Analysis in the Social Sciences*, New York: Cambridge University Press.

Mailand, M. (2006) "Dynamic Neo-Corporatism – Regulating Work and Welfare in Denmark", *European Review of Labour and Research*, 12 (3): 371–387.

Majone, G. (1996) *Regulating Europe*, London: Routledge.

Majone, G. (1994) "The European Community: An 'Independent Fourth Branch of Government'?" in: G. Brüggemeier (ed.) *Verfassungen für ein ziviles Europa*, Baden-Baden: Nomos Verlag, 23–43.

Majone, G. (1989) *Evidence, Argument and Persuasion in the Policy Process*, New Haven: Yale University Press.
Mandel, H. and Semyonov, M. (2006) "A Welfare State Paradox: State Interventions and Women's Employment Opportunities in 22 Countries", *American Journal of Sociology* 111 (6): 1910–1949.
Mandle, J.R. (2003) *Globalization and the Poor*, Cambridge: Cambridge University Press.
Manning, N. and Shaw, I. (2000) *New Risks, New Welfare. Signposts for Social Policy*, Oxford: Blackwell.
Manow, P. (2005) "Globalisierung, 'Corporate Finance' und koordinierter Kapitalismus. Die Alterssicherungssysteme als (versiegende) Quelle geduldigen Kapitals in Deutschland und Japan", in: P. Windolf (ed.). *Finanzmarkt-Kapitalismus. Analysen zum Wandel von Produktionsregimen. Sonderheft 45 der Kölner Zeitschrift für Soziologie und Sozialpsychologie*, Wiesbaden: VS Verlag für Sozialwissenschaften, 242–275.
Marin, D. (2006) "A New International Division of Labor in Europe: Outsourcing and Offshoring to Eastern Europe", *Journal of the European Economic Association*, 4 (2–3): 612–622.
Marshall, T.H. (1964) *Class, Citizenship and Social Development*, Westport, CT: Greenwood Press.
Marske, C.E. (1987) "Durkheim's 'Cult of the Individual' and the Moral Reconstitution of Society", *Sociological Theory*, 5 (1): 1–14.
Martin, C.J. (2004) "Reinventing Welfare Regimes. Employers and the Implementation of Active Social Policy", *World Politics* 57 (1): 39–69.
Marttila, T. (2010) *The Spectres of Entrepreneur: Construction of the Entrepreneur in Swedish Political Discourse 1991–2004*, Dissertation, Bamberg: University of Bamberg.
Marwah, S. and Deflem, M. (2006) "Revisiting Merton: Continuities in the Theory of Anomie-and-Opportunity-Structures", in: M. Deflem (ed.) *Sociological Theory and Criminological Research: Views from Europe and the United States*, Oxford, UK: Elsevier.
Mau, S. (2010) *Social Transnationalism. Lifeworlds Beyond the Nation State*, London: Routledge.
Mau, S. (2005) "Europe from the Bottom: Assessing Personal Gains and Losses and its Effects on EU Support", *Journal of Public Policy*, 25 (3): 289–311.
Mau, S. (2004) "Welfare Regimes and the Norms of Social Exchange", *Current Sociology*, 52 (1): 53–74.
Mau, S. (2003) *The Moral Economy of Welfare States: Britain and Germany Compared*, London: Routledge.
Mau, S. and Veghte, B. (eds) (2007) *Social Justice, Legitimacy and the Welfare State*, Aldershot: Ashgate.
Mau, S., Mewes, J. and Zimmermann, A. (2008) "Cosmopolitan Attitudes through Transnational Social Practices?", *Global Networks*, 8 (1): 1–24.
Mayer, K.U. and Solga, H. (eds) (2008) *Skill Formation – Interdisciplinary and Cross-National Perspectives*, Cambridge: Cambridge University Press.
Mead, L.M. (2004) *Government Matters. Welfare Reform in Wisconsin*, Princeton, NJ: Princeton University Press.
Meinecke, F. (1907/1962) "Weltbürgertum und Nationalstaat", in: H. Herzfeld (eds) *Meinecke Werke*, Vol. 5, Stuttgart: Koehler.
Merck, J. (1998) "Sozialverantwortung im Handel. Der SA 8000 als Element der Strategie des Otto Versand", *Forum Wirtschaftsethik*, 6 (4): 7–10.

Merkel, W. (2002) *Social Justice and the Three Worlds of Welfare Capitalism*, Archives Européennes de Sociologie XLIII (1): 59–91.
Merton, R.K. (1949/1968) "Social Structure and Anomie", in: R.K. Merton, *Social Theory and Social Structure*, New York: Free Press, 185–214.
Messner, S.F. and Rosenfeld, R. (1997) "Political Restraint of the Market and Levels of Criminal Homicide: A Cross-National Application of Institutional-Anomie Theory", *Social Forces*, 75(4): 1393–1416.
Messner, S.F. and Rosenfeld, R. (1994/2007) "Crime and the American Dream", Belmont: Wadsworth.
Messner, S.F., Baumer, E.P. and Rosenfeld, R. (2004) "Dimensions of Social Capital and Rates of Criminal Homicide", *American Sociological Review*, 69 (December): 882–903.
Messner, S.F., Thome, H. and Rosenfeld, R. (2008) "Institutions, Anomie, and Violent Crime: Clarifying and Elaborating Institutional Anomie Theory", *International Journal of Conflict and Violence*, 2 (2): 163–181.
Meyer, B.D. and Holtz-Eakin, D. (eds) (2001) *Making Work Pay. The Earned Income Tax Credit and Its Impact on America's Families*, New York: Russel Sage Foundation.
Meyer, J.W. (1997) "The Changing Cultural Content of the Nation State", in: G. Steinmetz (ed.) *State/Culture: State Formation after the Cultural Turn*, Ithaca, NY: Cornell University Press, 123–143.
Meyer, J.W. and Jepperson, R. (2000) "The 'Actors' of Modern Society: The Cultural Constitution of Social Agency", *Sociological Theory*, 18 (1): 100–120.
Meyer, J.W. and Rowan, B. (1977) "Institutionalized Organizations. Formal Structure as Myth and Ceremony", *American Journal of Sociology* 83 (2): 340–363.
Meyer, J.W., Boli, J., Thomas, G.M. and Ramirez, F.O. (1997) "World Society and the Nation State", *American Journal of Sociology*, 103 (1): 144–181.
Miller, P. and Rose, N. (2008) *Governing the Present*, Cambridge: Polity Press.
Mills, M., Blossfeld, H.-P., Buchholz, S., Hofäcker, D., Bernardi, F. and Hofmeister, H. (2008) "Converging Divergencies? An International Comparison of the Impact of Globalization on Industrial Relations and Employment", *International Sociology*, 23 (4): 561–595.
Mirowski, P. and Plehwe, D. (eds) (2009) *The Road from Mont Pèlerin. The Making of the Neoliberal Thought Collective*, Cambridge, MA: Harvard University Press.
Mishel, L., Bernstein, J. and Bonshey, H. (2003) *The State of Working American 2002/2003*, Ithaca and London: ILR Press.
Mitchell, K. (2006) "Neoliberal Governmentality in the European Union: Education, Training, and Technologies of Citizenship", *Society and Space*, 24 (3): 389–407.
Moffit, R.A. (2003) *Means-Tested Transfer Programs in the United States*, Chicago: The University of Chicago Press.
Monopolkommission der Bundesregierung (1998) *Systemwettbewerb. Sondergutachten der Monopolkommission gemäß § 24 b Abs. 5 Satz 4 GWB*. Bonn.
Morenoff, J.D., Sampson, R.J. and Raudenbush, S.W. (2001) "Neighbourhood Inequality, Collective Efficacy, and the Spatial Dynamics of Urban Violence", *Criminology*, 39: 517.
Mouw, T. and Kalleberg, A.L. (2010) "Occupations and the Structure of Wage Inequality in the United States, 1980s to 2000s", *American Sociological Review*, 75 (3): 402–431.
Münch, R. (2010) *European Governmentality. The Liberal Drift in Multilevel Governance*, London: Routledge.
Münch, R. (2008) "Constructing a European Society by Jurisdiction", *European Law Journal*, 14 (5): 519–541.

Münch, R. (2001a) *The Ethics of Modernity. Formation and Transformation in Britain, France, Germany, and the United States*, Lanham, MD: Rowan & Littlefield.
Münch, R. (2001b) *Nation and Citizenship in the Global Age. From National to Transnational Ties and Identities*, Houndmills, Basingstoke: Palgrave.
Münch, R. (1998) *Globale Dynamik, lokale Lebenswelten. Der schwierige Weg in die Weltgesellschaft*, Frankfurt a.M.: Suhrkamp.
Münch, R. (1995) *Dynamik der Kommunikationsgesellschaft*, Frankfurt a.M.: Suhrkamp.
Münch, R. (1993a) *Das Projekt Europa. Zwischen Nationalstaat, regionaler Autonomie und Weltgesellschaft*, Frankfurt a.M.: Suhrkamp.
Münch, R. (1991) *Dialektik der Kommunikationsgesellschaft*, Frankfurt a.M.: Suhrkamp.
Münch, R. (1986/1993b) *Die Kultur der Moderne*, Frankfurt a.M.: Suhrkamp.
Münch, R. (1984/1992) *Die Struktur der Moderne*, Frankfurt a.M.: Suhrkamp.
Münch, R. (1982/1988) *Theorie des Handelns. Zur Rekonstruktion der Beiträge von Talcott Parsons, Emile Durkheim und Max Weber*, Frankfurt a.M.: Suhrkamp.
Münch, R. and Guenther, T. (2005) "Der Markt in der Organisation. Von der Hegemonie der Fachspezialisten zur Hegemonie des Finanzmanagements", in: P. Windolf (ed.). *Finanzmarkt-Kapitalismus. Analysen zum Wandel von Produktionsregimen. Sonderheft 45 der Kölner Zeitschrift für Soziologie und Sozialpsychologie*, Wiesbaden: VS Verlag für Sozialwissenschaften, 394–417.
Münch, R., Lahusen, C., Kurth, M., Borgards, C., Stark, C. and Jauß, C. (2001) *Democracy at Work: A Comparative Sociology of Environmental Regulation in the United Kingdom, France, Germany and the United States*, Westport, CT: Praeger Publishers.
Münkler, H. (1997) "Der kompetente Bürger", in: A. Klein and R. Schmalz-Bruns (eds) *Politische Beteiligung und Bürgerengagement in Deutschland. Möglichkeiten und Grenzen*, Baden-Baden: Nomos, 153–172.
Murswieck, A. (1998) "Gesellschaft", in: W.P. Adams and P. Lösche (eds) *Länderbericht USA*, Bonn: Bundeszentrale für politische Bildung, 621–718.
Murswieck, A. (1997) "Soziale Unsicherheit als Entwicklungsmotor? Die Erfahrungen der USA", in: *Jahrbuch für Europa- und Nordamerikastudien 1: Standortrisiko Wohlfahrtsstaat?*
Myrberg, E. and Rosén, M. (2006) "Reading Achievement and Social Selection into Independent Schools in Sweden – Results from IEA PIRLS 2001", *Scandinavian Journal of Educational Research*, 50 (82): 185–205.
Narr, W.-D. and Schubert, A. (1994) *Weltökonomie. Die Misere der Politik*, Frankfurt a.M.: Suhrkamp.
Naschold, F. (1995) *Ergebnissteuerung, Wettbewerb, Qualitätspolitik, Entwicklung des öffentlichen Sektors in Europa*, Berlin: edition sigma.
Naschold, F. (1993) *Modernisierung des Staates. Zur Ordnungs- und Innovationspolitik des öffentlichen Sektors*, Berlin: edition sigma.
Naschold, F., Oppen, M. and Wegener, A. (1997) *Innovative Kommunen. Internationale Trends und deutsche Erfahrungen*, Stuttgart, Berlin, Cologne: Kohlhammer.
Nash, R. (2004) "Equality of Educational Opportunity: In Defence of a Traditional Concept", *Educational Philosophy and Theory*, 36 (4): 361–377.
Neckerman, K.M. and Torche, F. (2007) "Inequality: Causes and Consequences", *Annual Review of Sociology*, 33: 335–357.
Nelson, J.I. (1995) *Post-Industrial Capitalism. Exploring Economic Inequality in America*, Thousand Oaks, CA: Sage.
Neumayer, E. (2003) "Beyond Income: Convergence in Living Standards, Big Time", *Structural Change and Economic Dynamics*, 14 (3): 275–296.

Noelle-Neumann, E. and Köcher, R. (1997) *Allensbacher Jahrbuch der Demoskopie 1993–1997*, Vol. X, Munich: K.G. Saur.
Norberg-Schönfeldt, M. (2008) "Children's School Achievement and Parental Work: An Analysis for Sweden", *Education Economics*, 16 (1): 1–17.
Nullmeier, F. (2000) *Politische Theorie des Sozialstaats*, Frankfurt/New York: Campus.
O'Brien, R., Goetz, A.M., Scholte, J.A. and Williams, M. (2000) *Global Governance. Multilateral Economic Institutions and Social Movements*, Cambridge, MA: Cambridge University Press.
O'Sullivan, M.A. (2000) *Contests for Corporate Control*, Oxford: Oxford University Press.
OECD (2011a) *Family Database: Paris*. Online. Available at: www.oecd.org/dataoecd/13/19/43857755.xls (accessed 9 March 2011).
OECD (2011b) *Participation in Voluntary Work*. Online. Available at: www.oecd.org/dataoecd/1/24/43200180.xls (accessed 9 March 2011).
OECD (2011c) *Benefits and Wages*, Paris: OECD.
OECD (2011d) *Family Database*, Paris: OECD.
OECD (2011e) *StatExtracts*, Paris: OECD.
OECD (2011f) *Employment Database*, Paris: OECD.
OECD (2010a) *Education at a Glance*, Paris: OECD.
OECD (2010b) *Economic Outlook*, Paris: OECD.
OECD (2010c) *Employment and Labour Market Statistics*, Paris: OECD.
OECD (2010d) *Factbook*, Paris: OECD.
OECD (2010e) *Labour Market Statistics*, Paris: OECD.
OECD (2010f). *PISA 2009 Results*, Paris: OECD.
OECD (2010g) *Statistics*, Paris: OECD.
OECD (2009a) *Society at a Glance 2009*. Online. Available at: http://dx.doi.org/10.1787/550365522422 (accessed 9 March 2011).
OECD (2009b) *Science, Technology and Industry Scoreboard 2009*, Paris: OECD.
OECD (2009c) *Factbook*, Paris: OECD.
OECD (2008) *Employment Outlook*, Paris: OECD.
OECD (2007) *Science, Technology and Industry Scoreboard 2007. Innovation and Performance in the Global Economy*, Paris: OECD.
OECD (2006) *Employment Outlook*, Paris: OECD.
OECD (2004a) *Economic Outlook No. 75, 2004*. Paris: OECD.
OECD (2004b) *Corporate Data Environment, Labour Force Statistics*. Online. Available at: www1.oecd.org/scripts/cde/members/lfsdataauthanticate.asp.
OECD (2003a) *Employment Outlook*, Paris: OECD.
OECD (2003b) *Historical Statistics*, Paris: OECD.
OECD (2003c) *Labour Market Statistics*, Paris: OECD.
OECD (2003d) *Main Economic Indicators*, Paris: OECD.
OECD (2003e) *Quarterly Labour Force Statistics*, Paris: OECD.
OECD (2002) *Society at a Glance*, Paris: OECD.
OECD (2001a) *STI Scoreboard 2001*, Paris: OECD.
OECD (2001b) *Knowledge and Skills for Life*, Paris: OECD.
OECD (2001c) *OECD in Figures*, Paris: OECD.
OECD (2001d) *Education at a Glance*, Paris: OECD.
OECD (1999) *The Knowledge-based Economy. A Set of Facts and Figures*, Paris: OECD.
OECD (1996) *Employment and Growth in the Knowledge-based Economy*, Paris: OECD.

Oesch, D. (2010) "What Explains High Unemployment among Low-Skilled Workers? Evidence from 21 OECD Countries", *European Journal of Industrial Relations*, 16 (1): 39–55.
Olsen, G.M. (2008) "Labour Market Policy in the United States, Canada and Sweden: Addressing the Issue of Convergence", *Social Policy & Administration*, 42 (4): 323–341.
Olson, M., Jr. (1982) *The Rise and Decline of Nations. Economic Growth, Stagflation, and Social Rigidities*. New Haven/London: Yale University Press.
Olson, M., Jr. (1965) *The Logic of Collective Action*, Cambridge, MA: Harvard University Press.
Olssen, M. and Peters, M.A. (2005) "Neoliberalism, Higher Education and the Knowledge Economy: From the Free Market to Knowledge Capitalism", *Journal of Education Policy*, 20 (3): 313–345.
Ostner, I. (1998) "Quadraturen im Wohlfahrtsdreieck. Die USA, Schweden und die Bundesrepublik im Vergleich", in: S. Lessenich and I. Ostner (eds) *Welten des Wohlfahrtskapitalismus*, Frankfurt/New York: Campus, 225–252.
Pager, D. (2007) *Marked. Race, Crime, and Finding Work in an Era of Mass Incarceration*, Chicago: University of Chicago Press.
Palier, B. (ed.) (2010) *A Long Goodbye to Bismarck? The Politics of Welfare Reform in Continental Europe*. Amsterdam: Amsterdam University Press.
Park, S. and Vetterlein, A. (eds) (2010) *Creating Policy Norms in the IMF and the World Bank*, Cambridge: Cambridge University Press.
Parsons, T. (2007) *American Society. A Theory of the Societal Community*, ed. G. Sciortino, Boulder, CO: Paradigm Publishers.
Parsons, T. (1971) *The System of Modern Societies*, Englewood Cliffs, NJ: Prentice Hall.
Parsons, T. and White, W. (1964) "The Link between Character and Society", in: T. Parsons (ed.) *Social Structure and Personality*, New York: Free Press, 183–235.
Pastore, A.L. and Maguire, K. (ed.) (2003) *Sourcebook of Criminal Justice Statistics 2001*, Washington, DC: US Dept. of Justice, Bureau of Justice Statistics.
Patchin, J.W., Huebner, B.M., McCluskey, J., Varano, S.P. and Bynum, T.S. (2006) "Exposure to Community Violence and Childhood Delinquency", *Crime and Delinquency*, 52 (2): 307–332.
Pattilo, M.E., Weiman, D.F. and Western, B. (2004) *Imprisoning America: The Social Effects of Mass Incarceration*, New York: Russel Sage Foundation.
Pauly, L.W. (1998) *Who Elected the Bankers? Surveillance and Control in the World Economy*, Ithaca, NY: Cornell University Press.
Peck, J. (2001) *Workfare States*, New York: Guilford Press.
Peet, R. (2003) *Unholy Trinity: The IMF, World Bank and WTO*, London: Zed Books.
Peredo, A.M. and McLean, M. (2005) "Social Entrepreneurship: A Critical Review of the Concept", *Journal of World Business*, 41 (1): 56–65.
Perlmutter, F.D. (1997) *From Welfare to Work. Corporate Initiatives and Welfare Reform*, Oxford: Oxford University Press.
Peters, M.A. (2005) "The New Prudentialism in Education: Actuarial Rationality and the Entrepreneurial Self", *Educational Theory*, 55 (2): 123–137.
Petersmann, E.-U. (2007) "Multilevel Judicial Governance of International Trade Requires a Common Conception of Rule of Law and Justice", *Economics & Law*, 10 (3): 529–551.
Petersmann, E.-U. and Pollack, M.A. (eds) (2003) *Transatlantic Economic Disputes. The EU, the US and the WTO*, Oxford: Oxford University Press.

Pettit, B. and Western, B. (2004) "Mass Imprisonment and the Life Course: Race and Class Inequality in US Incarceration", *American Sociological Review*, 69 (2): 151–169.

Phillips, J.A. (2002) "White, Black, and Latino Homicide Rates: Why the Difference?" *Social Problems*, 49: 349–373.

Picht, G. (1964) *Die deutsche Bildungskatastrophe*, Olten: Walter-Verlag.

Pierson, P. (2004) *Politics in Time: History, Institutions and Social Analysis*, Princeton, NJ: Princeton University Press.

Pischke, J.-S. (2005) "Labour Market Institutions, Wages, and Investment: Review and Implications", *CESifo Economic Studies*, 51 (1): 47–75.

Plehwe, D., Walpen, B. and Neunhöffer, G. (eds) (2006) *Neoliberal Hegemony. A Global Critique*, London: Routledge.

Polanyi, K. (1944) *The Great Transformation*, New York: Rinehart Press.

Pontusson, J. (2005) *Inequality and Prosperity. Social Europe vs. Liberal America*, Ithaca, NY: Cornell University Press.

Prasad, E.S. (2000) "The Unbearable Stability of the German Wage Structure: Evidence and Interpretation", *IMF Working Paper* 00/22, February 2000.

Priller, E. (2002) "Zum Stand empirischer Befunde und sozialwissenschaftlicher Theorie zur Zivilgesellschaft und zur Notwendigkeit ihrer Weiterentwicklung", in: Enquête-Kommission "Zukunft des Bürgerschaftlichen Engagements" Deutscher Bundestag (ed.) *Bürgerschaftliches Engagement und Zivilgesellschaft*, Opladen: Leske + Budrich, 39–54.

Priller, E. and Zimmer, A. (1997) "Ehrenamtliches Engagement in Deutschland – Defizite, Chancen und Potentiale", in: Bank für Sozialwirtschaft (ed.) *BFS-Informationen* 10: 13–16.

Pruijt, H. and Dérogée, P. (2010) "Employability and Job Security, Friends or Foes? The Paradoxical Reception of Employacurity in the Netherlands", *Socio-Economic Review*, 8 (3): 437–460.

Putnam, R. (2000) *Bowling Alone: The Collapse and Revival of American Community*, New York: Simon & Schuster.

Putnam, R. (1995a) "Bowling Alone: America's Declining Social Capital", *Journal of Democracy*, 6 (1): 65–78.

Putnam, R. (1995b) "Turning In, Turning Out: The Strange Disappearance of Social Capital in America", *Political Science and Politics*, 28 (4): 664–683.

Putnam, R., Leonardi, R. and Nanetti, R.Y. (1993) *Making Democracy Work. Civic Traditions in Modern Italy*, Princeton: Princeton University Press.

Randow, G. von (1999) "Kapitalisten der Nächstenliebe", *Die Zeit*, No. 15, 8 April 1999, 25–26.

Rawls, J. (2001) *Justice as Fairness. A Restatement*, ed. Erin Kelly, Cambridge, MA: Harvard University Press.

Rawls, J. (1993) *Political Liberalism*, New York: Columbia University Press.

Rawls, J. (1971) *A Theory of Justice*, Cambridge, MA: Harvard University Press.

Rawls, J. (1958) "Justice as Fairness", *The Philosophical Review*, 67 (2): 164–194.

Reich, R. (1991) *The Work of Nations*, New York: Vintage Books.

Rhodes, M. (2001) "The Political Economy of Social Pacts: 'Competitive Corporatism' and European Welfare Reform", in: Paul Pierson (ed.) *The New Politics of the Welfare State*, Oxford: Oxford University Press, 165–196.

Ricardo, D. (1817/1977) *On the Principles of Political Economy and Taxation*, Hildesheim: Olms.

Ridley-Duff, R. (2008) "Social Enterprise as a Socially Rational Business", *International Journal of Entrepreneurial Behaviour & Research*,14 (5): 291–312.

Riedel, B. (2003) "Öffentliche Engagementförderung im europäischen Vergleich. Beispiele aus Dänemark, England und den Niederlanden", in: Enquête-Kommission "Zukunft des bürgerschaftlichen Engagements" Deutscher Bundestag (ed.) *Bürgerschaftliches Engagement im internationalen Vergleich*, Opladen: Leske + Budrich, 91–145.

Rieger, E. and Leibfried, S. (2001) *Grundlagen der Globalisierung. Perspektiven des Wohlfahrtsstaates*, Frankfurt a.M.: Suhrkamp.

Rifkin, J. (2000) *Access – Das Verschwinden des Eigentums*, Frankfurt a.M.: Campus.

Risse, T., Ropp, S.C. and Sikkink, K. (eds) (1999) *The Power of Human Rights. International Norms and Domestic Change*, Cambridge, MA: Cambridge University Press.

Rodrik, D. (2011) *The Globalization Paradox: Democracy and the Future of the World Economy*, New York: W.W. Norton.

Rodrik, D. (2007) *One Economics, Many Recipes: Globalization, Institutions and Economic Growth*, Princeton: Princeton University Press.

Rodrik, D. (1997) *Has Globalization Gone too Far?* Washington, DC: Institute of International Economics.

Rodrik, D. (1996) "Why do More Open Economies have Bigger Governments?", *NBER Working Paper* 5537.

Roemer, J.E. (1998) *Equality of Opportunity*, Cambridge, MA: Harvard University Press.

Room, G. (2000) "Commodification and Decommodification: A Developmental Critique", *Policy & Politics*, 28 (3): 331–351.

Rose, N. (1999) *Powers of Freedom: Reframing Political Thought*, Cambridge: Cambridge University Press.

Rosenbladt, B. von. (1991) "Arbeitslose in einer prosperierenden Wirtschaft. Empirische Befunde zu 'neuer Armut' und 'Arbeitsunwilligkeit' unter Arbeitslosen", *Mitteilungen aus der Arbeitsmarkt- und Berufsforschung*, 1991, 1: 146–156.

Rosenfeld, J. (2006) "Widening the Gap: The Effect of Declining Unionization on Managerial and Worker Pay, 1983–2000", *Research in Social Stratification and Mobility*, 24 (3): 223–238.

Rothenberg, L. (1992) *Linking Citizens to Government: Interest Group Politics at Common Cause*, Cambridge: Cambridge University Press.

Rothenbuhler, E.W. (2005) "The Church of the Cult of the Individual", in: E.W. Rothenbuhler and M. Coman (eds) *Media Anthropology*, London: Sage, 91–100.

Rubio-Marin, R. (2000) *Immigration as a Democratic Challenge. Citizenship and Inclusion in Germany and the United States*, Cambridge: Cambridge University Press.

Rueda, D. (2007) *Social Democracy Inside Out. Partisanship & Labor Market Policy in Industrialized Democracies*. Oxford: Oxford University Press.

Rueda, D. and Pontusson, J. (2000) "Wage Inequality and Varieties of Capitalism", *World Politics*, 52 (3): 350–383.

Sachweh, P. and Olafsdottir, S. (2010) "The Welfare State and Equality? Stratification Realities and Aspirations in Three Welfare Regimes", *European Sociological Review* (201) doi: 10.1093/esr/jcq055.

Sainsbury, D. (2006) "Immigrants' Social Rights in Comparative Perspective: Welfare Regimes, Forms in Immigration and Immigration Policy Regimes", *Journal of European Social Policy* 16 (3): 229–244.

Salamon, L.M. and Anheier, H.K. (1998) "Social Origins of Civil Society: Explaining the Nonprofit Sector Cross-Nationally", *Voluntas*, 9 (3): 213–247.

Salamon, L.M., Anheier, H.K., List, R., Toepler, S. et al. (1999) *Global Civil Society: Dimensions of the Nonprofit Sector*, Baltimore, MD: Johns Hopkins Center for Civil Society Studies, Comparative Nonprofit Sector Project.

Sampson, R.J. and Groves, W.B. (1989) "Community Structure and Crime: Testing Social Disorganization Theory", *American Journal of Sociology*, 94: 774–802.

Sampson, R.J. and Raudenbush, S.W. (1999) "Systematic Social Observation of Public Spaces: A New Look at Disorder in Urban Neighbourhoods", *American Journal of Sociology*, 105 (3): 603–51.

Savolainen, J. (2000) "Inequality, Welfare State, and Homicide: Further Support for the Institutional Anomie Theory", *Criminology*, 38: 1021–1042.

Schäfer, A. (2005) *Die neue Unverbindlichkeit. Wirtschaftspolitische Koordinierung in Europa*. Frankfurt/New York: Campus.

Scharpf, F.W. (2000) "Economic Changes, Vulnerabilities, and Institutional Capabilities", in: F.W. Scharpf and V.A. Schmidt (eds) *Welfare and Work in the Open Economy*, Oxford: Oxford University Press, 21–124.

Scharpf, F.W. (1998) "Jenseits der Regime-Debatte: Ökonomische Integration, Demokratie und Wohlfahrtsstaat in Europa", in: S. Lessenich and I. Ostner (eds) *Welten des Wohlfahrtskapitalismus*, Frankfurt/New York: Campus: 321–49.

Scharpf, F.W. (1997a) "Balancing Positive and Negative Integration: The Regulatory Options for Europe", *MPIfG Working Paper* 97/8, November 1997.

Scharpf, F.W. (1997b) "Employment and the Welfare State: A Continental Dilemma", *MPIfG Working Paper* 97/7, July 1997.

Scharpf, F.W. (1996) "Negative and Positive Integration in the Political Economy of European Welfare States", in: G. Marks, F.W. Scharpf, P.C. Schmitter and W. Streeck, *Governance in the European Union*, London: Sage, 15–39.

Scharpf, F.W. and Schmidt, V.A. (eds) (2000) *Welfare and Work in the Open Economy*, Oxford: Oxford University Press.

Scharpf, F.W., B. Reissert and F. Schnabel (1976) *Politikverflechtung: Theorie und Empirie des kooperativen Föderalismus in der Bundesrepublik*, Kronberg: Scriptor.

Schelsky, H. (1965) *Auf der Suche nach Wirklichkeit. Gesammelte Aufsätze*, Düsseldorf und Köln: Diederichs.

Scherer, A.G. and Löhr, A. (1999) "Verantwortungsvolle Unternehmensführung im Zeitalter der Globalisierung. Einige kritische Bemerkungen zu den Perspektiven einer liberalen Weltwirtschaft", in: B.N. Kumar, M. Osterloh and G. Schreyögg (eds) *Unternehmensethik und Transformation des Wettbewerbs: Shareholder Value, Globalisierung, Hyperwettbewerb*, Stuttgart: Schaefer-Poeschel.

Scherer, A.G. and Smid, M. (1998) "The Downward Spiral and the US Model Business Principles. On the Responsibility of Multinational Enterprises to Establish World-Wide Social and Environmental Standards", *Manuskript Universität Erlangen-Nürnberg*.

Schluchter, W. (1979) *Die Entwicklung des okzidentalen Rationalismus*, Tübingen: Mohr Siebeck.

Schmid, G. (2002) *Wege in eine neue Vollbeschäftigung. Übergangsarbeitsmärkte und aktivierende Arbeitsmarktpolitik*, Frankfurt/New York: Campus.

Schmid, J. (1996) *Wohlfahrtsverbände in modernen Wohlfahrtsstaaten*, Opladen: Leske + Budrich.

Schmidt, M.G. (1998) *Sozialpolitik in Deutschland. Historische Entwicklung und internationaler Vergleich*, Opladen: Leske + Budrich, 2nd edn.

Schmidt, V.A. (2000) "Values and Discourse in the Politics of Adjustment", in: F.W. Scharpf and V.A. Schmidt (eds) *Welfare and Work in the Open Economy, Vol. I*, Oxford: Oxford University Press, 229–309.

Scholte, J.A. (2004) "Civil Society and Democratically Accountable Global Governance", *Government and Opposition*, 39 (2): 211–233.

Schulze, G. (1992) *Die Erlebnisgesellschaft*, Frankfurt a.M.: Campus.
Schulze-Cleven, T. (2009) *Flexible Markets, Protected Workers: Adjustment Pathways in Europe's New Economy*, PhD Thesis, University of Berkeley, California.
Schumpeter, J.A. (2004) *Capitalism, Socialism & Democracy*, New York: Routledge.
Schumpeter, J.A. (1983) *The Theory of Economic Development*, New Brunswick, NJ: Transaction Publishers.
Schwengel, H. (1999) *Globalisierung mit europäischem Gesicht*, Berlin: Aufbau Verlag.
Scourfield, P. (2007) "Social Care and the Modern Citizen: Client, Consumer, Service User, Manager and Entrepreneur", *British Journal of Social Work*, 37 (1): 107–172.
Scruggs, L. and Allan, J. (2006) "Welfare–State Decommodification in 18 OECD Countries: A Replication and Revision", *Journal of European Social Policy*, 16 (1): 55–72.
Seeleib-Kaiser, M. (2001) *Globalisierung und Sozialpolitik. Ein Vergleich der Diskurse und Wohlfahrtssysteme in Deutschland, Japan und den USA*, Frankfurt/New York: Campus.
Seeleib-Kaiser, M. (1997) "Der Wohlfahrtsstaat in der Globalisierungsfalle: Eine analytisch-konzeptionelle Annäherung", in: *Jahrbuch für Europa- und Nordamerika-Studien1: Standortrisiko Wohlfahrtsstaat?*, 73–106.
Seifert, H. and Massa-Wirth, H. (2005) "Pacts of Employment and Competitiveness in Germany", *Industrial Relations Journal*, 36 (3): 217–240.
Sennett, R. (1998) *The Corrosion of Character: The Personal Consequences of Work in New Capitalism*, New York: Norton.
Serrano Pascual, A. and Magnusson, L. (eds) (2007) *Reshaping Welfare States and Activation Regimes in Europe*, Brussels: P.I.E. Peter Lang S.A.
Sharman, J.C. (2006) *Havens in a Storm. The Struggle for Global Tax Regulation*, Ithaca, NY: Cornell University Press.
Shaw, C.R. and McKay, H.D. (1942) *Juvenile Delinquency in Urban Areas*, Chicago: University of Chicago Press.
Siaroff, A. (1999) "Corporatism in 24 Industrial Democracies: Meaning and Measurement", *European Journal of Political Research*, 36: 175–205.
Siebert, H. (2006) "Locational Competition: A Neglected Paradigm in the International Division of Labour", *The World Economy*, 29 (2): 137–158.
Siegel, N.A. (2005) "Social Pacts Revisited: 'Competitive Concertation' and Complex Causality in Negotiated Welfare State Reforms", *European Journal Relations*, 11 (1): 107–126.
Simmel, G. (1908/1992) *Soziologie. Untersuchungen über die Formen der Vergesellschaftung*, Frankfurt a.M.: Suhrkamp.
Sincavage, J.R., Haub, C. and Sharma, O.P. (2010) "Labor Costs in India's Organized Manufacturing Sector", *Monthly Labor Review*, 133 (5): 3–22. Online. Available at: www.bls.gov/opub/mlr/2010/05/art1full.pdf (accessed 16 March 2011).
Sirianni, C. and Friedland, L. (2001) *Civic Innovation in America*, Berkeley and Los Angeles: University of California Press.
Skocpol, T. (1998) "Don't Blame Big Government. America's Voluntary Groups Thrive in a National Network", in: E.J. Dionne Jr. (ed.) *Community Works. The Revival of Civil Society in America*, Washington, DC: Brookings Institution Press, 37–43.
Skocpol, T. and Fiorina, M.P. (eds) (1999) *Civic Engagement in American Democracy*, Washington, DC: Brookings Institution Press.
Smeeding, T.M. and Grodner, A. (2000) "Changing Income Inequality in OECD Countries: Updated Results from the Luxembourg Income Study (LIS)", in: R. Hauser and I. Becker, *The Personal Distribution of Income in an International Perspective*, Berlin: Springer, 205–224.

Smith, A. (1776/1937) *The Wealth of Nations*, New York: Modern Library.
Smith, A.D. (1986) *The Ethnic Origins of Nations*, Oxford: Blackwell.
Smith, K.B. (2004) "The Politics of Punishment: Evaluating Political Explanations of Incarceration Rates", *The Journal of Politics*, 66 (3): 925–938.
Soederberg, S., Menz, G. and Cerny, P.C. (eds) (2005) *Internalizing Globalization: The Rise of Neoliberalism and the Erosion of the National Varieties of Capitalism*, London and New York: Palgrave Macmillan.
Solga, H. (2003) "Das Paradox der integrierten Ausgrenzung von gering qualifizierten Jugendlichen", *Aus Politik und Zeitgeschichte*, 27, B 21–22: 19–25.
Solga, H. (2002) "'Ausbildungslosigkeit' als soziales Stigma in Bildungsgesellschaften", *Kölner Zeitschrift für Soziologie und Sozialpsychologie*, 54: 476–505.
Sørensen A. (2006) "Welfare States, Family Inequality, and Equality of Opportunity", *Research in Social Stratification and Mobility*, 24 (4): 367–375.
Soysal, Y.N. (1994) *Limits of Citizenship. Migrants and Postnational Membership in Europe*, Chicago: University of Chicago Press.
Spear, R., Defourny, J., Favreau, L. and Laville, J.-L. (eds) (2001) *Tackling Social Exclusion in Europe*, Aldershot: Ashgate.
Spencer, H. (1972) *On Social Evolution. Selected Writings*, ed. J.D.Y. Peel, Chicago: University of Chicago Press.
Starke, P. (2006) "The Politics of Welfare State Retrenchment: A Literature Review", *Social Policy & Administration*, 40 (1): 104–120.
Statistisches Bundesamt (1999) *Stand und Entwicklung der Erwerbstätigkeit*, Bonn.
Statistisches Bundesamt (1997) *Datenreport 1997. Zahlen und Fakten über die Bundesrepublik Deutschland*, Bonn.
Statistisches Bundesamt (1996) *Statistisches Jahrbuch für die Bundesrepublik Deutschland*, Stuttgart: Metzler-Poeschel.
Steffek, J., Kissling, C. and Nanz, P. (eds) (2007) *Civil Society Participation in European and Global Governance. A Cure for the Democratic Deficit?*, Houndmills, Basingstoke: Palgrave.
Stehr, N. (1994) *Knowledge Societies*, London: Sage.
Stiglitz, J.E. and Charlton, A. (2005) *Fair Trade for All. How Trade Can Promote Development*, Oxford: Oxford University Press.
Stone Sweet, A. and Caporaso, J.A. (1998) "From Free Trade to Supranational Polity: The European Court and Integration", in: W. Sandholtz and A. Stone Sweet (eds) *European Integration and Supranational Governance*, Oxford: Oxford University Press, 92–133.
Straubhaar, T. (1996) "Standortbedingungen im globalen Wettbewerb", in: R. Biskup (ed.) *Globalisierung und Wettbewerb*, Bern et al.: Paul Haupt, 217–239.
Streeck, W. (2009) *Re-Forming Capitalism. Institutional Change in the German Political Economy*, Oxford: Oxford University Press.
Streeck, W. (2004) "Hire and Fire: Ist der amerikanische Arbeitsmarkt ein Vorbild für Deutschland?" Contribution presented in the framework of the lecturing series "Endstation Amerika? Sozialwissenschaftliche Innen- und Außenansichten", *Duisburger Akzente 2004*, Universität Duisburg-Essen, Campus Duisburg, 29 April 2004.
Streeck, W. (2000) "Competitive Solidarity: Rethinking the 'European Social Model'", in: K. Hinrichs, H. Kitschelt and H. Wiesenthal (eds) *Kontingenz und Krise: Institutionenpolitik in kapitalistischen und postsozialistischen Gesellschaften*, Frankfurt/New York: Campus, 245–261.
Streeck, W. (1999) *Korporatismus in Deutschland. Zwischen Nationalstaat und Europäischer Union*. Frankfurt/New York: Campus.

Streeck, W. (1998) "Globale Wirtschaft, nationale Regulierung", in: Bruno Cattero (ed.) *Modell Deutschland – Modell Europa*, Opladen: Leske + Budrich, 13–32.

Streeck, W. (1991) "On the Institutional Conditions of Diversified Quality Production", in: Egon Matzner and Wolfgang Streeck (eds) *Beyond Keynesianism: The Socioeconomics of Production and Full Employment*, Aldershot: Elgar, 21–61.

Streeck, W. (1987) "Vielfalt und Interdependenz. Überlegungen zur Rolle von intermediären Organisationen in sich ändernden Umwelten", *Kölner Zeitschrift für Soziologie und Sozialpsychologie*, 39 (3): 452–470.

Streeck, W. and Höpner, M. (eds) (2003) *Alle Macht dem Markt? Fallstudien zur Abwicklung der Deutschland AG*, Frankfurt/New York: Campus.

Streeck, W. and Thelen, K. (eds) (2005a) *Beyond Continuity. Institutional Change in Advanced Political Economies*, Oxford: Oxford University Press.

Streeck, W. and Thelen, K. (eds) (2005b) "Introduction: Institutional Change in Advanced Political Economies", in: W. Streeck and K. Thelen (eds) *Beyond Continuity. Institutional Change in Advanced Political Economies*, Oxford: Oxford University Press, 1–39.

Süddeutsche Zeitung (2009) "Liberale sacken wieder ab" *Süddeutsche Zeitung* 65, No 37, 14/15 February 2009, 6.

Süddeutsche Zeitung (2004) "Deutsche liegen mit Arbeitszeit im Mittelfeld", *Süddeutsche Zeitung* No. 112, 15/16 May 2004, V1/17.

Sutherland, E.H. (1939) *Principles of Criminology*, Philadelphia: Lippincott.

Swank, D. (2002) *Global Capital, Political Institutions, and Policy Change in Developed Welfare States*, Cambridge: Cambridge University Press.

Swedberg, R. (2003) *Principles of Economic Sociology*, Princeton, NJ: Princeton University Press.

Swedberg, R. (1998) *Max Weber and the Idea of Economic Sociology*, Princeton, NJ: Princeton University Press.

Taylor-Gooby, P. (2008) "The New Welfare Settlement in Europe", *European Societies*, 10 (1): 3–24.

Taylor-Gooby, P. (ed.) (2004) *New Risks, New Welfare. The Transformation of the European Welfare State*, Oxford: Oxford University Press.

Thelen, K. (2002) "The Explanatory Power of Historical Institutionalism", in: Renate Mayntz (ed.) *Akteure – Mechanismen – Modelle. Zur Theoriefähigkeit makro-sozialer Analysen*, Frankfurt/New York: Campus, 91–107.

Thelen, K. and Kume (2006) "Coordination as a Political Problem in Coordinated Market Economies", *Governance* 19 (1): 11–42.

Thompson, J. (2002) "The World of the Social Entrepreneur", *International Journal of Public Sector Management*, 15 (5): 412–431.

Thompson, J. and Doherty, B. (2006) "The Diverse World of Social Enterprise: A Collection of Social Enterprise Stories", *International Journal of Social Economics*, 33 (5/6): 361–375.

Thorlindsson, T. and Bernburg, J.G. (2004) "Durkheim's Theory of Social Order and Deviance: a Multi-level Test", *European Sociological Review*, 20 (4): 271–285.

Thurow, L.C. (1996) *The Future of Capitalism: How Today's Economic Forces Shape Tomorrow's World*, New York: William Morrow and Co.

Tiberghien, Y. (2007) *Entrepreneurial States. Reforming Corporate Governance in France, Japan and Korea*, Ithaca, NY: Cornell University Press.

Tilly, C. (1978) *From Mobilisation to Revolution*, Reading, MA: Addison-Wesley.

Tinbergen, J. (1965) *International Economic Integration*, 2nd ed. Amsterdam/London, New York: Elsevier.

Titmuss, R. (1958) *Essays on the Welfare State*, London: Allen and Unwin.
Tocqueville, A. de (1945) *Democracy in America*, 2 vols, New York: Alfred A. Knopf.
Traxler, F. (2005) "Geldpolitik, Tarifsystem und Korporatismus", in: P. Windolf (ed.) Finanzmarkt-Kapitalismus. Special Issue of *Kölner Zeitschrift für Soziologie und Sozialpsychologie* No. 45. Wiesbaden: Verlag für Sozialwissenschaften, 372–393.
Traxler, F. (2003a) "Bargaining, State Regulations and the Trajectories of Industrial Relations", *European Journal of Industrial Relations* 9: 141–161.
Traxler, F. (2003b) "Bargaining Institutions and the Monetary Regime: A Cross-national Comparison and its Implication for European Monetary Union", *Journal of European Public Policy*, 10 (4): 596–615.
Traxler, F. (2001) "Die Metamorphosen des Korporatismus", *Politische Vierteljahresschrift*, 42: 590–623.
Traxler, F. and Kittel, B. (2000) "The Bargaining System and Performance: A Comparison of 18 OECD Countries", *Comparative Political Studies*, 33: 1154–1190.
Traxler, F., Kittel, B. and Blaschke, S. (2001) *National Labour Relations in Internationalized Markets*, Oxford: Oxford University Press.
Triplett, J.E. and Bosworth, B.P. (2004) *Productivity in the US Service Sector. New Sources of Economic Growth*, Washington, DC: The Brookings Institution.
Tsebelis, G. (2002) *Veto Players. How Political Institutions Work*, New York: Russel Sage Foundation.
Tumin, M.M. (1953) "Some Principles of Stratification: A Critical Analysis", *American Sociological Review*, 18: 387–394.
US Bureau of the Census (1992) *Current Population Reports, Consumer Income*, Washington, DC: Government Printing Office.
US Bureau of the Census (1973) *Current Population Reports, Consumer Income*, Washington, DC: Government Printing Office.
US Census Bureau (2009) *Current Population Reports*, Washington. DC: Government Printing Office.
US Census Bureau (2002) *Statistical Abstract of the United States*, Washington, DC: Government Printing Office.
US Department of Justice (2003) *Prison and Jail Inmates at Midyear 2002*, Bureau of Justice Statistics Bulletin. Online. Available at: www.ojp.usdoj.gov/bjs/pub/pdf/pjim02.pdf.
UN (2003) *United Nations Online Data*.
Vail, J. (2010) "Decommodification and Egalitarian Political Economy", *Politics & Society* 38 (3): 310–346.
Veysey, B.M. and Messner, S.F. (1999) "Further Testing of Social Disorganization Theory: An Elaboration of Sampson and Groves's 'Community Structure and Crime'", *Journal of Research in Crime and Delinquency*, 36 (2): 156–174.
Viebrock, E. (2009) "Flexicurity and Welfare Reform: A Review", *Socio-Economic Review*, 7 (2): 305–331.
Vis, B. (2007) "States of Welfare or States of Workfare? Welfare State Restructuring in 16 Capitalist Democracies, 1985–2002", *Policy & Politics*, 35 (1): 105–122.
Visser, J. (2006) "Union Membership Statistics in 24 Countries", *129 Monthly Labor Review* (January): 38–49.
Visser, J. and Hemerijck, A. (1998) *Ein holländisches Wunder? Reform des Sozialstaats und Beschäftigungswachstum in den Niederlanden*, Frankfurt a.M.: Campus.
Vobruba, G. (2009) *Die Gesellschaft der Leute. Kritik und Gestaltung der sozialen Verhältnisse*, Wiesbaden: VS Verlag.

Vogel, S.K. (1996) *Freer Markets. More Rules. Regulatory Reform in Advanced Industrial Countries*, Ithaca/London: Cornell University Press.
Vogt, W.P. (1993) "Durkheim's Sociology of Law: Morality and the Cult of the Individual", in: S.P. Turner (ed.) *Emile Durkheim Sociologist and Moralist*, London: Routledge, 69–92.
Voß, G. and Pongratz, H.J. (1998) "Der Arbeitskraftunternehmer. Eine neue Grundform der Ware Arbeitskraft?", *Kölner Zeitschrift für Soziologie und Sozialpsychologie*, 50 (1): 131–158.
Wacquant, L. (2010) "Crafting the Neoliberal State: Workfare, Prisonfare, and Social Insecurity", *Sociological Forum* 25 (82): 197–220.
Wacquant, L. (2009) *Punishing the Poor: The Neoliberal Government of Social Insecurity*, Durham: Duke University Press.
Wacquant, L. (2008) *Urban Outcasts: A Comparative Sociology of Advanced Marginality*, Polity Press.
Wacquant, L. (1997) "Vom wohltätigen Staat zum strafenden Staat: Über den politischen Umgang mit dem Elend in Amerika", *Leviathan* 25: 50–63.
Warham, J., Cochran, J.K., Dembro, R. and Sellers, C.S. (2005) "Community, Strain, and Delinquency: A Test of a Multi-Level Model of General Strain Theory", *Western Criminology Review*, 6 (1): 117–133.
Weber, M. (1976) *Wirtschaft und Gesellschaft*, Tübingen: Mohr Siebeck.
Weber, M. (1927) *General Economic History*, trans. F.H. Knight, New York: Greenberg Publisher.
Weingart, P. (2001) *Die Stunde der Wahrheit? Zum Verhältnis der Wissenschaft zu Politik, Wirtschaft und Medien in der Wissensgesellschaf*, Weilerswist: Velbrück Wissenschaft.
Weiss, L. (1998) *The Myth of the Powerless State*, Ithaca. NY: Cornell University Press.
Weizsäcker, C. von. (1999) *Logik der Globalisierung*, Göttingen: Vandenhoek & Ruprecht.
Western, B. and Beckett, K. (1998) "Der Mythos des freien Marktes. Das Strafrecht als Institution des US-amerikanischen Arbeitsmarktes", *Berliner Journal für Soziologie*, 8: 159–180.
Western, B. and Pettit, B. (2005) "Black-White Wage Inequality, Employment Rates, and Incarceration", *American Journal of Sociology*, 111 (2): 553–578.
Westgaard-Nielson, N. (2008) *Low-Wage Work in Denmark*, New York: Russel Sage Foundation.
Westling, A. (2007) "Equal Opportunities in Educational Systems: the Case of Sweden", *European Journal of Education*, 42 (1): 133–146.
Whyman, P. (2003) *Sweden and the 'Third Way'. A Macroeconomic Evaluation*, Aldershot: Ashgate.
Wikipedia (2009) *Ergebnisse der Landtagswahlen in Hessen*, Online. Available at: http://de.wikipedia./org/wiki/Ergebnisse_der_Landtagswahlen_in_Hessen (accessed 19 January 2009).
Wildenmann, R. (ed.) (1991) *Staatswerdung Europas? Optionen für eine Europäische Union*, Baden-Baden: Nomos.
Wilke, U. (2002) *Sozialhilfe in den USA. Die Reform in Texas und Wisconsin*, Frankfurt/New York: Campus.
Wilkinson, R.G. and Pickett, K.F. (2007) "The Problems of Relative Deprivation: Why Some Societies do Better than Others", *Social Science & Medicine*, 65 (9): 1965–1978.
Wilson, J.W. (1990) *The Truly Disadvantaged. The Inner City, the Underclass and Public Policy*, Chicago: University of Chicago Press.

Wisconsin Department of Children and Families (2011) *Total Participant*. Online. Available at: http://dcf.wi.gov/researchandstatistics/rsdata/w2data.htm#Participant%20Placements (accessed 9 March 2011).
Wolf, A. (2002) *Does Education Matter? Myths about Education and Economic Growth*, London: Penguin Books.
World Bank (2002) *Globalization, Growth and Poverty*. Oxford: Oxford University Press.
World Bank (2011) "Fertility Rate, Total (Births per Woman)". Online. Available at: http://data.worldbank.org/indicator/SP.DYN.TFRT.IN (accessed 14 March 2011)
Wright, E.O. (1997) *Class Counts. Comparative Studies in Class Analysis*, Cambridge: Cambridge University Press.
Yerkes, M. and Tijdens, K. (2010) "Social Risk Protection in Collective Agreements: Evidence from the Netherlands", *European Journal of Industrial Relations*, 16 (4): 369–383.
Zajac, E.E. (1995) *Political Economy of Fairness*, Cambridge, MA: MIT Press.
Zempel, J. and Frese, M. (1997) "Arbeitslose: Selbstverantwortung überwindet die Lethargie", *Psychologie Heute*, June 1997: 36–41.
Zugehör, R. (2003) *Die Zukunft des rheinischen Kapitalismus. Unternehmen zwischen Kapitalmarkt und Mitbestimmung*, Opladen: Leske + Budrich.
Zukunftskommission der Friedrich Ebert Stiftung (1998) *Wirtschaftliche Leistungsfähigkeit, sozialer Zusammenhalt, ökologische Nachhaltigkeit*, Bonn: Dietz.

Index

Page numbers in **bold** denote figures, those in *italic* denote tables.

Acocella, N. 107
activation 5, 24, 98, 105, 119, 123, 130–1, 136, 138, 192, 206
Addison, J.T. 225
Adloff, F. 123
advantage, competitive 18, 21, 122, 169, 170, 186
Agell, J. 43
Agion, P. 61
Agnew, R. 216
Alber, J. 4
Albert, M. 11
Albin, C. 79
Alcock, P. 104
Alderson, A.S. 230
Alesina, A. 4, 75
Alexander, J.C. 123
Allan, J. 140
Allmendinger, J. 222
Alon, S. 73
Altvater, E. 99
Amoore, L. 82
Anderson, B. 40
Anderson, K.M. 193, 199
Andreß, H.-J. 75
Angeletos, G.M. 4, 75
Anheier, H.K. 123, 127, 133
Anhut, R. 221
anomie 5, 40, 59, 62, 101, 107–9, 157, 213, 215–16, 234, 236, 241, 245, 259–**60**
Antonczyk, D. 122, 230
Antony, J. 245
Anxo, D. 111
Archibugi, D. 76, 99
Armingeon, K. 23, 46, 163, 225
Arrow, K. 73
association 12, **16**, **18**, 23, 38, 47, 86–7, 95–**6**, 101–2, 113, 116–17, 120, 123–**4**, 126–7, 130–4, 147, 162, 173, 185, 187, 189, 192, 195, 197, 199, 210–11, 215–16, 218, 226–7, 245, 247, 256–8, **260**–1
Austin, J. 134
Axford, B. 54

Bach, M. 101
Backhaus-Maul, H. 105
Bambra, C. 86, 197, 217
Banfield, E.C. 123
banks **17**, 21, 23, 118, 120–2, 150, 261
Banting, K.G. 150
Barnett, M. 84
Bartels, L.M. 154
Batey, P.W.J. 66
Batton, C. 241
Baumert, J. 179, 191
Beck, U. 80, 99, 110
Becker, G.S. 158, 237, 245
Beckert, J. 9–10
Beckett, K. 59, 219, 245
Beckfield, J. 89
benchmarking 9, 28, 94, 98, 119, 134, 139, 247, 257, 262
Benner, C. 118
Benner, M. 105, 192, 194, 197–8
Bennet, W.L. 133
Berger, J. 10
Berger, P.L. 262
Berger, R. 133
Berger, S. 9
Berkel, R. van 102
Bernburg, J.G. 218, 236, 239
Bernhard, S. 94, 247
Berthold, N. 63–4, 99

Beyer, J. 9, 22, 259
Bhagwati, J.N. 64
Bischoff, G. 94, 103
Björklund, A. 200, 204
Blechschmidt, P. 252
Bleses, P. 173
Blomqvist, P. 202, 204
Blonigen, B.A. 66
Bluhm, K. 253
Blyth, M. 99
Bode, I. 131
Boiral, O. 82
Boli, J. 82
Bornschier, V. 22
Börsch, A. 188
Bosworth, B.P. 109
Bourdieu, P. 69, 75, 95, 165, 247
Bradley, D.H. 60
Bradshaw, Y.W. 79
Brady, D. 98
Brinkmann, C. 113
Brinkmann, U. 23
Bröcker, J. 66
Bröckling, U. 92, 250
Brown, P. 54, 65, 225
Brubaker, W.R. 40
Bruce, M.A. 216, 218, 241
Brunkhorst, H. 3
Bude, H. 191, 251
Bukodi, E. 73
Bundgaard Vad, T. 105, 192, 194, 197
Bursik, R.J. 241

Cahn, E.S. 132
Campbell, J.L. 193, 201
capital, economic **96**, **263**; political 95, 247; symbolic 95–6
capitalism 27, 53, 80–1, 112, 118, 137, 141, 162, 184, 194, 196
Caporaso, J.A. 88
Card, D. 155
Carr, F. 116
Casper, S. 13
Castells, M. 134
Cattero, B. 99, 115
Cerny, P.G. 1, 55, 99, 114–15, 213, 232
Chamlin, M.B. 245
change, economic 5, 7, 45, 259, 261–2; institutional 5, 7, 9–10, 22–3, 140; social **6–7**, 9–10, 49, 90–1, 216, 259, 262; structural 10, 23–4, 30, 38, 45, 55, 57–9, 61, 63, 64, 99, 107, 111, 197–9, 201, 207, 221–2, 248–9, 259–63; symbolic 5, 7–9, 90, 92–4, 98–9, 110

Charlton, A. 64
Charnovitz, S. 81
Choi, M. 228
citizen/citizenship 2, 23, 38, 40, **51**, 65, *67*, 72–4, 84, 87, 99, 101, 107, 125–6, 129, 137, 141–2, 157, 177–8, 183–4, 194–6, 202, 221, 232, 238, 241, 248–50, 256, 258; private 129, 184
Clasen, J. 140, 173
class, lower 30, 65, 68, 70, 179, 190, 251, 253–**5**, **260**; middle 10, 30, 41, 62, 65, 147–8, 150, 155–6, 162, 171, 186, 191, 197, 207, 214–15, 225, 250–1, **253–4**, 258; working 41–2, 65, 146–7, 153, 166, 171, 186, 189–91, 197, 207, 225, 250–1; upper 168, 128, 179, 214, 251–5, **260**
class society, middle 214, **260**, 262–3
class structure 7, 28, 48, 125, 154, 251–5, 258–**63**
Clegg, D. 173
Cloward, R.A. 157, 217
Cochran, J.K. 245
Cogneau, D. 73, 79
Cohen, J. 123
commitment/work, voluntary 82, 120, 125–9, 131, 133, 137
communication *29–30*, 37–8, 41, 53–7, 84, 111–12, 117, 173, 186, 230, 259, **260**
community 40, 74, 81–2, 86, 88, 97, 104, 109, 129, 139, 168, 177, 210, 216, 231, 238, 241, 251, 254
competition 1, 4–7, 10, 12–13, 15, 20–1, 27, 30, 34, 36–7, 45, 49, 55–7, 59, 62–3, 65–6, 68, 71–6, 78, 81, 84, 93, 99–103, 107, 111–12, 114–17, 119–21, 131–2, 134, 140–3, 148–53, 155–6, 161–2, 166, 168–72, 175–6, 183–5, 188–9, 192–201, 203, 206, 208, 211–13, 218, 222–3, 228, 230, 232, 234–**5**, 239, 246–50, 253, 255–6, 259, **260**, 261–2
competitiveness 58, 83, 99–100, 121–2, 149, 176, 187–8, 199–200, 206, 210, 232
competitor(s) 40, 56, 59–60, 65, 84, 133, 189, 223, 228
complexity 96–7, 171, 262
conflict(s) 5, 7, 39–40, 46, 48, 52–3, 70–1, 75, 88, 101, 125, 129, 139, 162, 164–5, 173, 177–8, 182, 208, 214, 248, 251
conformity 206, 216, 237
Conroy, M.E. 82
contract 27, 41, 46, 63, 86–7, 109, 114, 118, 126, 135, 164, 185, 188, 248, 257

control 1, 8, 12, **17**, 21–3, 58–9, 79, 82, 87, 95, 101, 118, 131, 153–4, 157–8, 161, 166, 173, 185–6, 206, 212, 219, 239, 241, 245, 257
Cooke, P. 66
cooperation 12, 19–20, 37, 39, 40, 43, 47, 50, 52–5, 82, 85, 87, 102, 107–8, 115, 117, 128, 138–9, 162, 169, 185, 193, 195–6, 199, 208–10, 217–18, 226, 237, 245, 256
Cornia, G.A. 60, 82
countries, developing 24, 36, 38, 64, 79, 110, 123, 229, 248–9, 254, 261; industrialized 14, 53, 127, 143, 170, 228, 246, 248–9
Court of Justice, European 2, 93, 247
Cox, R.H. 173, 193, 199
Crepaz, M. 154
crime (rate) 4, 40, 58–9, 64, 84, 158–**9**, 161, 191, 204–5, 215–**20**, 236–7, 239, 241, 245, 259, **260**
Crouch, C. 93, 222
Culpepper, P.D. 103
Curbach, J. 130, 254–5
Cusack, T.R. 10

Daguerre, A. 140
Dahl, C.M. 122, 188, 225
Dahrendorf, R. 190
Danziger, S. 61, 64
Daun, H. 204
Davey, J.D. 245
Davis, J.A. 147
Davis, K. 165
Davis, S.J. 157
Dean, M. 1
Deflem, M. 215–16, 236
Dehousse, R. 101
de-industrialization 221–2, 232, 234, **235**
Delhey, J. 101
delinquency 5, 58–9, 83, 107, 157–8, 161–2, 191–2, 204–5, 207, 231, 215–16, 218–19, 221, 233–4, 236–41, 245, 259
Dembour, C. 66
deprivation, relative 58, 83, 107, 161, 191, 213–15, 218–21
deregulation 19–20, 28, 60, 62, 107, 109, 114, 141–2, 149, 169, 176, 178, 212, 246, 256
Dérogée, P. 107
Dettling, W. 73, 131–3, 139
Deutsch, K.W. 40
Deutschland AG 118
Deutschmann, C. 60, 84

Dickens, W.T. 230
differentials, income/wage 3–4
differentiation 1, 4, 10, 14, 37, 42, 50, 66, 74, 76, 80–1, 84–5, 87, 100–1, 107, 110, 116–19, 121, 125, 141, 149, 166, 168, 186, 188–90, 208, 222, 225, 232, **235**, 250
DiMaggio, P.J. 262
Dingeldey, I. 105
discourse 2–3, 6–8, 38, 43, 45, 48, 52–3, 71, 90–5, 97–8, 103–4, 109, 112, 114, 119, 123, 128, 134, 138–9, 162, 196, 208–11, 259–62
discrimination 90–1, 130, 149, 160, 162, 259–**60**
disorganization 83, 103–4, 106–9, 156, 189, 192, 203, 207, 216, 221, 234–6, 241
Doherty, B. 134
Donziger, S.R. 58–9, 64, 219
Dore, R. 9
Dörre, K. 10, 23
Dostal, J.M. 105
Drass, K.A. 245
Dreas, S.A. 119
Dreher, A. 54, 117
Drori, G.S. 9, 95
Dubet, F. 221
Dunford, M. 53
Dunne, T. 2
Durkheim, E. 2, 5, 38–9, 41–2, 62, 74, 83–8, 93, 113, 184–5, 213–15, 231, 234, 239, 247, 259
Dustmann, C. 73, 153, 167

Ebbinghaus, B. 116, 140
economy, global 7, 24, 36, 43, 53, 66, 112, 115, 118, 151; national 54, 100, 115, 246–7; world 1, 53, 80, 82, 115, 186–7, 222, 231
education 2, 5–6, 14–15, **17**, 23–4, *25*, 31–5, 41–2, 49–50, 55–7, 59, 61–6, 68–73, **77–8**, 91, 93, 104–5, 112, 118–19, 125, 140–1, 152–*4*, 160, 165–72, 176, 178, 180–3, 186, 189–92, 195, 198–200, 202–7, 222–5, 233–6, 238–*42*, *244*, *6*, 248–53, 255–6, 258
Edwards, B. 126
efficiency 63, 71, 257
Elias, N. 40
elite(s) 2, 28, 50, 66, 68, 71, 95–**6**, 99, 103, 111, 152, 166, 186, 204, 251, 253, **254–5**, 258
Elliot, M.A. 94

employment rate/quota 21, *25*, 30–*5*, 47, 102, 104, 107–9, 113, 122, 126, *144–5*, 151–**2**, 163, 170, 174, 176–7, 179–80, 193, 238, 240, *242*, *244*
empowerment 24, 50, 92, 94, 98, 103, 106, 114, 119–20, 123, 134, 136, 138–9, 238, 247, 250, 255–6, 258, **260**
Enjolras, B. 123
Entorf, H. 218, 241, 245
equality 2, 6–7, 40, 43, 47, 55, 73–4, 79, 81–2, 89, 91, 102, 104, 114, 178, 199, 201, 204, 206, 209, 215, 238, **260**; of opportunity 50, 52, 72–3, 141, 147–9, 153, 171, 190, 206, 249–50, **260**; of results 1, 37–8, 54, 73–4, 76–8, 102, 141–2, 147, 149, 168, 189, 203, 217, 238, 250
Eriksen, E.O. 99
Esping-Andersen, G. 15, 41–2, 46, 85–6, 102, 109, 113, 140–1, 178–9, 197, 202–3, 217, 225, 241, 250
Estevez-Abe, M. 14–15, 152
Etherington, D. 193
ethnic 7, 40–2, 52, 91, 146, 150, 202, 251, **260**
ethnicity 42, *126*, 146–7, 149–50, *154*, 160, 162
Evers, A. 139
exchange 50, 85, 87, 92, 101–2, 134, 137, 188
exclusion 81, 104, 161, 172, 214–15, 222, 233, 236, 238, 246; relative 5, 58–9, 140, 161, 189, 191, 204–5, 213–16, 220–1, 228, 233–41, 245, 259–**60**
experts 2, 8–9, 79, 92, 95, 97, 103, 139, 202, 211, 247, 256–8, **260**

Fagan, C. 111
fairness 1, 4–5, 7, 37–8, 52, 73–5, 79–82, 101, 126, 249–50
Featherstone, R. 215–16, 236
Fejes, A. 63, 223
Field, J. 63, 223
Fiöretos, O. 14
Fiorina, M.P. 128
Firebaugh, G. 82
Fitzenberger, B. 172, 225
Fligstein, N. 8, 88
foreign, the/foreigner 79–81, 90, 225, 249
Fossum, J.E. 99
Foucault, M. 1, 56, 58, 92, 98, 213, 232, 247
Fougner, T. 55
Fourcade, M. 84, 97, 261

Freeman, G.P. 154
Freeman, R.B. 234
Frerichs, S. 239–40, 243–4
Frese, M. 113
Friedland, L. 129
Friedrich, P. 66
Frietsch, R. 13
Fromm, S. 246
frustration 191, 214–15
Fuchs, S. 226

Gabriel, O.W. 128
Gans, H.J. 62
Garhammer, M. 72
Garland, D. 245
Gartner, R. 218
Gaskin, K. 123, 133
Gaston, N. 54, 117
Gellner, E. 40
generation contract 164, 248
Genschel, P. 54
Gensicke, T. 71
Gerhards, J. 66
Gibbons, M. 96
Giddens, A. 1
Gilbert, B. 1
Gilbert, N. 1, 105
Gillies, V. 232
globalization **6**, 8–11, 20, 37–8, 42–9, 49–50, 53–4, 56, 71–2, 75, 81, 89, 92–3, 99, 111, 114–16, 118, 120, 139, 148, 153, 156, 169–70, 176, 183, 186–7, 189, 207, 211, 213, 220–2, 232, 234–**5**, 245, 251, 259–60, 262–**3**
Goff, P.M. 9
Goldstein, K.M. 101
Goldthorpe, J. 73
Goodin, R.E. 4, 86, 140, 217, 241
Gordon, M.M. 42
Gorlov, V. 203
Gorter, C. 109, 151
Gottschalk, P. 59, 61, 64, 160, 219
governance 9, 92, 94–7, 128, 169, 193, 247, 257, **260**, 262
Gramsci, A. 99, 247
Grasmick, H.G. 241
Grodner, A. 217, 219
Gross, P. 72
groups 3, 6–8, 13, 19, 37, 40–2, 44–5, 49, 72–4, 80, 82, 87, 95, 100, 119, 125, 129–30, 132–4, 137, 146–7, 149–50, 153–4, 164–5, 167–9, 173–5, 183–7, 189, 195, 202–3, 214, 221, 223, 225, 227, 234, 238, 248, 250–3, 258

Groves, W.B. 216, 236, 241
Grubb, W.N. 103
Guéhenno, J.-M. 77
Guenther, T. 18
guideline 3, 6, 94, 101, 116, 197, 246, 257

Haas, E.B. 88
Habermas, J. 2–3, 80, 99
Hacker, J.S. 150, 154
Hall, P.A. 6, 11–12, 19–22, 24, 26–7, 52, 90, 150, 152, 169–70, 199, 241, 262
Hammerschmidt, P. 131
Handler, J.F. 105
Harrysson, L. 105, 199
Hart, D. 125
Hay, C. 55
Hayek, F.A. von 63, 247
Heidenreich, M. 24, 94, 103, 116, 199–200
Heinze, R.G. 133
Heinze, T. 21–2
Heitmeyer, W. 221
Held, D. 53, 57, 76, 99, 228
Helfert, M. 225
Helgøy, I. 204
Hengsbach, F. 53
Henrekson, M. 157
Hesketh, A. 225
Heuser, U.J. 134, 136–7
hierarchy 59, 72–4, 76, 153, 164, 166–8, 184, 217
Hirsch, J. 55, 99, 114–15
Hirst, P. 54
Hiß, S. 130, 253
Hobbes, T. 86
Hobsbawm, E.J. 40
Höffe, O. 38
Hoffman, S.D. 106
Holden, C. 86
Holtz, Eakin, D. 106
Homme, A. 204
Hondrich, K.O. 225
Hoogenboom, M. 140
Höpner, M. 21–3, 54, 118, 188, 246–7
Huaco, G. 165
Huber, E. 10, 46–7, 142, 260
Hudson, J. 140, 173
Huo, J. 201

Immergut, E. 262
imprisonment (rate) 59, **159**, **161**, 219–**20**
Imrohoroğlu, A. 241
inclusion 1–2, 5–9, 24–5, 40, 50, 52, 64, 90–2, 94–5, 103–7, 109–10, 116, 119–20, 128, 132, 138–40, 142, 146, 150, 160, 171, 179, 189–92, 197, 202–7, 211, 213, 216, 221–2, 225, 227–8, 232–8, 240–1, 245, 249; collective, collectivistic 5, 162, 213, 216, 221–2, 232, 234–6, 259, 261; individual, individualistic 5, 77, 204–5, 207, 213, 232–6, 238, 240, 245, 250, 259–62
income, basic 99, 168, 170
income (re)distribution 100, 157, 166–7, 217, 240
individual 2–4, 6, 24, 35, 39–42, 50, 63, 72, 74–6, 80, 83, 85, 87–8, 93–4, 103, 113, 115–16, 123, 130, 141, 164, 166, 169, 177, 181, 184–5, 189, 195–6, 205, 213–14, 218, 222–3, 232, 234, 237, 239, 249, 256; cult of the 2, 5, 93–4; empowerment of the 50, 92, 94, 98, 103, 106, 119, 120, 123, 134, 138–9, 256, 259
individualism/individualistic 2, 5, 37, 50, 86, 184, 189
individuality 3, 138
individualization 4, 42–3, 46, 48–50, 54, 86, 92, 98, 110–11, 113, 116, 118, 139–41, 184–7, 189, 192, 200, 202, 206, 208, 210, 212–13, 222, 234, 238, 249–50, **260**, 262
inequality 4, 7, 15, 21, 38–9, 47, 72, 100, 109, 149, 162, 190, 195, 201, 239, *242*, *244*, **260**; of income/wage 15, 21, 43, 60, 72, 82, 89, 150, 153–7, 166–8, 170, 172, 190, 217–19, 225, 233–4, 236, 239–41; of opportunity 1, 141
innovation 7, 11, 12, 14–18, 20, 22, 24, 30, 40, 60, 62, 94–5, 102–3, 107–8, 115–16, 119–20, 138, 152, 158, 182, 186–7, 197–203, 208, 216, 236, 248; incremental 7, 11, **16**, 20, 24, 26, 35, 152, 169–70, 187, 199, 259; radical 11–12, **16–17**, 23–4, 26–8, 35, 152, 169, 188, 199, 201, 246, **260–3**
institutionalization 9, 121, 216, 236
institutions 6–7, 9, 15, 20–2, *25*, 44–5, 49–50, 52–3, 56, 77, 80, 94, 97, 115, 118, 127–8, 140–1, 146, 164, 169–70, 187, 207, 218, 221, 231, 262
integration, social 6–7, 20, 36, 38, 40–1, 43, 47–8, 52, 79, 91–2, 98–101, 106–7, 112, 115–16, 123, 125, 127–32, 135, 138–9, 142, 161, 163, 188, 210, 212–13, 221–2, 233, 241, 248–50
interest, economic 257–8
investor(s) **17**, 55–6, 58–60, 257–8
Iversen, T. 10, 15, 114, 120–2, 196, 199, 260

Jachtenfuchs, M. 39
Jackson, G. 21–2
Jackson, M. 73
Jacobs, D. 245
Jaeger, M.M. 75
Jahoda, M. 113
Jakobi, A.P. 1, 63
Jansen, M. 54
Jauß, C. 95, 101
Jensen, G. 241
Jepperson, R. 5
Jessop, B. 1, 105, 114, 247
job(s) 7, 15, 19, 22–3, 27, 30, 34, 45, 54, 56–8, 60, 65, 73, 102–11, 113, 117, 120–1, 126, 133, 137, 148–50, 153, 155–6, 165–6, 168, 170–3, 176, 178–9, 188, 191, 197–9, 202–4, 207, 227–8, 230–3, 237, 248–9, 256
Jones, M. 193
Joppke, C. 2, 93
Jordan, B. 79
jurisdiction 2, 39, 129
justice 1–2, 5–7, 9–10, 35, 37–8, 50, 52, 68–9, 72–6, 79–85, 89, 92, 140, 142, 148, 150, 164, 168, 194, 217, 248–9, 259, **260–3**

Kangas, O. 199
Kant, I. 38
Kaplow, L. 74
Katz, M.B. 150
Katzenstein, P.J. 53, 195
Kaufmann, F.-X. 250
Kawachi, I. 241
Keane, J. 82
Kelly, M. 245
Kern, H. 171, 225
Keupp, H. 133
Keynesianism 121–2, 261
Kim, C.H. 61, 65, 73, 153, 230
King, D. 105
Kittel, B. 122
Klages, H. 71, 139
Klages, P. 257
Klug, W. 139
Knieper, R. 77
Knijn, T. 109
Koch, C. 72
Koch, M. 162
Koch-Arzberger, C. 225
Köcher, R. 70–1
Koenig, M. 3, 93
Kolpin, V. 66
Korpi, T. 140, 204

Kowalsky, W. 116
Krawczyk, O. 28–9
Kronauer, M. 221, 233
Krueger, A.O. 64
Kuhn, T.S. 52, 97
Kühner, S. 140
Kuipers, S. 108
Kurdelbusch, A. 188

La Free, G. 245
labour 8, 10, 14, **18–19**, *25*, 41, 44–7, 55, 63–4, 81, 92, 94–5, 103, 106, 108–9, 112, 114, 116, 118–19, 126, 139, 162, 164, 176, 183, 186, 192, 194, 199, 229–32; division of 1, 3–4, 19, 37, 38, 43, 50, 54, 83–7, 95, 98–9, 103, 110, 112–13, 115, 139–40, 169, 171, 183–4, 187, 228, 232, 234, 247, 259, 261; force 98, 102–3, 106, 113, *126*, 150, 203
Laclau, E. 99, 247
Lahusen, C. 95–6, 101
Lang, S. 123, 129, 131, 136
Lange, W. de 109
Langer, S. 64
Langley, P. 82
Lapeyronnie, D. 221
Larsen, F. 192
law 8, 39, 41, 50, 77, 82–3, 85–6, 88–9, 92, 95, 101, 103, 105, 115–16, 125–6, 129–1, 136, 139, 158, 215–16, 219, 247, 257–8, 261; economic 88, 257
Lazerson, M. 103
Leadbeater, C. 134
Leat, D. 123
Lebaron, F. 97
legitimacy 4–5, 8–9, 23, 80, 92, 94–5, 98, 123, 190, 247, 261, 262
legitimation 5–**6**, 10, 70, 79, 83, 89, 92, 99, 114, 170, 206, 221, **260**, 262
Legler, H. 12, 23–4, 28–9
Leibfried, S. 45, 52, 68, 116, 148, 222, 259–60
Leigh, A. 106
Leira, A. 205
Lemke, T. 1
Leoni, R. 107
Lessenich, S. 4, 189, 217, 241
liberalism 2, 42, 44, 48, 52, 75, 92, 98, 107, 121, 123–5, 139, 142, 164, 167, 208, 256, 261
liberalization 1, 10, 19–21, 27–8, 57–8, 62, 91, 99–101, 114, 126, 131, 141–2, 149, 230, 246, 247, 256–7, 261
Liebig, S. 68

lifestyle 2, 74, 85, 162, 186–7, 189, 202, 208, 210, 212, 251
Lindbom, A. 199
Lindsay, C. 193, 201
Lipset, S.M. 130, 146–8, 166, 168, 173
location 7, 18, 23, 54–6, 59, 60, 63, 78, 102, 114, 137, 186, 222, 230–2, **235**
Lødemel, I. 102
Löhr, A. 82
Lowenkamp, C.T. 241
loyalty 80, 187, 209
Luckmann, T. 262
Luhmann, N. 80

McDonald, C. 105
McGrew, A. 76, 99
McKay, H.D. 216, 236, 241
Mackert, J. 5
McLean, M. 134
McNamee, S.J. 65, 73, 157
McQuaid, R.W. 193
Magnusson, L. 102
Maguire, K. 219
Mahnkopf, B. 99
Mahoney, J. 10
Mailand, M. 192–3, 201
Majone, G. 79, 95, 247
management 15, **17**–19, *67*, 71, 84, 115–18, 136, 147, 188, 223, 257
manager 3, 9, 15, 71, 95, 110, 167–8, 186, 203, 252–**3**, 257
Mandel, H. 151
Mandle, J.R. 64
Manning, N. 116
Manow, P. 23
Marin, D. 54
market(s) 1–2, 7, 10–13, 15, 18–24, 26, 28, 38–9, 41–2, 45–6, 52, 55–60, 63–5, 71–3, 79, 82, 85, 88, 97, 99–101, 104, 109, 111, 114–15, 117–18, 120–3, 131–2, 134, 138, 141, 146, 149–50, 153–4, 156–8, 160–2, 164, 166–8, 176, 184, 186, 188–9, 195–6, 198, 212, 215–18, 222, 228–32, 234–8, 248, 250, 257, **260**; European single 53–4, 77, 79, 94, 114, 230; financial 1, 20–2, 162; job 23, 60, 99, 171; labour 62, 64–5, 104, 106–7, 109, 113–14, 118–20, 134–5, 138, 141–2, *144*, 170–2, 177–9, 181, 183, 186–7, 192, 194–8, 203, 204, 207–8, 228, 237, 246, 250, 259
market capitalization **17**, 21, 23
market "closure" 80, 249

market economy, coordinated/social 7, 11–13, 15–24, 26–8, 30, 34–5, 164, 169, 176, 246–7; liberal 7, 11–13, 15–21, 22–4, 26–8, 30, 35, 121, 169
market opening 15, 22, 57, 248–9
Marks, G. 146–7, 166
Marshall, T.H. 40, 194
Marske, C.E. 93
Marston, G. 105
Martin, C.J. 193
Marttila, T. 98, 208, 258
Marwah, S. 215, 217, 236
Massa-Wirth, H. 188
Massey, A. 116
Mau, S. 66, 68, 79, 250
Mayer, K.U. 222
Mead, L.M. 150
Meinecke, F. 40
Merck, J. 82
Merkel, W. 217
Merton, R.K. 58, 62, 157, 213–16, 234, 236
Messner, S.F. 215, 218, 236, 241
Meyer, B.D. 106
Meyer, J.W. 3, 5, 9, 94, 119, 247, 262
Miller, P. 1
Miller, R.K. 65, 73, 157
Mills, M. 98
minorities 2, 139, 150, 202, 205
Mirowski, P. 98
Mishel, L. 154, 200
Mitchell, K. 223
mobility **18**, 55, 63, 107, 114, 146, 156, 190–1, 207, 213
modernity 38, 53, 86, 138
Moffit, R.A. 148
monopoly of power 40, 77, 83
Moore, W.E. 165
moral hazard 4, 63, 93, 185
morality 79–81, 86, 88–9; in-group 1, 10, 79, 249; out-group 1, 5, 10, 79–80, 249, 259–**60**, 262–3
Morenoff, J.D. 245
Mouffe, C. 99, 247
Mouw, T. 61, 65, 153, 230
Müller, H.P. 5
Münch, R. 3, 5, 18, 41, 53, 66, 72, 77–8, 80, 92, 96, 101, 211, 247
Münkler, H. 127
multiculturalism 149
Murswieck, A. 68, 130, 216
Myrberg, E. 204

Narr, W.-D. 72

304   Index

Naschold, F. 131
Nash, R. 73
nation, national 1–5, 7–10, 14, 24, 28, 36–8, 40–3, 48–50, 52–6, , 59, 64–9, 73, 75–6, 79–80, 82–3, 85–9, 92–4, 95–102, 110, 112, 114–16, 118, 120–3, 129, 131, 139–43, 146, 163, 184–7, 197, 200, 202, 208, 218, 228–32, 241, 245–52, 254–**60**, 262
nation state(s) 1–2, 4, 9–10, 37–8, 40–3, 48, 50, 52–6, 66, 77, 82, 84–7, 92–4, 100–2, 110, 112, 115–16, 123, 126, 128, 138–9, 194, 202, 262
Naudet, J.-D. 73, 79
Neckerman, K.M. 89
Neef, R. 221
Nelson, J.I. 61
neo-liberalism, neo-liberal 1, 48, 56, 62–3, 75, 80, 92, 97–9, 103–4, 107, 139, 142, 208, 261
network(s) 1, 3, 12, **16**, 38, 52, 54, 69, 75–6, 82, 87, 92, 95, 97, 102, 110, 113, 116, 118, 131–8, 141, 147, 184–7, 189, 195, 231, 234, 240
Neumayer, E. 245
Nicoll, K. 63, 223
Noelle-Neumann, E. 70–1
Norberg-Schönfeldt, M. 204
norm(s) 2, 115, 215–16, 221
Nullmeier, F. 250

O'Brien, R. 2
Oesch, D. 223
Olafsdottir, S. 75
Olk, T. 139
Olsen, G.M. 140
Olson, M., Jr. 130, 246–7
Olssen, M. 63, 223
Open Method of Coordination (OMC) 94, 139, 247, 257
order, economic 7, 30; social 7, 30, 62, 164, 250; institutional 4–5
Ostner, I. 4, 179, 217, 241
O'Sullivan, M.A. 11–12, 21

Pager, D. 160
Palier, B. 183
paradigm, change of 2, 5, 7, 10, 30, 52, 90–1, 139, 248, 250, 259–**60**, 262
Park, S. 84
Parsons, T. 5, 41, 146
particularism, particularistic 2, 41, 80, 101–2, 114, 121, 185, 208–9
party 3, 10, 41–2, 48, 75, 87, 96–7, 108, 111, 128, 147, 164, 181–2, 193, 210–11, 218, 250–7, 259–**60**, 262–3
Pastore, A.L. 219
Patchin, J.W. 241
path dependency 9, 139–40, 142, 212, 259
Pattilo, M.E. 160
Pauly, L.W. 99
payment(s) **18**, 63, 79, 175, 217, 231, 238
Peck, J. 105
Pedersen, O.K. 193, 201
Peet, R. 84
Peredo, A.M. 134
Perlmutter, F.D. 134
Peters, M.A. 63–4, 223
Petersmann, E.-U. 81–2
Petersson, J. 105, 199
Pettit, B. 59, 160, 219, 245
Phillips, J.A. 218
Picht, G. 190
Pickett, K.F. 218, 245
Pierson, P. 9, 116, 154, 259
pioneers, moral 2–5, 254
Pischke, J.-S. 73, 153, 167
Plehwe, D. 98
pluralization 42–3, 46, 48–50, 54, 85, 87, 92, 111, 116–18, 139, 185–7, 189, 200, 202, 208, 210–12, 222
Polanyi, K. 80
policy, social 2, 6–8, 10, 24, 35, 45–6, 52, 62, 78–9, 90–5, 98, 102–3, 107, 115, 138, 141, 164, 222, 248, 261
Pollack, M.A. 82
Pongratz, H.J. 71
Pontusson, J. 101, 155
poverty 38, 47, 61, *62*, 64, 82, 104, 109, 138, 179
Powell, W.W. 262
Prasad, E.S. 73, 153, 167
Priller, E. 123, 133, 137
prisoner's dilemma 173
privatization 10, 28, 246
production 7–8, 11–12, **16**–19, 22, 24, 27–8, 30, 48–9, 54–5, 57, 60, 63–4, 73, 81, 96, 102, 109, 114, 123, 127–8, 138–9, 150, 152, 155, 165, 167, 169, 171, 178, 185–7, 190–1, 194, 198, 202–4, 226–30, 236–8, 241, 247–8, 250; chain 22, 54, 141, 229–30; diversified quality 12, 19–20, 22, 24, 34, 36, 169–70, 172, 175, 188; jobs/work 7, 15, 23, 106, 109–10, 165, 172, 190, 206–7, 222, 225, 228, 230; mass 15, 19, 60, 117–18, 246
property crime **159**–**60**, 204, 216, 219–**20**, 236; rights 39, 54, 134

protectionism, protectionist 45, 249, 260–1
Pruijt, H. 107
Putnam, R. 123, 133

"race to the bottom" 52–3, 114, 248–9
Randow, G. von 134, 136–7
rationalization 106, 109, 172, 191, 198, 203, 210
Raudenbush, S.W. 241
Rawls, J. 74–5
rebellion 4, 73, 75, 216, 259, **260**
reciprocity 64, 81
redistribution 15, 40, 43, 46,-7, 54–5, 63, 68, 75, 78, 100–2, 114, 157, 195, 206, 217–18
regime 6, 8, 27, 47, 50, 52, 90, **96**, 98, 117, 118, 127, 164, 257; conservative 15, 140, 173, 190, 199, 204–5, 212, 217, 256; innovation 7, **16**, 22–3, 35, 170, 246; liberal 7, 15, 18–19, 23, 47–8, 98, 110, 121–2, 140, 179, 189–91, 199, 204–7, 212–13, 217, 219, 236, 241, 245, 250, 256, 258–60; production 15, 19, 22, 46–8, 246; social democratic 7, 15, 47, 140, 190, 207, 213, 217, 221–2, 250; welfare 6–7, 8, 15, 98–9, 107, 113, 122, 140, 142, 174–5, 207, 213, 217, 219, 221, 225, 232, 237–8, 241, 245, 256
Reich, R. 54–5
relation(s), industrial 109, 118, 147, 169
religion, religious 7, 40–2, 81, 83–4, 97, 146, 185, 216, 249, **260**
research (and development) 11–12, 15–**16**, 20, 23–5, 56, 71, 96, 198, 230, 240
retirement, early 103, 109, 170, 176, 248
Rhodes, M. 107
Ricardo, D. 83
Richardson, A.M. 245
Ridley-Duff, R. 134
Riedel, B. 131
Rieger, E. 45, 52, 68, 148, 259–60
Rifkin, J. 134
rights 2, 6, 39, 41, 50, 85, 87, 89, 93, 112, 115, 129–31, 177–8, 183–4, 194, 247, 254, 257; civil 2, 4, 6, 130, 149–50, 162, 178, 194; human 2, 4, 53, 82, 93, 194; individual 2, 41, 88, 93; minority 2, 6, 91
risk 21, 28, 30, 39, 43, 45, 48–9, 62, 86, 93, 100, 103, 109, 123, 134, 149, 158, 174, 248–9, 257, 259, 260
Risse, T. 2
ritualism 216

Rodrik, D. 43, 72, 148, 259
Roemer, J.E. 73
Room, G. 86
Rose, N. 1
Rosén, M. 204
Rosenbladt, B. von 113
Rosenfeld, J. 61, 117, 157
Rosenfeld, R. 215, 218, 236, 241
Rothenberg, L. 130
Rothenbuhler, E.W. 93
Rowan, B. 94, 119, 262
Rubio-Marin, R. 184
Rueda, D. 155, 183
Rueschemeyer, D. 10

Sachweh, P. 75
Sainsbury, D. 150
Sakamoto, A. 61, 65, 73, 153, 230
Salamon, L.M. 123
Sampson, R.J. 216, 236, 241
Savolainen, J. 245
Schäfer, A. 247
Scharpf, F.W. 4, 24, 39, 79, 102, 107, 111, 113, 173, 193, 198, 200, 209, 230
Schelsky, H. 214
Scherer, A.G. 82
Schettkat, R. 226
Schluchter, W. 80
Schmid, G. 24, 119, 225
Schmid, J. 41
Schmidt, M.G. 41
Schmidt, V.A. 4, 113, 193, 196, 198, 200, 208
Scholte, J.A. 82
Schubert, A. 72
Schulze, G. 71
Schulze-Cleven, T. 35, 172, 191, 201
Schumann, M. 171, 225
Schumpeter, J.A. 37, 56–7, 62, 99
Schwengel, H. 99
Scourfield, P. 134
Scruggs, L. 140
security, social 9, 15, 24, 41, 43, 46, 49, 63, 66, 68, 93, 98, 102, 132, 148, 164, 175, 195, 199, 230, **235**, 238, 245, 250, 255–6
Seeleib-Kaiser, M. 53, 106, 142, 173
Seidman, L.S. 106
Seifert, H. 188
self-organization, civic 98, 102, 123, 125, 128–30, 194–5
Semyonov, M. 151
Sennett, R. 64, 100, 156
Serrano Pascual, A. 102

service(s) 11, 23–4, 27–35, 37, 39, **44**, 54, 63, 66, 84–5, 87, 101–2, 106, 107, 109, 111–12, 117, 119–20, 123, 127, 130–2, 135–8, *144–5*, 150, 155, 157, 162, 165–8, 172, 179–80, **182**, 186, 188, 195–7, 201–3, 210, 222, 226–8, 232, **235**, 246, 249, **253–4**
service employment/job/work 7, 15, 19, *67*, 105–6, 109–11, 113, 150, 154, 165, 173, 175, 179, 202, 207, 228, **235**
shareholder **17**, 21, 118, 257–8
Sharman, J.C. 54
Shavell, S. 74
Shaw, C.R. 216, 236, 241
Shaw, I. 116
Siaroff, A. 120
Siebert, H. 55
Siegel, N.A. 107, 109, 140
Simmel, G. 3, 88
Sincavage, J.R. 229
Sirianni, C. 129
Sivesind, K.H. 123
Skocpol, T. 128
Smeeding, T.M. 217, 219
Smid, M. 82
Smith, A. 83, 164
Smith, A.D. 40
Smith, K.B. 160
Smith, T.W. 147
society, market 168, 215; model of 4, 75, 138, 170, 185, 246, 250; national 2, 5, 9, 94–5, 184, 258
Soederberg, S. 99
Solga, H. 65, 221–3, 232–3
solidarity, mechanical 38, 41, 84–7, 141, 231; national 1, 8–9, 37, 40–2, 48, 52, 55, 65–6, 68, 75–6, 85, 92, 110, 118, 1412 186, 200, 251–2, 255; organic 41–2, 85–7, 92, 167–8, 170, 172–3, 177, 184–7, 189–90, 192, 231; transnational 1, 4, 48, 50, 80, 85, 87, 231
Sørensen A. 157
Soskice, D. 10–12, 19–22, 24, 26–7, 150, 152, 169–70, 199, 241
Soysal, Y.N. 2, 93
Spear, R. 120
Spencer, H. 83
Spengler, H. 218, 241
spirit, civic/common 39, 85, 89
standard(s), social 49, 248–50
Starke, P. 140
state 1, 10, 15, 19–20, 37, 39–41, 43, 47, 52, 55, 66, 76, 87, 92, 99, 102, 104–5, 107–8, 111, 117, 119–20, 123–7,
129–32, 134, 136–40, *149*, 185, 192–5, 199, 205, 213–14, 217, 226
Steffek, J. 82
Stehr, N. 1
Stephens, J.D. 10, 15, 46–7, 60, 142, 260
Sterrie, D. 111
Stiglitz, J.E. 64
Stone Sweet, A. 88
stratification 165, 189, 262–**3**
Straubhaar, T. 56
Streeck, W. 9–10, 12, 22–4, 52, 54, 56, 76, 90, 114, 117–18, 162, 169–70, 175, 185, 188–9
Sutherland, E.H. 217
Swank, D. 10, 19, 49, 140, 260
Swedberg, R. 10
system, educational 14, **17**, 62–4, 152–4, 165–6, 170–1, 189, 191–2, 204, 249; welfare 15, 54, 63–4, 77, 79, 163–4, 175, 185–6, 192–4, 202, 209

Tahlin, M. 204
takeover **17**, 21, 23, 257–8
Tannock, S. 54
Taylor, R.C.R. 262
Taylor-Gooby, P. 140
technology 7, 11–13, 16, 18, 20, 23–4, *26*–35, 53, 55, 60, 118, 141, 150–2, 176, 186, 190, 195, 198–9, 201–2, 206; high 19, 23, *26*–7, *30*–5, 201
tertiarization (of the economy) 186, 258
Thelen, K. 9–10, 21, 52, 90, 259
Thomas, G.M. 82
Thompson, G. 54
Thompson, J. 134
Thorlindsson, T. 239
Thurow, L.C. 55, 57, 61, 65
Tiberghien, Y. 55
Tienda, M. 73
Tijdens, K. 107, 109
Tilly, C. 166
Tinbergen, J. 39
Titmuss, R. 42, 196, 258–9
Tocqueville, A. de 126–8
Toepler, S. 123, 127
togetherness, feeling of 88
Torche, F. 89
trade 3, 23, 28, *30*, 43–6, 50, 53–4, 56, 81, 185, 201; free 45–6, 79, 82–3, 248; world 45, **51**, 53, 64, 230
trade union 5, **18**–20, 23, 35, 41, 45–6, 48, 54, 87, 95, 106, 108, 113–18, 120, 126–7, 142, 157, 161–2, 171–2, 187, 189, 193, 195–7, 200, 202, 206, 209–11,

215–18, 225–8, 234–**5**, 238, 241–*2*, *244*, 253, 256
tradition 4–5, 9, 12, 38, 58, 63, 81, 94, 97–8, 100, 104, 115, 122, 136–7, 140–2, 147, 153, 162, 180, 182, 202, 208–9, 212, 226, 236, 247, 257, 249
transaction costs 9, 83, 174, 259
transaction(s), economic 4, 53, 185, 261
transnationalization 1, 5, 48, 93–4, 103, 139, 168, 247, 250, 255–6, 258–**63**
Traxler, F. 23, 122, 261
Trickey, H. 102
Triplett, J.E. 109
trust 127–8, 162, 196, 209
Tsebelis, G. 10, 260
Tumin, M.M. 165
Turrini, A. 54

Uhlendorff, U. 131
unemployed/unemployment 14, 19–20, 22–4, *25*, 41, 45–6, 52, 58–60, 64, *67*–8, 72, 75–7, *76*, 85, 102–14, 119–20, 125, *126*, 133, 136–7, 141–3, *144*–6, 163, 170–6, 180, 182–3, 187–8, 192–3, 196–204, 207–8, 210, 217, 220–**4**, **235**, 237–8, 241, *243*–*4*, 248, 256
universalism, universalistic 2, 3, 80, 93, 104, 178, 183–4, 194, 217
utility maximization 237

Vail, J. 197
Valkenburg, B. 102
Van Voorhis, R.A. 105
Veghte, B. 68
Vetterlein, A. 84
Veysey, M.M. 241
Viebrock, E. 140
violence 61, 64, 125, 138, 218, 240
Vis, B. 105
Visser, J. 107–8, 119, 225
Vobruba, G. 10
Vogel, S.K. 88
Vogt, W.P. 93
Voß, G. 71
vote(s/rs) 10, 44, 71, 96–7, 130, 210–11, 251–3, **255**, 260

Wacquant, L. 58, 62, 64, 105, 160–1, 219
Wallace, M. 79

wealth 3–5, 15, 44, 52–3, 68, 70, 72–3, 75, 82–4, 88–9, 101, 110, 114, 117, 128, 131, 137, 142, 154, 164, 168, 175, 183, 190–1, 194, 214, 226, 232–3, 237–8, 241, 250
Weber, M. 40, 80–1
Weingart, P. 96
Weiss, L. 99
Weizsäcker, C. von 99, 114
welfare 1, 5, 8, 37, 39–41, 43–7, 49, 76–7, 89, 91–4, 98, 102, 105, 107, 112–13, 123, 128–33, 138–9, 148, 150, 189, 194–6, 199, 204–5
welfare state(s) 1–2, 5, 9–10, 30, 37–8, 41–3, 45–50, *46*, 54, 59–60, 62–4, 66, 68, 72, 74–6, 78–82, 85–7, 91, 93, 98–102, 104–7, 109–10, 113–15, 117, 119, 125–9, 131–2, 137–42, 146–8, 156–8, 160–3, 167–70, 173, 175–83, 185–7, 189, 191–209, 212–14, 217–18, 220–3, 225, 228, 232–3, 236, 240–1, 245–6, 250, 255, 258–62, **260**
Western, B. 59, 160, 219, 245
Westgaard-Nielson, N. 207
Westling, A. 204
Wheeler, N.J. 2
White, W. 5
Whyman, P. 196–7, 199
Wildenmann, R. 76
Wilke, U. 105–6
Wilkinson, E.G. 218, 245
Wilson, J.W. 216
withdrawal 37, 104, 129, 131, 138, 210, 216
Wolf, A. 103
workforce 7, 14–15, 19, 20, 24, 35, 54–6, 63, 65, 99–100, 114, 116–19, 141, 149–50, 171, 174–6, 186, 188, 192, 197, 203, 222, 225–32, 246, 251, 254–5, 259
world society 10, 43, 48, 53, 74, 76, 82, 94, 99–101, 112, 119, 139, 254
Wright, E.O. 64

Yerkes, M. 107, 109

Zajac, E.E. 74
Zempel, J. 113
Zimmer, A. 123, 133
Zugehör, R. 188

Taylor & Francis
eBooks
FOR LIBRARIES

ORDER YOUR FREE 30 DAY INSTITUTIONAL TRIAL TODAY!

Over 23,000 eBook titles in the Humanities, Social Sciences, STM and Law from some of the world's leading imprints.

Choose from a range of subject packages or create your own!

Benefits for you
- ▶ Free MARC records
- ▶ COUNTER-compliant usage statistics
- ▶ Flexible purchase and pricing options

Benefits for your user
- ▶ Off-site, anytime access via Athens or referring URL
- ▶ Print or copy pages or chapters
- ▶ Full content search
- ▶ Bookmark, highlight and annotate text
- ▶ Access to thousands of pages of quality research at the click of a button

For more information, pricing enquiries or to order a free trial, contact your local online sales team.

UK and Rest of World: online.sales@tandf.co.uk
US, Canada and Latin America:
e-reference@taylorandfrancis.com

www.ebooksubscriptions.com

A flexible and dynamic resource for teaching, learning and research.